"Why should not the New Englander be in search of new adventures?"
THOREAU: *Walden*

NORTH AMERICA
Country Inns and Back Roads

21st Year — Revised Annually

New England, West Coast,
Canada, Middle Atlantic, South, Midwest,
Rocky Mountains

By Norman T. Simpson
The Berkshire Traveller

PERENNIAL LIBRARY

HARPER & ROW, PUBLISHERS, New York
Cambridge, Philadelphia, San Francisco,
London, Mexico City, São Paulo, Singapore, Sydney

TRAVEL BOOKS BY NORMAN T. SIMPSON

Country Inns and Back Roads, North America
Country Inns and Back Roads, Britain and Ireland
Country Inns and Back Roads, Continental Europe
Bed and Breakfast, American Style

TX
910
.G7
557
1986
153474
nov.1991

COVER PAINTING: Rockhouse Mountain Farm, Eaton Center, New Hampshire,
by Marge Kendrick, a local New Hampshire artist
DRAWINGS: Janice Lindstrom

First Perennial Library edition published 1986. Earlier editions of this book were
published by Berkshire Traveller Press.

ISSN: 70-615664
ISBN: 0-06-096066-3

86 87 88 89 10 9 8 7 6 5 4 3 2 1

Contents

Pennsylvania

Rhode Island

Tennessee

Vermont

CANADA

Ontario

Prince Edward Island

Quebec

PREFACE

This is the twenty-first year for *Country Inns and Back Roads*. I must say that I am somewhat impressed myself. We frequently are all so impressed by chronological milestones; I guess I'm no exception. However, in many ways I am preparing already for the twenty-fifth year.

The first edition of this book had sixteen pages and included twelve inns. I wrote under the nom de plume, "The Berkshire Traveller." Early on, I dropped that idea as being a sort of conceit, but still retained the term, "The Berkshire Traveller," as a kind of subtitle.

Like the man in the TV washing machine ads, I felt pretty much alone for about the first eight years; it was just the innkeepers, the readers, and me. Of course, I was growing all the time, learning my trade as it were, and making many new friends—people who were learning about country inns and appreciated them.

The book grew slowly at first, partly because there weren't very many inns during the late 1960s. However, I soon realized that there were a great many other people out there who really loved country inns, and it was clear that country inns needed guests.

So I began to apply myself more seriously to the business of finding good country inns, and in the process, I gradually gave up my other business interests to concentrate more fully on this book. Each year saw the number of inns in the book increasing, until about eight years ago when I felt that with 210 inns we had reached the optimum number.

Soon, what had begun as a little booklet became a bona fide book, and what had been a small sideline for me blossomed into a publishing venture that included a number of other books. As a small publishing house, I believe we have gained a reputation for producing books of integrity and interest.

Almost from the beginning, I found that innkeepers had no forum where they might exchange ideas and views and simply talk shop, so a small informal innkeepers' association was formed, and meetings were held every year to provide such a forum. From one meeting a year, this idea grew into the Independent Innkeepers' Association, where upwards of twenty meetings a year are held throughout North America. There is one large meeting held every year to which hoteliers from Britain and the

Continent are also invited. As a matter of fact, this year for the second time there was a meeting in England.

I learned about innkeeping from innkeepers, and it never stops. The inn picture has changed radically in the past ten years. Whereas in the early days the book was really a guide to almost every existing country inn, now with the marked proliferation of inns, the book has become highly selective—based, of course, on my own personal choices. With the limitation on the number of inns to be included, there is a waiting list each year. Because inns are omitted when they change owners, and occasionally for other reasons, the principle behind this book is each year to find a few good replacement inns in various parts of North America; to keep in touch and visit all of them as frequently as possible, and to concentrate on quality rather than quantity.

I guess our own "coming of age" took place in late 1984, when one of the most prestigious and reputable publishing firms in the world, Harper & Row, evinced an interest in the four books I write. After a few quiet discussions, it was decided that they would become the new publishers of *Country Inns and Back Roads, North America; Country Inns and Back Roads, Britain and Ireland; Country Inns and Back Roads, Continental Europe;* and *Bed & Breakfast, American Style.*

I hasten to add that my agreement with Harper & Row permits me to be the sole arbiter of the contents of all of these books, and they are in complete agreement with the standards that have been built up over the past twenty years. It is a most agreeable marriage, I can assure you.

We will all be here for the rest of the day if, like the winners of the Academy Awards, I recognize all of the people who have made marvelous, unselfish contributions to the growth of the original idea. I thank them all.

I will, however, mention the people who have written me letters over the years, recommending that I visit inns, sharing their inn-adventures with me, and from time to time, penning a letter of complaint. The latter are taken very seriously, and I reply to each one and also discuss the complaint with the innkeeper concerned. It has worked out very well over the years.

To our readers in Great Britain and other countries in Europe:

Welcome to North America! Many of you are making your first visit and we're delighted that you'll be experiencing some of the *real* United States and Canada by visiting these country inns. Incidentally, all of them will be very happy to help you make arrangements and reservations at other inns in the book.

For your further convenience, automobile rental reservations for the United States can be made before your departure through AutoEurope, a world-wide rental corporation.

In Europe, AutoEurope may be reached at a London number: 02934-71583.

In North America, the toll-free number for AutoEurope is 1-800-223-5555.

Further Notes:

Here are some basic guidelines for reservations and cancellations in most of the inns listed in this book:

A deposit is required for a confirmed reservation. Guests are requested to please note arrival and departure dates carefully. The deposit will be forfeited if the guest arrives after date specified or departs before the final date of reservation. Refund will be made only if cancelled from 7 to 14 days (depending on the policy of the individual inn) in advance of arrival date and a service charge will be deducted from the deposit.

A number of inns have nearby airports where private planes may land, and further information may be obtained directly from each inn. We have indicated those inns near such airports by putting the following symbol at the end of each inn's directions.

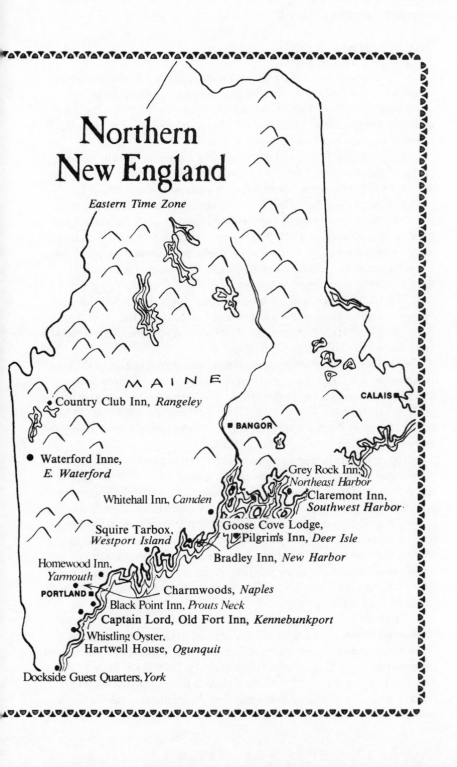

Northern
New England

Eastern Time Zone

M A I N E

• Country Club Inn, *Rangeley*

CALAIS ■

■ BANGOR

• Waterford Inne,
  E. Waterford

Grey Rock Inn,
Northeast Harbor

Whitehall Inn, *Camden*

Claremont Inn,
Southwest Harbor

Squire Tarbox,
Westport Island

Goose Cove Lodge,
Pilgrim's Inn, *Deer Isle*

Homewood Inn,
Yarmouth •

Bradley Inn, *New Harbor*

PORTLAND ■

Charmwoods, *Naples*

Black Point Inn, *Prouts Neck*

Captain Lord, Old Fort Inn, *Kennebunkport*

Whistling Oyster,
Hartwell House, *Ogunquit*

Dockside Guest Quarters, *York*

THE BIRCHWOOD INN
Temple, New Hampshire

"We as a young nation of Americans are really just developing a true nostalgia of our own. Just since the Bicentennial has this craving grown tremendously, and an old country inn allows guests to turn back the clock and immerse themselves almost totally in an atmosphere of the roadside travel of the 18th and 19th centuries in America."

Judy and Bill Wolfe and I were enjoying a quiet moment in the back parlor of the Birchwood Inn, and I could see by the light in his eye that Bill was most enthusiastic about being an innkeeper.

The Birchwood Inn, sitting on one corner of the village green, is listed on the National Register of Historic Places and is believed to have been in operation since 1775. The present Federal-style brick building, along with the adjacent barn, was probably built about 1800, and the records document a history of changing uses that mirror the evolution of the small-town tavern in New England.

The small village of Temple has no telegraph wires in the center of the town, and it's pretty much the same as it's been for two hundred years, with the Grange Hall, Congregational Church, village store, Revolutionary cemetery, and old blacksmith shop.

In 1965, probably the most interesting and prized feature of the inn was discovered when some early wall murals were uncovered under layers of old wallpaper. The paintings proved to be the work of the well-known muralist Rufus Porter, painted between 1825 and 1833. Fortunately, they were restored and are now being carefully preserved by Bill and Judy.

Today, the inn is characterized by comfortable furniture, a Steinway square grand piano, wide floorboards, checked tablecloths of yellow, red, brown, and blue, music in the background, and many tiny little areas where guests can enjoy a tête-à-tête. On the other hand, there is much opportunity for sociability. Judy said, "We have developed countless friendships with lovely people from all over the world without ever leaving the comforts of our little inn. The opportunity to reach out to people of all interests is a rare privilege afforded to both innkeepers and their children alike." The Wolfes find that their three children enjoy being involved with inn activities.

There are seven most original guest rooms sharing two bathrooms. Each of them has its own theme. For example, the Seashore Room has a lobster trap and shore pictures; the Music Room is decorated with old instruments, including a violin lampstand; the Train Room reflects the fact that Bill is a train buff; and the Editorial Room has a collection of framed original front pages of newspapers with headlines about the moon walk and "Nixon Quits."

The kitchen is handled in an interesting way because Bill does the cooking. Judy bakes breads and desserts, including blueberry-lemon bread, blueberry cobbler, chocolate cake, and various pies and tortes. The evening menu is on a slate blackboard, and on the night of my visit included broiled lamb chops and scallops kabob.

Bill remarked, "Serving meals as innkeepers is like hosting a dinner party each evening, except it's a lot easier since you don't have to sit down with the guests. By the time they're finished, you're nearly finished as well."

Temple is sort of tucked out of the way on a paved back road, and I don't think I would have ever found it on my own, but thanks to one of my readers, I'm glad I did.

THE BIRCHWOOD INN, Rte. 45, Temple, NH 03084; 603-878-3285. A 7-guestroom (2 baths) village inn in southern New Hampshire. Open year-round. Dinner not served on Sun. or Mon. Hiking, xc skiing, hayrides, summer theater, ice skating, superb backroading, and numerous historic houses nearby; also the Cathedral in the Pines. No credit cards. Judy and Bill Wolfe, Innkeepers.

Directions: Take Rte. 3 north to Nashua. At Exit 7W follow Rte. 101 west through Milford to Rte. 45. Turn left 1½ mi. to Temple. From I-91 at Brattleboro take Rte. 9 east to Keene to Rte. 101 through Peterborough, over Temple Mtn. to Rte. 45. Turn right, 1½ mi. to Temple.

COLBY HILL INN
Henniker, New Hampshire

Following Don Glover's suggestion, I turned off Route 202 just outside Hillsborough, following the sign that says, "West Henniker." One of the interesting things about this road is that at one point there are two bridges across the river almost side by side. They are both two-way bridges and I couldn't for the life of me figure out why anyone would want two bridges across the same river at the same point. Later, while standing in front of the long window in the dining room, overlooking the barns shown in Jan Lindstrom's sketch, Don laughed and said that the early inhabitants of New Hampshire certainly had some most interesting ideas.

This dining room has seen the major change at Colby Hill in recent years, with additional space providing more tables. The atmosphere is enhanced by wide pine floorboards, and the pine furniture causes me to run my hands over the tabletops and backs of chairs. The wood-chunk stove provides comfortable and welcome warmth when needed.

"Oh, I see you're watching our birds," Don said. "Many of our guests are confirmed bird watchers. Yesterday, one of them said that he saw a bobolink—I haven't seen one for many years. The new wider window really provides a much more intimate view of the birds."

Don and his wife, June, were friends of mine at Bucknell University, and Don recently held a reunion of several of his Phi Kappa Psi brothers and was good enough to send me a photograph of the group. I knew all of them.

A few years ago Don and June, along with their son, Don Jr., and his wife, Margaret, acquired this classic New Hampshire inn on the outskirts of the small village of Henniker, the home of New England College. The ceilings are low, the walls are hung with old paintings and

prints, and the furnishings are country antiques. A grandfather clock ticks away in one corner. There are birds during all seasons and a gorgeous flower garden during spring and summer. In earlier times, the living room fireplace was used for baking bread.

Guest rooms at the inn are typical country New England. Many have candlewick bedspreads, hooked rugs, and old bowl-and-pitcher sets, reminiscent of the days when water was brought in from the outside. Some of them have shared bathrooms, and all of them have that wonderful "old home" feeling.

"This is great cross-country skiing terrain," commented Don. "There are forty miles of trails in this vicinity and a great many of our guests, including the children, come up for long weekends, or even, when possible, during the week."

At that moment, I caught the aroma of freshly baked bread coming from the kitchen, so Don and I wandered back to where Don Jr., was discussing the evening fare with the chef. I had a short conversation with him about the ever-expanding menu. "We serve chicken Colby House," he said, "and this, along with our fresh seafood, has been received very well. We have specials almost every day and usually a fresh fish of the day. My mother, June, has her own little baking corner here and she does the chocolate cakes, the cinnamon buns, the biscuits, and the applesauce."

One of my favorite things at this inn is a delightful swimming pool sheltered by an ell, formed by the two huge barns adjacent to the inn. It is most welcome on the hot days of the southern New Hamsphire summer.

This inn is enjoyable in many seasons because this section of New Hamsphire has many lakes, state parks, golf courses, summer theaters, and antique shops that add to the attraction for vacationers or weekenders.

COLBY HILL INN, Henniker, NH 03242; 603-428-3281. A 12-guestroom (mostly private baths) inn on the outskirts of a New Hampshire college town. European plan. Breakfast served to houseguests only. Dinner served to travelers Tues. through Sun., except Thanksgiving, Christmas, and New Year's Day. Open year-round. Swimming pool on grounds. Tennis and xc skiing one short block; alpine, 3 mi.; golf, canoeing, hiking, bicycling, and fishing nearby. No children under 6. No pets. The Glover Family, Innkeepers.

Directions: From I-89, take Exit 5 and follow Rte. 202 to Henniker. From I-91, take Exit 3 and follow Rte. 9 through Keene and Hillsborough to Henniker. From the blinking light in town center, go west ½ mi. on West Main St. (Western Ave.) to the Oaks. Inn is on the right.

THE DARBY FIELD INN
Conway, New Hampshire

There's a real sense of adventure involved in just making the last stage of the journey to reach Darby Field Inn. I turned off Route 16 and followed the Darby Field sign, plunging into the forest on a wonderful dirt road that seems to climb ever upward. Following this road through the forest, I again had the great feeling of expectation that something would emerge at the top of the mountain that was going to be grand, and grand it is.

The Darby Field Inn has a most impressive panoramic view from its terrace dining room and many of the bedrooms. On this particular day Marc and Marily Donaldson, the innkeepers, had taken a short holiday on the coast of Maine, but I was extremely well attended by Marion Cram and Sandra Gass, the assistant innkeepers. Although they were very busy, in and out of the kitchen, answering the telephone, and attending to the other guests' needs, they took turns making sure that I saw all of the redecorating that had been accomplished in the inn, and we also had a chance to talk about the great view of the mountains.

"Over there is South Moat Mountain," Marion explained, "and that's Mount Washington just to the right. We can also see Adams and Madison and White Horse Ledge in the center."

The Darby Field Inn, run by Marc and his wife, Marily, sits on the edge of the White Mountain National Forest, where guests can cross-country ski, snowshoe, and hike to nearby rivers, waterfalls, lakes, and open peaks. Fortunately, there's a very pleasant swimming pool on the terrace, providing guests with not only a cooling dip in the hot days of summer, but still another view of the mountains.

Marion seemed to hand me over to Sandra at this point, while we did a short tour of the rooms. "Each room has its own country personality," she observed. "Some have four-poster beds, patchwork quilts, and braided rugs. Most of them have private baths and, as I'm sure you've noticed, many face our special view of the valley."

I was curious about the origins of Darby Field Inn. "Samuel and Polly Chase Littlefield first came up here in 1826, when it was hard work farming through all those generations of hard winters and long distances," Sandra recounted. "Later on, the home took in summer guests, and it was then that the innkeeping tradition began. In the 1940s, a man from Boston and his family came here, and the original farmhouse became the living room section of what was to be known as the Bald Hill Lodge. The barn and blacksmith shop came down and in its place the dining room and kitchen section was built. The swimming pool was added and even a small ski lift for guests."

Marc and Marily met in Venezuela, Marily's homeland, and came to Darby Field in 1979. They saw it as a country home for their children and an opportunity to meet guests from all parts of the world.

Many guests at Darby Field really enjoy going through the three volumes of scrapbooks containing brochures from inns all over New England. They provide a very pleasant few hours of relaxation in the living room in front of the big fireplace and invariably lead to making new acquaintances among other guests.

As Marion and Sandra walked me out to the car, Sandra said, "We can't let you go without pointing out our garden where we get so many of the good things we serve at the inn, including snow peas, peppers, cabbage, corn, lettuce, and brussels sprouts."

THE DARBY FIELD INN, Bald Hill, Conway, NH 03818; 603-447-2181. A 17-guestroom White Mountain country inn, 3 mi. from Conway. Modified American plan. Open all year. Bed and breakfast offered at various times and I would suggest checking with the inn in advance. Within convenient driving distance of all of the Mt. Washington Valley cultural, natural, and historic attractions, as well as several internationally known ski areas. Swimming pool and carefully groomed xc skiing trails on grounds. Tennis and other sports nearby. Marc and Marily Donaldson, Innkeepers.

Directions: From Rte. 16: Traveling north turn left at sign for the inn (½ mi. before the town of Conway) onto Bald Hill Rd., and proceed up the hill 1 mi. to the next sign for the inn and turn right. The inn is 1 mi. down the dirt road on the left.

DEXTER'S INN AND TENNIS CLUB
Sunapee, New Hampshire

Some of my innkeepers write most interesting and informative letters. As a case in point let me share with you some portions of a letter I received from Frank Simpson at Dexter's Inn, high in the mountains in the Lake Sunapee area of New Hampshire:

"The greatest change in the inn is a result of our remodeling, enlarging, and redecorating our old lounge, which has become a focal point for after-dinner activities, leaving the lovely living room as a comfortable spot for reading and quiet after-dinner conversation. The transformation is a result of a combined effort. Michael Durfor, who is married to my daughter, Holly, did a great deal of the hard work, including sanding the floors. But it was really Shirley's deft hand at decorating that sets it all off. It was a successful combined operation.

"We hosted two modern dance concerts on the last two Sundays in July. These are open to the public, but free to our houseguests. They were produced and directed by Larkin Medas of the Malabar Dance Company out of Boston. Larkin's husband is our tennis host. The dances were performed on the lawn with the deep woods as the background."

Although the words "tennis club" have been included in Dexter's name, it is really a resort-inn, with something for everybody to enjoy, with the lovely lakes just a short distance away, splendid backroading, and good, easy trails for moderate hiking, plus nearby entertainment. Many guests stay quite a few days at a time.

As far as the tennis activities are concerned, the opening senior tournament starts early in May. It's for 65s and 70s, singles and doubles. The other tennis tournament is the Senior Sixties, held right after the 4th of July. For non-competitive tennis guests, the tennis host and instructor can arrange games for mid-June through August, and there is always lots

of activity on the courts. Incidentally, the courts are all-weather, and play is possible early in the sprir g and even on warmish days late in the fall.

Guest rooms at Dexter's are fun. The accent is on very bright and gay colors in wallpaper, curtains, and bedspreads. The rooms in the main house are reached by using funny little hallways that zigzag around various wings. There are also guest rooms with a rustic flavor in barns across the street.

Lake Sunapee is the only remaining Grade A lake in New England. It has many islands, and has seen few changes since 1900, when steamboats delivered homeowners to their own docks. There are also three fine golf courses—two of championship quality, one of which was redesigned by famous pro-golfer Gene Sarazen.

Frank's final word was, "Hope you can come up soon. We'll have your pitcher of fresh lemonade waiting."

The really last word from Frank is a happy note announcing that his daughter, Holly, has given birth to a beautiful baby boy, Hartwell Simpson Durfor—another little innkeeper in the making.

DEXTER'S INN AND TENNIS CLUB, Box R, Stagecoach Rd., Sunapee, NH 03782; 603-763-5571. A 17-guestroom resort-inn in the western New Hampshire mountain and lake district. Mod. American plan; European plan available in late June and Sept. only. Breakfast, lunch, and dinner served to travelers by advance reservation; closed for lunch and dinner on Tues. during July and Aug. Lunches served only July, Aug. Open from early May to mid-Oct. Three tennis courts, pool, croquet, and shuffleboard on grounds. Lakes, hiking, backroading, and championship golf courses nearby. Limited activites for children under 12. Pets allowed in Annex only. No credit cards. Frank and Shirley Simpson, Innkeepers; Michael Durfor, Manager.

Directions: From north & east: use Exit 12 or 12A, I-89. Continue west on Rte. 11, 6 mi.—just ½ mi. past Sunapee to a sign at Winn Hill Rd. Turn left up hill and after 1 mi., bear right on Stagecoach Rd. From west: use Exit 8, I-91, follow Rte. 103 east into NH—through Newport ½ mi. past junction with Rte. 11. Look for sign at "Young Hill Rd." and go 1½ mi. to Stagecoach Rd.

A number of inns have nearby airports where private airplanes may land. An airplane symbol at the end of the inn directions indicates that there is an airport nearby. Consult inn for further information.

HICKORY STICK FARM
Laconia, New Hampshire

I'm going to share a letter I received from one of our readers, Collette Compton, about her trip to Hickory Stick Farm:

"Vacationing by car in Vermont and New Hampshire last month was a great experience, but by the time we reached the resort area of Lake Winnipesaukee, my friends and I were ready for a change of pace from fast motorways, motels, and coffee shops.

"One evening we saw a sign pointing off the main road to 'Hickory Stick Farm' with a carved duck decoy underneath. Turning off into the woods we were immediately in a different world of unbelievable peace

and quiet, and we drove 1½ miles of winding roads. 'Round a bend in the road could be seen a picture-perfect red farmhouse on a hill overlooking a splendid panorama. The sun was still shining on the valley and Ragged Mountain in the distance was a misty purple.

"Entering the converted farmhouse was like entering the house of a dream grandmother. We were shown into the living room, which is used as a waiting room, while the hostess checked on the availability of a table for dinner. During the short wait we admired the antiques in the living room, including a spinning wheel, and enjoyed visiting the Gift Shop, where many locally made gifts were for sale.

"Scott Roeder, the innkeeper, introduced himself and recounted the history of the farm, which dates back a number of years when his mother and father first bought it.

"The atmosphere in the dining room was relaxed and happy, surrounded by antiques and pewter and red accessories. Our waiter, a student from Boston, suggested we order the famous roast duckling, available in one quarter-pound, one half-pound, or a whole duck that is carved at the table. I have never enjoyed such a tender and delicious duckling, and Mr. Roeder explained the very special way he has of cooking them so that they have a brown, crisp skin and tender, moist meat. It was served with an orange sherry sauce, stuffing, wild rice, and delicious vegetables.

"After a leisurely dinner Mr. Roeder happened to mention that he had room cancellations for the following night, so we immediately booked the rooms and returned to the farm on the following late afternoon. Our rooms were a welcome sight.

"The Rose Room had a queen-sized cannonball bed and pretty flowered wallpaper. The Gold Room had twin-sized cannonball beds under the eaves, and a comfortable sitting area with antique furniture. Both rooms had large bathrooms with baths, showers, and dressing areas.

"Breakfast was served in a small dining area in the living room and Mary Roeder cooked the eggs, bacon, and french toast. They were both very friendly and we all parted most reluctantly."

Thank you, Colette Compton, for sharing your letter with us and I hope you'll share with us more of your *CIBR* inn-going adventures in the future!

HICKORY STICK FARM, R.F.D. #2, Laconia, NH 03246; 603-524-3333. A 2-guestroom hilltop country inn and restaurant 4 mi. from Laconia in the lake country of New Hampshire. Guestrooms and breakfast available most of the year. Please telephone ahead. Open from Memorial Day to Columbus Day; closed Mon. except July and Aug. Dinners served from 5:30 to 9 p.m. Sun. dinner served all day from noon to 8 p.m. Extended hours during fall foliage season—call ahead. The Shaker Village in Canterbury is nearby, as well as the Belknap recreational area (10 mi.) with crafts and antique shows, concerts, Oktoberfests, alpine and xc skiing, and other New Hampshire attractions. Scott and Mary Roeder, Innkeepers.

Directions: Use Exit 20 from I-93. Follow Rte. 3 toward Laconia approx. 5 mi. over bridge over Lake Winnisquam. A short distance past this bridge, turn right on Union Rd. immediately past Double Decker, a drive-in restaurant, and follow Hickory Stick signs 1½ mi. into the woods. If you do not turn onto any dirt roads, you are on the right track. From Laconia, go south on Rtes. 3 & 11 (do not take Rte. 106) and turn left on Union Rd. (about ½ mi. past the Belknap Mall) and follow signs.

THE INN AT CROTCHED MOUNTAIN
Francestown, New Hampshire

The first thing that comes to mind when I think of this inn is the fabulous view.

One of the intriguing things about this view, which can be enjoyed from a great many lodging rooms as well as from the dining room, living room, the terrace, and the swimming pool, is that it gets better with each visit.

When I mentioned this to Rose Perry, she laughed merrily and said, "Oh, we think so, too. Even though John and I have been looking at this view for many years, it becomes more and more meaningful to us."

There were many other most intriguing aspects beside the fabulous view with which this very attractive Indonesian-Chinese woman acquainted me. Rose's father is a hotelier in Singapore, and she lived a number of years in Hong Kong. Rose and John met while attending Paul Smith College, a hotel school in the Adirondacks. In complete charge of the kitchen, she does most of the cooking, and I was surprised at the unusual number of main dishes, many of which are her own recipes.

The inn was originally built as a farmhouse in 1822. The original owner had strong political convictions and constructed a secret tunnel from his cellar to the Boston Post Road, incorporating his home as a way station to shelter runaway slaves on the Underground Railroad.

During the late 1920s, it was to become one of the most spectacular farms in New England, boasting an internationally recognized breed of sheep, champion horses, and Angora goats.

The house was destroyed by fire in the mid-30s, rebuilt, and John and Rose came on the scene in 1976.

I first visited Crotched Mountain early in June, when the late New England spring is at its most delicious with apple blossoms and lilacs, and I was smitten by the wonderful panorama stretching out for miles.

Since then I have visited in all seasons of the year, but it seems to me that September would be one of the most ideal times to be here. It isn't generally known, but the southern New Hampshire foliage comes a little earlier than other places in New England. So, I think the advantages are self-evident.

Recently I had a leisurely dinner with John and Rose, and the menu had roast duck with plum sauce, sautéed bay scallops, and Indonesian-style scallops with sautéed tomatoes, onions, pepper, and ginger. There was a glowing fire in the low-ceilinged parlor of the little pub, where after-dinner guests and other couples dropped in during the evening.

My lodging room had a fireplace and windows overlooking the mountains and valleys; also, a door through which I could step directly outside to the swimming pool.

The next morning I took a few moments to wander around on the broad green lawn and look out over the valley. "It looks this way in Indonesia," Rose said, as she joined me for a few minutes. "It's just like the mountains and valleys in Djakarta. The floating mist on the mountains has an Indonesian look."

As I walked toward the car, John remarked that this was a different world in the winter, when Crotched Mountain skiers would be walking the short path to the lift line, and the cross-country skiers would be headed into the woods.

The views are many at the Inn at Crotched Mountain.

THE INN AT CROTCHED MOUNTAIN, Mountain Rd., Francestown, NH 03043; 603-588-6840. A 14-guestroom (5 rooms with private baths) mountain inn in southern New Hampshire, 15 mi. from Peterborough. European plan. Open from mid-May to the end of Oct., and from Thanksgiving thru the ski season. During winter dinner is served on Fri. and Sat., and during holiday periods. Dinner is served from Tues. thru Sat. during the remainder of the year. Within a short distance of the Sharon Arts Center, American Stage Festival, Peterborough Players, Crotched Mt. ski areas. Swimming pool, tennis courts, xc skiing, volleyball on grounds. Golf, skiing, hill walking, and backroading in the gorgeous Monadnock region nearby. No credit cards. Rose and John Perry, Innkeepers.

Directions: From Boston, follow Rte. 3 north to 101A to Milford. Then Rte. 13 to New Boston and Rte. 136 to Francestown. Follow Rte. 47, 2½ mi. and turn left on Mountain Road. Inn is 1 mi. on right. From New York/Hartford: I-91 north to Rte. 10 at Northfield to Keene, N.H. Follow 101 east to Peterborough, Rte. 202 north to Bennington, Rte. 47 to Mountain Rd. (approx. 4½ mi.); turn right on Mountain Rd. Inn is 1 mi. on right.

JOHN HANCOCK INN
Hancock, New Hampshire

The previous day's late-winter storm had dropped about eight inches of snow on the Monadnock region, and the roads that twist and turn with a very pleasant roller coaster effect through the woods, past occasional farmhouses, and over brooks were piled high with snow on each side.

The village of Hancock could not have been more attractive, with gleaming white clapboards and occasional red brick Colonials glistening in the high-noon sun. I passed the village green, with its now-dormant bandstand, and the high-steepled church and school. In the center of the village there was the hospitable door of the John Hancock Inn.

"John Hancock never slept here. In fact I don't think he ever came here." Pat Wells pointed to a print of Mr. Hancock. "He was a land speculator in Boston and in those days the man who owned the land had everything named after him."

Pat's husband, Glynn, was seated on the low oaken counter that serves as a main desk in the lobby, and I sat on a restored buggy seat next to the low fire. The lobby resembles a country store of 100 years ago, with many of the trappings that would have been in such an establishment.

Through the open door I could see into the unusual lounge, where the tables are gigantic bellows imported from Nova Scotia. The wood in that room came from old horse stalls.

The John Hancock is a prime model for a village inn. It is the continuing center for community activity and is small enough that villagers and visitors have the opportunity to get acquainted. It is New Hampshire's oldest continuously operating inn, and all of the guest rooms have been appropriately furnished. Many have double and twin canopy beds.

I first met Pat and Glynn when they visited me in Stockbridge many years ago to talk about the possibility of finding a country inn to buy. They fell in love with the John Hancock Inn and have been here ever since, becoming an integral part of this small community.

Pat and Glynn have their own ideas about Sunday brunch. For example, instead of having a buffet table, they prefer to offer their guests table service, and in many cases Hancock neighbors join with the out-of-town guests—it's becoming a regular stop-off after church or after the "morning-trip-out-for-the-paper."

For many years I have shared a portion of a yearly letter from Pat that has proven to supply an insight into country innkeeping. Here's a sampling of one of her notes:

"I think that the whole business of innkeeping has been an act of faith for us. Back in 1972, the realization that we were going to be somewhere else was the controlling factor that led us to Hancock. God has been good these years. We believe that with His strength and guidance we can make the inn what it richly deserves to be—a haven for others, a source of pride for the town, and a deep and rich experience for our family. It is all that, I believe, but never could be without the faith that has supported us in every kind of problem.

"We find that many guests are including the John Hancock Inn in a kind of New England sampler. They plan a circle trip that includes Boston and its many attractions, the seacoast of Maine, the higher mountains of northern New Hampshire, and then a stay in our land of picturebook

villages, twisty roads among the hills, and inviting vistas that make up the Monadnock region. Many of these visitors are from the West Coast and they tell us that New England is everything they hoped it would be."

Latest news from the Wells family is that Glynn and Pat's son, Andrew, is with the 82nd Airborne Division of the U.S. Army, working as a night baker, and Pat says he's soaking up the challenge. Susan has developed a great love for the world of fashion, Pat's former world, and will probably continue her education in that direction. As Pat says, "It's rewarding to see these new adults—strangers, really—and then to realize they're the same lovable creatures that we've known in years past."

THE JOHN HANCOCK INN, Hancock, NH 03449; 603-525-3318. A 10-guestroom village inn on Rtes. 123 and 137, 9 mi. north of Peterborough, in the middle of the Monadnock region of southern N.H. European plan. Breakfast, lunch, and dinner served daily to travelers. Sun. brunch. Closed Christmas Day and one week in spring and fall. Bicycles available on the grounds. Antiquing, swimming, hiking, alpine and xc skiing nearby. Glynn and Pat Wells, Innkeepers.

Directions: From Keene, take either Rte. 101 east to Dublin and Rte. 137 north to Hancock or Rte. 9 north to Rte. 123 and east to Hancock. From Nashua, take 101A and 101 to Peterborough. Proceed north on Rtes. 202 and 123 to Hancock.

LOVETT'S BY LAFAYETTE BROOK
Franconia, New Hampshire

Charlie Lovett was explaining his philosophy of innkeeping, which he has been practicing here at Lovett's for nearly forty years. "The whole idea is to run a comfortable inn. We think ours accommodates itself to the landscape."

Looking out over the striking White Mountains and then glancing back at the distinctive New England lines of this white clapboard building, I fully agreed with him.

"This is a mountain inn, and you know there are many reasons for coming to the White Mountains and especially to our little village of Franconia. We have antiquing, and flower shows and horse shows, summer theater, auctions, and country fairs. There also is the fall foliage, good winter and spring skiing, and cross-country skiing as well. I think that our guests like to escape from city life by visiting us.

"There are walks all over these mountains and all kinds of places to motor to," Charlie pointed out. "Most of the ski areas run their lifts during the summer and autumn. Shopping seems to intrigue our guests as well. We have several superior places right here in Franconia and a sprinkling of country stores and crafts shops throughout the mountains."

Charlie and I were in the sitting room with its deep couches, overhead beams, and woodburning stove. There is a painting of the inn showing Cannon Mountain in the background.

Lovett's has several country-inn-type guest rooms in the main house and in two nearby houses. There are more contemporarily furnished small chalets on the grounds with living rooms and mountain views, many of them with fireplaces. A few poolside chalets are also available.

An outdoor terrace faces Cannon Mountain on the south and great sunsets on the west.

With Lovett's impressive reputation for its food, it is difficult to make a choice from the tempting menu.

"We're particularly proud of our cold wild blueberry soup, hot mussel bisque,and curried fresh sorrel soup. The pleasure of three-course breakfasts is heightened by coffee made with Mount Lafayette's purest water," Charlie commented.

The nearby New England Ski Museum is the only ski museum I know of, and it has photographs and films of the early days of North American skiing, which had its beginning at nearby Peckett's Inn on Sugar Hill.

The establishment of the New England Ski Museum was one of Charlie's dreams. "It is for all the New England states and contains much memorabilia and history of some of the great early Austrian ski instructors such as Hans Schneider, who really provided the impetus that eventually resulted in the American ski industry. Lovett's was in on the early part of everything around 1930 and we had our own Swiss ski instructor here. He took the guests up on Cannon Mountain every day, and in those days you herringboned up the side of the mountain because there was no ski lift as there is now."

Winters in this part of New Hampshire are dominated by the presence of ski areas, principally Cannon Mountain, which looms in all of its snow-clad glory just a few minutes from Lovett's. Cannon is one of the principal downhill ski areas in New England, and its well-known tramway carries skiers to the top of the mountain for some really great skiing.

Lovett's is a sophisticated country inn with considerable emphasis on excellent food and service. It is well into its second generation of

one-family ownership and many of the guests have been returning for years. Their fathers and mothers came before them. There is a very definite spirit that pulls everybody together. As one guest remarked, "It's almost like a club."

LOVETT'S BY LAFAYETTE BROOK, Profile Rd., Franconia, NH 03580; 603-823-7761. A 32-guestroom country inn in New Hampshire's White Mountains. Modified American plan omits lunch. Box lunches available. Breakfast and dinner served by reservation to travelers. Open daily from June 29 to Oct. 8 and from Dec. 26 to Apr. 1. Swimming pool, pond and streams for fishing, xc skiing, lawn sports on grounds. Golf, tennis, alpine skiing, hiking nearby. Mr. and Mrs. Charles J. Lovett, Jr., Innkeepers.

Directions: South of Franconia 2½ mi. on N.H. business loop, at junction of N.H. 141 and I-93 South Franconia exit; 2¾ mi. north of junction of U.S. 3 and 18.

THE LYME INN
Lyme, New Hampshire

The letter from Judy Siemons told of removing layers and layers of wallpaper from brick walls, plastering and painting, uncovering fireplaces, and finally stenciling borders, and creating a gift area in the upstairs hall. They were able to save one wall of strawberry wallpaper in the guest room that is part of the old ballroom. All of which comes under the heading of the never-finished sprucing-up jobs that innkeepers are ever engaged in. On all my visits with innkeepers Judy and Fred Siemons, there has always been another refurbishing project just finished or under way.

On my last visit, Judy was overflowing with news about the "Garrison stove in our third dining room. What a difference it makes, both in direct heat and warming up the atmosphere. We found a wonderful source of braided rag rugs, and have replaced many of our older rugs and covered previously bare floors with some of the nicest braided rugs I've ever seen. We've also added quite a few Hitchcock chairs and tables to our dining rooms."

The Lyme Inn is an antique-laden gem that sits at the end of a long New England common. The ten guest rooms with private baths and five rooms with shared baths have poster beds, hooked rugs, hand-stitched quilts, wide pine floorboards, stenciled wallpaper, and winged chairs. I feel certain that children would not be comfortable, because there is no entertainment particularly designed for them.

This inn is a treasure-trove of nostalgic memorabilia; one room displays old farm tools, and reminds us that this is good snowshoeing country. The house boasts a number of antique maps and salt-glazed pottery, and one of its bedrooms is outfitted in a rare suite of 19th-century painted "cottage" furniture, reminiscent of Eastlake.

My attention was drawn to the unusual collection of framed samplers on the wall of the dining room. "Oh, I am definitely into samplers," exclaimed Judy. "I am always anxious to know more about them and sometimes our guests are able to be of assistance.

"Samplers are a form of American folk art," she continued, "and I find that the real old ones are fast disappearing. A friend of mine who lives nearby does most of our framing and we are doing everything we can to preserve them, including using acid-free paper."

Breakfast, included in the room rate, features juice, fresh fruit in season, fried or scrambled eggs, french toast with local maple syrup, and blueberry muffins.

Chef Hans Wickert, trained in Germany and Switzerland, has introduced several Continental specialties, including hasenpfeffer. He offers a different menu for summer and winter, but always a veal dish and a shrimp dish, and always makes his own soups from scratch.

Guests are intrigued with the four sheep, two black and two white ewes. Judy says they are kept as added "lawn mowers." They're sheared every spring and she talked about possibly trading their wool for blankets at one of the crafts shops in the area. These sheep are kept in line by Duffy, the sheep dog, who is well known to almost every guest who stays at the inn. As Judy says of him, "He's just a people's dog and has never led a dog's life."

Although the village feels quite remote, it is nonetheless just ten miles from Hanover, New Hampshire, the home of Dartmouth College, and inn guests have the opportunity to enjoy some of the sporting and

theatrical events taking place there. It is just a few minutes from the Dartmouth Skiway, and there's plenty of cross-country skiing nearby. In fact, new snowmaking equipment at the Skiway has caused Fred and Judy to offer a midweek MAP special to take advantage of the uncrowded week days.

THE LYME INN, on the Common, Lyme, NH 03768; 603-795-2222. A 15-guestroom (10 with private baths) village inn 10 mi. north of Hanover on N.H. Rte. 10. Breakfast included in room rate. Dinner served daily to travelers except on Tues. Closed from Sun. following Thanksgiving to Dec. 26, and 3 wks. in late spring. Convenient to all Dartmouth College activities, including Hopkins Center, with music, dance, drama, painting, and sculpture. Alpine and xc skiing, fishing, hiking, canoeing, tennis, and golf nearby. No children under 8. No pets. Fred and Judy Siemons, Innkeepers.

Directions: From I-91, take Exit 14 and follow Rte. 113A east to Vermont Rte. 5. Proceed south 50 yards to a left turn, then travel 2 mi. to inn.

MOOSE MOUNTAIN LODGE
Etna, New Hampshire

"We have lots of things to do here in the summer!"

I must say that the weather on this wonderful snowy day in January certainly belied the subject of our conversation. Innkeepers Kay and Peter Shumway and I were seated around the Lazy Susan table in the dining room at Moose Mountain Lodge, and I was enjoying some marvelous blueberry pancakes. With snowflakes dancing merrily and the sounds of cross-country skiers waxing their skis in the adjacent shop, this was a far cry from mid-August.

Kay poured us all another cup of coffee and continued. "Our guests hike, swim, and canoe on the Connecticut River, visit Dartmouth College and Hanover, and perhaps what is most outstanding, sit on the porch, enjoy the view, and watch the birds. Children are welcome, providing they are old enough to get out and hike, ski, and do outdoor things."

Sitting on the porch and watching the birds is very easy at Moose Mountain Lodge. The lodge is a rustic building high on the western side of Moose Mountain, built in the late 1930s, mostly of logs and stones gathered from the surrounding forests and fields. The broad porch extends across the entire rear of the lodge, and has views, in the foreground, of the rolling New Hampshire countryside and, in the distance, of famed Vermont peaks as far away as Rutland.

There are twelve "lodge-type," rustic bedrooms with colorful quilts, lots of books and magazines, bunk beds and conventional single and double beds, and a rustic air that I seldom find these days.

"Many things are different here in the summer, including the menus," Kay remarked. "Summer meals have lots of fish and some meats with light sauces; all the vegetables from the garden and all the fresh fruits that I can pick; sometimes cold soups. We have salads and homemade breads and generally fruit desserts.

"However, in the wintertime we serve stuffed squashes, lots of potatoes and big roasts, and always a huge salad and all kinds of desserts. Everything is put out on the buffet table so guests can have whatever they want and they can sit wherever they wish."

Meanwhile, on this particular day, the new soapstone stove at the far end of the dining room was sending out rays of welcome heat. In the adjacent room, a huge fire was crackling away, and gathered around it were guests reluctant to leave their morning coffee to take to the cross-country ski trails. One guest was even playing lightly on one of the two pianos. It was sort of between meals, but people were pouring cups of coffee from the ever-present pot and nibbling at the offerings in the seemingly bottomless cookie jar.

Peter was called away, and I followed Kay into another one of the

centers of activity at Moose Mountain Lodge—the kitchen. "We run an open kitchen here," Kay said. "I like it when guests wander in and ask 'what's for lunch!' Incidentally, most of the time it's soup and salad." This was Kay's domain and it revealed her many interest besides cuisine, including flowers and plants. In the middle of the big butcher-block table was a copy of *Webster's New Collegiate Dictionary*. How can you go wrong in a kitchen that is also a haven for the intellectually curious!

Peter breezed in to say that he was going to take some of the guests out on the cross-country trails. He gave Kay a hug and said "so-long" to me. As the door shut behind him, Kay turned back to me and said, "We love innkeeping and we've had a lots of fun doing it ever since we've been here."

MOOSE MOUNTAIN LODGE, Etna, NH 03750; 603-643-3529. A 12-guestroom (5 shared baths) rustic lodge a few miles from Hanover, New Hampshire. Closed April and May, and from Nov. 15 thru Dec. 26. Breakfast, lunch, and dinner served to houseguests only. Xc skiing for all abilities on grounds or nearby. Ski equipment available. Hiking, biking, walking, canoeing, backroading, and many recreational and cultural attractions nearby, including Dartmouth College. No pets. Peter and Kay Shumway, Innkeepers.

Directions: If arriving for the first time, stop in Etna at Landers Restaurant or the Etna Store and telephone the lodge for directions. The last mile up the mountain is steep, and when the road is icy, guests are met at the bottom parking lot with a 4-wheel-drive vehicle. Etna is on the map, a few miles east of Hanover.

PHILBROOK FARM INN
Shelburne, New Hampshire

One of the happiest moments of my life (and I've had quite a few happy moments) was when I was presented with an official Philbrook Family Reunion T-shirt and made an official Philbrook adoptee. All of this tomfoolery took place at Philbrook Farm on the eve of their great family reunion, for which at least 80-odd Philbrooks were going to arrive for the once-every-five-years occasion.

In the last edition, I began the account of my visit to this almost-ancient farm country inn in northern New Hampshire by saying that some things never change. I guess I failed to realize that some changes were coming then, which are very much in effect now.

First of all, there is now a swimming pool. The sketch of the inn does not show the pool, but it would be on the left corner and it has already been used for a full summer to the great delight of the guests.

The second change is that Nancy Philbrook and her sister, Connie Leger, and Connie's son, Larry, have been joined by Larry's sister, Ann, and her friend, Madonna, which has swelled the family members of the staff considerably. Perhaps I'd better describe this inn and then refer to Ann's letter for other interesting changes.

The main house of Philbrook Farm was built in 1834 and the first addition with the blue porch and old-fashioned door was put on in 1861. The east end was built in 1905 and the dining room, along with the "new kitchens," was added when the big barns burned in 1934.

The Philbrook Farm *is* New Hampshire. There are New Hampshire prints, paintings, and photographs, some of them really irreplaceable. There are some tints of old prints, hooked rugs, and many, many books about New Hampshire. A whole library of books is just on the White Mountains, some of them written by former guests of the farm.

A new project is making cross-stitch door plaques with the names of many of the long-time returning guests. The plaques are being done with the help of guests, friends, and the rest of the family. More about that in the next edition.

One of the fascinating aspects of Philbrook Farm is the fantastic collection of ninety-eight jigsaw puzzles, all cut by Larry and Ann's great-grandfather and kept in their own special cupboard. "He was quite a diabolical gentleman because he really liked to befuddle people," Ann said. "They would hear him chuckling to himself down in the shop as he cut these puzzles. He would bring a puzzle upstairs for the guests, and if they finished it too quickly he would take it right back downstairs and recut it to make it harder. Each puzzle is dated and has a title, but there are no pictures to follow."

I'm afraid that this piece is becoming a bit of a jigsaw itself, so

perhaps we'd better save the account of the remaining changes at Philbrook for another year, but let me reassure you that with or without changes, things go on beautifully at Philbrook Farm.

PHILBROOK FARM INN, North Rd., Shelburne, NH 03581; 603-466-3831. A 20-guestroom country inn in the White Mountains of northeastern N.H., 6 mi. from Gorham and just west of the Maine/N.H. line. American, mod. American, and European plans available. Open May 1 to Oct. 31; Dec. 26 to Apr. 1. Closed Thanksgiving, Christmas. Swimming pool, shuffleboard, horseshoes, badminton, ping-pong, croquet, billiards, hiking trails, xc skiing, snowshoeing trails on grounds. Swimming, golf, hiking, backroading, bird watching nearby. Pets allowed only during summer season in cottages. No credit cards. The Philbrook and Leger Families, Innkeepers.

Directions: The inn is just off U.S. Rte. 2 in Shelburne. Look for inn direction sign and turn at Meadow Rd., cross R.R. tracks and river, and turn right at North Rd. The inn is at the end of the road.

"European Plan" means that rates for rooms and meals are separate. "American Plan" means that meals are included in the cost of the room. "Modified American Plan" means that breakfast and dinner are included in the cost of the room. The rates at some inns include a continental breakfast with the lodging.

ROCKHOUSE MOUNTAIN FARM INN
Eaton Center, New Hampshire

"Our headline news," the letter from Libby and John Edge proclaimed, "is that Rockhouse will be forty years old in 1986!" This makes Rockhouse Mountain Farm one of the very select few country inns that have been operated by the same family for four decades.

I've been visiting the Edge family for many years, and have watched as son Johnny and daughter Betsi took on many responsibilities around the inn with ease and affability—Betsi as a superlative cook and Johnny as farm manager and animal handler. Johnny, a virtual dynamo on the farm, has gained not only county but state recognition by the New Hampshire Conservation District with an award for "Outstanding Accomplishment in the Conservation of Soil, Water, and Related Sources." This was in recognition of the improvement, embellishment, and beautification of the Rockhouse land. Libby tells me that with all of this, Johnny still finds time to cook the breakfasts, grill steaks and chickens for outdoor barbecues, and socialize with the guests.

Guest-friends have been returning to this farm-inn, in some cases, for as many years as it has been open, bringing their children and their grandchildren. It is definitely oriented for family vacations. Just imagine the fun a youngster can have in a barn filled with new-mown hay, where there are horses, cows, pigs, geese, and ducks—all, incidentally, with their own names.

There are fascinating things to do for everyone—milking cows, feeding the animals, riding horses, hiking to the old Indian cave, canoeing or sailing on Crystal Lake, or sunbathing or picnicking on the private beach. Farther afield there is tennis, golf, bicycling, fishing, summer theater, or antiquing. Or you can sit under the glorious maples in front of the white buildings of the inn and dream, as I have done. The cover of this book depicts Rockhouse Mountain Farm in autumn.

Food is bounteous and hearty and mealtimes are informal, with separate dining for children. Fresh vegetables from the gardens tended by Alana, Johnny's wife, fresh-baked breads, roasts, outdoor barbecues, and scrumptious desserts, many with blueberries from nearby Foss Mountain, are all part of the home-style fare. I especially remember Libby's apple-rhubarb pie. Johnny doesn't stint on breakfasts either, with fresh eggs and blueberry pancakes with real maple syrup.

A new living room, with a big picture window opening out on a panoramic view of the beautiful pastures and a new pond, is the most recent addition to the main building. The music room was converted into a dining room, providing further dining space.

On my last visit, I had the delightful surprise of being the first person to occupy the newly redecorated "Norman Simpson Room," furnished with, as Johnny explained, his great-grandmother's bureau and other nice antiques. As I reported, I slept like a top, feeling very much at home in the friendly, homey atmosphere of Rockhouse Mountain Farm.

ROCKHOUSE MOUNTAIN FARM INN, Eaton Center, NH 03832; 603-447-2880. A complete resort in the foothills of the White Mountains (6 mi. south of Conway), combining a modern 18-guestroom country inn with life on a 350-acre farm. Some rooms with private bath. Mod. American plan. Open from June 15 through Oct. Saddle horses, milk cows, and other farm animals; haying, hiking, shuffleboard; private beach on Crystal Lake with swimming, rowboats, sailboats, and canoes—canoe trips planned; stream and lake fishing; tennis and golf nearby. No credit cards. The Edge Family, Innkeepers.

Directions: From I-93, take Exit 23 to Rte. 104 to Meredith. Take Rte. 25 to Rte. 16, and proceed north to Conway. Follow Rte. 153, 6 mi. south from Conway to Eaton Center.

SPALDING INN & CLUB
Whitefield, New Hampshire

Many years ago the White Mountains in New Hampshire had numerous summer resorts where "mother and children" might come up early in the season and where "father" joined them for the last four weeks or so. These resorts were wonderful, gay places where everything that was needed for a long, complete vacation was either on the grounds or nearby. The lure of the mountains drew people in great numbers from Boston and New York.

Now, with few exceptions, all of these family-run resorts have disappeared, but not the Spalding Inn & Club, which is thriving under second- and third-generation owners and innkeepers. Many of the amenities of earlier times are still preserved; for example, gentlemen wouldn't think of going to dinner without a jacket and tie. The inn is a focal point for the sports of lawn bowling and tennis, with several tournaments scheduled from mid-June to mid-September, including the U.S. National Singles and Doubles Lawn Bowling Championships.

The Spalding Inn & Club is an excellent example of entertainment and hospitality that can be provided for a family with many different preferences. For example, on the inn grounds there are four clay tennis courts, a swimming pool, a nine-hole par-3 golf course, two championship lawn bowling greens, and shuffleboard. Five golf courses are within fifteen minutes of the inn, and plenty of trout fishing and boating, and enticing back roads are nearby. The Appalachian Trail system for mountain climbing is a short walk from the inn.

There is also a well-blended balance of vigorous outdoor activity and quiet times, including an extensive library, a card room, and a

challenging collection of jigsaw puzzles. Groves of maples, birches, and oak trees native to northern New Hampshire are on the inn grounds and there are over 400 acres of lawns, gardens, and orchards. There are real country-inn touches everywhere. The broad porch is ideal for rocking, and the newly decorated main living room has a fireplace with a low ceiling, lots of books and magazines, baskets of apples, a barometer for tomorrow's weather, a jar of sour balls, and great arrangements of flowers.

Those country-inn touches also include the traditional hearty menu items so satisfying after a day of outdoor activities in the White Mountains. Among other offerings in the air-conditioned dining room are delicious clam chowder, oyster stew, broiled scrod, poached salmon, pork chops, roast duckling, roast tenderloin, and sweetbreads. Children love the Indian pudding. All of the pies, including hot mince, and the breads and rolls are made in the bakery of the inn.

I am just as pleased as I can be that Bill and Michael Ingram continue keeping their standards high, and that this delightful, elegant resort-inn continues to offer its unique White Mountain hospitality.

SPALDING INN & CLUB, Mountain View Road, Whitefield, NH 03598; 603-837-2572. A 70-guestroom resort-inn in the center of New Hampshire's White Mountains. American and modified American plans (MAP omits lunch.) Open late May to mid-Oct. Breakfast, lunch and dinner are served daily to travelers. Heated pool, tennis courts, 9-hole par-3 golf course, 18-hole putting green, 2 championship lawn bowling greens, and shuffleboard on grounds. Also Sunday night movies. Guest privileges at 5 nearby golf clubs. Trout fishing, boating, summer theater, and backroading nearby. William A. and Michael B. Ingram, Innkeepers.

Directions: From New York take Merritt Pkwy. to I-91; I-91 to Wells River, Vt./Woodsville, N.H. exit; then Rte. 302 to Littleton, then Rte. 116 thru Whitefield to Mtn. View Rd. intersection—3 mi. north of village. From Boston take I-93 north thru Franconia Notch to Littleton exit; then Rte. 116 thru Whitefield to Mtn. View Rd. intersection—3 mi. north of village. From Montreal take Autoroute 10 to Magog; then Autoroute 55 and I-91 to St. Johnsbury, Vt.; then Rte. 18 to Littleton, N.H. and Rte. 116 as above. The inn is situated 1 mi. west on Mountain View Rd.

STAFFORD'S IN THE FIELD
Chocorua, New Hampshire

The first sight that caught my eye was the family of ducks. Two good-sized adults and at least ten baby ducklings were waddling their way across the parking lot down toward the new tennis court, in its final stages of construction. I tried as unobtrusively as possible to get a closer view of the duck family, but they would have none of it and kept moving farther away into the high grass, with mama and papa duck carefully herding the little ones out of harm's way.

The muted tan shades of the main building had a fresh look, with the gay accents of window boxes and a summer garden of black-eyed Susans and other seasonal flowers. The big, old red barn, which I have admired since my first visit in 1971, was still intact.

Next to the kitchen door a small table, shaded by a bright blue umbrella, had a sign saying, "Bakery." Another small sign indicated that cookies, sandwiches, and other things would be available for guests for noontime forays into the countryside. I found Ramona Stafford in the

kitchen and had a nice chat with her while she was doing the morning muffins. On the wooden table were the necessities and trappings of baking: a large bowl of eggs, a blender, a box of oats, a brush with melted butter, five or six recipe books, and on the shelf all kinds of tempting flavorings, in addition to a contraption for weighing and measuring the ingredients.

As early as the 1972 edition of *Country Inns and Back Roads* I pointed out that this was an inn of many faces. It sits at the end of the road at the top of a small hill, with broad meadows on three sides and a beautiful woods behind. There is an apple orchard, stone walls, a series of small cottages, and that famous barn. A great many of the winter guests are fond of cross-country skiing and there are trails all around the inn. Today, there is a nine-hole country golf course among the trees.

Still another face of this old inn is seen in summer when the New Hampshire mountains offer many diversions, including water sports like canoeing, sailing, fishing, and swimming. It's possible to find a place of unusual peace and contentment by disappearing into the woods surrounding the inn. For the more vigorous climber, Mount Chocorua offers a worthy challenge.

Still another side of Stafford's in the Field is Ramona's gourmet cooking. I hasten to point out that "gourmet" is a word I never use lightly, but my original conversation with her convinced me that she was not merely a good cook but a dedicated searcher for true expression in the culinary art. Breads and pastries are home-baked and there is a very generous selection of Russian, French, Italian, and German dishes with a knowledgeable use of herbs and spices. One of my favorite dishes is the spareribs cooked in maple syrup from the Staffords' own trees.

I joined Fred Stafford at breakfast, where the houseguests were seated around the long tables, and many of them, it seems, were traveling with *Country Inns and Back Roads*. Some of them had used the book to visit Europe.

Having watched Ramona turning out those muffins, my mouth was watering for them. I can report that I ate three, hot from the oven and deliciously buttered; with the fourth I tried something new—cutting it up in several slices and pouring some delicious hot maple syrup over it.

Mmmm, terrific!

STAFFORD'S IN THE FIELD, Chocorua, NH 03817; 603-323-7766. A 14-guestroom resort-inn with 5 cottages, 17 mi. south of North Conway. Modified American plan omits lunch. Dinner is offered to the public with reservations. Open all year. Bicycles, square dancing, tennis, country golf, and xc skiing on grounds. Golf club, swimming, hiking, riding, and fishing nearby. No pets. The Stafford Family, Innkeepers.

Directions: Follow N.H. Rte. 16 north to Chocorua Village, then turn left onto Rte. 113 and travel 1 mi. west to inn. Or, from Rte. 93 take Exit 23 and travel east on Rtes. 104 and 25 to Rte. 16. Proceed north on Rte. 16 to Chocorua Village, turn left onto Rte. 113 and travel 1 mi. west to inn.

WOODBOUND INN
Jaffrey, New Hampshire

I have just finished as engrossing a piece of writing as I have ever read. It is the history of the Woodbound Inn, written by Ed Brummer for the 50th anniversary of the inn, celebrated in the summer of 1984. I'm going to share some of this with you after we set down the basic information about the inn, so that everyone will know how enjoyable it can be.

The Woodbound is a genial family resort-inn. Ed and Peg Brummer started it all, and their son and daughter-in-law, Jed and Mary Ellen, are continuing it. There is even a third generation of Brummers on the scene.

Open in all four seasons, the Woodbound provides unlimited winter sports, including downhill and cross-country skiing on the grounds, ice skating, tobogganing, sleigh riding, and even showshoeing.

The Woodbound especially welcomes families, and has cottage units designed especially for them, with maid service and with meals at the inn. There are regular programs and activities for children and a baby-sitting service as well.

For me, one of the most rewarding experiences at Woodbound is the early morning nature walks with a local ecologist along a unique half-mile nature trail, covering three separate ecological environments with an unusual number of uncommon flora.

As might be expected in a resort-inn of this nature, food is most important, and Ed's son, Jed, pointed out in a recent letter, "The Woodbound dining experience has been completely refined. The dining room has been redecorated and our new chef is doing a wonderful job." The Woodbound menu features such traditional offerings as roast turkey, roast leg of lamb, country ham, lobster, roast pork, as well as lamb chops, pork chops, veal piccata, veal scallopini, chicken amaretto, baked haddock, and broiled bay scallops.

In addition to the Woodbound's 1,200-yard par 3 golf course with 9 holes, there are four full-length 18- and 9-hole golf courses nearby. There is a half-acre trout pond developed in a natural setting, and Lake Contoocook has wide-mouth bass, perch, and pickerel.

Now to some excerpts from Ed Brummer's history:

"The operation could be classified as Fifty Years of Putting In Private Baths! Using one room to put in baths and closets for two others, squeezing space where possible. There was not only that process over a period of years, but many of those baths have again been completely renovated.... That first year, rates were $3 a day with three meals and a special of $17.50 a week at the beginning of the season.... For the first twelve years of Brummer operation the cooking continued to be done with a large hotel wood stove and there were plenty of cooks who knew how to cook with wood. Until after World War II, refrigeration was provided by ice boxes. The ice was cut out of the lake each winter and hauled by horses to the inn icehouse..... For several years a female Brooklyn librarian of middle age came to the inn and enjoyed nude sunbathing...."

One guest appointed himself the croquet master, instructing new guests on the rules and maintaining the lines, equipment, and blackboard scores. He returned for years, keeping up his unremitting activities until he was ninety. The Woodbound has had its share of celebrities over the years, including Vice President George Bush, former Vice President Henry Wallace, and Libby Holman (the torch singer of the twenties). And there is much more fascinating lore in Ed Brummer's history. He ends his account with a declaration:

"Woodbound has been ringing a bell at mealtimes for fifty years under the Brummers and will continue to do so."

WOODBOUND INN AND COTTAGES, Jaffrey, NH 03452; 603-532-8341. A 44-guestroom resort-inn on Lake Contoocook, 2 mi. in the woods from West Rindge or Jaffrey. Modified American plan. Breakfast, lunch, and dinner served daily to travelers. Open year-round. Par-3 golf course, swimming, beach, sailing, water skiing, tennis, hiking, nature walks, children's programs, downhill ski area, 22 miles of groomed ski-touring trails, tobogganing, lighted skating rink, summer carriage rides, hayrides, and sleigh rides. Ed and Peggy Brummer, Jed and Mary Ellen Brummer, Innkeepers.

Directions: From Boston, follow Rte. 2 then Rte. 119 to Rindge where there are directional signs to inn. From New York, follow I-91 to Bernardston, Mass. Proceed on Rte. 10 to Winchester, then Rte. 119 to Rindge and watch for signs to inn.

BARROWS HOUSE
Dorset, Vermont

There was a beautiful full September moon coming up over the Barrows House. As I drove past the house to the parking area, I noticed Earl, the orange cat, lazily washing himself on a patio table under a Cinzano umbrella. I decided to take a short walk around the grounds past the many colorful gardens, the two tennis courts, and the huge swimming pool.

Then, heading back toward the inn, I rounded a curve in the path and came upon a wonderful view of the new extension to the dining room, called "The Greenhouse." It was indeed a captivating scene with the gracefully curved solarium-style glass ceiling and walls, through which I could see the flickering candles at each table and the impressive candelabra. The many hanging plants created a true garden feeling.

Plants and flowers are an important part of the ambience of the Barrows House. Earlier, Marilyn Schubert explained that her garden started in early spring with tulips, violets, daffodils, iris, and lupine. Later on, there were the flowers of summer—columbine, day lilies, bleeding hearts, phlox, bee balm, shasta daisies, dahlias and many others. In fact, I don't believe I realized before just what a large part flowers play in Marilyn's life. She had spent a number of years as an airline hostess before she and her husband, Charlie, and their young son came to the Barrows House in Dorset.

The main house, as you can see from the Jan Lindstrom sketch, is of Federalist design with some Victorian additions. There are also seven other buildings on six acres. "I think we've become a mini resort-inn," is the way Charlie puts it. "Many of our guests can spend much of their time right here, but when the spirit moves them they can go antiquing in the

little villages like Pawlet or Wells, drive up and down the Mettowee River, or into the mountains to Weston and the famous Vermont Country Store. In winter, it's just a short drive to Bromley or Stratton Mountain for downhill skiing. Of course, we have all the cross-country skiing equipment and trails right here at the Barrows House."

Besides the Greenhouse, many other exciting things have happened since my last visit. For example, the country inn bedrooms have almost all been redecorated, and the hallways have been adorned with some wonderful stenciling. The result is an attractive, gay atmosphere, with each bedroom having its own distinctive feeling, and with views of the lawns or gardens from every window.

A little earlier, Marilyn and I had walked through the gardens past Charlie's touch-football field and sat in the gazebo. She was very enthusiastic about the cuisine and said with a self-deprecating air, "I think we're getting a very good reputation locally. Our chef does things like blackened fresh red snapper, turkey breasts stuffed with prosciutto and cheese, broiled lamb chops in the French provincial style, and a roast country duckling with green peppercorn sauce. We are on the modified American plan, although lunch is served every day."

She leaned forward and put her hand on my arm, "You know, I've always been so pleased that Charlie dedicated this gazebo to me and it is so romantic that we've had several weddings performed right here. One of them was a 50th-anniversary renewal of original vows by a lovely couple who visit the inn regularly."

BARROWS HOUSE, Dorset, VT 05251; 802-867-4455. A 31-guestroom village inn on Rte. 30, 6 mi. from Manchester, VT. Modified American plan. Breakfast, lunch, and dinner served daily to travelers. Swimming pool, sauna, tennis courts, paddle tennis, bicycles, skiing facilities, including rental equipment and instruction on grounds. Golf, tennis, trout fishing, and alpine skiing nearby. No credit cards. Charles and Marilyn Schubert, Innkeepers.

Directions: From Rte. 7 in Manchester, proceed 6 mi. north on Rte. 30 to Dorset. ⌐⊿

I do not include lodging rates in the descriptions, for the very nature of an inn means that there are lodgings of various sizes, with and without baths, in and out of season, and with plain and fancy decoration. Travelers should call ahead and inquire about the availability and rates of the many different types of rooms.

BIRCH HILL INN
Manchester, Vermont

Life takes some interesting twists and turns, doesn't it? For many, many years I used to drive north from Stockbridge on Route 7 to Manchester, Vermont, and then turn left at the Johnny Appleseed Bookstore, taking a shortcut around Manchester Center to reach Route 30 and continue on west to Dorset, and up the valley of the Mettowee through Pawlet on up to Lake St. Catherine.

I'm sure that almost every time I took this Manchester shortcut I was attracted to a very large, handsome white house that sat on a rise in a grove of trees. In the winter the snow would be shoveled out and piled high around the entrance, which was reached by a circular driveway. I used to imagine what kind of people lived in that house and what the interior was like.

In 1981 I learned that my lovely white house had indeed become an intimate inn. In the course of events I visited it and met Pat and Jim Lee, who were then new innkeepers, and I subsequently included it in the 1982

edition of this book. Pat's family has lived in that house since 1917, so the chances are I may have seen various members of the family outside as I passed to and fro en route.

The interior is every bit as attractive as the exterior. For example, there are windows on three sides of the living room, which has a wonderful warm feeling, aided by a low ceiling, a sizeable fireplace, a spinet piano, the ongoing, never-ending jigsaw puzzle, and innumerable books and magazines. Over the big fireplace is a print of George Washington's triumphal entry into New York City after the Revolutionary War.

For 190 years Birch Hill was a family home and today it has retained that same homelike feeling. It's obvious that the Lee family has a great deal of interest in art, music and history.

Accommodations are in five comfortable and cheerful guest rooms in the main house, all of which have views toward the mountains, farm, and pond. They are well decorated with paintings and furniture from the family home. A nearby cottage on the grounds has been converted into an ideal family-style accommodation as well.

Dinner is offered only to houseguests every night except Wednesday and Sunday, and I was most interested in what Pat Lee had to say about the "Beefalo" that she often serves. "Beefalo," she explained, "is a breed of cattle originally developed by the introduction of American bison (buffalo) genes into domestic cattle. Beefalo meat contains less than 15% of the fat of supermarket beef, and only 3% of the cholesterol.

"We have small steers and heifers here in the fields around the inn. They are always a great source of conversation among our guests."

One of the things that I enjoy at Birch Hill Inn is the custom of having the guests sit down around the big table together and really get acquainted. By the way, Pat serves a full breakfast every morning.

The well-groomed cross-country ski trails start out right from the inn's property and continue over hill and through the woods. These become excellent jogging or running trails at other times of the year.

In summertime there's good swimming and a trout pond, where the fish are reproducing at such a rate that guests can bring them back to the inn to be cooked for breakfast.

I think it's wonderful that my beautiful white house has become an inn that I can share.

BIRCH HILL INN, Box 346, West Rd., Manchester, VT 05254; 802-362-2761. A 5-guestroom extremely comfortable country-home inn, with a family cottage, 5 min. from downtown Manchester Center. Breakfast included in the cost of the room. Dinners offered to houseguests only, every night except Wed. and Sun. Open after Christmas to mid-April, and May to late Oct., 2-night minimum preferred (be sure to make reservations). Swimming pool, xc skiing, trout fishing, and walking trails on grounds. Alpine skiing at major areas nearby as well as tennis and golf facilities; great biking. Children over 6 welcome. No pets. No credit cards. Pat and Jim Lee, Innkeepers.

Directions: From Rte. 7 in Manchester, take left fork at Johnny Appleseed Bookstore and continue on for about 3 mi. Birch Hill is on the right.

BLUEBERRY HILL
Goshen, Vermont

I first visited Tony Clark at Blueberry Hill in midsummer of 1972, when the idea of opening up an inn exclusively for cross-country skiers was just taking shape in his mind. It became a reality the following year, and, as I guess all of New England knows, Tony was an innovator in what has become a very popular winter pastime. Today, most inns in New England, or in fact anywhere in the mountains, have some kind of cross-country skiing facilities on the premises or nearby.

In the meantime, Tony has continued to look for new paths to follow (see following paragraph for *double entendre*). Let me put it in his words:

"As you know, Norman, we are open for skiing from December through March. But, May through October, and especially summertime here in the Green Mountains is just fabulous. We have a program of inn-to-inn hiking and we're very popular with summer and fall backpackers and walkers. Many, many of our cross-country trails are used for walking and hiking, and it's possible to use the inn as a central point for such activities or to include it on an itinerary. We use our ski trails as nature and educational paths, providing all kinds of guides to help our guests learn the names of the trees and birds."

Tony looked at me with a chuckle. "Here's something rather odd, we are also on an inn-to-inn canoeing program." For a while I thought he was putting me on, but it turns out that the inn is indeed on such a program, and I think that the reader who is interested best make his own inquiries. Of course, there is no river going past Blueberry Hill because it's high in the mountains, but Tony can tell you all about it.

"Actually," he said, pronouncing it as only a native-born Britisher can, "we have a lot of other summertime activities here, including a kite-flying weekend during the second week in September. There are all kinds of kite contests, and with this wonderful open field immediately across from the inn, it's ideal for such activity. We also have a Mozart festival and a chamber music festival in the offing."

Blueberry Hill is very definitely family style. Everyone sits around the big dining room table and there is one main dish for each meal, cooked in the farmhouse kitchen. This main dish is likely to be something quite unusual, depending upon the cook's gourmet proclivities.

Bedrooms are plain and simple with hot water bottles on the backs of doors and handsome patchwork quilts on the beds. It is truly like visiting a Vermont farm.

In late July, to continue the summer saga, there has been an annual cross-country footrace and Blueberry Festival. The course covers 6.5 miles on the paved and gravel roads, leading the runner down through the cool, shaded heart of Goshen, Vermont, up a series of hills and back

through the woods and pastures, with beautiful views of the Green Mountains. Following the race, the Blueberry Festival, open to competitors and spectators alike, features a chicken barbecue with salads, homemade breads, and blueberry baked goods. An old-time square dance wraps up the festivities.

The newest thing is the fact that last June Blueberry Hill hosted the first annual Vermont croquet competition, and all competitors were asked to wear whites.

Blueberry Hill is an unforgettable experience, whether it's early-morning coffee in the greenhouse, a day-long ski tour, or a romantic evening of relaxation in front of a roaring fire. There is great fishing, hiking, biking, and tennis nearby and always a refreshing dip in the pond.

Reservations for winter accommodations should be made as early as possible, as the inn is often booked solid for weeks at a time in winter.

BLUEBERRY HILL, Goshen, VT 05733; 802-247-6735. An 8-guestroom (private baths) mountain inn passionately devoted to xc skiing, 8 mi. from Brandon. Modified American plan for overnight guests. Open from May thru Oct. and Dec. to March. Public dining by reservation only. Closed Christmas. Swimming, fishing, hiking, nature walks, and xc skiing on grounds. Much other recreation nearby. Tony Clark, Innkeeper.

Directions: At Brandon, travel east on Rte. 73 through Forest Dale. Then follow signs to Blueberry Hill.

"European Plan" means that rates for rooms and meals are separate. "American Plan" means that meals are included in the cost of the room. "Modified American Plan" means that breakfast and dinner are included in the cost of the room. The rates at some inns include a continental breakfast with the lodging.

INN AT SAWMILL FARM
West Dover, Vermont

"They said we couldn't grow roses in Vermont, but just look at those!"

Rodney Williams pointed to some gorgeous rose bushes of many varieties that line the pleasant little terrace of the Inn at Sawmill Farm. Three sides of this secluded little enclave with its tidy swimming pool are formed by a farmhouse and a series of connecting barns, some of which were moved into place by Rodney and Ione Williams, when they escaped Atlantic City, New Jersey, to open a country inn quite a few years ago.

"The early Vermont settlers tried to build their houses in little green valleys beside a stream with an apple orchard on the southern slope," he said. "That's why there are so many beautiful houses with beautiful

surroundings." Even as Rod was expounding on this idea I realized how closely this description fits his country inn. Looking south across the swimming pool, past the picturebook Christmas tree, I could see the white spire of the West Dover church. Just below the swimming pool and beyond the Spring House, I caught a glimpse of the two-acre pond that provides ice skating in the winter and trout fishing and boating in the summer. The warm sunshine (on the south side, naturally) also provides perfect light for the profusion of apple and maple trees. It is a scene that has been photographed and painted quite a few times during the past few years. The original pond has now been augmented by a second pond stocked with bass. Rod explained to me that the first pond is stocked with rainbow trout, and you can't mix the two kinds of fish because the bass will eat up the trout. Some guests come to Sawmill with the idea of doing some good pond fishing and fly casting.

When Rod and Ione Williams made the "big break" from the pressures of urban life, they brought their own particular talents and sensitivities to this handsome location, and it is indeed a pleasing experience. There was plenty of work to do—a dilapidated barn, a wagon shed, and other outbuildings all had to be converted into lodgings and living rooms. However, over the years, the transition has been exceptional. The textures of the barn siding, the beams, the ceilings, the floors, and the picture windows combine to create a feeling of rural elegance.

Guest rooms have been both added and redecorated, and again I was smitten with the beautiful quilted bedspreads, the bright wallpaper and white ceilings, the profusions of plants in the rooms, and all of the many books and magazines that add to their guests' enjoyment. Lodgings are also found in outbuildings, including the Cider House Studio, which has a bedroom, dressing room, bath, and living room. The king-sized bed is in an alcove facing a fireplace.

In the living room of the inn there is a superb conversation piece that perhaps symbolizes the entire inn—a handsome brass telescope mounted on a tripod, providing an intimate view of Mount Snow rising majestically to the north.

Brill Williams, Rod and Ione's son, was a teenager when the family moved to West Dover. Now, he is the chef and officially one of the owners of the inn. The menu selection and quality of the food has been praised by many national restaurant and food reviewers. The menu changes with the seasons; for example, the fall menu includes rabbit, grouse, duck, quail, and always a fresh Florida fish.

Taken all in all or in separate parts, Sawmill Farm is spoken of as a model for country inns.

INN AT SAWMILL FARM, Box 8, West Dover, VT 05356; 802-464-8131. A 23-guestroom country resort-inn on Rte. 100, 22 mi. from Bennington and Brattleboro. Within sight of Mt. Snow ski area. Modified American plan omits lunch. Breakfast and dinner served to travelers daily. Closed Nov. 7 thru Dec. 7. Swimming, tennis, and trout fishing on grounds. Golf, bicycles, riding, snowshoeing, alpine and xc skiing nearby. No children under 8. No pets. No credit cards. Rodney, Brill, and Ione Williams, Innkeepers.

Directions: From I-91, take Brattleboro Exit 2 and travel on Vt. Rte. 9 west to Vt. Rte. 100. Proceed north 5 mi. to inn. Or take U.S. 7 north to Bennington, then Rte. 9 east to Vt. Rte. 100 and proceed north 5 mi. to inn.

THE INN AT WEATHERSFIELD
Weathersfield, Vermont

Perkinsville is a real "Vermont" village. On Route 106, north of Springfield, its long main street has several very interesting early 19th-century Vermont homes, many of them of brick. Here and there are some samplings of other architectural styles pleasant to the eye.

I mention Perkinsville because it is right near the Inn at Weathersfield. This time I came to the inn during the Christmas holiday season, and with six inches of snow on the ground it was indeed a picture of Christmas celebration, with candles in all of the front windows and green garlands and red ribbons festooning the balustrade above the second floor. An old sleigh on the front porch was laden with gaily wrapped Christmas packages.

As soon as I walked through the front door, Ron Thornburn came to greet me. He was showing some other guests through the inn for the first time, and I tagged along, learning that the dining room had at one time been the old carriage house. It has low ceilings and a beautiful old stone fireplace. "We save our tree every year for our guests to trim," he explained. "It is in the front parlor, and I think they've done a wonderful job."

We moved on into the Gathering Room, which had been completed since my last visit. It has a fireplace and mantel at one end where there were several Christmas stockings. Everything was beautifully decorated with greens, Christmas tree balls, and in the center of the table—would you believe—real live daisies.

High tea was being served, as it is every day. So I realized that I had arrived at just the right time.

Mary Louise Thornburn came bustling in, gave me a big hug, and plunged right into the fascinating information that they had done an entire Thanksgiving meal in the beehive oven, a part of the original fireplace, situated in the entrance area of the inn. "We cooked everything that you would have had for a meal at the end of the 18th century," she said. "Beans, custards, pies, bread, and things like that. It was such a good idea that we are going to continue doing it at least once a week during the summer, and we are going to use it for baked goods, including breads and rolls, muffins, indian pudding, and the like. I learned how to do this over in Old Sturbridge Village last year."

The Inn at Weathersfield is located in the mountains of eastern Vermont, just west of the Connecticut River. The original farmhouse was built nearly two centuries ago. It was enlarged in 1796, a carriage house was added in 1830, and the graceful pillars on the front porch were built by a homesick Southern minister around 1900.

The inn is set back from Route 106 and has seventeen large guest rooms and suites furnished with period antiques. Each room has a private bath, some have canopied beds, and most have working firplaces.

I wandered back into the Gathering Room and sat down next to the fireplace. Meanwhile, several tables were set up, candles were put in the candelabra, and the early winter evening took over the mood.

Now tea was being served and, wonder of wonders, there was a piece of the most delicious pumpkin pie imaginable. Yes, I am certainly glad that I stopped in at the Inn at Weathersfield today.

Would I stay on for dinner? You bet I would!

THE INN AT WEATHERSFIELD, Route 106 (near Perkinsville), Weathersfield, VT 05151; 802-263-9217. A 17-guestroom Vermont country inn a few mi. west of I-91 and north of Springfield. European plan, with breakfast and a high English tea included in the cost of the room. Dinner also served. Closed for dinner, Sun., Mon., and Tues. (although also available on those evenings during the high season). Horseshoes, badminton, croquet, billiards, sauna, exercise room, sleigh riding on grounds. Also a natural amphitheater with music and theater offered during the summer. Many footpaths and back roads. Bicycles available. Berry and apple picking, golf, downhill skiing (Ascutney and Okemo), xc skiing, horseback riding nearby. Children under 8 years old are not conveniently accommodated. No pets. Mary Louise and Ron Thorburn, Innkeepers.

Directions: Traveling north on I-91, use Exit 7 at Springfield and follow Rte. 106. Traveling south, take Exit 8 and follow Rte. 131 to Rte. 106 and turn south. From Boston, leave I-89 and follow Rte. 103 across New Hampshire west into Vermont, where it becomes Rte. 131, and then go south on Rte. 106.

THE INN ON THE COMMON
Craftsbury Common, Vermont

Penny Schmitt was explaining her philosophy of gardening, particularly perennial gardens. "As all gardeners know," she declared, "a perennial bed needs constant attention—lifting and changing and moving around of plants. Well, this year we found a gardener who knows what it's all about and the gardens at the Inn on the Common are going to be more beautiful in years to come. We're working towards a kind of gardening Nirvana that should produce a series of beds in which there is something colorful happening at all times during the growing season. It's a true labor of love and one that I hope I can devote more time to next summer. Our gardens provide the guests with beautiful flowers and that wonderful view, and are really a place where one can renew oneself, body and soul. There's no more harmonious blending of man and nature than in a flower garden."

For many people, if I said nothing else about the Inn on the Common, that would be enough, but there is much more to say.

Penny and Michael Schmitt left New York City early in the 1970s and decided to start an entirely new way of life by opening an inn in Craftsbury Common, a beautiful Vermont hill-town, north and west of St. Johnsbury. They had been summering in this section of the state for many years so the area was most familiar.

According to the new brochure (please do not hesitate to write for one), the Inn on the Common is located in a beautiful, peaceful, unspoiled New England town. Each of the three inn buildings dates from the early 19th century and has been handsomely restored. The seventeen rooms are filled with antiques, folk art, original art, lovely wallpapers, hooked rugs, and custom quilts in wonderful colors.

At dinnertime guests are seated at three oval tables and, as a result of a very pleasant pre-dinner social hour, by the time the first course is served almost everybody is acquainted.

Some of the unusual main courses are shrimp marinara served with sour cream and fresh Parmesan; tournedos Béarnaise; scallops with herbs, white wine, and cream; locally grown lamb served with sorrel sauce; chicken served in a spicy nut and wine sauce garnished with shrimp and tomato.

Recognizing that more and more guests are enjoying longer stays, Michael and Penny have, in recent years, provided an expanding program of outdoor recreation that includes a swimming pool, tennis court, and English croquet in summer, and cross-country skiing and other outdoor sports in the winter.

The inn is just a short cross-country trail from the sports center on Big Hosmer Lake. There is lots of waterfront activity—swimming and

sun bathing, as well as canoeing and small sailboats. An additional interesting note is that sculling lessons are also provided.

For the guests who prefer a contemplative vacation, the bookshelves are most generously stocked with best sellers and mysteries, and the guest lounge with a fireplace is equipped with a library of films on tape.

In talking about the inn, Penny said, "People feel good about the inn and good about themselves when surrounded by beauty. Our wonderful, experienced staff backs this up with super food and attentive, caring service. The net result of all this seems to be more and happier guests than ever before, and I think that is what this business is all about. One important plus to that—Michael and I still love our work."

THE INN ON THE COMMON, Craftsbury Common, VT 05827; 802-586-9619. An 18-guestroom resort-inn in a peaceful Vermont town, 35 mi. from Montpelier. Modified American plan omits lunch. Breakfast and dinner served to houseguests only. Open 365 days a year. Swimming, tennis, croquet, xc skiing, snowshoeing on grounds. Golf, tennis, swimming, sailing, horseback riding, canoeing, fishing, xc and downhill skiing, skating, hiking, and nature walks nearby. Attended pets allowed. Michael and Penny Schmitt, Innkeepers.

Directions: From the south take I-91 to St. Johnsbury exit. Take Rte. 2 west, to Rte. 15 west, to Hardwick. Then take Rte. 14 north for 8 mi., turn right and go 3 mi. up long curving hill to inn. From Canada and points north, use Exit 26 on I-91 and follow Rte. 58W to Irasburg. Then Rte. 14 southbound 12 mi. to marked left turn, 3 mi. to inn.

THE MIDDLETOWN SPRINGS INN
Middletown Springs, Vermont

My connections with the town of Middletown Springs go back at least forty years. At that time I made frequent visits to nearby Lake St. Catherine, and it was part of the fun to drive over the Poultney hills and to take the lovely curving road that followed the tumbling brook to this sequestered Vermont village.

The Middletown Springs Inn is located on a picturesque green in the middle of this village. The green itself has a brave Civil War laddie on top of a pedestal and an American flag on a slightly bowed flagpole. These are protected by a cannon of some indefinite years. Around the square is the church and a nice Vermont home with a porte cochere, and across the way is a Federal-period brick house.

The inn is an 1879 Victorian mansion, built at the time when Middletown Springs was quite a thriving place, mostly because of the springs that still bubble up. At one time the town's reputation for its waters rivaled that of Saratoga Springs.

After searching for an inn, Nancy and Dee Schnitzler moved here from western New York State, and have been very happy with their choice ever since. Nancy showed me into the parlor with its impressive curved wall on the left of the central hall. This leads into the library, which is a little less formal, and then on into still another large center room, with several rooms leading off of it.

One of these rooms is the storybook country kitchen where, as Dee points out, "Eventually, all our guests find their way to talk to me in the morning or evening."

Throughout the inn there are antiques of every kind, some of them actually older than the mansion. There are two dining rooms, which have extremely impressive tables and breakfronts. One of the windows in one dining room has little glass shelves, where Nancy has a very fetching collection of colored glassware that sparkles when the sun shines through it.

A handsome carved stairway to the second floor reminds me of the one at the Mainstay Inn in Cape May, New Jersey. Again, there is a center hallway with antique-furnished guest rooms on either side. Terrycloth bathrobes are provided for rooms that have shared baths.

I was back downstairs having a cup of tea with Dee and Nancy, and we got to talking about the evening menu. This is where Nancy took over once again: "We have specially prepared dinners by prior reservation, and in fact encourage our guests to have dinner here. Some of the main dishes include rolled fillet of sole, stuffed with Vermont cheddar and minced onions, and then breaded and baked at a very high temperature for a few minutes." Dee could not resist saying, "Several of Nancy's recipes are called Chicken Supreme but every one is a different recipe. One is a boneless breast of chicken placed on slices of chipped dried beef, and bacon slices are criss-crossed on top of that. It's cooked for a while, and then the juices and fats are taken off and a cheddar cheese–mushroom–sherry sauce is poured over it and it is baked forty-five minutes."

"We treat all of our guests like company. We have freshly baked muffins and breads at the hearty breakfast, cookies in the cookie jar, and freshly prepared dinners, featuring Vermont country cooking.

"We're always delighted to assist in planning the day's activities; arranging bike rentals and sharing our favorite meandering routes. Actually, we're located near some of the best hiking, biking, skiing, and picture-taking in New England, and there's lots of jogging and running, and cross-country or downhill skiing."

The entire town is on the National Register of Historic Places, and once again I was particularly happy to find the Middletown Springs Inn—a perfect complement to the village.

THE MIDDLETOWN SPRINGS INN, Middletown Springs, VT 05757; 802-235-2198. A 10-guestroom (5 with private bath) Victorian mansion on the green of a lovely 18th- and 19th-century village. Full breakfast included; arrangements can be made for dinner. Open year-round; however, call in advance for reservations. Within easy driving distance of all central Vermont summer and winter recreation. Mt. Killington, state parks, summer theater, trout fishing, hiking, xc and alpine skiing, bicycling, swimming, golf, tennis nearby. Not suitable for young children. Dee and Nancy Schnitzler, Innkeepers.

Directions: From Manchester Center, Vt., follow Rte. 30 to Pawlet and turn north on Rte. 133 to Middletown Springs. From Poultney, Vt., follow Rte. 140 to East Poultney and on to Middletown Springs.

NORTH HERO HOUSE
North Hero, Lake Champlain, Vermont

Caroline Sorg and I were rocking on the front porch of the North Hero House, which looks to the east out over Lake Champlain. In the distance we could see Mount Mansfield at Stowe, Vermont. "The inn was open longer in 1985 for the first time," she commented. "We stayed open into mid-October for fall travelers enjoying Vermont's wonderful color and beautiful weather. Previously, we have always closed after Labor Day because, as you know, Roger always returned to his dentistry practice in Flemington, New Jersey, and it was necessary for David and Lynn to go back to school. Now things have changed; Roger is no longer in the practice of dentistry."

"Let's just saw that I've withdrawn!" Roger came across the porch and flopped down in one of the comfortable rockers. "That's an old tooth term," he said. "Anyway, I've withdrawn from the practice of dentistry, and it was just wonderful to have guests here so late in the season. You might tell your readers that the first three weeks of October are already booked. There are still some good bookings in September 1986, however."

During the fifteen years I've been visiting and writing about North Hero House, I've become very attached to the entire Sorg family, particularly David and Lynn, whom I've known since they were just kids playing around the inn with the other inn guests' children. Now, after getting a degree in hotel administration at the University of Vermont, David has opened his own restaurant, "Old Timbers," in Randolph, New Jersey. Lynn, on the other hand, is now a fully qualified dental hygienist, but will be spending each summer at North Hero House with the family.

The North Hero House provides guests at this island inn on the sandy shore of Lake Champlain the opportunity to enjoy many wonderful

adventures nearby. It is just an hour and fifteen minutes from Old Montreal, Canada; forty-five minutes from the famous Shelburne Museum, with its impressive collection of early Americana; and only a short distance from Mount Mansfield and Stowe to the east, which can be reached entirely by back roads.

We stopped talking long enough to watch two of the youngsters out in the lake struggling to pull the sail of the windsurfer up out of the water. Roger pointed out that this is one of the really fun things to do here.

Over the years I have always been intrigued by the extent of the menu at the North Hero House, where so many of the vegetables have been supplied by the garden, watched over by almost all of the staff members. Caroline is particularly proud of this variety, including their chicken Marfasso, veal with hollandaise, asparagus, and artichokes, grilled salmon "mayonnique," apple and raisin bread pudding, and a green grape dessert.

Guest rooms are situated in the main inn building, as well as in Cove House and Southwind, both of which date to 1800. All have some rooms with a lake view, and some with private porches.

For those people with boats, North Hero Island can be reached by water, as it is part of the inland waterway stretching from Key West, Florida, to the St. Lawrence Seaway.

During my visits to the inn, I've had lots of happy moments on the tennis courts; on the lake, canoeing, windsurfing, waterskiing; on the country roads, jogging or bicycling; or simply on the porch, rocking and looking. I've also been thrilled by the sight of the moon rising over the lake, and the refreshing early morning swims before breakfast.

NORTH HERO HOUSE, Champlain Islands, North Hero, VT 05474; 802-372-8237. A 23-guestroom New England resort-inn on North Hero Island in Lake Champlain, 35 mi. north of Burlington and 65 mi. south of Montreal. Modified American plan. Breakfast, lunch, and dinner served daily to travelers. Open from June to mid-Oct. Reservations highly recommended. Swimming, fishing, boating, waterskiing, icehouse game room, sauna, bicycles, and tennis on grounds. Horseback riding and golf nearby. No pets. No credit cards. Roger and Caroline Sorg, Innkeepers.

Directions: Travel north from Burlington on I-89; take Exit 17 (Champlain Islands) and drive north on Island Rte. 2 to North Hero. From N.Y. Thruway (87 north), take Exit 39 at Plattsburg and follow signs "Ferry to Vermont." Upon leaving ferry, turn left to Rte. 2, then left again to North Hero. Inn is 15 min. from ferry dock on Rte. 2. By water: follow sectional maps to North Hero–City Bay. Enter bay and proceed in westerly direction to North Hero House.

OLD NEWFANE INN
Newfane, Vermont

I first heard of Eric Weindl and his wife, Gundy, because of the cuisine at the Old Newfane Inn. However, my visit convinced me that this historic hostelry has several other highly attractive aspects that make it an ideal objective for country inn enthusiasts.

Eric, like his fellow countryman, Guenther Weinkopf, at the Queen Anne Inn in Chatham, Massachusetts, originally came from a small village near Munich, and both he and Gundy speak English with a very intriguing Bavarian accent.

I was visiting in the middle of a warm August afternoon, just a few minutes before Eric would find it necessary to start preparations for the evening meal. The three of us were seated on the side porch overlooking the village green, the fountain, the maples and oaks, and the Windham County Courthouse.

The Courthouse was built in 1825, the same year the inn was moved to its present location from the top of Newfane Hill, which at that time was really the center of the village. The Town Hall is a mixture of Greek Revival and Colonial, and there are several other buildings around the square that are much older.

I had just been escorted on a tour through every one of the ten meticulously decorated and furnished lodging rooms. It was like visiting a Vermont farmhouse of a hundred years ago. There were elaborate samplers and wall hangings such as I have never seen before. The second-floor rooms, at one time part of a ballroom, are light and airy, and there's a very pleasant little side balcony overlooking the green.

Eric, who was trained as a chef in one of the best hotels in Switzerland, warmed up to the subject of the Old Newfane Inn menu: "I think we could be characterized basically as Swiss-Continental," he said. "Our maitre d' does such dishes as chateaubriand or one of several flaming specialties at the tableside, which is always a lot of fun."

"This I can tell you," said Gundy, "Eric is a very good-natured man who loves good fun, but he takes cooking very seriously and is most particular about everything on the menu, including frog legs, shrimp scampi, lobster, tournedos of beef, and medallions of veal. He is too modest to say this, but people drive for many, many miles just to enjoy dinner with us. You see, I'm the hostess, so I meet them all."

Dinner was served in the low-ceilinged dining room, with its mellowed beams overhead and windows along one side. The floorboards of varying widths were highly polished and there were pink tablecloths with white undercloths, candles on the table, and pistol-handled knives. The maitre d' was wearing an elegant-looking tuxedo, and the waitresses were wearing black uniforms trimmed in white.

I was entranced with the salad, which was very simple and served with one of the most extraordinary, but simple, dressings I have ever tasted—just my preference for salads. I've never tasted better calves' liver, served in a Tyrolean sauce, and I had the opportunity to sample the medallions of veal served with creamy mushrooms that were delicious. Everything could be cut with a fork.

Because both Eric and Gundy are highly involved throughout the day with food and dining room preparation, casual visitors cannot be accommodated for tours of the inn. If you have a reservation and find the front door locked, ring the bell and they will be delighted to show you to your room.

OLD NEWFANE INN, Court St., Newfane, VT 05345; 802-365-4427. A 10-guestroom village inn 12 mi. west of Brattleboro, on Rte. 30. European plan. Lunch and dinner served to travelers during summer. Closed for rooms on Mondays. Open mid-Dec. to first of April; May to end of Oct. Closed Thanksgiving, Mother's Day. Near many downhill ski areas, Marlboro Music Festival. Backroading, tennis, swimming nearby. No facilities for children under 7. No credit cards. Eric Weindl, Innkeeper.

Directions: From New York: Follow 684 to 84 to Hartford; I-91 to Brattleboro, Exit 2. Follow Rte. 30 for 12 mi. to Newfane. From Boston: Follow Rte. 2 to Greenfield. I-91 to Brattleboro, Exit 2; follow Rte. 30 to Newfane.

I do not include lodging rates in the descriptions, for the very nature of an inn means that there are lodgings of various sizes, with and without baths, in and out of season, and with plain and fancy decoration. Travelers should call ahead and inquire about the availability and rates of the many different types of rooms.

THE QUECHEE INN AT MARSHLAND FARM
Quechee, Vermont

I have often said that I would like to be able to spend Christmas at every one of the more than two hundred inns in this book. Obviously, this has some built-in impossibilities. However, I was now doing the next best thing: I was visiting the Quechee Inn during Christmas week. Wouldn't you know that it was on a day when there was a light snowfall, and the Vermont landscape, as always, responded to this lovely natural phenomenon with its usual grace and beauty. Pine trees at the inn entrance had caught a few errant flakes on their outspread branches, and posts and fence rails took on a new sculptured look.

En route I had paused for a moment to look down at the Quechee Gorge, which cuts through the granite bedrock on its way to newer levels, and also had stopped for a moment in the village to visit Simon Pearce's glass-blowing establishment.

Now I sat with Rebecca Carson Rogers and Barbara Yaroschuk, as they enthusiastically reviewed all of the things that have happened at the Quechee Inn since my last visit.

"As you see, we extended the front of the building and constructed the second-floor porch. The Marsh family, who originally built the house, used that porch, and we thought it would be fun to have the porch back. It also gives us a wonderful place to entertain. The rocking chairs make it very peaceful."

Rebecca had a few thoughts. "As you see, we have increased the size of our Common Room, and now, during the Christmas season, we have wonderful holiday entertainment. We have Christmas caroling by a high school group, and before Christmas we had a puppet show, stories, and songs for children. We've had folk singers and jazz, and this afternoon we are having the Vermont Flute Ensemble. With this additional space, we are going to be doing a lot more year-round entertaining for our guests."

The Quechee Inn is the 1793 farmstead of Colonel Joseph Marsh, the first lieutenant governor of Vermont. The original carriage house is now a comfortable Common Room, and while I was there, guests were seated in front of the big fireplace, having come in from a morning of cross-country skiing or walking.

Period furniture, wide pine-board floors, brass four-poster beds, and braided rugs help to recreate the atmosphere of a time past. The Yaroschuks have added several modern conveniences as well.

Inn guests enjoy privileges at the Quechee Club, where they can play two of the best golf courses in New England. The clubhouse has an indoor and outdoor pool, and there is a beautiful little lake, just right for the Sunfish sailboats and paddleboats. There are ten tennis courts.

I was delighted to find a first among inns: a fly-fishing school, run at various times throughout the fishing season. I would suggest contacting the inn for further details. Other special things include bike, canoe, and fishing equipment rentals, Sunday afternoon watercolor workshops; the Quechee hot air balloon festival, summer concerts, a Scottish festival, and myriad other special days. As Barbara says, "Our weekends are actually seven days long."

Barbara pointed out that one of the nicest things that happen is that Quechee guests come on a vacation and discover that they would like to bring their business associates back for small meetings and seminars. "The inn is well suited and equipped to handle such events," she commented.

THE QUECHEE INN AT MARSHLAND FARM, Clubhouse Rd., Quechee, VT 05059; 802-295-3133. A 22-guestroom country inn in central Vermont just a few minutes from Woodstock, Dartmouth College, and many other Vermont attractions. Continental buffet breakfast for houseguests only. Dinner by reservation only served daily (except Tues.) to travelers July thru Oct.; Wed. thru Sun., Nov. thru June. Jackets requested. Closed 3 wks. in Apr. and 1 wk. in early Dec. Spectacular foliage, sugaring, hiking, fishing, canoeing, bird watching, and cidering available. Historic sites, antique shops, covered bridges, and especially the Quechee Gorge, all within short distance. Tennis, golf, swimming, tubing, squash, sauna, sailboats, xc and downhill skiing nearby. Barbara Yaroschuk, Innkeeper.

Directions: From intersection of Interstate 91 and 89, take 89 north to Exit 1 (Rte. 4, Woodstock–Rutland). West on Rte. 4 for 1.2 mi. Right on Clubhouse Rd. to inn.

RABBIT HILL INN
Lower Waterford, Vermont

Many of my readers make inquiries about what Christmas is like at a country inn. In thinking it over, I realized that while Christmases at country inns all share many of the same traditional joys, many of them have their own individual touches and traditions. Eric and Beryl Charlton, who are originally from Great Britain, follow time-honored English traditions in celebrating Christmas at Rabbit Hill. I thought it would be fun to share some of their festivities with my readers.

Before we plunge into the Yuletide activities at this northern Vermont country inn, I'd like to point out that Lower Waterford is truly picturebook New England. The village is situated along just one street and consists of the Rabbit Hill Inn, the village church, the 150-year-old post office, the library (which has an honor system for signing out books), and about eight early-19th-century classic New England homes. The view from Rabbit Hill Inn is of the magnificent Presidential Range of New Hampshire. What a sight it is in the distance with the sun lighting up its snow-clad peaks.

All of the inn's country bedrooms have their own private baths and all but two have a view of the mountains. The guest rooms are generously furnished with antiques and a collection of coal miners' lamps that originally came from England. There are lace-trimmed canopy beds and flowered wallpapers and other decorations in the country-inn theme.

In sharing their Christmas activities at the inn with me, Beryl and Eric pointed out that at Christmas the inn is open to a very limited number of guests. The staff is not on duty on Christmas Eve and Christmas Day, and the Charltons like to celebrate this Christian holiday as a family—the family spirit enhanced by everyone helping a little! "We are principally geared to an adult group at this time," explained Beryl.

On Christmas Eve afternoon, tea is served in a typically English manner. What else? At seven o'clock there is a candlelight service in the church across the street, and this is an interdenominational service that Rabbit Hill guests normally attend. Anyone having any vocal or musical ability is most welcome at this informal service.

After the service, there is a wassail bowl at the inn, and hors d'oeuvres are available.

The grand Christmas Eve supper is served between 8:30 and 9:00, and afterward everybody takes a welcome walk for carol singing in the village.

On Christmas Day after breakfast, and providing there is snow, there are morning and afternoon sleigh rides. A noon soup-pot follows for anyone feeling hungry. Afternoons might be spent building a snowman, cross-country skiing, or taking a good walk, perhaps followed by an afternoon nap. And then it's time for Christmas dinner. As a finale the lights are lowered and the flaming Christmas pudding is brought out while all raise their voices in song.

After dinner there are exchanges of presents, disorganized games, and more good fun.

By the way, plum puddings are available at the inn gift shop, as well as oat cookies from a Charlton family Scottish border recipe, and crunchy, crumbly, buttery Scottish shortbread.

I'm sure we all realize that Rabbit Hill Inn is open most of the year and is an ideal vacation and holiday experience for outdoor-minded guests.

If this description of Christmas at Rabbit Hill sounds enticing to you, may I suggest that you make your reservations no later than September 1.

RABBIT HILL INN, Pucker St., Lower Waterford, VT 05848; 802-748-5168. A 20-guestroom country inn with a view of mountains on Rte. 18, 10 mi. from St. Johnsbury, Vt. European plan. Open all year except Apr. and Nov. Breakfast and dinner served to travelers. Swimming, fishing, xc skiing on grounds. Tennis, swimming, walking, alpine skiing, sailing, backroading nearby. The Charlton Family, Innkeepers.

Directions: From I-91, take Exit 19 (I-93 south), then Exit 1 onto Rte. 18 south. From I-93, exit at Rte. 18 junction, turn north (left) on Rte. 18.

ROWELL'S INN
Simonsville, Vermont

This is how it happened: I was asleep in the first-floor bedroom at Rowell's Inn, and was awakened by the jingle of harnesses and the sounds of horses stamping on the ground at the front doorway. I could hear voices saying, "Yes, this is Rowell's Inn; we're about halfway between Londonderry and Chester. Yes, we can put you up for the night; just hand down your portmanteau."

After that I drifted back to sleep again, but was awakened a little later by still another sound—that of an early 1920s automobile, such as an Overland or a Marmon. Once again, I could hear voices, this time inquiring about stopping off for lunch and how far to Lake Sunapee, New Hampshire. Once again, another voice responded that they could stop for lunch because they were expected!

In the morning, I joined innkeepers Lee and Beth Davis at a very hearty and splendid breakfast. I remarked that probably all of the discussion at dinner the previous evening about how Rowell's Inn had originally

been a stagecoach stop and later on a regular stop on the Ideal Auto Tours of the early 20s had remained in my mind. I mentioned that I had heard these voices in the night. Beth passed me another slice of breakfast quiche, looked at Lee with a trace of a smile, and I caught a glance between the two of them. "So you heard them, too," Lee smiled.

Rowell's Inn is an authentic historic inn, built for that purpose in 1820 by Major Simons, who was the founder of the village, located at a bend in Route 11, across from Lyman Brook. This handsome red brick building, with the highly distinctive wooden porches added to the front, is on the National Register of Historic Places. The five guest rooms are furnished in the tradition of the inn's prosperous past, as are the front common parlors and a tavern room in the rear, which has a colorful past of its own.

I was very much interested in Lee and Beth's own story. Originally from the Midwest, they traveled in the East a few years ago, using (I report modestly) *CIBR*. They became smitten with the idea of owning their own country inn. Oddly enough, I had been admiring this building for a great many years since it is on one of the principal east-west roads in Vermont.

Today, with a great deal of hard work and loving care, they have restored the inn to its Colonial effulgence. Along with a great collection of antiques, there are also many modern touches, making it totally up to date with added bathrooms and a very excellent antique and gift sh'p.

Five-course meals are offered with a nightly entrée that might include roast leg of lamb, stuffed veal marsala, beef tenderloin, rolled turkey breast, or the guest may opt for the house specialty—pan-fried trout. In addition to offering dinner to houseguests, the inn accepts a few outside reservations.

From the moment I stepped through the gorgeous stained-glass front door, saw the alternate floorboards of cherry and maple in the dining room, toured the bedrooms, and enjoyed dinner and breakfast with these enthusiastic innkeepers, I knew that Rowell's Inn belonged in *Country Inns and Back Roads*.

ROWELL'S INN, RR 1, Box 269, Simonsville, VT 05143; 802-875-3658. A 7-guestroom (5 with private baths) inn in the mountains of central Vermont. Open all year. Mod. American plan with 2-day minimum on weekends. During week bed-and-breakfast plan is available. Dinner is served by request. Convenient to all the cultural, recreational, and historic attractions in the area, including, hiking, biking, trail riding, golf, tennis, fishing, theaters, downhill and xc skiing. Children over 6 welcome. No pets. No credit cards. Beth and Lee Davis, Innkeepers.

Directions: Rowell's Inn is located on Rte. 11, 7 mi. west of Chester, and 7 mi. east of Londonderry.

SHIRE INN
Chelsea, Vermont

If the word "idyllic" had not already been created, I would certainly have invented it myself just to describe this bucolic scene.

Standing on a sturdy wooden bridge immediately behind the Shire Inn, gazing down on a branch of the White River below, I caught the flash of a trout slipping through the cool, rushing waters. Some early owner of the house so appreciated this scene, he placed a bench long enough to hold eight people here on the bridge.

I had just driven through some exceptionally beautiful Vermont country, following Route 14 north from Lebanon, alongside the White River, to Chelsea. The village is listed on the National Register of Historic Places, and has two commons and several early-18th-century homes and buildings.

Built of Vermont brick in 1832 and surrounded on all sides by gardens and lawns, the Shire Inn, with its fanlight doorway and black shutters, is certainly one of the most attractive of these historic homes.

The entrance hallway is dominated by a handsome circular staircase. On one side of this hallway is a most comfortable living room with deep chairs and sofas, as well as lots and lots of books. "This is the gathering room for our guests," remarked Ingeborg Davis, who with her husband, De, is the innkeeper.

"We're open year around," De told me, "and it's a good base from which guests can explore the variety of recreational and cultural opportunities that abound up here in this area. We've got good cross-country skiing here in Chelsea—actually, right from our own backyard. There's also downhill skiing at the Sonnenberg Ski Area near Woodstock, and there's hiking and bicycling in fair weather, as well as swimming and boating in the summer, and skating in the winter, on Lake Fairlee. Of course, everybody enjoys going over to Hanover, New Hampshire, where there are art galleries, theater, cinema, and many other attractions."

The six guest rooms are most attractively furnished and four of them have working fireplaces. Ingeborg referred to the one on the right side of the entranceway as "our toasty room, because the boiler is just underneath." Upstairs, there are two high-ceilinged rooms with fireplaces on the front, one with a delightful canopy bed. Each has a little sign that says, "Good night, rest well. Breakfast at 8:30." Another has a spool bed and ruffled curtains. Very pleasant country bedspreads and comforters are found in each of the guest rooms, and all the beds have triple sheets. The beautiful "pumpkin pine" floorboards have been brought back to their lovely natural finish with lots of hard work by De and Ingeborg. All the guest rooms, named after Vermont counties, have a bountiful supply of books and magazines, but each has its own distinctive quality.

Breakfast, included in the room rate, is most unusual; in fact, when people are staying on for additional days the entire table setting is changed, and this includes the colors and the dishes and all the decorations. Ingeborg is obviously very much at home in the kitchen, and guests often wander back to ooh and aah.

A five-course, single-entrée dinner is offered at the Shire Inn by advance reservation. "I usually serve things that go with the time of year," Ingeborg said, "as there is no point in serving a heavy meal in the midst of a Vermont warm spell."

You will, as I did, have some fun getting there, and after you arrive I hope you'll agree with me that Chelsea and the Shire Inn have just the kind of "withdrawn New England" atmosphere that you hoped to find.

SHIRE INN, Chelsea, VT 05038; 802-685-3031. A 6-guestroom (2 with private bath) village inn in a beautiful central Vermont setting. Open all year with a vacation break in Nov. and Apr. Breakfast included in room rate. Evening meal available by advance reservation. The Justin Morgan horse farm, the Joseph Smith memorial, xc and downhill skiing, fishing, swimming, boating, walking, and bicycling are all available. No children under 12. No pets. No smoking. De and Ingeborg Davis, Innkeepers.

Directions: From I-89 use Exit 2, proceed west on Rte. 14, then northward on Rte. 110 to Chelsea. From I-91, take Exit 14 and turn left on Rte. 113 proceeding northwest to Chelsea. Both of these roads are extremely picturesque.

THREE MOUNTAIN INN
Jamaica, Vermont

"I have skied Stratton many times," I remarked, "but tell me about the summertime activities here in the valley."

Charlie Murray and I were seated in the snug little living room at Three Mountain Inn, located in a very tucked-away southern Vermont village. The house was built in the 1870s, and has expanded considerably since my first visit a few years ago.

Charlie waxed enthusiastic. "Stratton hosted the Volvo Tennis Tournament in early August 1985 for the first time, with approximately 60,000 people in attendance over the five-day period. It could not have gone better. We received many unsolicited comments from our dinner and house guests about how tastefully it was all presented and how great the tennis was. John McEnroe, Jimmy Connors, Ivan Lendl, and many other tennis celebrities were here competing for the big prize money. McEnroe won, as you may recall. Since Three Mountain Inn is the closest inn to Stratton, we were very busy all week. We're certainly looking forward to many more years of the Volvo at Stratton."

In 1985 I reported visiting the Three Mountain Inn during construction of two new guest rooms over what used to be the stable. It all turned out very well, and Elaine Murray points out these new rooms are the largest and nicest, and both have private baths. Incidentally, Rod Williams from the Inn at Sawmill Farm was very helpful on the project. There is a queen-sized authentic four-poster "pencil bed" in one and a king-sized four-poster in the other. One of them has a newly completed balcony/deck for relaxing in the sun in the summer and fall.

Third-floor renovation has also been completed, and there are two lovely, cozy rooms tucked away up there, each with a private bath. This means that the Three Mountain Inn now has ten rooms, all with private baths.

Sage Hill House, a small farmhouse across the street, is part of Three Mountain Inn, too. It's a wonderful, compact little house with three bedrooms, a kitchen, a bathroom and a half, and a living room with a wood-burning stove. It's often used by families with a number of children or younger families with babies. A sitter is available, allowing parents to have a quiet meal in the dining room by themselves.

There's much to do in this part of Vermont in all seasons of the year, and Charlie told me that the spring fishing vacations are working out very well. "I've lined up some outstanding local guides who can almost guarantee that our guests will catch fish on either the West River or the Battenkill." The mention of fish reminds me that locally caught corncob-smoked trout is one of the specialties of the kitchen, which is carefully supervised by Elaine. I can remember now that at the time of my first visit

I had chicken paprikash. The breads and desserts are all homemade, and the muffins, doughnuts, and breakfast rolls are also baked right at the inn.

Some of our readers have been following my occasional mentions of Claire Murray, who was my first guide a few years ago, when she was only seventeen years old. She returned to the United States after spending ten months in Siena, Italy, in connection with her studies at the University of Vermont and the Experiment in International Living. Her Italian is

spectacular, and she's already talking about returning to Italy. She worked all summer as a waitress at the inn and will probably be here during the summer of 1986 as well.

THREE MOUNTAIN INN, Rte. 30, Jamaica, VT 05343; 802-874-4140. A 10-guestroom inn located in a pleasant village in southern Vermont. Modified American plan (rates include breakfast and dinner). Dinners also served to other than inn guests nightly except Wed. Closed Apr. 15 to May 15; Labor Day to Sept. 15; Oct. 31 to Thanksgiving. Swimming pool on grounds. Tennis, golf, fishing, horseback riding, nature walks and hiking trails in Jamaica State Park, downhill and xc skiing, Marlboro Music Festival, Weston Playhouse, all within a short drive. No pets. No credit cards. Charles and Elaine Murray, Innkeepers.

Directions: Jamaica is located on Rte. 30, which runs across Vermont from Manchester (U.S. 7) to Brattleboro (I-91).

TUCKER HILL LODGE
Waitsfield, Vermont

"I'd say that we were casual with classical overtones," Zeke Church declared, "Our goal is to present a refined, country-style elegance, along with our particular brand of outgoing, down-home hospitality." Emily Church nodded in agreement. The Churches are the innkeepers of Tucker Hill Lodge. We were having dinner in the "sun room" with its expansive skylights and many varieties of hanging plants.

The drive north on the Wednesday before Columbus Day weekend (incidentally one of the busiest, and reservations should be made no later than midsummer) had been almost entirely on Route 100, which begins at the Massachusetts border. I arrived in the Sugarbush Valley, sometimes called the Mad River Valley, and made the turn off Route 17 and up the dirt road, to find this attractive inn of grey clapboards with blue trimming. Cars in the parking lot had many different license tags.

The pretty young waitress presented my dessert, an apple strudel served with a scoop of homemade vanilla ice cream. I wasn't sure that I'd still have room after the generous portion of duckling and homemade pasta. "Homemade" is one of the key words here because the vinegars, jellies, and even the ice cream are all made in the inn kitchen.

I asked the Churches to describe their guest rooms. "They're all relatively simple," Emily replied. "They have handmade quilts on all the beds and fresh flowers in all the rooms. There are antiques in the rooms, but they are not fancy antiques. The rooms are simple. I wouldn't like to say that the meals are more sophisticated than the rooms, but people don't come here looking for fancy rooms."

"I'd say we have a mood of rustic elegance that we try to carry through to the public rooms as well, including the living room with its fieldstone fireplace," chimed in Zeke.

"We have the modified American plan here," he went on. "The accommodations include a full breakfast and a full dinner; however, our standard booking periods are for two-day weekends on Friday and Saturday nights and we also have a special five-day week planned from Sunday night through Friday morning."

During the winter season, the Valley is a skier's paradise with such major downhill areas as Sugarbush and Mad River Glen; and the Tucker Hill Ski Touring Center is just about twenty-five paces from the front door. There are guided mountain hikes during the summer, and the inn is affiliated with the Country Inns Along the Trail hiking program, as well as the Vermont Country Cyclers.

"I'd call us a sort of mini resort inn," Zeke said, as we went down the stairway to the very attractive little lounge area, which has a barn motif. There were several people seated downstairs having a good time

just visiting. "However, our guests enjoy horseback riding, polo games, canoeing, sailboarding, trout fishing, soaring, summer theater, covered bridges, back roads, and all those things that you love."

In spite of all these things, I think one of the most memorable impressions I have of the Tucker Hill Lodge is the flowers. They can be found everywhere. Both Zeke and Emily, who originally came from North Carolina, have an obvious enthusiasm for these messengers of good cheer and happiness. There are forty hanging baskets on the deck, and the gardener is clearly devoted to his art.

TUCKER HILL LODGE, RD 1, Box 147, Waitsfield, VT 05673; 802-496-3983 or 1-800-451-4580 (except from Vermont). A 20-guestroom (14 with private baths) inn in the Mad River/Sugarbush Valley of North-Central Vermont. Modified American plan. Open for lodgings every day. Closed for dinner from late Oct. to the weekend before Thanksgiving and closed again from Mon. after Thanksgiving until mid-Dec. Also not serving dinner between Easter and the first week in June. Two-day minimum on weekends. Xc skiing, tennis, swimming pool on grounds. A wide variety of all summer and winter recreation nearby. Children are welcome. Sorry, no pets. Zeke and Emily Church, Innkeepers.

Directions: In Waitsfield turn west off Rte. 100 and follow Rte. 17 a short distance to the inn sign on the left.

THE VILLAGE INN
Landgrove, Vermont

This time I traveled to Landgrove from Weston, taking the road that leads west, passing the Weston Playhouse, over the bridge and up the hill. At the fork I took the road marked "Peru" and "Landgrove."

This is an ideal back road. For one thing, it becomes a dirt road almost immediately, something that is now hard to find in Vermont, and it passes through some good woods and marshlands where I could see beaver lodges. At one point I crested a hill to discover a beautiful 19th-century home with spectacular flower plantings, enjoying unexcelled views of both Stratton and Magic Mountain, two well-known central Vermont ski areas. It's possible to turn off to Danby, Vermont, on

another dirt road leading to the right. Preoccupied as I was with the beautiful bucolic Vermont scenery, before I realized it, there were the familiar red clapboard buildings with the white trim of the Village Inn in Landgrove.

It's interesting that my visits to Jay and Kathy Snyder have almost always been at noon, and we have had several lunches seated by the swimming pool, giving us a chance to "talk shop," and for me to catch up on the details and news of the inn. Their two daughters, Kim and Heidi, are now both at Northfield-Mount Hermon School, and as Kathy says, "Instead of having one call home *regularly*, we have two calling home regularly!"

The inn is a real family affair, with Pop continuing to preside in the kitchen at the breakfast hour, and his blueberry pancakes—"a berry in every bite"—are always in demand. Mom is at the front desk and has lost count of the number of inn tours given. Jay's aunt, Norma Quinn, helps serve breakfast, greet guests, do desk duties with Mom, and she tells great stories.

The Snyders were filled with other news of the inn, including the horse-drawn sleigh rides, now offered during the wintertime. "We usually start off at sunset," Jay said, "and then continue on the snowy roads, getting back in time for dinner. It is a nice country experience. We have some very interesting midweek package plans, all of which include combinations of alpine and Nordic skiing, and our skiing guests are also very enthusiastic about the hot tubs."

We finished a leisurely lunch and then roamed around the inn grounds, while Jay and Kathy pointed out different types of hybrid day lilies, including one very special lavender species, in the extensive flower beds.

There is also an extensive vegetable garden, and Kathy laughingly told me that one year she and Jay had gotten their signals mixed. "He would come out and plant a row of something, and then I would come and, not realizing, would plant the same row with something else. The result was that we had carrots coming up with the lettuce. There are some wonderful peas that are good enough to eat raw and many species of onions and other garden goodies."

The Village Inn has been owned and operated by the Snyders for twenty-five years. It first opened its doors as an inn in 1939, and for many guests the main interest was skiing. However, in recent years the Snyders have developed an all-season resort-inn that is particularly attractive to families with children of all ages.

Summertime amenities on the grounds include tennis courts with a ball machine, a 4-hole pitch-and-putt golf course, a heated pool, volleyball, hiking trails, fishing, and a new paddle tennis court.

In winter the outdoor-minded guest can enjoy downhill skiing at five major areas nearby, plus cross-country skiing, snowshoeing, and sledding in the woods right behind the inn. There is also an ice skating pond.

THE VILLAGE INN, Landgrove, VT 05148; 802-824-6673. A 21-guest-room rustic resort-inn in the mountains of central Vermont, approx. 4½ mi. from Weston and Londonberry. Lodgings include breakfast. Breakfast and dinner served to travelers by reservation during the summer except Wed. dinner. Open from Nov. 23 to Apr. 15; July 1 to Oct. 17. Swimming, tennis, volleyball, pitch-and-putt, paddle tennis, xc skiing, fishing on grounds. Downhill skiing, riding, indoor tennis, antiquing, backroading, alpine slide, golf, summer theater nearby. Children most welcome. No pets. Jay and Kathy Snyder, Innkeepers.

Directions: Coming north on I-91 take Exit 2 at Brattleboro, follow Rte. 30 to Rte. 11 and turn right. Turn left off Rte. 11 at signs for Village Inn. Bear left in village of Peru. Coming north on Rte. 7 turn east at Manchester on Rte. 11 to Peru. Turn left at signs for Village Inn. Bear left in village of Peru.

WEST MOUNTAIN INN
Arlington, Vermont

"A lot of things have happened since your last visit." Mary Ann and Wes Carlson and I were having hors d'oeuvres, along with the other guests at the West Mountain Inn. "This is a wonderful way to introduce all of our guests," Mary Ann remarked, "and many of them join each other for dinner as well. I'm so glad that we have started it."

There have been a few architectural changes since my first visit, including a parking lot that is barrier-free and an enlarged front entry room with a striking slate floor, windows on three sides, and wicker furniture. "Our guests can now enjoy our side porch with a view of Red Mountain or our front enclosed porch with the panoramic view of the Green Mountains," Wes pointed out.

"On the second floor we've enlarged Governor Chittenden's room, just above the new entryway, added on a new bathroom and redecorated. We were able to make the cedar closet in Robert Todd Lincoln's room into a cedar bathroom. So now only two of our thirteen inn rooms share a bath."

This southern Vermont inn has an air of easy informality and friendliness, owing, I'm sure, to the attractive personalities of innkeepers Mary Ann and Wes Carlson and their two teenagers. There is a wide variety of outside diversions on the 150 acres of meadows and hills, where wilderness trails abound and the cross-country ski trails have been extended considerably, especially with the novice skier in mind.

The guest rooms are in many sizes and shapes; some with outside porches, one with a working fireplace, one with a bedloft for children, two with high, pine-paneled cathedral ceilings, and all attractively and comfortably furnished. There is one barrier-free room on the first floor equipped for disabled persons. This room is available for one month in advance only to disabled persons.

There are many other memorable qualities to be found at the West Mountain Inn, not the least of which is Wes and Mary Ann's tremendous interest in flowers. For instance, in the spring there are hundreds of parrot and rare orchid tulips, double peonies, and daffodils everywhere. There is also a collection of over forty different varieties of day lilies, along with gigantic begonias in the window boxes. In the fall, dahlias and mums dazzle the guests as they walk to the front door, and in the winter the flowers come inside. There are over thirty amaryllis bulbs in bloom from Christmas through February. Guests receive an African violet plant when they leave. What a remembrance!

However, there's even more. Wes is now into collecting rabbits and other small animals, and this story is really too extensive for me to cover it completely, but I'm sure you're going to be surprised and delighted with some of the new pets that have been added to the West Mountain staff, including two African pygmy goats who love to be petted.

The inn has recently changed its policy and now operates on the modified American plan. The menu has been expanded and it includes a five-course dinner with a choice of entrée and a choice of dessert. These are usually pretty hearty dishes, because the Vermont outdoor experience

brings guests back with huge appetites in all seasons of the year. Incidentally, they offer apple pie or chocolate pancakes à la mode for a unique breakfast dessert.

The West Mountain Inn is an ideal base for enjoying all of the activities in the Vermont mountains in all seasons, and there are many diversions for young people.

WEST MOUNTAIN INN, Arlington, VT 05250; 802-375-6516. A 13-guest-room comfortable hilltop country estate with a view of the Green Mountains. Private and shared baths. Mod. American plan. Open year-round. Breakfast and dinner served to travelers daily; a Sun. brunch served 9 to noon. Swimming, canoeing, hiking, fishing, nature walks, xc skiing, and tobogganing on grounds. Special weekend programs from time to time; call for information. Children welcome. No pets. Mary Ann and Wes Carlson, Innkeepers.

Directions: Take Historic Rte. 7 to Arlington. Follow signs for West Mountain Inn, ½ mi. west on Rte. 313; bear left after crossing bridge.

BLACK POINT INN
Prouts Neck, Maine

I drove up the circular driveway to the canopied entrance of the Black Point Inn, and there sat a sedate black London taxicab. I couldn't help but reflect that it was, like the inn itself, a throwback to the days of New England's past.

Normand Dugas, the innkeeper, had seen me through his office window and came out to tell me about "Wally, the cab." "In 1981, an English company sent over a couple of their famous London taxicabs as samples, hoping to corner the market left open by the demise of the Checker Cab Company. However, it all came to naught, and after a number of adventures I acquired one of the cabs. The staff named it 'Wally.' With a four-cylinder diesel engine, Wally has a top speed of fifty miles an hour and gets about fifty miles to the gallon. He seats five people comfortably, and we use him for transporting people back and forth to the airport and for sedate afternoon rides."

We walked upstairs into the lobby, where the grandfather's clock tolled exactly twelve noon, which meant it was thirty minutes before lunch. A few of the guests were on the porch overlooking the bay side of Prouts Neck, and a few others were in the enclosed sunporch playing cards or knitting. Ordinarily, lunch would be served poolside, but today being a bit too foggy, it was served in the regular inn dining room.

I strolled about for a moment, particularly interested in seeing the lovely roses, planted in full view of the glassed-in addition to the dining room. There must have been at least three dozen varieties. Just beyond, some of the guests were taking advantage of the putting green. On this particular side of the inn, many of the second-floor rooms have their own balconies.

Normand and I walked into the new indoor swimming pool room, which he tells me has been extremely well received by all of the inn guests. Those staying slightly off season have particularly appreciated this pool since the ocean is too cold before mid-June and after mid-September. The walls of the room are lined in beautiful California red cedar and the pool overlooks the rose garden and the putting green. This also includes a group jacuzzi, sauna, and exercise area. Normand pointed out that the pool is accessible to any guest staying in the main hotel.

The Black Point Inn is one of the few remaining American plan hotels that were so numerous on the New England coast sixty and seventy years ago. It has quiet dignity, personal service, and attention to details.

For the active, sports-minded guest, there's just about everything: an 18-hole golf course, tennis courts, sailing, fishing, swimming, beach walking, and clambering over rocks.

In many respects the Black Point is a throwback to the F. Scott

Fitzgerald era. Gentlemen wear coats and ladies don colorful dresses for dinner. The small orchestra plays for dancing in the evening and at poolside during lunches.

Rooms are more readily available during the months of June and July. During recent years, the weather in early June has been exceptional, and it is sometimes possible to call and make a reservation a day ahead; however, August is always a full month.

One hundred years ago, the American painter Winslow Homer found in this section of the rocky Maine coastline the inspiration and atmosphere that enabled him to create some of his greatest works. In fact, he walked these sandy shores and climbed these same rocks. His studio is located just a few minutes' walk from the front door of the inn.

Prouts Neck became popular as a summer resort at the end of the 19th century, and time has brought few changes to this lovely neck of land stretching out into the Atlantic. The sea, birds, water, sky, and trees, all of which go to make such desirable tranquility, are still here today.

BLACK POINT INN, Prouts Neck, ME 04070; 207-883-4311. An 80-guestroom luxury resort-inn on Rte. 207, 10 mi. south of Portland. Open May thru Oct. American plan during July and Aug. Optional MAP May, June, Sept., Oct. Indoor pool, jacuzzi, and sauna, fresh-water whirlpool, heated salt-water pool, bicycles, sailing, dancing, golf, tennis, and ocean bathing all within a few steps. No facilities for children under 12. No pets. Normand H. Dugas, Innkeeper.

Directions: From Maine Tpke., take Exit 7. Turn right at sign marked Scarborough and Old Orchard Beach. At second set of lights turn left on Rte. 207. Follow 4.3 mi. to Prouts Neck.

THE BRADLEY INN
Pemaquid Point, New Harbor, Maine

I reached out and put my hands on the firm stone base of the Pemaquid Point Lighthouse. It radiated a wonderful warmth borrowed from the brilliant September sun, so I sat down and rested against it, attempting to draw into myself some of its strength and nobility. It was my lighthouse.

Immediately in front of me, this selfsame sun created momentary jewels where the Atlantic gently lapped against the striated rocks that stretched out toward Spain. Overhead, sea birds wheeled and turned and talked to each other incessantly. I closed my eyes and my thoughts drifted back to my arrival at the Bradley Inn, just a short, pleasant walk from my lighthouse.

This time I had taken Route 32 off Route 1 at Waldoboro, south of Rockland. This is a delightful experience through back-country Maine. Travelers who are trying to get pell-mell from one inn to another may never leave I-95 for Route 1, and that's unfortunate, for here is a good alternate back road that's hard to beat. It comes out just a few moments from the Bradley Inn. If you're traveling north from the Bradley Inn, ask any member of the Ek family and they will put you on Route 32.

Well, I found the Ek family, Ed, Louine, and Grandma, in excellent spirits because many new features had been added to the inn; in fact, the front of it was quite different from the last time I visited. The dining room has also been enlarged to encompass the former old-fashioned screened-in porch, with an addition that forms a lounge with a piano, all done in knotty pine and bentwood chairs. Both the dining room and lounge have a pleasant view across the fields.

A visit to this country inn on the rocky coast of Maine is in many respects a step backward in time. Most of the guest rooms share bathrooms and conveniences "down the hall," and the furniture came from Ed and Louine's former home. Besides decorator sheets and pillowcases in bright colors, these moderately sized rooms have firm mattresses. Smoking, incidentally, is not permitted in the guest rooms.

The menu includes such hearty offerings as prime ribs of beef, several chicken and veal dishes, and much seafood from the local waters, when available, including scallops, sole, swordfish, haddock, and lobster. Sunday brunch is always a happy occasion.

With new areas in the inn and much new decorating, the Bradley Inn has taken on wonderful new dimensions; however, there is a simplicity and purposefulness, in some ways personified by a small plaque in each room, which reads in part: "Let the guest sojourning here know that in this home our life is simple. What we cannot afford we do not offer, but what good cheer we can give, we give gladly. We make no strife for appearance's sake. We will not swerve from our path for you. . . .

"For, while you are with us, we would have you enjoy the blessings of a home, health, love and freedom, and we pray that you may find the final blessing of life—peace."

In this edition for the first time I have asked Janice Lindstrom, our artist, to reproduce the Pemaquid Point Lighthouse, which I, along with, I'm sure, most of the guests at the Bradley Inn, find delightful.

THE BRADLEY INN, Rte. 130, 361 Pemaquid Point, New Harbor, ME 04554; 207-677-2105. A 12-guestroom (shared baths) country inn near Pemaquid Lighthouse on Maine's rocky coast, 15 mi. from Damariscotta. Rooms are available year-round. Continental breakfast included in room rate. Open daily to the public for dinner from mid-June to mid-Oct.; on weekends only Oct. to Jan., March to June. Restaurant is closed Christmas Eve, Christmas Day, Jan., Feb. Tennis, swimming, golf, canoeing, backroading, woodland walks, xc skiing all available nearby. Many cultural, historical, and recreational facilities nearby. No pets. No smoking in rooms. Edwin and Louine Ek and Grandma, Innkeepers.

Directions: From south: Maine I-95 to Brunswick/Bath Coastal Rte. 1 Exit. Follow Rte. 1 through Brunswick, Bath, and Wiscasset. Exit Business Rte. 1 at Damariscotta. Turn right at top of hill (white church), follow Rte. 130, 14 mi. to Pemaquid Pt. From north: Rte. 1; exit at Business Rte. 1, Damariscotta. Turn left at white church onto Rte. 130. Follow 130, 14 mi. to Pemaquid Pt.

THE CAPTAIN LORD MANSION
Kennebunkport, Maine

I remember it very well; in fact, it was only last summer. It was a Wednesday morning in mid-July and I joined the Captain Lord breakfast group at nine-thirty. (There had been an earlier breakfast group at eight-thirty.) Many of the guests were seated in a large but somewhat formal dining room enjoying coffee and planning the day's activities. A large jigsaw puzzle was on the dining room table and a couple of guests were playing chinese checkers in one corner. The Chippendale chairs, beautiful cabinets, and crystal chandelier were indications that this was indeed an important room during the many years of the mansion's existence.

Meanwhile, Vicki rang the morning breakfast chimes, and almost as one, the waiting guests rose and crossed the hallway and walked into the ample Captain Lord kitchen, where breakfast is served.

I took advantage of the moment to walk around and admire the handsome woodwork and lovely period wallpapers of this mansion, built during the War of 1812. Captain Nathaniel Lord answered the needs of idle carpenters and sailors by engaging them to build this stately home, using timbers intended for ships.

I walked to the front of the house where a beautiful curving banister led up a rather formal staircase to the third floor. Throughout the mansion, Rick and Bev have collected antiques, oriental rugs, and other tasteful objets d'art. One parlor has been set aside as a gift shop offering attractive mementos of the area, as well as smaller items such as cups, saucers, plates and the like.

Ample use has been made of the generously sized hallways, both on the second and third floors, with handsome cabinets, antique children's sleighs, duck decoys, quilts, prints of sailing ships, a spinning wheel,

and even a basket of washed wool. Many of the rooms have been named after ships that probably sailed from Kennebunkport.

I peeked into a few of the guest rooms whose doors were open, and once again, fluffy comforters, handmade quilts, or 100% wool blankets and Posturepedic mattresses reigned supreme. There are eight rooms with queen-sized beds and two rooms with king-sized beds.

Well, we were quite a group at breakfast. There were several couples from New Jersey, and a couple who had been married in Francestown, New Hampshire, just the day before. We all had great fun guessing what our various occupations were and also how long we had been married. There was lots of laughter and also many comments about the fact that breakfast, consisting of orange juice, homemade breads, muffins, or toast and coffee and, if desired, a soft-boiled egg, was not only plentiful, but extremely tasty as well.

We were all seated around the lovely harvest table, which provides just the right amount of intimacy to make this whole experience even more fun. Our conversation turned to what we looked for at an inn, and we decided that congeniality among the guests was a very important quality. It was definitely agreed by all present that the Captain Lord should get very high marks for having congenial guests!

Before I departed, I had a chance to talk to Rick about their newly acquired wonderful copper eagle weathervane. "It was actually originally here at the Captain Lord Mansion," he said. "I was the most persistent bidder for it at an auction in Lebanon, Maine, and as the auctioneer gaveled my winning bid, he told the crowd, 'the eagle is going back home to the Captain Lord Mansion in Kennebunkport.' "

THE CAPTAIN LORD MANSION, Box 800, Kennebunkport, ME 04046; 207-967-3141. A 16-guestroom mansion-inn in a seacoast village. Lodgings include breakfast. No other meals served. Open year-round. Near the Rachel Carson Wildlife Refuge, the Seashore Trolley Museum, the Brick Store Museum, and lobster boat tours. Bicycles, hiking, xc skiing, deep sea fishing, golf, indoor swimming, and tennis nearby. No children under 12. No pets. No credit cards. Bev Davis and Rick Litchfield, Innkeepers.

Directions: Take Exit 3 (Kennebunk) from the Maine Tpke. Take left on Rte. 35 and follow signs through Kennebunk to Kennebunkport. Take left at traffic light at Sunoco station. Go over drawbridge and take first right onto Ocean Ave., then take fifth left off Ocean Ave. (³⁄₁₀ mi.). The mansion is in the second block on left. Park behind building and take brick walk to office.

CHARMWOODS
On Long Lake, Naples, Maine

Charmwoods is a unique type of inn. Set in an area of great natural beauty and maintained by conscientious hosts, the inn provides a perfect setting for an escape to the countryside.

Once a private lakefront estate, Charmwoods radiates all the flavor and ambience of the Maine woods, but is a mere 2½-hour drive from downtown Boston.

As hosts, Marilyn and Bill Lewis make for a perfect combination. Marilyn is attractive and vivacious, and delights in giving her guests personal attention so as to ensure them the most pleasurable of vacations.

Bill, a former editor at the *Boston Globe* and *Boston Herald,* has unusual interests that Charmwoods guests find to be a pleasant diversion. For example, he often entertains with his 1890 Thomas A. Edison phonograph, drawing from a collection of about 500 cylindrical recordings. The newest acquisition is an antique player-piano, complete with rolls of the old favorites. Evenings, it is the center of attraction for guests addicted to sing-alongs with a keen nostalgia for this lusty entertainment of yesteryear.

Marilyn's penchant for decorating is particularly evident in all the spacious bedrooms with their selection of handsome, coordinated sheets, blankets, towels, and other accessories in distinctive colors. The master suite boasts a sunken Roman-style bathtub. Every suite enjoys a view of the lake.

The focus of activity at Charmwoods is frequently the commodious and gracious living room with its massive fieldstone fireplace and panoramic view of lake and mountains. Everything about this room encourages friendly discussions with a free exchange of information and ideas. The striking undersea photographs are provided by the Lewises' son, Jonathan.

Within fifteen minutes after my arrival, Bill and Marilyn had introduced me to their guests and we were immediately on a first-name basis—chatting as would old friends. Several guests were regulars at Charmwoods, having returned year after year.

Adjoining the living room and sharing center stage during much of the year is a broad deck with an unobstructed view of Long Lake. It is equally ideal for sunny breakfasts or for chatting under the stars.

A path leads down a few steps to the shoreline of this delightfully clear lake where a rowboat and canoe are docked in the boathouse. Swimming from the white sandy beach or private sundeck is ideal, and a trim cabana provides numerous amenities, including telephone service.

The village of Naples, a short stroll down the road, offers guests some interesting upcountry diversions, not the least of which is a seaplane

flight providing an excellent overview of the entire resort area. The *Songo River Queen,* an old-fashioned paddleboat, and the U.S. mailboats run excursion trips across the ten-mile lake. There is plenty of backroading and quite a few antique shops in the immediate area.

During my visit at Charmwoods nearly all the guests clutched tennis rackets, and the all-weather court saw plenty of play. There's a lakeside golf course and riding stables just a few minutes away.

Visiting Charmwoods is like being a guest at a houseparty for friends.

CHARMWOODS, P.O. Box 217, Naples, ME 04055; 207-693-6798 (winter: 617-469-9673). A 4-guestroom (private baths) lakefront bed-and-breakfast inn, with a guest cottage, on the west shore of Long Lake, approx. ½ hr. from Maine Tpke. Open early June into Oct. Breakfast is the only meal served (to houseguests only). Tennis, swimming, boating, canoeing, shuffleboard, and horseshoes on grounds; horseback riding, golf, and para-sailing nearby. Summer playhouse just down the road. Not suitable for children under 12. No pets. No credit cards. Marilyn and Bill Lewis, Innkeepers.

Directions: From Boston: follow Rte. 1 north to I-95 to Exit 8 (Portland-Westbrook). Turn right and follow Riverside St. 1 mi. to Rte. 302. Turn left (west) to Naples, which is about 30 mi. ahead. Charmwoods is just beyond the village on the right with an unobtrusive sign. From North Conway, N.H.: follow Rte. 302 through Bridgton. Charmwoods sign and driveway off Rte. 302 just before Naples village.

THE CLAREMONT HOTEL AND COTTAGES
Southwest Harbor, Maine

The year was 1884. Grover Cleveland (Democrat) defeated James G. Blaine (Republican) for president. London opened the first underground railroad. Auguste Rodin created his famous sculpture *Burghers of Calais*. Harry Truman was born. The Ringling Brothers circus was organized in Baraboo, Wisconsin. The Statue of Liberty was completed and presented to the United States. Women first competed in Wimbledon tennis, and the Washington Monument was completed.

It was also the year that the Claremont Hotel was opened. Its creator was Captain Jesse Pease, a native of Rockland and a well-known sea captain. During that first year, 146 names were entered on the register. Many of these came from New York and Boston and enjoyed a simple, modest vacation at the Claremont. There were oil lamps and pitchers and basins in each room. Hot baths were ordered in advance for twenty-five cents.

Considerable contribution to the progress of this now-century-old establishment came during the long tenure of the Philips family, who owned it for sixty years. During that time, more bedrooms and a new dining room were added, and such improvements as an elevator and a sprinkling system were installed.

In 1968, the Claremont was sold to Mr. and Mrs. Allen McCue of Yarmouth, Maine, who have continued in all of the traditions, as well as adding new cottages and making many improvements, particularly in 1978.

During 1984, the Claremont celebrated its centennial in a most auspicious way with a series of very interesting events, some of which I suspect will be continued during many summers to come. The official birthday was celebrated on August 18, and I told Jay Madeira, who has been the innkeeper for most of the ten years I have been visiting the Claremont, how sorry I was to miss such an important affair.

On the waters of Somes Sound, the Claremont is situated in a most interesting community with an identity of its very own. It always intrigues me that there are two different aspects to Southwest Harbor. On one side of the small peninsula is a working harbor with lots of fishing boats and the hustle and bustle of people who make their living with the cooperation of the sea. On the other side is a more tranquil scene, with sailboats and launches. This view over the water to Northeast Harbor is the one which is enjoyed by Claremont guests as they sit in the boathouse or on the front porch of the inn itself.

On each visit I have been struck by the wide variety of entertainment and recreation available for people vacationing on Mount Desert Island. All of the natural attractions of the area are within a very convenient distance; however, in recent years the Claremont has become well known for an important tournament of 9-wicket croquet—a game which has been played on the lawn of the inn since its earliest days. Players and spectators alike enjoy the Claremont Croquet Classic, a unique event for Claremont visitors. Many guests and staff return year after year to enjoy the serene atmosphere and the beautiful views.

Now the Claremont, on the National Register of Historic Places, is in its second hundred years!

THE CLAREMONT HOTEL AND COTTAGES, Southwest Harbor, ME 04679; 207-244-5036. A 22-guestroom (mostly private baths) rambling summer hotel with rooms also in two adjacent guest houses; on Somes Sound, Mt. Desert Island, 24 mi. south of Ellsworth. Hotel and dining room open mid-June thru mid-Sept. Breakfast and dinner served to guests and the public. Lunch served in the boathouse during July and Aug. Guest-house rooms and housekeeping cottages available May thru Oct. Hotel and Phillips House rooms available only on mod. American plan during the season. Off-season, all rooms available either EP or MAP while hotel is open. Tennis, rowboats, croquet, badminton, golf, bicycles, riding, boating, and sailing rental nearby. No credit cards. Personal checks accepted. The McCue Family, Owners; John Madeira, Jr., Manager.

Directions: From Maine Tpke., exit at Augusta and proceed east on Rte. 3 to U.S. 1. At Ellsworth, pick up Rte. 3 again and follow Rte. 102 on Mt. Desert Island to Southwest Harbor. Follow inn signs approaching and in Southwest Harbor.

THE COUNTRY CLUB INN
Rangeley, Maine

We were all gathered at one of the focal points at the Country Club Inn—the deck, with its sweeping panorama of sky, lake, and mountains. There were innkeepers Bob and Sue Crory, their daughter, Marge, and her husband, Steve Jameson, and the Crorys' son, Bob, Jr. There was also an extra guest, Ann Leger, from Philbrook Farm Inn in Shelburne, New Hampshire, who had driven up with me for the day. Sue was telling me how pleasant it was to have Marge, Steve, and Bob Jr. with them at the inn.

"I think a lot of it is with the returning guests," she said. "They look for them as soon as they arrive. It's always a case of 'Oh, where's Margie?' Or, 'Is Bob here this year?' Our staff is small enough anyway so that they all become like a family. Of course, we all change our hats around here and move from one job to another, but having members of the family makes everything a lot more personal."

There's no doubt that there are two emphases at the Country Club Inn; the first is the familylike atmosphere and the second is the really incredible scenery. Rangeley, Maine, is one of those places in the world

that has a special kind of charisma. There are few locations that offer such beauty and grandeur in all seasons. It's a combination of wide skies, vast stretches of mountain woodland, and the placid aspect of the Rangeley Lake that has been drawing people to this part of western Maine since long before the roads were as passable and numerous as they are today.

Bob Crory joined in: "I spent my boyhood summers working in Maine resorts and then went on to major in hotel administration at the University of New Hampshire. Sue and I had many different jobs, but all the time we knew that what we wanted was to have our own resort inn, small, cozy and comfortable. We found it in the Country Club Inn because we're small, but this coziness plus all the things there are to do here, like the swimming pool, the golf course, and the backroading make it a really good experience."

All of the guest rooms at the Country Club Inn have a picture window with a view of the lake and each one has a double bed and a twin bed, which, as Bob says, "makes everybody happy." The dining room also has this same view of the lake that reminds me of a similar stretch of lake and mountains in certain sections of Scotland, Loch Ness being one.

Sweeping an arm towards the view, Bob said, "September is a golden month. This whole panorama becomes a pageant of changing colors. You can see the colors coming down from the top of the mountains into the valley enveloping the countryside in brilliance. We also frequently can see the northern lights at that time. Of course, our big fireplace is going all the time."

The Country Club Inn has been open in both summer and winter in the past few years as there are lots of wintertime activities in the woods of western Maine, including tobogganing, snowmobiling, cross-country skiing, and downhill skiing at Saddleback and Sugarloaf. It's at times like these that guests appreciate the sauna most.

As Ann and I were leaving, Ann remarked, "I didn't realize how close the front door of the lodge is to the first tee on the golf course. Next time let's come earlier and play at least nine holes!"

THE COUNTRY CLUB INN, P.O. Box 680C, Rangeley, ME 04970; 207-864-3831. A 25-guestroom resort-inn on Rangeley Lake in western Maine, 45 mi. from Farmington. European, modified American plans. Open mid-May to mid-Oct. and mid-Dec. to mid-Mar. Breakfast, lunch, dinner served to travelers. Near many cultural, historic, and recreational attractions. Swimming pool and lake swimming, horseshoes, bocci, and 18-hole golf course on grounds. Fishing, saddle horses, water skiing, canoeing, hiking, tennis nearby. Winter sports—snowmobiling and xc skiing at doorstep. Downhill skiing at Saddleback and Sugarloaf Mts. Bob and Sue Crory, Innkeepers.

Directions: From Maine Tpke., take Auburn Exit 12 and follow Rte. 4 to Rangeley. From Vt. and N.H., take I-91 to St. Johnsbury; east on Rte. 2 to Gorham, and Rte. 16 north to Rangeley. From Bar Harbor, Rte. 1A to Rte. 2 to Rte. 4. From Montreal, Rte. 10 to Rte. 112 to Rte. 147, to Rte. 114; then Rte. 26 to Rte. 16 to Rte. 4.

DOCKSIDE GUEST QUARTERS
York, Maine

"There must be something special that happens here on the Fourth of July; don't I remember that you have a special little celebration?"

Harriette Lusty and I were having a light luncheon on the porch of the dining room at Dockside Guest Quarters. It was a day such as I have experienced here many times in the past, watching the wonderful harbor traffic as all kinds of craft make their way through the harbor to the ocean. Even though it had been a very hot day out on I-95, here on this lovely porch there was a wonderful breeze that made even sitting in the sun a joy.

"Oh, we do some very wonderful things here on the Fourth of July," Harriette exclaimed. "We have a very large flag that is brought out, unfolded, and placed on the lawn, because it is much too large for any flagpole. At noontime we set off our cannon, and the waitresses and all of our chambermaids come over and stand by. It's really quite a ceremony and we leave one of our postcards at each door, inviting all the guests to come up to the shoot. It takes place right over there by the flagpole. We use that little brass one-pounder cannon originally kept in the hallway near the front door. Everybody gets into a wonderful Independence Day mood."

The Dockside Guest Quarters is composed of the original New England homestead of the 1880s, called the Maine House, and other multi-unit cottage buildings of a contemporary design, each with its own porch and water view. Some have a casual studio feeling and some have kitchenettes.

The innkeepers are David and Harriette Lusty. David is a real "State of Maine" man, complete with a wonderful Down East accent. They have raised four strapping sons at Dockside, two of whom have stayed in the hospitality business.

Harriette continued, "The days in early June can be spent in many different ways. We have a number of sandy beaches, and swimming is at its best when the sun is highest at midday and in early afternoon. It's also great fun to wander around the stretches of beach and have them almost entirely to one's self. Golf and tennis are available at the golf club, and the marina has rental sailboats and outboards. We're doing something very interesting during the month of June; we have arranged a special bargain package that includes a sightseeing cruise with a luncheon stop at Portsmouth Harbor. We are arranging several other similar expeditions for our guests. It also includes a lobster dinner and very attractive pre-season rates."

There's always a great deal of history to share in the York area, and this time I learned about the famous statue that is the figure of a Confederate soldier, instead of a "Boy in Blue." David tells me that they have now

located the town somewhere in South Carolina where the statue of the Union soldier has been resting for almost a hundred years. Everybody has decided that they're going to leave the statues the way they are. "After all," said David, "that war has long been over."

So the combination of Dockside life, generous dollops of history, the pleasant vista from Dockside of the harbor craft, and the opportunity to enjoy a good dinner at the Dockside dining room, managed by Steve and Sue Roeder, makes staying at this little seaside inn an enjoyable experience in any season of the year—perhaps just a tad more satisfying in June.

DOCKSIDE GUEST QUARTERS, P.O. Box 205, Harris Island Rd., York, ME 03909; 207-363-2868. An 18-guestroom (some studio suites with kitchenettes) waterside country inn 10 mi. from Portsmouth, N.H. American plan available. Continental breakfast served to houseguests only. Dockside Dining Room serves lunch and dinner to travelers daily except Mon. Open from Memorial Day weekend in May thru Columbus Day (in Oct.). York Village is a National Historic District. Lawn games, shuffleboard, badminton, fishing, sailing, and boating from premises. Golf, tennis, and ocean swimming nearby; safe and picturesque paths and roadways for walks, bicycling, and jogging. Credit cards are not welcome for amounts over fifty dollars. Personal checks accepted for payment of food and lodgings incurred by registered guests. David and Harriette Lusty, Innkeepers.

Directions: From I-95, take the last exit before the northbound toll gate at York to U.S. 1, then to Rte. 1A. Follow 1A thru center of Old York Village, take Rte. 103 (a side street off Rte. 1A leading to the harbor), and watch for signs to the inn immediately after crossing bridge.

GOOSE COVE LODGE
Deer Isle, Maine

I was singing in the shower; in fact, I was singing quite loudly in the shower. Fortunately, my particular cottage, "Azalea," was, like all of the other cottages at Goose Cove, considerably separated from the others, with a resulting lovely sense of privacy.

I hopped out of the shower, dashed into the bedroom, and toweled myself off in front of the crackling fire that was just right for a rather chilly early June morning.

My cottage, like most of the others, had an excellent native stone fireplace, and the basic motif was unfinished aromatic wood that was used for the walls, beams, shelves, bookcases, and the like. It had a peaked roof and exposed overhead beams. The entire structure sits on a great granite rock up over Goose Bay, and from all the windows I was able to look down through the pine trees to the waters of the bay. Entirely in keeping with the eclectic ambience of Goose Cove, one of the wooden walls had a very large non-objective modern painting. A comfortable love seat was in front of the fireplace and the furnishings were completed with two hooked rugs and a bed with wool blankets and a very colorful quilt. Each of the rustic lodges has its own bathroom facilities and in some cases there's an extra bedroom.

Goose Cove Lodge is a resort-inn on Deer Isle. It is on the modified American plan and all guests take breakfast and dinner in the newly-expanded dining room. During breakfast, one of the other guests asked George Pavloff about their one-week-minimum- stay policy during July and August.

"We have found it works wonders for guests during that peak season," he declared. "Typically, our guests will arrive about 5:30 on the appointed Saturday after driving a long time. Our gentle Priscilla quietly greets them, shows them to their cottage or room, and explains that hors d'oeuvres have just been set out in the Lodge, and reminds them that the dinner bell will ring at 6:30. A bit later over hors d'oeuvres, Elli and I greet them and introduce them to other guests. Then it's time for the Saturday evening buffet, and already they are beginning to realize that many of the other guests have been coming here for quite a few years, and anxiety starts to recede. That night they sleep surprisingly well on a full stomach and a firm mattress." We all laughed at that one.

"We take the time during and after breakfast the first morning to orient them to Deer Isle and the many choices they have for various activities, and that evening they're all eager to share the day's experiences—perhaps a boat ride to the outer islands, a drive to Bar Harbor, a day walking the nature trails, visits to the crafts and antique stores, a deep muscle massage, a sailing lesson or expedition—and already acquaintances are beginning to multiply and deepen. This sharing continues throughout the week.

"Our guests are further acquainted by reading our own in-house newspaper, 'Mother Goose Says,' which rolls out of our copying machine each Saturday. It has news of all the goings-on at or near the lodge.

"On Friday night the lobster cookout on the beach is like the last night of summer camp—physical and mental tensions are gone, faces are relaxed, fellowship is high. Guests are exchanging addresses at breakfast the next morning and the innkeepers and staff are all saying goodbye. The result is obvious and a marked contrast to those guests who are trying to "do" New England in a week by touching down briefly in a different place each night."

GOOSE COVE LODGE, Sunset, Deer Isle, ME 04683; 207-348-2508. A 22-guestroom (60 people) resort-inn on beautiful Penobscot Bay approx. 1 hr. from Rte. 1 at Bucksport. Open mid-May to mid-Oct. Modified American plan mid-June to mid-Sept.; 7-day minimum stay (Sat.–Sat.) in July and Aug.; 2-day minimum stay other times. Meals served to houseguests only. Swimming, boating, canoeing, hiking, and bird watching all available at the inn. Other outdoor sports, including backroading, golf, tennis, etc., nearby. Especially adaptable for children of all ages. Elli and George Pavloff, Innkeepers.

Directions: From Bucksport, drive 4 mi. north on Rte. 1 and turn right on Rte. 15 down the Blue Hill Peninsula to Deer Isle Village. Turn right in village at sign to Sunset, Maine. Proceed 3 mi., turn right at Goose Cove Lodge sign. Follow dirt road 1½ mi. to inn.

GREY ROCK INN
Northeast Harbor, Maine

Janet Millet and I were seated in a new, trim sitting room that had been created on the second floor of the Grey Rock Inn since my last visit. Bathed in the afternoon sunshine, it's a perfect place for a quiet cup of tea, and that's exactly what we were having.

"I call it a little upstairs sitting room," she said. "I put on the last of the wallpaper in June, and as you see I've decorated it with other things of which I am very fond. I put some wicker furniture in here, including a Victorian bird cage with some colorful peacocks, and there is some geranium ivy. It's supposed to have pink blossoms, but they haven't come out just yet. That Japanese screen is one of my favorites and it's decorated with jade and mother-of-pearl."

Janet is British and she has an innate admiration for things British. For example, she loves, as do most Britons, "a lovely fireplace." Fortunately, Grey Rock is on the coast of upper Maine and there is plenty of firewood right from her own little forest to supply the two living-room/parlor fireplaces with ample wood.

I usually tease her about being British and this time I asked, "What are some British touches that you use here at Grey Rock?"

"Well, we serve a very good strong cup of tea. English breakfast tea," she replied rather firmly. "Another English touch is the unusual reception and drawing room, also used as our breakfast room. We have a very large selection of books and British magazines."

"Is there anything that you particularly liked and remembered from growing up in England that you have introduced in the bedrooms?" I asked.

"Yes, my lovely down-feather pillows. We used to have down-feather mattresses when I was a girl, but I've got the very best down-feather pillows here for Grey Rock. We have all kinds of other English touches too, with lots of flowers and bright and gay fabrics in all of the guest rooms."

I must admit that Grey Rock has a very authentic English country house feeling—the same feeling I enjoy so much when visiting in England. Some of the guest rooms on the second floor have very good views of the corner of the harbor.

One of the focal points is a porch off the reception area that gives one the sensation of sitting in the treetops. There are evergreen trees all around it and big hanging tuberous begonias. It's a very pleasant place for breakfast in the morning.

"Elegant" is an excellent word to describe Grey Rock, and almost immediately new arrivals are struck by Janet's unusual collection of wicker pieces, which are rare art forms. For example, there is a tea table on wheels, a chaise lounge, three or four wicker table lamps, a wicker floor lamp, wicker love seats, a wicker desk, a wicker plant stand for two plants, and wing chairs in wicker. These are all in the main sitting room and another smaller adjacent parlor.

These wicker pieces blend beautifully with the unusual collection of oriental memorabilia that Janet has gathered over the years, making the inn somewhat reminiscent of a New England house of a century ago, when sea captains brought back the wonderful treasure of the Orient on

their clipper ships. Particularly impressive are the collection of fans and the exquisite framed oriental paintings on silk. As part of the harmonious whole, fresh flowers complete the picture.

Grey Rock literally sits on a rocky ledge above the town of Northeast Harbor, well within its own forested area, where trails lead into the woods. There is no amusement or recreation on the grounds for smaller children. The entire kaleidoscope of the wonderful natural attractions of Mount Desert Island is literally at the front door.

GREY ROCK INN, Harborside Rd., Northeast Harbor, ME 04662; 207-276-9360. A 12-guestroom village inn adjacent to Acadia National Park and all of the attractions of this unusual region. European plan. Continental breakfast served to houseguests only. No other meals served. Small cottage available for minimum 4-night stay. Season from early spring to Nov. 1. Children 14 yrs. and older preferred. No pets. No credit cards. No smoking in guest rooms. Janet Millet, Innkeeper.

Directions: Located on the right side of Rte. 198 approaching the town of Northeast Harbor. Note sign for inn. Do not try to make a right turn at this point, but proceed about one block, turn around and approach the inn on the left, up the steep hill.

HARTWELL HOUSE
Ogunquit, Maine

The story of my first visit to this inn begins with a sumptuous dinner at the Whistling Oyster overlooking Perkins Cove in Ogunquit. I was telling John Parella that we seemed to be back at "square one" as far as being able to recommend an overnight accommodation in Ogunquit.

Many years ago when I first included the Whistling Oyster, John recommended that I visit the Island House, at that time just a few steps beyond the "Oyster," and for many years the combination worked very well. Then, unfortunately, the Island House went out of business, and again we were faced with the original problem.

"Wait a minute!" he exclaimed, "I think I have just the place for you to see. It's called the Hartwell House, run by Trisha and Jim Hartwell, and it's a beautiful, elegant, sophisticated small bed-and-breakfast inn, actually within walking distance of where we are right now."

My first glimpse of the Hartwell House on Shore Road leading back to the center of Ogunquit was most favorable. It was a two-story, pleasantly designed building with a facade of many Moorish arches. There were some gardens in the front and what appeared to be some considerable grassy acreage in the rear.

The unusually large and attractively decorated front porch area had beautiful summer furniture with lighthearted slipcovers. There were several groups of comfortable chairs and sofas, stacks of books and magazines, and many varieties of flowers. Four houseguests were playing bridge. It had the kind of atmosphere that invited me to sit down and feel at home.

Trisha Hartwell suggested that this would be a good time for us to see the accommodations at Hartwell House, since many of the guests were having dinner at the Whistling Oyster, so I embarked on a rather happy journey through a group of attractively furnished rooms, some with four-poster beds, with many antiques and beautiful bedspreads. The rooms in the back of the inn also had balconies overlooking the lawn.

"We're planning on making some conservative additions, including tennis courts and a gazebo," explained Trisha. "Nothing that will interfere with the very pleasant country-house atmosphere. I imagine it will be a couple of years before it's all completed. Our lawn leads down to the river and our guests presently enjoy sitting quietly under the trees."

There are nine accommodations at Hartwell House, including two efficiency apartments and two studios. All have private baths. These have full-sized kitchens, if the guests desire. A complimentary continental breakfast is served either on the patio or in the elegant dining room.

On winter weekends the Hartwell House is happy to provide a special package with welcome hors d'oeuvres on Friday evening, late

breakfast on Saturday, dinner at the Whistling Oyster on Saturday night, Sunday brunch, and a late checkout time. As Trisha says, "Bring a good book and a good friend."

Hartwell House is within walking distance of the beach, Perkins Cove, churches, and the Marginal Way. It's also on the minibus route that serves the town.

So once again I'm happy to be able to recommend lodging accommodations in Ogunquit in keeping with the elegance and tone of the Whistling Oyster, which does not have lodgings but serves both lunch and dinner. I'm certain that our readers will find the Hartwell House a very pleasant experience.

I would hope that readers who are planning a visit to the southern coast of Maine with an overnight stay in Ogunquit, would call ahead sufficiently in advance to be able to make reservations here, because it is well worth the effort.

HARTWELL HOUSE, 116 Shore Rd., Ogunquit, ME 03907; 207-646-7210. A 9-guestroom inn providing a very compatible atmosphere for a limited number of guests (4 rooms may be rented as a complete apartment). Complimentary continental breakfast. Open year-round. The ocean, Perkins Cove, the Marginal Way, Ogunquit Playhouse, all within walking distance. Fishing, golf, swimming, bicycles, sailing nearby. Tennis, swimming pool, and golf privileges available at Cliff Country Club. Not suitable for children under 14. No pets. Trisha and Jim Hartwell, Innkeepers.

Directions: Follow I-95 north through New Hampshire into Maine; take last exit before Maine toll booth; north on Rte. 1, 7 mi. to center of Ogunquit. Turn right on Shore Rd. approx. ¾ mi. Hartwell House is on right.

HOMEWOOD INN
Yarmouth, Maine

"Tell me about the kind of guests who come to Homewood," I said to Fred Webster as we were strolling about the grounds.

"Well, I think that we appeal to a great many people of all ages and preferences," he said. "For instance, we have one guest who comes for three weeks in late June each year and tells us to put through no phone calls and not to bother him and his wife for clambake reservations or anything else. It happens that he's about to leave now and we haven't seen him once! Of course, there are others who like to chat with the staff and the family and who mix well around the pool and the tennis courts with the other guests. One of the things that attracts almost every guest is the L. L. Bean store."

The L. L. Bean store in nearby Freeport is just one of the many reasons to remain several nights at the Homewood Inn. The inn has been operated for a number of years by the Webster family and has a view of some of the 365 Calendar Islands. Many of the single and double cottages that make up most of the inn complex have fireplaces and are set among the juniper, cedar, maple, and Norway pine trees. There is a multitude of flowers, including roses, phlox, snapdragons, marigolds, petunias, and dozens of other flowering plants and shrubs.

Guests are frequently delighted to discover that they are sharing their waterside environment with many varieties of land and shore birds. Colleen Webster told me that a few years ago she looked out of her window and saw a moose walking on the property. "It seemed to me to be as big as a house," she declared. "Eventually it strolled down the road, passed some of our cottages, and entered the water and swam off into the distance. We do have seals on our offshore rocks, but this is the first time I've ever seen a moose. As a matter of fact, I hope it's the last time!"

Homewood Inn has been on this particular spot on Casco Bay for many, many years. It was originally started by Fred Webster's mother and father and is being continued by Fred and his wife, Colleen.

The Inn Shop has been operated by Fred's mother, Doris Gillette, and her husband, Ted. They scout around the crafts shops in Maine seeking out unusual gifts. Incidentally, they are still very active people at 85 and 86 years of age.

In the summer, I've always enjoyed being at Homewood on a Monday night so that I can have fun at the regular Monday night clambake—a real Down East feast, with lobster, steak, clams, and chicken served outdoors at rustic tables. On the other nights, the restaurant menu has a great many features that reflect both the agricultural and water-oriented location of the inn. This includes chicken and beef dishes, as well as lobster, scallops, and broiled fish native to Maine waters. The chef is Joe Gricus, whom I knew for many years at the Inn at Starlight Lake in Pennsylvania, and the cuisine consultant is the Websters' daughter, Julie, who has literally grown up at Homewood.

Meanwhile, Fred and I walked over the path he had cut in the field by the woods, through the new pine-tree farm, and we were accompanied by Bonnie, a full-bred collie. She flushed out a pileated woodpecker and a cedar waxwing as we strolled along.

The Homewood is certainly well named; it's very homelike and looks happily settled among the woods, fields, and harbor. Its informal atmosphere invites vacationers, especially those with children, to enjoy a real country resort-inn experience. Sooner or later everyone meets at the lodge, around the pool, or at the tennis courts.

HOMEWOOD INN, Drinkwater Point, P.O. Box 196B, Yarmouth, ME 04096; 207-846-3351. A 42-guestroom (including suites and cottages) waterside inn on Casco Bay, 20 min. north of Portland. European plan. Breakfast and dinner served to travelers daily except Mon., when a steak or lobster cookout at night is available (by advance reservation). Open June 12 through Oct. 14. Bicycles (including tandems), pool, tennis, croquet court, hiking, salt-water swimming on grounds. Golf, riding, fishing, boating, state parks, theater nearby. Fred and Colleen Webster, Julie Webster Frank, and Ted and Doris Gillette, Innkeepers.

Directions: From the south, take Exit 9 from Maine Tpke. (I-95) to Rte. 1-N, or Yarmouth exit from I-295 to Rte. 1-N and follow signs to inn. From north (Brunswick area) take I-95 to Yarmouth exit. Then take Rte. 88 and follow signs to inn.

OLD FORT INN
Kennebunkport, Maine

"Beaches are fun and I enjoy salt water, but to me there's something very special about having the privacy and quietness of a swimming pool."

A group of us were seated around the pool at the Old Fort Inn when this particular observation was made by a Canadian guest. Someone else had said, "I like to play tennis and I like to know that not only is there a good tennis court here, but there are frequently people who play a good game."

The Old Fort Inn is a very special kind of country inn that provides a complete change of pace from the hustle and bustle of Kennebunkport. A few years ago, the main building of the hotel that originally had been on the property was torn down, and the handsome stone carriage house was converted into twelve large bedrooms with electric heat, fully equipped kitchen facilities, Laura Ashley wallpapers, and daily maid service. The rooms are large enough so that guests can stay for longer periods without feeling cramped.

Guests gather at the main lodge in a converted barn, built around 1880. It has a big fireplace that serves as a focal point on spring and fall evenings, and its open deck next to the swimming pool makes it a very comfortable place where guests may gather in the warmer weather.

The innkeepers are David and Sheila Aldrich, two very attractive people from California, who came here a few years ago and have made the Old Fort Inn and Kennebunkport their new home. They are considerably assisted by their perky daughter, Shana, who must be at least nine years old by this time.

I think it might be fun if I shared a description of my bedroom at the Old Fort Inn. For one thing, it's large enough to be comfortable for two people, with plenty of room for a third person on the little sofa bed. There is a big double cannonball bed with blue sheets and a harmonizing blue comforter, blue carpeting, and a blue cover on the daybed. There are good reading lights on both sides of the bed. A fully equipped kitchenette, including a stove with an oven and separated from the rest of the room by a divider, gives guests the option of preparing their own meals. A wood table and chairs for two, a Victorian table with an attractive lamp, a wicker armchair, and a beautifully refinished chest of drawers complete the picture. A painting of a duck is part of the great collection of duck decoys and paintings found throughout the inn.

A large over-sized closet contains extra pillows (something I commend at all times). By the way, David and Sheila have provided such thoughtful things as a laundry with a dryer in the same building.

I think I can safely say that Kennebunkport, Maine, is one of the few fast-disappearing places in the world that lives up to its advance billing.

The village still retains much of the ambience it had when clipper ships sailed from its shores. The lovely old sea captains' houses remain, and the beautiful streets and winding river make it a very pleasant vacation experience.

During my most recent visit I found that guests spend quite a bit of time in the antique shop that's mainly Sheila's project. "David and I feel that it has added considerably to the attractiveness of the inn," she said.

Spring is an excellent time to visit this part of the Maine coast, and between April 29 and June 14, David and Sheila have arranged for a very special midweek "Escape Plan" that I'm sure many of our readers would find most attractive.

OLD FORT INN, Old Fort Ave., Kennebunkport, ME 04046; 207-967-5353. A 12-guestroom resort-inn within walking distance of the ocean in a historic Maine town. Includes an ample continental breakfast, and a full kitchen is provided with each apartment. Daily maid service. Fireplace lodge. Open from May 1 to Oct. 31. Heated pool, tennis court, shuffleboard on grounds. Bicycles, golf, salt-water swimming, and boating nearby. Not comfortable for children under 7. No pets. Sheila and David Aldrich, Innkeepers.

Directions: Take Exit 3 (Kennebunk) from the Maine Turnpike. Take left on Rte. 35 and follow signs through Kennebunk to Kennebunkport. Take left at traffic light at Sunoco station. Go over drawbridge and take first right on Ocean Ave. Take Ocean Ave. to the Colony Hotel; turn left in front of the Colony, go to the Y in the road, go right ¼ mi. Inn is on left.

THE PILGRIM'S INN (originally The Ark)
Deer Isle, Maine

Travelers really have to be looking for Deer Isle and the Pilgrim's Inn. It's a good hour's drive from U.S. 1, east of Bucksport, to the Blue Hill Peninsula. Deer Isle sits just off the southern flank of the mainland, and no matter how you arrive it's necessary to cross over the suspension bridge at Eggemoggin Reach.

This is really "down home" Maine and even the 1939 bridge has failed to disturb the naturalness of either the islanders or the area.

Jean and Dud Hendrick moved here a few years ago after acquiring the Pilgrim's Inn (the name of which is gradually being changed back to "The Ark").

A four-story gambrel-roofed grey house, this building has overlooked the long harbor on the front and the mill pond in the rear since 1793. Much of the original building has remained almost completely unchanged, with the original Colonial feature of two large rooms and a kitchen on the ground floor still intact. One of these rooms is the common room of the present-day inn.

Most of the guest rooms are quite large, with richly hued pine floorboards, wood stoves, country furniture, and a selection of books and magazines. They are enhanced by coordinated Laura Ashley fabrics, used for curtains, lampshades, quilts, and cushions.

In answer to my question about why there are so many returning guests, Jean said, "I think it's the little touches. We pride ourselves on attention to such details as apples in the rooms, a welcoming letter to each guest establishing the ground rules and identifying some of the recreational options. And we're so proud of our new soft towels and washcloths and our beautiful quilts."

Dud had a few things to add. "We give each guest a tour of the inn that includes the common room and the lounge and the kitchen, where they meet our baker, Rebekah of Tennessee, who does great homemade breads, tortes, and cakes. We continue on into the barn/dining room, where we have local artists' exhibits.

"There are really a lot of wonderful things to do around here. For instance, the mail boat to Isle au Haute is a most romantic day trip, and the sailing here is terrific. There are many, many art galleries and crafts shops a short distance away and Arcadia National Park is just close enough for a day trip."

Jean excused herself to head for the kitchen and Dud told me somewhat confidentially, "Jean continues to do all of our dinners, with the exception of the weekly lobster, crab, mussel, and clam cookout. This year, a favorite is Tournedos Neptune—tenderloin topped with crabmeat and Béarnaise sauce, garnished with shrimp and halibut and served with artichoke hearts. Her poached salmon with beurre blanc is also a winner."

Pilgrim's Inn is a special place, so tell only your very special friends about it.

THE PILGRIM'S INN (originally The Ark), Deer Isle, ME 04627; 207-348-6615. A 12-guestroom (some shared baths) inn in a remote island village on the Blue Hill Peninsula on the Maine coast. Modified American plan, May 15 to Nov. 1, includes a hearty breakfast and a creative dinner. In season, outside dinner reservations are accepted. A 4-day minimum reservation is requested in Aug. Bicycles, badminton, ping-pong, regulation horseshoes, croquet, and a rowboat for the mill pond on the grounds. All types of cultural and recreational advantages, including golf, fishing, sailing, hiking, and browsing nearby. No pets. Dud and Jean Hendrick, Innkeepers.

Directions: From Boston, take I-95 to Brunswick exit. Take coastal Rte. 1 north past Bucksport. Turn right on Rte. 15, which travels to Deer Isle down the Blue Hill Peninsula. At the village, turn right on Main St. (Sunset Rd.) and proceed one block to the inn on the left side of the street, opposite the harbor.

THE SQUIRE TARBOX INN
Westport Island, Maine

"The town of Wiscasset and Westport Island were purchased in 1664 from an Indian chief named Robinhood (honestly, that's really his name)," Bill Mitman assured me, "but Indian harassment prevented permanent settlement until eighty years later. When Sam Tarbox arrived in the early 1800s, he was considered the richest and most influential man on the island, and he expanded this house to its current rambling structure. Actually, the oldest part dates from 1763, and it was recently added to the National Register of Historic Places. Tarbox family neighbors have donated some fascinating historical memorabilia too."

Bill and Karen Mitman, the innkeepers of the Squire Tarbox Inn, and I were strolling down the pine-needled path to the salt water, where there's a screened shed at the water's edge for guests to relax and enjoy the view and the birds. I was once again enjoying a most pleasant visit to this lovely world set apart on the Maine coast.

The Squire Tarbox is a very quiet inn in a section of Maine that is sufficiently off the beaten track to be unspoiled and natural. It has both the wainscoting of the early 1800s and the rustic wide-board construction of the 1700s. It is quite small—nine guest rooms have a cozy "up country" feeling with Colonial prints and colors and some working fireplaces. A large hearth with the original bake oven, pumpkin pine floors, and hand-hewn beams set the tone for this rambling Colonial farmhouse with its hip roof and pale yellow narrow clapboards and apple green shutters. There are several choices for sitting around in front of fireplaces to enjoy reading or conversation, especially in a captivating barn with large doors that open out on a screened-in sundeck. And there is a player piano, an antique music box, Colonial wooden toys, and English wooden puzzles for further amusement.

Bill and Karen are very friendly, conversational people, who make innkeeping seem almost deceptively simple. Their background at the Copley Plaza in Boston must have much to do with this. The conversation turned toward some of their menu ideas.

"Our sole paupiettes (fillet of sole stuffed with spinach and Parmesan cheese) and the chicken Madeleine (a boneless breast of chicken in a sherried mushroom sauce on a bed of chipped beef and rice) are two dishes that are most appreciated by our guests," Karen said. "We also have pork chops cooked in a brandied sauce of onions, apples, and prunes, and we serve fresh native seafood, because it is so available, and fiddlehead ferns with their delicate flavor are often featured as a garnish."

Bill laughed and added, "You've got to try the Squire's 'Sin Pie,' the ultimate chocolate experience."

I noticed that Karen was steering our walk through the woods to an

immaculately neat shed, down the road a few paces from the main inn. Here I found a very pleasant surprise—a small herd of attractive, friendly, pure-bred Nubian goats. They have become the center of quite a lot of attention, including a two-page spread in the *Washington Post's* Sunday Food section.

"These are really my charge," Karen explained. "I milk them twice a day and the guests all seem to enjoy them. They are very clean and friendly and provide us with a smooth-tasting, soft cheese that is herbed and served when all of our guests reassemble at the end of the day." The goats have recently been joined by two burros and a garden scarecrow, much to the amusement of the guests.

THE SQUIRE TARBOX INN, Westport Island, R.D. 2, Box 2160, Wiscasset, ME 04578; 207-882-7693. A 9-guestroom (some private baths) restored Colonial home on Rte. 144 in Westport, 10 mi. from Wiscasset. Modified American plan. All lodgings include continental breakfast and full leisurely dinner. Also serving dinner to travelers. Open late May to late Oct. Within a 30-min. drive of beaches, harbor shops, and museums of mid-coast Maine. No amusements for children under 12. No credit cards. Bill and Karen Mitman, Innkeepers.

Directions: From Maine Tpke. take Exit 9 and follow Rte. 95 to Exit 22. Take Rte. 1 to Rte. 144, 7 mi. north of Bath. Follow Rte. 144 to Wiscasset–Westport Bridge. The inn is located 6 mi. south of bridge on Westport Island.

A number of inns have nearby airports where private airplanes may land. An airplane symbol at the end of the inn directions indicates that there is an airport nearby. Consult inn for further information.

THE WATERFORD INNE
East Waterford, Maine

Three of us were seated on the newly screened-in porch, which has a lovely view of the meadows and had actually only been completed the day before, so both Rosalie and Barbara Vanderzanden, innkeepers at the Waterford Inne, were feeling very proud and happy.

"This is something that we've been wanting to do for years," said Barbara. "It seems that we have about one major project every year; one year it was the new kitchen and, of course, this year it's the porch. It also provides us with additional dining space on warm evenings."

My eye happened to travel to what was one of the most sumptuous-looking vegetable gardens I have ever seen, and it prompted a question: "What are some of the things that you grow in your own garden for your kitchen?"

"Well, we grow practically all our own herbs," explained Rosalie, who is Barbara's mother and the cook. "We like fresh herbs in the salad dressing. We also have tomatoes, brussels sprouts, broccoli, peppers, squash, and pumpkins. I'm surprised at how fussy pumpkins are to grow."

"What about some of your other main dishes?" I asked. "You have one main dish every night, don't you?"

"Well, we like baked ham with peach glaze, breast of chicken with heavy cream, various kinds of roasts, and beef Stroganoff. We serve a fixed-price dinner every evening for both houseguests and visitors. We do all our own baking, and our guests seem to enjoy it very much."

At the Waterford Inne, located in the little-known Oxford Hills area of western Maine, "small and tidy" is beautiful. It can be truthfully said that the Waterford Inne is an intimate inn. The inn is small enough to provide a really cozy country inn experience. The original house was built in 1825 and has five upstairs bedrooms that step out of the 19th century. These are augmented by four additional rooms created in a wing leading to a very large barn.

All of the bedrooms have been carefully decorated, usually with some theme in mind. For example, the Chesapeake Room has a fireplace stove and a private porch. The decorations are in the Eastern Shore theme, with duck decoys and water fowl. Even the sheets and towels have colorful water fowls on them. All of the rooms have either antiques or attractive country furniture. My bed was a four-poster with a lace canopy.

Guests gather in the main living room, where there are many different books and magazines, including several from England, because Barbara and Rosalie are Anglophiles and in fact followed *Country Inns and Back Roads, Britain and Ireland* in a trip they made to England.

Well, our chat was over, and as Rosalie went to the kitchen, Barbara

and I strolled around to take a closer look at the big barn. "The Oxford Hills section of Maine abounds in much beautiful scenery," she remarked. "It's hard to drive more than four or five miles without coming to a lake. It's quite a popular area for summer camps, so we are rather well booked in advance for the camp visitation weekends. Many camp parents stay at the inn and then stay on extra days, because it's such a lovely, tranquil experience."

THE WATERFORD INNE, Box 49, East Waterford, ME 04233; 207-583-4037. A 9-guestroom farmhouse-inn in the Oxford Hills section of southwest Maine, 8 mi. from Norway and South Paris. Closed March and April. Breakfast and dinner served to travelers by reservation. European plan. Within a short distance of many recreational, scenic, and cultural attractions in Maine and the White Mountains of New Hampshire. Cross-country skiing and badminton on grounds. Lake swimming, golf, rock hunting, downhill skiing, hiking, canoeing nearby. Alcoholic beverages not served. Well-behaved pets welcome; however, advance notification is required and a fee is charged. No credit cards. Rosalie and Barbara Vanderzanden, Innkeepers.

Directions: From Maine Tpke.: use Exit 11, follow Rte. 26 north approx. 28 mi. into Norway, then on Rte. 118 west for 8 mi. to Rte. 37 south (left turn). Go ½ mi., turn right at Springer's General Store, up the hill ½ mi. From Conway, New Hampshire: Rte. 16 to Rte. 302 east to Fryeburg, Me. Take Rte. 5 out of Fryeburg to Rte. 35 south, thence to Rte. 118, which is a left fork (with Rte. 35 going right). Continue on Rte. 118 east, past Papoose Pond camping area, then watch for right turn onto Rte. 37. Go ½ mi. to Springer's General Store. Take immediate right turn, ½ mi. up hill.

WHITEHALL INN
Camden, Maine

We were quite a group. There was Ed and Jean Dewing, the inn-keepers at the Whitehall Inn, along with several other members of their family. There was their daughter, Heidi, who covers several different areas of the inn, including innkeeping at the Maine House, across the street, which offers the weary traveler bed and breakfast during the winter. Then there was Chip and Kathy, who were married a few years ago, and both of whom work at the inn; and Jonathan, who was a little tyke of only fourteen when the Dewings acquired the inn a number of years ago. The other member of the family is Jean's brother, Don Chambers, who is the chef.

I believe this is a record number of seven members of the same family working at an inn in what is obviously marvelous harmony.

If ever an inn and a setting were made for each other, the Whitehall Inn and Camden are perfectly matched. The neoclassic buildings of the inn are connected by a large porch filled with plenty of comfortable wicker furniture. The inn sits back from the main street among huge elm and pine trees, and there are many window boxes and arrangements of summer flowers.

On the first floor there are several parlors and a large lobby, all of which are furnished with Maine antiques. The lounge has sewing machines ingeniously converted into tables, chess sets that invite competition, and a large collection of unusual shells displayed under glass. Guest rooms are country-style.

Ed said that most of the guests still are interested in the Edna St. Vincent Millay Room, designed as a tribute to her, with many volumes of her poems, along with memorabilia that would be of interest to her numerous admirers. It was here at the Whitehall Inn on a warm August evening in 1912 that young Edna first recited her poem, "Renascence."

The inn is just a short, tree-lined walk from the center of the village.

An excellent folder provided by the inn has dozens of suggestions about activities in and around this part of Maine, including golf, sightseeing, art exhibitions, boating, swimming, hiking, and fishing.

I believe that a major part of everyone's country inn experience is the food. In reference to the Whitehall Inn, here's a letter I have from a gentleman from Vermont: "Because I have been connected with the food industry most of my life, I instinctively notice the small considerations that lift an establishment head and shoulders above the rest. During the past few years, we have enjoyed quite a few meals at the inn, and this year we were guests for a delightful week. The food is certainly exceptional."

Ed recently sent me a copy of a letter written to him by an eight-year-old boy who had been a guest at the inn. "Thank you very much for the hospitality you showed our family on our visit to Camden. Thank you, too, for the lobster buoy. It is hanging in my room. It will be a nice remembrance of our trip to New England. I will always remember putting that old wooden puzzle together."

Well, even if the young man's mother gave him a little assistance with words like "remembrance," I'm sure we will agree that he caught the Whitehall spirit. As Ed says, "After fifteen years filled with ups and downs, Jean and I are still glad we chose this way of life and already look forward to our sixteenth season in 1986. We promise the same beautiful sunrises and sunsets, crisp, clean air, brilliant fall foliage, friendly neighbors, a bountiful table, and lots of people who look out for everybody's comfort and well being."

WHITEHALL INN, Camden, ME 04843; 207-236-3391. A 38-guestroom village inn in a Maine seacoast town, 75 mi. from Portland. Modified American plan omits lunch. Bed and breakfast offered in Maine House and Wicker House. Breakfast and dinner served daily to travelers. Open May 25 to Oct. 15. Tennis, bicycles, shuffleboard, arrangements for harbor cruises on grounds. Golf, hiking, swimming, fishing, day sailing nearby. No pets. The Dewing Family, Innkeepers.

Directions: From Maine Tpke. take Exit 9 to coastal Rte. 95. Proceed on Rte. 95 to Rte. 1 at Brunswick. Follow Rte. 1 to Rte. 90 at Warren, to Rte. 1 in Camden. Inn is located on Rte. 1, ½ mi. north of Camden.

THE WHISTLING OYSTER RESTAURANT
Ogunquit, Maine

A balance of traditional New England fare and Continental-American cuisine best describes the luncheon and dinner menus at this most picturesque restaurant on Perkins Cove. Innkeeper John Parella is particularly proud of the fine fresh fish, meats, and other ingredients and the presentation and preparation that vary frequently. The menu especially features foods that are in season.

All of the baking is done on the premises, and the Whistling Oyster chefs make their own ice creams, often with fresh fruits.

While feasting on such offerings as fresh baked haddock amandine, tenderloin of beef with forest mushrooms, casserole of fresh Maine crabmeat, and roast duckling with fruit sauce, guests may enjoy the especially appealing view of the waterside ambience and the ebb and flow of the fishing village water traffic.

After a pleasant meal, guests often visit the gift shop, filled with elegant and often exclusive items such as imported china and crystal, gold and sterling jewelry, and two gourmet food lines. A popular item has been gift certificates for the gift shop or restaurant.

THE WHISTLING OYSTER RESTAURANT, Perkins Cove, Ogunquit, ME 03907; 207-646-9521. A waterfront restaurant and gift shop in Perkins Cove at Ogunquit. Lunch and dinner served daily. Open throughout the year. Reservations advisable. No lodgings, but nearby CIBR overnight lodgings can be found at the Hartwell House, Ogunquit (207-646-7210). John Parella, Innkeeper.

Directions: From the south, take the York exit from I-95. Turn north on Rte. 1 to Bourne Lane. Turn right on Shore Rd. for about 1 mi. to Perkins Cove turnoff.

Favorite Back Roads

Route 35 is representative of one of the most delightful tour byways in this area, regardless of season. From Naples village, Route 35 winds its way, keeping in close touch with the eastern shoreline of Long Lake, for approximately twelve miles to the village of Harrison. The alert motorist can view both lake and the White Mountains in New Hampshire without ever leaving his vehicle. Besides, there are magnificent homes, working farms, and woods galore along this trail. From Harrison the motorist would jog over a mile to the storybook picturesque hamlet of North Bridgton, home of one of the oldest boys' preparatory schools in the nation. Campus, class buildings, dorms, and chapel—all wood frame and painted pristine white—are set above a huge rolling lawn. The Academy dominates the village which is also completely clothed in white—homes, church, firehouse, and post office. By the way, Bridgton Academy is my alma mater.

Here the motorist picks up Route 37, sister byway of Route 35, and wends his way through woodlands and lakes to the picture-perfect village of Waterford which, we are advised, is listed on the National Historic Register in its entirety. "High tea" served daily (except Tuesdays) at the Artemus Ward House in Waterford Common is a must before the "Backroader" returns to Naples and his Charmwoods base.

We suggest on the homeward trip that for the sake of variety the motorist take companion Route 35 back to Harrison and then on to Naples. The entire drive, with time out for tea in Waterford, can be conducted in leisurely fashion in an hour, more or less. The route is practically devoid of commercial establishments and is strictly for those who desire to commune with nature.

Bill and Marilyn Lewis
Charmwoods
Naples, Maine

Southern New England

Eastern Time Zone

● Sedgwick Inn, *Berlin*

ALBANY
Millhof Inn, *Stephentown, N.Y.*

■ **PITTSFIELD**
● Peirson Place, *Richmond*
| ● Village Inn, *Lenox*

● The Inn at Stockbridge, *Stockbridge*
Red Lion Inn, *Stockbridge*

Colonel Ebenezer Crafts Inn, *Sturbridge*

The Weathervane Inn, *South Egremont*

M A S S A

● Simmons' Way Village Inn,
Millerton

■ **HARTFORD**

● Boulders Inn, *New Preston*

C O N N E C T I C U T

Bee and Thistle Inn, *Old Lym*

● West Lane Inn, *Ridgefield*

Griswold, *Essex*

NEW HAVEN ■

Silvermine Tavern, *Norwalk*

● Homestead Inn, *Greenwich*

NEW YORK CITY

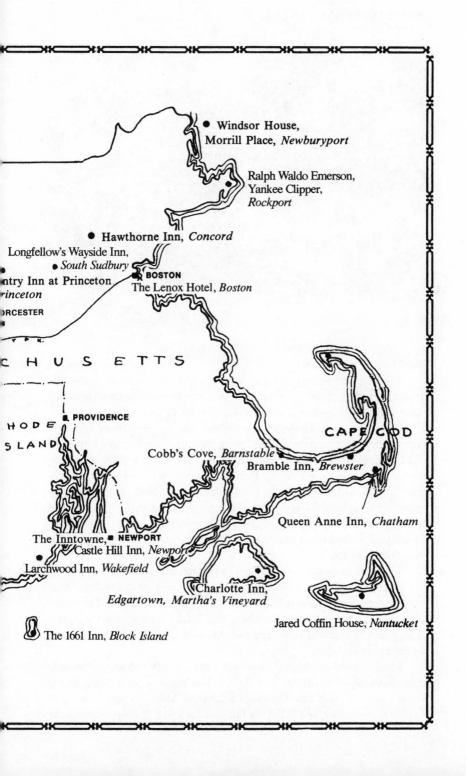

Windsor House,
Morrill Place, *Newburyport*

Ralph Waldo Emerson,
Yankee Clipper,
Rockport

Hawthorne Inn, *Concord*

Longfellow's Wayside Inn,
South Sudbury

ntry Inn at Princeton
rinceton

BOSTON

The Lenox Hotel, *Boston*

ORCESTER

T P K.

C H U S E T T S

HODE
SLAND

PROVIDENCE

CAPE COD

Cobb's Cove, *Barnstable*

Bramble Inn, *Brewster*

Queen Anne Inn, *Chatham*

The Inntowne, **NEWPORT**

Castle Hill Inn, *Newport*

Larchwood Inn, *Wakefield*

Charlotte Inn,
Edgartown, Martha's Vineyard

Jared Coffin House, *Nantucket*

The 1661 Inn, *Block Island*

BEE AND THISTLE INN
Old Lyme, Connecticut

"The natural beauty of Old Lyme was the ideal subject matter for American artists painting in the Barbizon and Impressionist styles. Old Lyme was one of the earliest art colonies in this country."

Penny Nelson, knowing my enthusiasm for American art, was sharing some of her appreciation for the beautifully preserved homes in Old Lyme. She had taken a pause for a moment from seating the many guests who were dining at the Bee and Thistle Inn, and was having a quick cup of coffee with me in front of the fire. "There are at least fifty houses here ranging from the late 17th century to the present, which are not only artistically captivating, but also worthy of study for their architecture and historical importance. Lyme Street was designated a historic district in 1970."

This love of beauty and fine things was reflected throughout the Bee and Thistle. The house was built in 1756 and many of the architectural features enhance an atmosphere of friendly open-heartedness. The many fireplaces, antiques, sunlit porches, the lovely carved staircase, the canopy and four-poster beds, and the old quilts and afghans are some of the engaging features.

I had arrived on this visit to the inn on a lovely fall afternoon and, after checking in with Bob and Penny, had taken a walk down Lyme Street, past the Florence Griswold Historical Museum, the Lyme Art Association Gallery, and the many fine antique and gift shops. Penny had offered me a bicycle for exploring, but after the drive up from New York on the Connecticut Turnpike, I opted for seeing the town on foot.

After I returned to the Bee and Thistle, my appetite, encouraged by such a pleasant stroll, felt the need of something hale and hearty. Bob Nelson suggested that either the veal sweetbreads, the roast duckling, or the breast of pheasant might be appropriate. In the course of making all these decisions I discovered that the inn has at least six separate menus, including one for breakfast, luncheon, appetizers for the evening meal, as well as another for the entrées. Still another had a handsome selection of inviting dishes served for Sunday brunch.

As a matter of fact, their food has been gaining the attention of food critics, and Jane and Michael Stern of the *Hartford Courant* have given their kitchen 2½ stars.

All of this emphasis on good eating is complemented by many different dining areas throughout the inn, including two porches with ample views of the more than five acres of grounds.

After dinner (I chose the country paté, made in the inn kitchen, and the breast of pheasant), Penny found me wandering around the parlors, admiring the paintings—hence our conversation in front of the fireplace. We took a few moments to see as many of the bedrooms as possible and it's hard to imagine a more comfortable atmosphere.

"Bob and I have had a wonderful time, even though there has been so much to do," she said, her eyes shining. "We're putting some more antiques in the bedrooms and we've also got a wonderful Welsh cupboard from one of the antique shops near you in Sheffield, Massachusetts. I think more than anything else we want the Bee and Thistle to be the warmest, friendliest, and most traditional New England inn imaginable. I'm certainly glad that we found it."

Penny and Bob, so am I—and I'm glad I found you.

BEE AND THISTLE INN, 100 Lyme St. (Rte. 1), Old Lyme, CT 06371; 203-434-1667. An 11-guestroom (2 rooms with shared bath) inn located in an as-yet-unspoiled Connecticut village, near the border of Rhode Island. À la carte breakfast served daily. Lunch and dinner daily, except Tuesday. Sunday brunch. Open year-round. Conveniently located to visit Gillette Castle, Goodspeed Opera House, and Essex steam train and train rides. Mystic Seaport, Essex Village, Ivoryton Summer Theater nearby. No pets. Bob and Penny Nelson, Innkeepers.

Directions: Coming north on I-95 take a left at the bottom of Exit 70. At the first light take a right. At the second light, take a left and then follow Rte. 1 (Lyme Street) to inn.

THE BOULDERS INN
Lake Waramaug, New Preston, Connecticut

Carolyn Woollen drew another cup of delicious tea from the samovar and I helped myself to two lumps of sugar and a dollop of cream. She passed me a plate of homemade breads and cakes.

For a moment we just sat there looking out across Lake Waramaug, now comfortably covered with a good blanket of snow and basking in the brillance of colors and hues created by the sinking sun. Blue waters, white sails, and ruddy swimmers give this same lake an altogether different look in summer.

Carolyn put her finger to her lips and then her hand to her ear. "If we listen quietly I think we can hear the Canada geese talking to each other."

There was a stamping of feet at the back door and I could hear the clatter of cross-country skis being stacked in the corner. Some red-cheeked guests came trooping across the living room and gathered around the fireplace warming their hands and exclaiming about the wonderful time they had had on the trails.

In an earlier edition of this book I reported on the progress that Carolyn and her husband, Jim, and their children, Peter, Mary, and Byron, had made at the inn. At that time their objective had been to provide a small intimate retreat where care, attention, and a homelike atmosphere would blend with the physical setting and facilities. Now I was ready for another update.

"Oh, we've all had a wonderful time." Carolyn reported. "In addition to attending to our guests, we've extended our outdoor dining area with two terraced decks overlooking the lake. We did this in time for last summer's guests and the shady area under the pine trees proved a very popular place for dining.

"We installed fireplaces in our cottages, making them even more cozy. They all have either patios or balconies.

"Summer and fall are well established here by a tradition of vacationers and by those enjoying the autumn foliage, but more and more of our guests are coming during the colder months because it's an area of such incredible beauty. I think it's quite reminiscent of the Scottish hills and it's hard to realize that New York City is just eighty miles south of us. Guests can skate on the lake, toboggan on our old ski hill, and hike the mountain trails starting from the back door. We're only twenty minutes away from the Mohawk Mountain ski center. For guests who are more inclined toward reading or conversation, we have a whole corner of the living room set aside as a library."

I picked up the menu to see what chef Marty Carlson was offering this season and found two familiar favorites: duck breast Maconnaise and chicken paprikash. "Each night a list of several specials supplements the

standard menu," Carolyn explained. "This keeps Marty's creative juices flowing and offers constant variety to our guests. His versatility is exciting."

The cross-country skiers and hikers would have a hearty meal at the Boulders Inn tonight.

One brief snatch of conversation caught my ear: "You know, Emily, it's so good here right now, can you imagine what it's like in the summer!"

BOULDERS INN, Lake Waramaug, New Preston, CT 06777; 203-868-7918. A 14-guestroom year-round resort-inn, 20 mi. north of Danbury, 40 mi. west of Hartford. Modified American plan Memorial Day to Labor Day. Breakfast, lunch, and dinner served to travelers, except Mon. dinner. Sept. thru May, breakfast served daily; dinner Tues. thru Sat. Open Thanksgiving, closed Christmas Eve and Christmas Day. Tennis, swimming, boating, sailing, fishing, antiquing, hiking, riding, and downhill skiing nearby; 40 min. from chamber music concert series July thru Aug. Not suitable for children under 6. The Woollen Family, Innkeepers.

Directions: From I-84, take exit 7 and follow Rte. 7 north to Rte. 202 (formerly 25) thru New Milford. Proceed 8 mi. to New Preston then 1½ mi. to inn on Rte. 45.

GRISWOLD INN
Essex, Connecticut

Somewhere in the considerable pile of brochures, information, notes, menus, and clippings and articles about the Griswold Inn, I discovered a phrase I think succinctly tells the Griswold story: "Catering to travelers and neighbors for two centuries."

Innkeeper Bill Winterer first visited Essex and saw the inn when he was an officer candidate at nearby New London Coast Guard Academy. After a few years in the world of high finance, he and his wife, Vicky, decided to start life anew here as innkeepers.

Only five families have owned the Griswold Inn since 1776. Bill reminded me that it was the first three-story structure in Connecticut, and except for a couple of small changes it has remained the same. The Tap Room was built in 1738 and was the first schoolhouse in Essex. It was rolled on logs drawn by a team of oxen down the main street to its present location.

Bill and Vicky, with their children, are great lovers of holidays, and there is always much holiday celebration at the "Gris," as it's called locally. The traditional holidays—Halloween, Thanksgiving, Groundhog Day, Valentine's Day, George Washington's Birthday, and Easter—are replete with special diversion and fun.

Within its many dining rooms and parlors, the inn has a remarkable collection of marine paintings, including some by Antonio Jacobsen, prints, ship models, firearms, binnacles, ship's clocks, a potbellied stove, humorous posters and prints, a genuine popcorn machine, and many, many other curiosities.

One of the dining rooms was constructed from an abandoned New Hampshire bridge, and in still another, the walls rock back and forth, creating the impression of being on board ship. Fresh flowers, warm woods, open fires, and candles abound, and for the guests' enjoyment, there are different kinds of entertainment almost every evening.

All of the twenty-two guest rooms at the "Gris" have private baths and are furnished in "early Essex." A lovely home next door to the inn has been converted into two suites. On the street floor of this building, a comfortable living room with a wood-burning fireplace and a game room provide houseguests with space for conviviality and relaxation.

"We have made a concerted effort to search out more New England specialties and include them on our menu," Bill declared. "These include our regular menu and our special holiday and festival menus. I daresay we serve many popular items that are simply unavailable in other dining rooms. Easily fifty percent of our patrons order fish, and all of it—with the exception of shrimp—is delivered daily fresh from the sea. While our emphasis has always been on the quality and freshness of our food, we continue to price our menus moderately, not to exclude anyone who would like to eat at the Griswold Inn."

A special luncheon menu features "Southern Secrets from Abigail Griswold's Carpet Bag." It seems that Abigail, a Louisiana lady, married Sala Griswold in June, 1775, and brought with her to Connecticut recipes for deep-fried catfish, barbecued ribs and chicken, and red beans and rice, served Cajun style. Bill swears to me that these recipes were found in Abigail's diary, discovered in 1906 in the attic of the inn.

I know that it was a great source of satisfaction to the entire Winterer family when their wonderful John-Alden design ketch, *Axia*, won the coveted prize for the Finest Sailing Yacht presented by *Nautical Quarterly*. Bill may be a landlubber now, but on weekends and special occasions and vacations you'll find him sailing up and down the New England coast with his family.

GRISWOLD INN, Main St., Essex, CT 06426; 203-767-0991. A 22-guest-room inn in a waterside town, steps away from the Connecticut River. European plan. Complimentary continental breakfast served daily to inn guests. Lunch and dinner served daily to travelers. Hunt breakfast served Sun. Closed Christmas Eve and Christmas Day. Near the Eugene O'Neill Theatre, Goodspeed Opera House, Ivoryton Playhouse, Gillette Castle, Mystic Village, Valley Railroad, and Hammonasset State Beach. Day sailing on inn's 44-foot ketch by appointment. Bicycles, tennis, and boating nearby. Victoria and William G. Winterer, Innkeepers.

Directions: From I-95 take Exit 69 and travel north on Rte. 9 to Exit 3, Essex. Turn right at stoplight and follow West Ave. to center of town. Turn right onto Main St. and proceed down to water and inn.

THE HOMESTEAD INN
Greenwich, Connecticut

As frequently as I have visited the Homestead over the years, I'm always delightfully re-surprised at the truly residential nature of its location. There's been an inn here for a very long time with a long procession of different innkeepers and many different types of accommodations; now, however, I believe the Homestead has reached the pinnacle of its success.

Today, the inn reflects the sensitivities and tastes of Lessie Davison and Nancy Smith, two attractive and talented women who saw the possibilities in restoring this 185-year-old farmhouse that is just a few moments from I-95.

The inn began its life as a farmhouse, built in 1799. In 1859 it was sold to innkeepers who completely remodeled it in the distinctive "Carpenter Gothic" architecture of the Victorian era.

The inn is set back from the road in a lovely old orchard and gardens, and the sloping lawn is highlighted by handsome hydrangea bushes. There are now twenty-four guest rooms, all with different decorative

themes. They are handsomely furnished, including many antiques and such comforts as clock radios, electric blankets, two pillows for every head, lots of books and magazines, and very modern bathrooms. In many ways, the guest rooms resemble those at Rothay Manor in the Lake Country of England.

Although many of the guest rooms are in the main house, some very careful attention has been given recently to the remodeling of other buildings on the property, and guests may now enjoy a variety of rooms, some with queen-sized beds and balconies or porches, as well as a queen-bedded suite, with a lovely, large, cathedral-ceilinged bedroom and a front porch overlooking the neighbor's apple orchard.

The Homestead is the perfect alternative to the busy, noisy New York hotels, and provides a very pleasant country-type atmosphere for city dwellers who want to leave the canyons of steel for the peaceful lanes of Greenwich.

One of the main reasons for the continuing success of the Homestead is La Grange Restaurant. The chef is Jacques Thiebeult from Paris, who trained in France, Switzerland, England, and at Le Cirque and Le Cygne restaurants in New York.

The *New York Times* restaurant reviewer awarded three stars to La Grange, pointing out that the restaurant "pays attention to every detail: salads, warm, crusty rolls, even a choice of loose tea, all are part of the seamlessly smooth dining performance."

The menu offerings include French country paté, cream of asparagus soup, scallops of veal with chestnuts, striped bass, and shad roe with bacon. Desserts include créme brulée, chocolate mousse cake, almond tart, and almond cake with chestnut filling.

Incidentally, I learned recently that William Inge wrote *Picnic* here during the 1950s. This, of course, was long before Lessie and Nancy arrived on the scene, bringing with them impeccable taste and a gratifying attention for detail. I'm sure, were he to revisit now, Mr. Inge would find the atmosphere and cuisine even more inspiring.

THE HOMESTEAD INN, 420 Field Point Rd., Greenwich, CT 06830; 203-869-7500. A 24-guestroom inn located in the residential area of a suburb, 45 min. north of New York City. Lunch served Mon. thru Fri.; dinner served daily except Labor Day, Christmas, New Year's. Located a short distance from Conn. countryside and shore scenes. Accessible by train from New York City. No amusements for children under 12. No pets. Lessie Davison, Nancy Smith, Innkeepers.

Directions: The inn is 3 min. from Rte. I-95. Take Exit 3 in Greenwich; from NYC, turn left; from New Haven, turn right off ramp. Turn left onto Horseneck Ln. at light, just before railroad overpass. Go to next traffic light; turn left onto Field Point Rd., and continue approx. ¼ mi. to inn on the right.

SILVERMINE TAVERN
Norwalk, Connecticut

"The fact of the matter is," Frank Whitman commented, "when Duke and Penny are not here we all miss them."

Duke and Penny are two swans in residence on the wonderful pond and waterfall at the Silvermine Tavern, and Frank was referring to the fact that the two seemed to have wandered off during the last two or three days and as yet had not returned.

We were seated in the dining room overlooking the summer deck at the inn, and the scene, which was set for Christmas with a package-laden sleigh, was quite a contrast to midsummer, when lunch is served with a full view of not only the pond and the water wheel, but also the flowers, birds, and other bucolic attractions.

On this Saturday before Christmas there happened to be two families enjoying a holiday luncheon and the atmosphere was most festive.

By an interesting coincidence, there was also a wedding party taking place, and while we were watching, the bride, bridesmaids, and ushers all came out to be photographed sitting in the sleigh.

The Silvermine Tavern has at various times served as a country inn, a gentleman's country seat, and a town meetinghouse. Today, it is not only a popular eating place for the residents of this Connecticut suburb, but also a very pleasant overnight stop, and especially a romantic honeymoon hideaway, with attractive double- and twin-bedded rooms, some with canopied beds.

The decorations in all of the public rooms are definitely Colonial and early-19th-century in nature, and each time I visit I learn that Frank has found even more interesting furnishings.

The menu, which is quite large, can best be characterized as "American cuisine with New England specialties." It's one of the few places I know north of Virginia that actually serves genuine Smithfield ham. Other menu offerings include indian pudding, bread pudding, native scrod, lobster, and scallops. On various nights during the week there are special buffets, and a brunch buffet on Sunday.

Whenever I visit the Silvermine, I never miss taking home a dozen of the absolutely scrumptious honey buns. I freeze them and enjoy them very sparingly, one at a time, to stretch out the memory of my visit.

You're probably wondering what happened to the swans. Well, Frank received several calls informing him of the progress of one of them down the river, as it stopped off at various riverside homes to pick up free snacks. "My neighbors are very interested in the swans and feed them during the winter and enjoy them in the summer," he explained. "Yesterday, I went to pick up the errant bird, but we couldn't get her into the trap. Then, this morning, I got her into the trap, but she climbed out. Now, I'm

going down this afternoon to see if we can outsmart this bird. One of them left the pond and ended up on the road recently. My wife saw it while she was out driving, and managed to herd it into the pond again."

I decided not to worry about the swans—I'm sure Frank has their best interests at heart.

You should look for them when you visit the Silvermine.

SILVERMINE TAVERN, Perry Ave., Norwalk, CT 06850; 203-847-4558. A 10-guestroom country inn in the residential section of Norwalk. European plan includes continental breakfast. Lunch and dinner served to travelers daily. Open year-round. Closed Christmas Day and Tuesdays during winter. Long Island Sound and beaches 6 mi. away. Golf, tennis, and fishing nearby. Francis C. Whitman, Innkeeper.

Directions: From New York or New Haven via I-95, take Exit 15. Pick up the new Rte. 7 going north. At the end of Rte. 7 (approx. 1 mi.) turn right, go to first stoplight, turn right. At next stoplight by firehouse turn right onto Silvermine Ave. Proceed down Silvermine Ave. about 2 mi. to Tavern. From I-84 and Danbury take old Rte. 7 south the Norwalk. Watch for Kelly Greens, ½ mi. south of Merritt Pkwy. on the left, turn right on Perry Ave., opposite Kelly Greens. Follow Perry Ave. 2 mi. to Tavern. From Merritt Pkwy. take Exit 39 south on old Rte. 7 and follow directions above.

WEST LANE INN
Ridgefield, Connecticut

"Basically, I think that we have three different types of guests that find their way to our little inn." Maureen Mayer and I were seated on the broad front porch of the West Lane Inn enjoying a generous continental breakfast. "By the way," she added, "if you'd like a bigger breakfast, we have an à la carte breakfast menu that offers, among other things, grapefruit, sliced bananas, berries, yogurt, corn flakes, and poached eggs."

I might add that this breakfast was served at a table with real linen tablecloths and napkins.

One of the things that sets West Lane Inn apart is the many additional amenities this attractive innkeeper provides for her guests. For example, there is a clock in every guest room, as well as a computerized phone system, a radio-TV, individual heating and air conditioning controls, and one-day laundry and dry-cleaning service, and a basket of fruit, cheese, and crackers is presented to newly arrived guests.

"Among our guests are families being relocated to the Ridgefield-Fairfield-Danbury area who need a comfortable, roomy place in which to stay while they look for a new home. Many come and stay for a week or two. I decided that they would be much more comfortable if we had accommodations that reflected the feeling of the area, so we have rooms with decks overlooking our lawn and the forest in the rear. Some of these have fireplaces and kitchen facilities. You see, guests can literally establish a little home for a short time. One of our bathrooms is designed for the handicapped, similar to the one at the West Mountain Inn in Vermont."

I observed that Ridgefield itself would be an ideal suburban place in which to live. Within commuting distance of New York and driving distance of the many corporations which are relocating in Fairfield County, Ridgefield is a most pleasant town with large graceful trees and excellent small shops. "There's also a very active community here," Maureen remarked. "We have a historical society, a library, the Ridgefield Symphony, the League of Women Voters, and various men's service clubs, sports groups, and business groups."

West Lane Inn is set back from the village street with a broad lawn enhanced by azaleas, tulips, roses, and maple and oak trees. It was originally built as a mansion in the early 1800s and the guest rooms are unusually commodious.

The other types of guests are commercial travelers, both men and women, and vacationers who enjoy country-inn hospitality. "I think we understand commercial travelers very well and we've done everything possible to have them feel that this is really a 'home away from home.'

"As far as the country-inn travelers are concerned, we're at sort of a

crossroads for north-south, east-west travel, and many couples on their way to or from New England come back and stay every year."

The West Lane could well be a model for other bed-and-breakfast inns everywhere. Every lodging room is spotless and the furnishings and decorating are all part of a harmonious color scheme. Overnight guests are coddled even further with heated towel racks and wonderful, new, large, fluffy bath sheets.

One of the things that also appeals to me is the 100%-cotton sheets on every bed in the inn. When was the last time you slept in a bed that had 100%-cotton sheets? Outstanding!

I have just received a letter from Maureen about her three new luxurious and individually decorated suites, all with separate living and dining rooms and large kitchens.

WEST LANE INN, 22 West Lane, Ridgefield, CT 06877; 203-438-7323. A 23-guestroom (several suites with kitchens) inn approx. 1 hour from N.Y.C., in a quiet residential village in southwest Connecticut. Open every day in the year. Breakfast and light snacks available until 10:30 p.m. Convenient to many museums and antique shops. Golf, tennis, swimming, and xc skiing and other outdoor recreation available nearby. No pets. Maureen Mayer, Innkeeper.

Directions: From New York: follow I-684 to Exit 6, turn right on Rte. 35, 12 mi. to Ridgefield. Inn is on left. From Hartford: Exit I-84 on Rte. 7 south and follow Rte. 35 to Ridgefield.

INN AT CASTLE HILL
Newport, Rhode Island

I was enjoying a few moments of quiet on the porch of one of the Harbor Houses at the Inn at Castle Hill watching the water traffic on Narragansett Bay. In the foreground, a young fisherman wearing very high orange boots was taking in his nets, and in the middle distance I counted at least seventeen sailboats, including one of the famous twelve-meter yachts that are used in the America's Cup Races. In the far distance there was the presence of the famous Newport Bridge, which soars over the bay to Jamestown.

Each one of the Harbor Houses is beautifully furnished with its own bathroom and is roomy enough to accommodate three people comfortably. All of them are newly decorated and the bright white walls and gay curtains and bedspreads are just perfect for the waterside atmosphere.

In addition to these lodgings, there are several rooms in the main mansion of the Inn at Castle Hill. This was once the property of the eminent naturalist Alexander Agassiz, who built Castle Hill one hundred

years ago as a summer residence. It has remained unchanged in character and many of the original furnishings, including oriental rugs and the handcrafted oak and mahogany paneling, are still intact. "This was done before Newport really became a chic society hideout," said Paul McEnroe, the innkeeper at Castle Hill. "Agassiz built this mansion for himself and was really one of the forerunners of Newport's later resplendence."

Paul and I strolled along the grassy bank to the deck of the main house where luncheon was served in full view of the everchanging panorama of sea, sky, and ships. The menu featured several enticing offerings, including a variety of omelets, crêpes, quiches, and salads.

Our conversation naturally led to the dinners at the inn, and Paul explained that the inn takes a limited number of diners each night. "They must be spaced just right. Dinner takes two to two-and-a-half hours, so we naturally cater to people who are not in a hurry. Our dinners are now 98 per cent by reservation, and we only hold a table ten minutes. We always request that they not be late in order to avoid any misunderstandings.

"The evening meal is oriented to French cuisine and includes hot and cold hors d'oeuvres, soups, salads, fish, fowl, lamb, veal, and beef, all cooked and served in the continental manner."

The European flavor of the Inn at Castle Hill is considerably reinforced by the road that leads from Ocean Drive through a small section of woods. It reminds me of the Barbizon Forest, about two hours south of Paris, which inspired a school of French painters, including Millet. When I remarked to Paul on this resemblence to inns that I have visited in Europe, he responded enthusiastically, "That's exactly what we've tried to achieve. After all, this inn was built as a mansion and we're trying to recreate the elegance of Newport's past by having a menu, service, and furnishings that best suit our ideals. Jackets are required at dinner and no jeans, not even designer style, are allowed in the dining rooms. I'm sure that's the way it was eighty years ago."

The dining rooms are closed from January 3 to Easter. However, rooms are available all winter with continental breakfast being served.

INN AT CASTLE HILL, Ocean Drive, Newport, RI 02840; 401-849-3800. A 20-guestroom mansion-inn on the edge of Narragansett Bay. European plan. Continental breakfast served to houseguests only. Lunch and dinner served daily to travelers. Dining room closed from Jan. 3 to Easter. Guestrooms open all winter. Lounge open winter weekends. Near the Newport mansions, Touro Synagogue, the Newport Casino, and National Lawn Tennis Hall of Fame, the Old Stone Mill, the Newport Historical Society House. Swimming, sailing, scuba diving, walking on grounds. Bicycles and guided tours of Newport nearby. No pets. Jens Thillemann, Manager; Paul McEnroe, Innkeeper.

Directions: After leaving Newport Bridge, follow Bellevue Ave. which becomes Ocean Dr. Look for inn sign on left, about 2 mi. out of town.

THE INNTOWNE
Newport, Rhode Island

No matter how many times I've done it, it still gives me a tremendous lift to cross over the bridge from Jamestown to Newport, Rhode Island. Not only is this approach one of the most convenient ways to reach Newport, it affords a wonderful view of Newport Harbor.

It was a lovely day in mid-May, and as soon as I parked the car I spied Paul McEnroe, well tanned and as young-looking as the day I met him in 1966. He immediately took me into the Mary Street House, a new addition to the main inn since my last visit. Each of the rooms has been decorated with care and subtlety by Ione Williams, who with her husband, Rod, is also the owner of the Inn at Sawmill Farm in West Dover, Vermont.

The Mary Street House proved to be a fitting complement to the Inntowne, and all of the decorations and furnishings were a continuation of the earlier themes that had been established a few years ago when Paul and his wife, Betty, relocated in Newport after living for many years in New York State. Paul is also the innkeeper of the Inn at Castle Hill. After spying the architectural integrity of the original, old, dilapidated brick building on the corner of Mary and Thames, he decided to convert it into an elegant bed-and-breakfast inn and call it the Inntowne Inn.

The lobby-living room area has some handsome antiques, including an old grandfather's clock in a beautiful inlaid antique case, and one wall is a bookcase decorated with ivy plantings and a beautiful model ship. It's like being in a living room of a very elegant house of two hundred years ago, because the atmosphere is decidedly Colonial, rather than Victorian.

Betty joined us, and while we were having a cup of afternoon tea, a regular event at the Inntowne, I heard the receptionist responding to a phone call, explaining that there were no TV's, no telephones, and no elevators. Upon checking in, guests are advised that arrangements can be made for parking in a special lot just up the street.

Breakfast at the Inntowne includes very tasty croissants and muffins, and something I am always delighted to find: freshly squeezed orange juice.

I asked Paul about the best time to come to Newport. "If someone is looking for a nice quiet time and a nice quiet country inn within the city, I think the fall or even the winter is lovely. The crowds are gone and you can get into all of the restaurants and there is still much to see and do.

"We're taking more and more reservations for people in the wintertime," he continued. "There are three mansions open on weekends in the winter. The indoor tennis facilities are open, the shopping and wharf areas, and the fine restaurants are all at their best. The drive along the ocean is magnificent."

Betty added, "Christmas in Newport is a wonderful time to come. The city is very active with many events scheduled, including parades, Christmas tree decorations, and there are candles in all the windows. The town is most tastefully decorated. There is a special calendar published for December, and there is something happening every day. Although we are closed Christmas Eve and Christmas Day, we are open throughout the rest of the Christmas season."

As I departed after a really pleasant visit with Paul and Betty, it occurred to me that there was a distinct resemblance between the Inntowne and the Residence du Bois in Paris. Each has a soothing air of quietude, somewhat away from the hustle and bustle of the city.

THE INNTOWNE, 6 Mary St., Newport, RI 02840; 401-846-9200. An elegant 20-guestroom bed-and-breakfast inn in the center of the city of Newport overlooking the harbor, serving continental breakfast and afternoon tea. Open every day. Reservations by telephone only between 9 a.m. and 5 p.m. Convenient for all of the Newport historical and cultural attractions, which are extremely numerous. No recreational facilities available; however, tennis and ocean swimming are nearby. Not adaptable for children of any age. No pets. Betty and Paul McEnroe, Innkeepers.

Directions: After crossing Newport bridge turn right at sign: "Scenic Newport." Drive straight to Thames Street; Inntowne is on corner of Thames St. and Mary St., across from Brick Marketplace.

LARCHWOOD INN
Wakefield, Rhode Island

Once again, I was overwhelmed with the wonderful trees that surround the Larchwood Inn. I had left Route 1 at the Pond Street exit and followed the road to its ending, right in front of the spacious lawns of the inn. It was a beautiful day in mid-June, the flowers and bushes were in wonderful profusion, and I could hear a piano being played somewhere in the inn. It was just a little after lunch, and indeed there were a few lingering lunchers enjoying themselves, but for the most part things were very quiet.

I wandered into one of the dining rooms, where there is a mural depicting the southern Rhode Island beaches. The tables were very attractively set for the next meal with green tablecloths. I noticed the living room had been redecorated since my last visit. It was very pleasant, with comfortable chairs and a fireplace with a very impressive ship model on the mantel. There was also an exotic bird in a cage.

At this point Frank Browning came in, and after a few hello-how-are-you's, I asked him about the ship model. "That is a three-masted schooner, called *L'Astrolabe,* and everything was built to scale by a friend of mine. See the little boys on the deck—he thought of everything."

The Larchwood is a large mansion, dating back to 1831, in the village of Wakefield, set in the middle of a large parklike atmosphere with copper, beech, ginkgo, pin oak, spruce, mountain ash, maple, Japanese cherry trees, evergreens, dogwoods, and a very old mulberry tree. In all there are three acres of trees and lawn.

The interior has many Scottish touches, including quotations from

Robert Burns and Sir Walter Scott, and photographs and prints of Scottish historical and literary figures.

The conversation naturally turned to menu items, since Frank was the chef here for many years and is now carefully supervising the kitchen and dining room.

"We're in the process right now of working with the South County Hospital. They are coming out with low-cholesterol items and they came to us to ask if we could cooperate with them. We're working on seven or eight items in our restaurant for their program. There will be lighter things, including different ways to serve chicken and fish. By the way, my brother and I were out a few days ago bluefishing and caught a lot of bluefish and put it right on the menu. You know you can't beat it; it has a wonderful taste."

I asked him about breakfasts, and I'm very glad I did. "We make the french toast with our own bread and then offer it with either sour cream or whipped cream and warm strawberries. The strawberries make it absolutely fantastic. It's something that our guests really appreciate, along with our selection of different omelets."

Frank was very anxious to show me some of the redecorating and refurnishing he has completed in the guest rooms, all of which overlook the splendid estatelike grounds. He pointed out that many rooms have a single and a double bed, quite a convenience for many travelers.

There are additional attractively furnished guest rooms in the Holly House, a 150-year-old building across the street from the inn. Guests at the Holly House can enjoy breakfast, lunch, and dinner at the Larchwood Inn dining room.

"One of the interesting parts of our summer dinner business is from people who are cruising on their boats. Our inn is about a mile and a half from Ram Point Marina, at the head of Point Judith Pond. It is the largest and best facility in the area. We frequently get calls from people at the marina asking for reservations and directions. We often transport them back to their boat."

By the way, the Larchwood Inn is a few miles from Point Judith, where the ferry leaves for Block Island. The Larchwood makes a nice overnight stop.

LARCHWOOD INN, 176 Main St., Wakefield, RI 02879; 401-783-5454. A 19-guestroom (some shared baths) village inn just 3 mi. from the famous southern R.I. beaches. European plan. Breakfast, lunch, dinner served every day of the year. Swimming, boating, surfing, fishing, xc skiing, and bicycles nearby. Francis Browning, Innkeeper.

Directions: From Rte. 1, take Pond St. Exit and proceed ½ mi. directly to inn.

1661 INN
Block Island, Rhode Island

The 1661 Inn has a wonderful, old "Block Island" feeling and atmosphere.

A few years before my first visit to Block Island, Joan, Justin, Rita, Mark, and Rick Abrams had discovered the 1661 Inn during one of their many sailing adventures from Providence. At that time it was a small hotel named the Florida House. Later, it was renamed the 1661 Inn by the Abramses, in honor of the year that Block Island was settled by colonists from New England.

"At that time, we gave each of the bedrooms the name of one of the original brave settlers," Joan explained. "Our family spent many hours consulting books for authentic New England decor and redoing all the rooms. We decorated with many of our own antiques and Early American paintings."

A few years later, after Rita Abrams and Steve Draper met, fell in love, and were married, the house next door to the 1661 Inn was acquired. Steve, who is a natural-born planner and builder, set about completely

remodeling what was to become the 1661 Guest House. All of the bedrooms were done over and private decks were added. The guest house is completely heated and is open all year.

Perhaps Steve did not know the Abrams family's penchant for remodeling and rebuilding, but he soon found out about it! Joan and Justin decided to restore one of the island's historic summer hotels, the Manisses Hotel, also owned by the Abrams family.

With the completion of the Manisses, the Abramses and Drapers looked for new opportunities and they found them. Three of the bedrooms overlooking the dining deck at the 1661 Inn were enlarged and now enjoy glorious views of the ocean from their own deck. Directly above them, three second-floor bedrooms have their own decks, so that there are seven rooms with sea views and decks. Each room has been decorated in Colonial-period furniture, wallpaper, and draperies.

Because there is so much activity on Block Island for outdoor-minded people who develop hearty appetites, breakfast and dinner at the 1661 Inn are very important times.

Breakfast is an extravaganza with fresh fruit, corned beef hash, scrambled eggs, quiche, choices of breakfast meat, small, red, roasted potatoes, cut and baked in the oven with spices, and at least one or two special dishes, such as chicken tetrazzini and vegetable casseroles. All the muffins, jams, and breads are homemade.

The evening menu features such regional dishes as Block Island clam chowder, flounder, lobster, swordfish, johnnycake, indian pudding, and blackberry flummery. I must say that the baked stuffed flounder with mussels and clams is a joy. Guests may take lunch at the Manisses.

May I take a moment to point out that Block Island is a very singular experience during what is usually known as the "off season." This is any time after the middle of October. There are wonderful beaches to walk, bikes to ride, and the island, with a population of only 600 during the winter, becomes a very private experience. Rita and Steve and their two boys are always on hand in the Guest House to help island winter visitors make it a really beautiful experience.

THE 1661 INN, Box 367, Block Island, RI 02807; 401-466-2421 or 2063. A 25-guestroom island inn off the coast of R.I. and Conn. in Block Island Sound; 11 private baths. Open from Memorial Day thru Columbus Day weekend. Breakfast served to travelers daily. (Guest House open year-round; continental breakfast included in off-season rates; dinner upon request.) Lawn games on grounds. Tennis, bicycling, ocean swimming, sailing, snorkeling, diving, salt and fresh water fishing nearby. Block Island is known as one of the best bird observation areas on the Atlantic flyway. The Abrams Family, Innkeepers.

Directions: By ferry from Providence, Pt. Judith, and Newport, R.I. and New London, Ct. Car reservations must be made in advance for ferry. By air from Newport, Westerly, and Providence, R.I., New London and Waterford, Ct., or by chartered plane. Contact inn for schedules.

THE BRAMBLE INN
Brewster, Cape Cod, Massachusetts

Every time I travel on Route 124, the road that leads from Exit 10 on the Mid-Cape Highway toward Brewster, I am most pleased with its wonderful "country" feeling. The bike trails leading off the road provide another diversion for travelers and natives alike. Among other things, it passes the Pleasant Lake General Store, another interesting step back into life as it was lived on the Cape a few years ago—just the battered red building in itself would indicate that.

Route 124 joins Route 6A, the north shore road of the Cape, also with many lovely villages and pleasant views. Upon turning right, one can almost see the Bramble Inn sign in the distance on the left-hand side.

There have been some very interesting changes at the Bramble Inn since our last edition. It is now owned and operated by Ruth and Cliff Manchester, who have had many years of experience in the accommodations field. Ruth is a very experienced gourmet cook, as we shall learn in just a few moments.

Other changes can be found, for example, in the handsome oriental rugs on the wide floorboards, and the dining room, which has changed almost completely with new decorations. The Manchesters have also worked hard redoing all of the bedrooms, and have put another bathroom in the 1849 House, adjacent to the present inn building. There are now five rooms, all with private baths.

Perhaps the most dramatic change is the fact that the Bramble is now open year around. This means it's possible to travel to the Cape in the off-season and have a very pleasant country inn experience and perhaps enjoy the Cape at a more leisurely pace.

The continental breakfast, served on the porch every morning and included in the cost of the room, consists of homemade muffins, which are invariably different every day, juice, coffee, and other items of that nature.

The dinner menu is quite different. Now, it's a four-course price-fixed dinner that changes almost nightly. As Ruth Manchester points out, "There's a choice of five items from each course and it's really given me the opportunity to offer some dinners that present me with a real challenge. Among our more popular main dishes are tenderloin of beef with Roquefort and a white wine sauce, and rack of lamb with a cracked peppercorn and mustard backing. However, our most sought-after recipes—also requested by both *Bon Appetit* and *Gourmet*—are the lettuce and scallion bisque and our chocolate terrine with coffee cream sauce.

"Dinner is served Tuesday through Sunday in season, and Thursday through Sunday off season," Ruth explained, "The Bramble, under Elaine and Karen, has never been open year around, so we need to help our local friends get adjusted to our new hours."

Guest rooms at the top of the stairs in the main inn have flowered wallpaper, antiques, country furniture, and share two baths. There's a definite tilt to the doors and the floors, adding to the fun. The same is true of the five additional guest rooms, all with their own baths, in the 1849 House.

So, we welcome the new owners of the Bramble Inn, Ruth and Cliff Manchester, to *Country Inns and Back Roads*.

For those readers who have already made the acquaintance of the previous owners, Karen Etsell and Elaine Brennan, the authors of *How To Open A Country Inn*, I'm happy to report that they have moved almost directly across from the inn on Route 6A, and when last I had a chance to chat with them, they were redoing an old Cape house and were going to make a portion of it into a gift shop.

THE BRAMBLE INN, Route 6A, Main St., Brewster, Cape Cod, MA 02631; 617-896-7644. An 8-guestroom (5 with private bath) village inn in the heart of one of Cape Cod's north-shore villages. Lodgings include continental breakfast. Dinner served Tues. thru Sun. in season; Thurs. thru Sun. in fall and winter. Open year-round. Swimming, sailing, water sports, golf, recreational and natural attractions within a short drive. Adjacent to tennis club. This is a small, intimate inn and does not meet the needs of most children. No pets. Cliff and Ruth Manchester, Innkeepers.

Directions: Take Exit 10 from Rte. 6. Turn left (north) and follow Rte. 124 to the intersection of Rte. 6A (4 mi.). Turn right, 1/10 mi. to inn.

CHARLOTTE INN
Edgartown, Martha's Vineyard, Massachusetts

There's always something new happening at the Charlotte Inn. Over the many years that I have been visiting it, Gery and Paula Conover and Gery's two strapping sons, Timmy and Gery, Jr., have been providing exciting innovations for Charlotte Inn guests.

It was just a few years ago that I included a description of the then newly-remodeled carriage house with its cathedral ceiling and unusual adornments.

On still another visit I had the opportunity to see for the first time the new "garden house," across the street from the main inn. It has been decorated with a French country look and, as is the case with the other guest rooms throughout the inn and the annex, the furnishings and decorations have been done with great care and taste. This house also provides houseguests with a private lounge of their own, where they may enjoy the fireplace, play games, watch TV, and get acquainted.

Like many other Edgartown houses, the main building of the Charlotte Inn is a classic three-story white clapboard with a widow's walk on the top. It is the former home of a Martha's Vineyard sea captain. Guest rooms are individually furnished with their own private baths and are very quiet. Several rooms have working fireplaces and there are many four-poster beds. There are lots of fresh flowers, books, magazines, good reading lamps, and a most romantic atmosphere.

Dinner at the Charlotte Inn is taken at the Chez Pierre dining room. The menu is both continental and American, with such interesting items as lobster with cognac cream sauce, fresh sea scallops sautéed with morels, and Nantucket pheasant in a black plum sauce.

Besides a complimentary continental breakfast, the inn offers a complete breakfast at an additional price, with such things as island fresh eggs delivered right to the back door, home-fries and bacon, maple walnut french toast, and spanish omelets or ham and swiss cheese omelets.

The inn also contains a most prestigious art gallery and one of the most handsome shops I have ever visited.

Now, to the latest news. Another house next to the inn has been completely renovated, and a beautiful old-fashioned porch filled with antique wicker and plants has been added. The landscaping is very English-looking, with many boxwoods and two urns from Strawberry Hill Farm overflowing with pale pink geraniums flanking the porch steps. There is even a small goldfish pond.

October is one of the greatest times to be out at Martha's Vineyard. The weather is usually pleasantly chilly in the morning and it warms up as the hours go by. The island is not crowded, the ferries are not crowded, and it is possible to really enjoy Martha's Vineyard as a place with its own personality rather than as a tourist objective.

By the way, if you are headed for the Woods Hole Ferry in the height of the season, there are a couple of ferry parking lots in Falmouth where it might be a good idea to leave your car. You can be bused to the ferry most conveniently.

CHARLOTTE INN, So. Summer St., Edgartown, Martha's Vineyard Island, MA 02539; 617-627-4751. A 24-guestroom combination inn-art gallery and restaurant on a side street, just a few short steps from the harbor. European plan. Continental breakfast served to inn guests. Open year-round. Chez Pierre restaurant open for dinner from mid-March through New Year's Day, also winter weekends. Boating, swimming, beaches, fishing, tennis, riding, golf, sailing, and biking nearby. No pets. Not suitable for children under 15. Gery and Paula Conover, Innkeepers.

Directions: Martha's Vineyard Island is located off the southwestern coast of Cape Cod. The Woods Hole/Vineyard Haven Ferry runs year-round and automobiles may be left in the parking lot at Woods Hole. Taxis may be obtained from Vineyard Haven to Edgartown (8 mi.). Check with inn for ferry schedules for all seasons of the year. Accessible by air from Boston and New York.

COBB'S COVE
Barnstable Village, Cape Cod, Massachusetts

"Come and see the changes we've made in the master suite." Evelyn Chester and I were once again touring all of the bedrooms at Cobb's Cove, a very small, quiet inn in Barnstable Village on the north shore of Cape Cod.

I saw immediately that she and Henri-Jean had created an attractive brick patio for the master suite and decorated it with large pots of petunias and geraniums. "Guests can take their before-breakfast coffee or afternoon refreshments out here," she said.

The lodging rooms at Cobb's Cove have massive exposed beams and posts, and natural wood walls and ceilings. One on the top floor has an atrium feeling with a studio-type window that sweeps from the eaves almost to the top of the cathederal ceiling. Each bedroom has a full bath, including a whirlpool tub, a dressing room, air conditioning, and private telephone lines which are available for extended stays. There are also big fluffy towels—something I always like to find in a country inn.

During a recent trip to Africa, Evelyn and Henri-Jean bought bolts of hand-woven fabrics, and have had them made into beautiful draperies for all the suites in the inn. The furniture, draperies, and adornments harmonize beautifully with the colors and textures of the handsome wood.

Our tour continued through the dining room with its long trestle table, where breakfast and dinner are served. Floor-to-ceiling bookshelves display works on many subjects, sharing space with a wide variety of shell, mineral, and fossil collections. In one corner is a baby grand piano, and the strains of Vivaldi wafted from a hi-fi system.

Henri-Jean, radiating good humor and the savory aromas of bluefish

Provençale, came out of the kitchen, and we all sat down in front of one of the most unusual fireplaces I've ever seen. "It's a Count Rumford fireplace," Henri-Jean explained. "You'll notice that it's quite shallow, but it was designed hundreds of years ago by a gentleman whose personal history would make a good book or movie. The design is such that it keeps the entire room bathed in generous heat."

That was the beginning of a long and most enjoyable conversation that continued throughout the remainder of the beautiful, sun-bathed December afternoon on Cape Cod. I heard all about how Henri-Jean, who is a civil engineer, designed, cut out, assembled, and physically built this beautiful Colonial saltbox manor on its 1643 historical site. "Actually, Evelyn and I worked side by side in every phase of its design and construction," he said, sending a most loving look in her direction.

There is much to share, both at Cobb's Cove itself and in that particular section of Cape Cod. "We are on the low-key side of the Cape," Evelyn remarked with a smile. "Because it's people-oriented, rather than a resort section. Most of the small crafts shops, like the weavers and the pottery and the Bird Barn, are open year-round, and in the so-called off-season the beaches are even more beautiful because there's hardly anyone on them except the seagulls."

The most recent news is that Henri-Jean has added a dormer to the third-floor "Honeymoon Suite." Glassed in on three sides, it affords a panoramic view of Barnstable Harbor, Sandy Neck, and Cape Cod Bay.

The extended flower and herb gardens with many bird feeders have created a virtual bird sanctuary to beguile guests while they breakfast on the terrace.

COBB'S COVE, Barnstable Village, Rte. 6A, Cape Cod, MA 02630; 617-362-9356. A 6-guestroom secluded inn on Cape Cod's north shore. Lodgings include a full breakfast. Houseguests can arrange for dinner. Closed Dec., Jan., Feb.; but call for specific information. Within a short distance of Cape Cod Bay and the Atlantic Ocean, the U.S. National Seashore, and Sandy Neck Conservatory, as well as many museums, art galleries, crafts shops, and other attractions of the Cape. Active sports nearby. No facilities to amuse children at the inn. No pets. Credit cards not accepted. Evelyn Chester, Innkeeper.

Directions: From Rte. 6 (Mid-Cape Hwy.) turn left at Exit 6 on Rte. 132 to Barnstable. Turn right on Rte. 6A, approx. 3 mi. through Barnstable Village, past the only traffic light and turn left just past the Barnstable Unitarian Church on to Powder Hill Rd. Look for small wooden sign on left at a gravel driveway saying: "Evelyn Chester."

JARED COFFIN HOUSE
Nantucket Island, Massachusetts

I receive letters almost every day from people who visit the country inns written about in *Country Inns and Back Roads*. I remember this one letter in particular.

"A few years ago, my husband and I ran across a copy of one of your books which shows a gentleman skater on the cover. (That would be about 1968!) On page 17 there was a map of Nantucket Island and a description of your visit there in February, and your stay at the Jared Coffin House. Later, we got an edition with a green cover showing what I presume was the same gentleman fishing with his dog, and again you were quite enthusiastic about visiting the Jared Coffin House on Nantucket Island. We read all about the Chippendales, the Sheratons, the Crewel Room, where you had accommodations, and the quahaug chowder, the bay scallops, the roses, the moors and beaches.

"Your most recent issue was the last straw. You mentioned spending part of the Christmas holiday there and talked about the winding cobblestone streets, bicycling out to the other end of the island, visiting the bird sanctuary, and again the excellent food and accommodations at the Jared Coffin House.

"We could stand it no longer. I must say that planning a trip to an island thirty miles at sea is not something that one does lightly. I'm glad you suggested that it wouldn't be necessary to take our automobile, so we left it at the Woods Hole parking lot. The ferry trip was just long enough to give us a feeling of being at sea and we were delighted with Nantucket.

"Mr. Read was a marvelous host and he went out of his way to show us some of the back roads on the moors. He even told us about the time you and he got lost on one of them.

"Of course, the inn is just like living in a museum and I am happy to say that we also were able to reserve the Crewel Room, and that fourposter bed with the crewel-embroidered spread and canopy was a beauty. The sun came in the windows in the morning and there was the aroma of breakfast, just as you promised."

There have been some changes since 1968. In addition to the main house of the inn, built in 1845, over the years innkeepers Phil and Peggy Read have acquired the Harrison Gray House (1841), the Henry Coffin House (1821), the Swain House (1700s), the Eben Allen Wing (1857), and the Daniel Webster House. Three of these are physically connected; the others are only thirty feet away. Each is unique in its own way. All of the rooms have private baths and telephones, and most have television.

When I asked Phil why Nantucket had been so marvelously preserved as an elite eighteenth and early nineteenth century environment, he said, "Nantucket was seriously damaged by the Great Fire of 1846.

This, coupled with the discovery of gold in California and oil in Pennsylvania, caused the depletion of the whaling oil industry on the island, and the young people left in great numbers to seek their fortunes in other places. This explains why the island has remained somewhat low-key, with very few new buildings constructed in the late nineteenth century, so that Nantucket was bypassed by the Victorian movement."

Today, in a very real and exciting way, the Jared Coffin House helps recapture the spirit of the glorious days of Nantucket's reign as queen of the world's whaling ports.

JARED COFFIN HOUSE, Nantucket Island, MA 02554; 617-228-2400; reservations: 617-228-2405 (M-F 10-6). A 56-guestroom village inn, 30 mi. at sea. European plan. Breakfast, lunch, dinner served daily (food service in Tap Room only in Jan., Feb., Mar.). Please verify accommodations before planning a trip to Nantucket in any season. Swimming, fishing, boating, golf, tennis, riding, and bicycles nearby. Philip and Margaret Read, Innkeepers.

Directions: Accessible by air from Boston, New York, and Hyannis, or by ferry from Woods Hole and Hyannis, Mass. Automobile reservations are usually needed in advance: 617-540-2022. Cars are not recommended for short stays. Ferry service from Hyannis available May thru Dec.: 617-426-1855; Woods Hole, Jan.-Mar. Inn is located 300 yards from ferry dock.

QUEEN ANNE INN
Chatham, Cape Cod, Massachusetts

The innkeeper of the Queen Anne Inn, handsome, athletic Guenther Weinkopf, throttled the *Boston Whaler* down to a very low speed as we headed toward the sandy beach. We had just finished one of the most pleasant hours of my summer, zooming around Chatham Harbor as Guenther pointed out the many landmarks and points of natural beauty.

"When time permits I love to take guests on this ride," Guenther said, as we edged in toward the shore. "What I enjoy the most, though, is the reaction of guests participating in our boat excursions to legendary Monomoy Island. Since I made my U.S. Coast Guard Captain's license in April, I am running those trips myself. The island, already known to the Vikings, extends fifteen miles into the Atlantic pointing towards Nantucket. Now a wildlife sanctuary, it provides a habitat for an abundance of animals—snow egrets, blue herons, terns, wild swans, Canada geese, ducks, seals, deer—you name it. In October the seals are here. A fairly large fresh-water lake also helps to create the environment for most unusual vegetation. The only human sign is an old lighthouse, closed in 1919. Its tower is still intact, and it's a great spot for a good view of all the island and the Nantucket coastline in clear weather."

Having moored the boat properly, we walked on up through the sand and beach grass toward the inn, which has undergone some really striking changes since my last visit. When I mentioned these to Guenther, he responded enthusiastically.

"Oh, yes, all of us, including Nicole, my wife, and our daughters, Sonja and Tina, have pitched in and made the inn into something that fills us with great pride. We have balconies on all the rooms on the garden side, so that every one of those bedrooms has a view over Oyster Pond Bay. We've expanded the garden and still have many other ideas."

The Queen Anne is open every day of the year and there is a program of fall and winter culinary events, including fowl and game dinners prepared with herbs from the inn's own garden.

My bedroom, typical of most of the bedrooms at the inn, had a spacious deck overlooking the garden in the rear, where many of the shrubs and flowers were in bloom even in late October. Furnished with beautiful antiques and matching quilts and draperies, my room had single beds, each with a carved headboard, put together with one mattress. There are private baths with every room, and in some there are working fireplaces.

The menu of the inn included a special dish called "Atlantic Delicacies"—lobster, scallops, mussels, and shrimp glazed with a white wine sauce. Lobsters are on the menu whenever they are available. Other items were fillets of duck sautéed in red wine and garnished with fresh

chervil; tenderloin of beef in Madeira sauce and foie gras; a double saddle of lamb roasted with the inn's own thyme and rosemary; and medallions of veal with a fresh chive sauce.

One of the activities that the inn guests enjoy the most is the opportunity to go on the whale-watching excursions that leave from nearby Provincetown. Guenther explains that an experienced crew of spotters and a sophisticated navigation system help to make the experience a great success. Arrangements are made through the inn for these truly unusual experiences in coexistence.

THE QUEEN ANNE INN, 70 Queen Anne Rd., Chatham, MA 02633; 617-945-0394. A 30-guestroom village inn on Cape Cod on the pictur-esque south shore. Full American, modified American, or European plans. Open year-round. Breakfast, dinner, Sunday brunch, and Tuesday clambake served to travelers. Restaurant hours limited in fall and winter. Call for reservations. Near all of the Cape's scenic, cultural, and histor-ical attractions. Water skiing, deep-sea fishing, sailing, bicycles, back-roading, beach walking nearby. No recreational facilities for children on grounds. Nicole and Guenther Weinkopf, Innkeepers.

Directions: From Boston: Take Rte. 3 south to Sagamore Bridge crossing Cape Cod Canal. Continue on Rte. 6 to Exit 11; take Rte. 137 south to Rte. 28 and turn left. This is Chatham's Main St. Turn right into Queen Anne Rd. From New York: Take I-95 north to Providence, RI, I-95 to Wareham, and Rte. 6 to Sagamore Bridge (see directions above).

THE LENOX HOTEL
Boston, Massachusetts

Quite a number of years ago, I broke my own precedent for evaluating country inns when I first included the Algonquin Hotel in New York as a "country inn in the city." My rationale, which I must modestly say has been successful, is that people who enjoy country inns eventually have to go to the city, and I would like to be able to recommend a city hotel that has the requirements I prize in a country inn: friendliness and warmth from the staff, private ownership, and conveniences that make a stay more enjoyable.

I'm happy to have discovered the Lenox Hotel, a small, turn-of-the-century establishment, conveniently located in the Back Bay area of Boston (next door to Copley Place and Lord & Taylor) and something of a rarity in these days of corporate ownership—a family-run hotel, whose owners are very visible.

Gary Saunders and his father, Roger, along with other members of the family have owned the hotel for the past twenty-five years. Gary's mother is very involved with the ongoing renovation of the guest rooms and his father tends to the myriad details that keep things looking spruce.

On the day of my visit, there was a crackling fire in the comfortably furnished lobby with its grandfather clock.

I have not seen every one of the 220 rooms, but I can assure the Gentle Reader that they are most pleasantly furnished in one of three decorative styles—Early American, French, or Oriental—and every room has a distinctive quality of its own. Some rooms have a telephone in the bathroom! There are eighteen corner rooms with working fireplaces.

I must also admit that I enjoy having my car valet-parked, eliminating the hassle of finding a garage that isn't full.

Now that I have established the hotel's *bona fides*, I'm delighted to say that there are some additional features that will set it apart from other city hotels.

Delmonico's, the main restaurant, with a Victorian decor, has an impressive menu. Hearty New England fare is served in the Olde London Pub and Grille, for which the main paneling, posts, and tables were shipped over from England. I, who have seen many places in Britain, have to tip my hat to the owners for creating a first-rate ambience.

Another feature is Diamond Jim's piano bar. In the big city, piano bars are no novelty, but this one is really good. It's been running about twenty years, and offers the opportunity for young vocalists to get a little "on stage" experience. It took me back to my own early days as an aspiring singer.

The breakfast menu is exhaustive, to say the least, including à la

carte choices of freshly hand-squeezed (always, Gary tells me) orange juice or other juices and fruits, cereals, eggs any style, bacon, ham, sausage, corned beef hash, pancakes, waffles, and on and on. There are also various set breakfasts ranging from the Continental to the Eye-Opener, featuring sirloin steak and homefries.

In 1900, the *Boston Post* ran a headline story on the opening of this "Magnificent New Hotel...Boston's Waldorf Astoria." Well, I would say that the Lenox Hotel is the "Algonquin in Boston," although it has its own personality.

As this edition goes to press, the Lenox Hotel is undergoing an extensive exterior renovation, which will end up, as Gary commented, with the hotel looking exactly as it did in 1900.

THE LENOX HOTEL, 710 Boylston St, Boston, MA 02116; 1-800-225-7676 (Mass.: 617-536-5300). A 220-guestroom conservative hotel in Boston's Back Bay area. Open all year. Breakfast, lunch, and dinner served every day. All contemporary hotel conveniences provided. Drive-in garage with valet parking service. Convenient to business, theaters, sightseeing, and shopping. The Saunders Family, Innkeepers; Jacques Gasnier, General Manager.

Directions: If arriving by automobile, take Exit 22 from the Mass. Tpke., the Copley Square ramp, turn left on Dartmouth St. for 2 blocks to Newbury St. Take a left on Newbury St. for 1 block to Exeter St., take a left on Exeter for 1 block and the hotel is ahead at the corner of Exeter and Boylston Sts. An airport limo service between Logan Airport and the Lenox is available for a nominal fee.

RALPH WALDO EMERSON
Rockport, Massachusetts

"When it comes to rocks, ocean, and sky, I think we have more than our share," said Gary Wemyss. Gary pointed out to the breakwater about three miles in front of the "Emerson," as it is known to most of its guests. "In 1946, it was about three times the length it is now, but storms and heavy seas have beaten it down until now in places it is barely visible. The far left end originally formed a harbor of refuge for sailing ships, but the builders ran out of money and gave up the construction.

"There is a reef out there beyond the breakwater known as 'Dry Salvages,' which was an inspiration for the T.S. Eliot poem. The town is trying to get the federal government to rebuild the breakwater because it protects us in winter's heavier storms."

Preoccupation with reefs, the ocean, and the swooping gulls is one of the big attractions at this country inn in Pigeon Cove. It is run by Gary Wemyss, the son of the innkeepers at the Yankee Clipper, about a mile away. The two inns make an interesting contrast, because the Emerson is built along somewhat conventional lines and has many rooms overlooking the water, whereas the Clipper is tucked away among the rocks overlooking the water and is much smaller.

Gary pointed to two lighthouses on Thatcher's Island. "They are the only twin lighthouses on the Eastern Seaboard. However, only one of them has a working light. People like to sit out here in the evening and watch the stars over the ocean and the circling beam from the lighthouse.

"In recent years there's been an increased interest in whale watching, and from May through November there are cruises with naturalists on board. We see some fin-backed whales, but there are humpbacked whales primarily. They come here to feed and they are so tame you can almost reach out and touch them. The naturalists can determine a great many things by looking at the flukes, and they can give you all kinds of information about the whales. The cruises leave primarily from Gloucester, although some leave from Rockport. Plane spotters are often used to determine where the whales are located. You can virtually always see whales. I think it's one of the most thrilling and touching experiences anyone can have to be so close to these wonderful creatures."

Gary explained that the guests include people of all interests and ages. "I think they mix well here," he said. "Everyone seems to enjoy the things that are here—the village, the shore, and of course the proximity to the sea. There is a real feeling of being relaxed and away from urban pressures, and I think that draws a lot of people together. It is such a relief just to have a few days' holiday."

Well, any kind of a holiday usually includes an emphasis on food, and at the Emerson the emphasis is on food from the nearby ocean waters, especially lobster. "People come to this part of New England for lobster, so we try to serve it as frequently as possible," Gary remarked. "Sometimes our guests go up to the Clipper for dinner, or people staying there come down here. It is part of the advantage of having two inns run by the same family."

Ocean, rocks, sky, reefs, lighthouses, bobbing lobster pots, plenty of home-cooked food—all close to Rockport, Massachusetts, one of the most picturesque towns on the New England coast—that's what the Ralph Waldo Emerson is all about. It has provided vacationers with diversion and relaxation for many years.

RALPH WALDO EMERSON, 1 Cathedral Ave., Pigeon Cove, Rockport, MA 01966; 617-546-6321. A 36-guestroom oceanside inn, 40 mi. from Boston. Modified American and European plans. Breakfast and dinner served daily from July 1 to Labor Day; bed and breakfast only during remainder of the year. Pool, sauna, and whirlpool bath on grounds. Tennis, golf nearby. Courtesy car. No pets. Gary and June Wemyss, Innkeepers.

Directions: Take I-95 to Rte. 128 to Rte. 127 (Gloucester). Proceed 6 mi. on Rte. 127 to Rockport and continue to Pigeon Cove.

YANKEE CLIPPER INN
Rockport, Massachusetts

Nineteen eighty-six bids fair to be a banner year at the Yankee Clipper Inn. It's the fortieth anniversary of the beginnings of the Clipper by Fred and Lydia Wemyss in 1946. It is also their fiftieth wedding anniversary year and the twenty-fifth wedding anniversary year for their daughter, Barbara, and her husband, Bob. This means that guests at the Clipper during 1986 are probably in for some additional treats.

The Clipper is actually three different buildings. One is The Inn, a gracious ocean-front mansion with antique furnishings, some canopy beds, glass-enclosed porches, and a dining room right on the ocean. All the meals are served in this building. The Quarterdeck, just a few paces away, features unsurpassed views of the ocean through large picture windows and lots of sitting space to enjoy the view. The Bulfinch House

was designed by the early-American architect Bulfinch, who also designed the Massachusetts State House. It is a classic early-19th-century New England house of clipper ship days with period furnishings.

The rooms in the Inn and Quarterdeck are offered with breakfast and dinner included in the spring and fall under the modified American plan, and with breakfast, lunch, and dinner included in the summer (American plan).

The inn is open in winter on a bed-and-breakfast basis in the two ocean-front buildings, and sitting in front of the fireplace in the afternoon sipping hot mulled cider and munching homemade goodies with the other guests is really a lot of fun. The innkeepers have a better chance to get to know the guests, and many of them come back two or three times during the winter and again during the summer.

Spring in Rockport, one of the most photographable and paintable villages on the New England coast, has become an annual musical treat. Starting in late March and continuing through June, there are events such as the Rockport Community Chorus, the Cape Ann Symphony, and the annual Rockport Chamber Music Festival.

One of the more exciting things for guests to do is to take a whale-watch boat trip out to the feeding grounds off Stellwagen Banks, the main fishing grounds for the local fleet. These boats have naturalists on board who give a commentary on each individual whale sighted, its habits, how often it's been seen, and much other information. These trips last from four to five hours, and at least a two-day stay at the Clipper would be necessary.

There is also much to occupy the time of both the active and the more contemplative guests at the Yankee Clipper. A heated saltwater pool is sheltered by lovely garden walls and beautiful shade trees. Many guests spend the greater part of the day in the comfortable deck chairs, looking out over the sunlit waters of the bay.

Whether active or contemplative, guests' appetites seem to increase, and the menu has been one of the special features over the past forty years. Incidentally, lobster dinners are always one of the most popular reasons that guests return to the Yankee Clipper.

YANKEE CLIPPER INN, P.O. Box 2399, Rockport, MA 01966; 617-546-3407. A 28-guestroom intimate inn on the sea, 40 mi. from Boston. Modified American plan from mid-May to July 1 and Labor Day to end of Oct. Breakfast, lunch, and dinner served during July and Aug. Meals served to travelers by reservation only. The Quarterdeck and main inn open Nov. 1 to April 15 on a bed-and-continental-breakfast basis. (Closed Dec. 24 and 25.) Heated outdoor pool, ocean view, shoreline walks. Many antique shops and other stores within walking distance. No facilities for infants and children. No pets. Fred and Lydia Wemyss, Proprietors; Barbara and Bob Ellis, Innkeepers.

Directions: Take I-95 to Rte. 128 to 127 (Gloucester). Proceed 6 mi. on Rte. 127 to Rockport and continue to Pigeon Cove. ✈

A number of inns have nearby airports where private airplanes may land. An airplane symbol at the end of the inn directions indicates that there is an airport nearby. Consult inn for further information.

I do not include lodging rates in the descriptions, for the very nature of an inn means that there are lodgings of various sizes, with and without baths, in and out of season, and with plain and fancy decoration. Travelers should call ahead and inquire about the availability and rates of the many different types of rooms.

MORRILL PLACE
Newburyport, Massachusetts

The scene bordered on the idyllic. I was on the screened-in summer porch of Morrill Place, with Monroe purring contentedly on the wicker couch beside me. Innkeeper Rose Ann Hunter was reading to me from John P. Marquand's account of Newburyport. "Newburyport appears at its best," she read, "on a clear October day, for October is usually the most genial month in northeastern Massachusetts. Our October skies are clear and soft blue. Such leaves as are left on the elms are an unobtrusive russet yellow.

"In October, you will find that Newburyport still offers an illusion of security, a blending of past and present, and the serene sort of disregard for the future that is one of the greatest charms of an old New England seaport.

"Newburyport is not a museum piece, although it sometimes looks it. It has some of the most perfect examples of early Colonial and Federal architecture in America, but it is a vital, tolerant place and still able to keep up with the times, if you get to know it."

I was seeing Newburyport through the eyes of this very enthusiastic young woman, who moved here a few years ago. In addition to having shown me through the graceful Newburyport mansion, which has been turned into a warm and receptive guest house, she was kind enough to take me on a comprehensive tour of the town and the Parker River National Wildlife Refuge on Plum Island.

"Morrill Place was built in 1806," Rose Ann said, "by Kathryn and William Hoyt. The owners include three Newburyport sea captains—that's why there's a widow's walk. We have fourteen guest rooms and we are always open, even through the holidays. There are twelve working fireplaces."

We were joined for a moment by Rose Ann's daughter, Kristen, who is an energetic almost-teenager.

Earlier in the afternoon, my house tour started at the front of the house in the formal living room, adorned with oriental *objets d'art*. I marveled at the double-hung staircase with the six-inch risers. "This was built at the time when women wore hoop skirts," Rose Ann explained. "Double-hung staircases are rare, even in Newburyport."

Many of the guest rooms have fireplaces, and are decorated with distinctive period wallpapers. I saw my first "Indian shutters" which, when closed, left a narrow horizontal open slit. "In the 18th century, the real danger was from marauding pirates," she explained.

My room was named after Daniel Webster, who was a frequent visitor to the house. There was a remarkably preserved print of Mr. Webster over the fireplace, and the furnishings were typical of other guest rooms, including an antique deacon's bench, two twin beds, each embellished with a pineapple motif, a lovely old chest of drawers, and a Boston rocker.

Our tour, as so many do, ended up in the kitchen, where we had a refreshing cup of tea, and I learned that the breakfasts include juice, coffee or tea, cereal, fresh baked rolls and english muffins, topped off by "mother's strawberry jam."

How could I help but like the Morrill Place with a cat named Monroe?

MORRILL PLACE, 209 High St., Newburyport, MA 01950; 617-462-2808. A 14-guestroom (mostly shared baths) mansion on one of Newburyport's beautiful residential avenues. Lodgings include continental breakfast, the only meal offered. Open every day in year. Within a very convenient distance of all of the Newburyport historic and cultural attractions and Plum Island Wildlife Refuge. Other recreational facilities nearby. Rose Ann Hunter, Innkeeper.

Directions: From Boston, follow I-95 north and take Historic Newburyport exit and follow Rte. 113. This becomes High St. Follow it for about 2 mi. Inn is on right-hand side at corner of Johnson and High St. From Maine, exit I-95 for Historic Newburyport and follow above directions.

WINDSOR HOUSE
Newburyport, Massachusetts

Judith Crumb was telling me how much Newburyport has to offer. "Bird watchers, nature lovers, hikers, and beachcombers love the Parker River Wildlife Refuge with its beautiful beaches, and there are day and evening whale-watch cruises with a marine specialist aboard, as well as harbor tours on a lovely river boat. We can make arrangements for bicycle touring, too, which is more and more popular. Of course," she said as she warmed to her subject, "if you want something really romantic, there's the historic Newburyport tour in a horse-drawn carriage.

"We have a wide variety of comedy, drama, and musicals in our year-round theater in Newburyport, and in the summer we have the Castle Hill Music Festival in Ipswich, the North Shore Music Theatre in Beverly, and the Hampton Playhouse in Hampton, New Hampshire. And there are regular outdoor concerts in our new waterfront park."

I thought she'd told me everything and we'd start our tour of the house, but she put a restraining hand on my arm. "And we mustn't forget that Newburyport is an increasingly important center for fine art, with 18th- and 19th-century painting and antiques, as well as contemporary art, in several excellent galleries. We've definitely moved away from the 'Sunday painter school,' and some very fine work is being exhibited."

Now we headed for the kitchen, as she continued her conversation. "The Windsor House was started in 1785 and completed in 1787 as a private residence. By 1796 it was being used as both a residence and a ship's chandlery. The kitchen here was the original shipping and receiving room, as you can see from those big outside doors.

"The brick wall with the fireplace is part of a firewall that also goes to the top story and separates the warehouse section from the living section. The posts and beams throughout the entire house were built by ships' carpenters, the same men who built the clipper ships."

The kitchen is really the pulse of the Windsor House. Not only do all the guests gather around in the morning to enjoy Judith's prandial skill, but, as she says, "It's the place where we all gather at any time during the day and tell tall tales and get acquainted."

There were interesting contrasts between the rooms on the warehouse side of the firewall and the residential section. The Merchant's Suite on the first floor was the original chandlery. It has its own street entrance and is filled with antiques from 19th-century provisioners' shops, including scales, display boxes, and a bootjack. It's ideal for folks who have difficulty with stairs, or a family with small children.

Rooms on the residential side of the house tend to have wood paneling and other graceful features that would befit a residence.

Judith and her colleague, Jim Lawbaugh, share the breakfast duties,

and he has developed his own sausage recipe. Incidentally, his two sons, Richard and Paul, are frequently in residence at the inn. A rather informal supper with the innkeepers may be enjoyed with special advance arrangement.

The door opened and two guests, who had been doing the walking tour of Newburyport with the Clipper Trail folder, returned for a warming cup of coffee and a little conversation. "We decided to stay for two more days, there's just too much to see."

We all readily agreed.

WINDSOR HOUSE, 38 Federal St., Newburyport, MA 01950; 617-462-3778. A 6-guestroom inn (private and shared baths) in the restored section of Newburyport. Open year-round. Breakfast served to all guests. Supper with the innkeepers by special arrangement. Located in the Merrimack River Valley, 3 mi. from Plum Island and the Parker River National Wildlife Refuge. A short walk from the restored 19th-century retail area, restaurants, and museums. Also nearby: deep sea fishing, swimming, art galleries, antique shops, family ski area, horseback riding, and year-round theater. Some trundle beds available for children. Babysitters provided. Small dogs welcome. Judith Crumb and Jim Lawbaugh, Innkeepers.

Directions: From Boston and Maine: From I-95 use exit to Rte. 113, turn right onto High St. (Rte. 1A) and proceed 3 mi. to Federal St., turn left. Inn on left across from Old South Church (Rte. 1A is scenic drive from Boston or New Hampshire).

LONGFELLOW'S WAYSIDE INN
South Sudbury, Massachusetts

Off Route 20 there's a wonderful country road marked "Wayside Inn" that leads past the Wayside Inn Gristmill, the Martha and Mary Chapel, and right to the inn itself on the left. Set in a beautiful grove of trees, high hedges, and wooden fences, the inn looks out over a pond. Never mind that it's the site of one of America's oldest country inns, or that history has been made within its walls, the point is that the setting and the building make it a wonderful country inn experience at any time.

Built around 1702, the inn originally was called Howe's Tavern. In 1775, led by innkeeper Ezekiel Howe, the Sudbury farmers were among the men at nearby Concord, and Revolutionary War soldiers found sustenance at the inn's tables. Today, all musters of the Sudbury Minutemen

take place at the inn as preparations are made for their annual reenactment of the march from Sudbury to Concord on April 19. The 200th anniversary of the Battle of Lexington and Concord was celebrated in 1975.

Henry Wadsworth Longfellow immortalized the inn in 1863 with his *Tales of a Wayside Inn,* and thereafter it was known by its new name. Thanks to a grant from the Ford Foundation, the buildings and priceless antiques have been preserved as a historical and literary shrine. The inn is filled with preserved and restored antiques. It combines being a museum with the more practical function of providing lodging and food.

The dining room specializes in such good New England fare as Massachusetts duckling in orange sauce, baked Cape Cod scallops, roast beef, stuffed fillet of sole, muffins made from meal stone-ground at the Gristmill, and indian pudding served with ice cream.

I must echo the advice of innkeeper Frank Koppeis that anyone who is expecting to visit Longfellow's Wayside Inn, either for a meal or lodgings, should be sure to make a reservation in advance.

The gift shop is well worth noting. It is filled with mementos, including prints of the inn and of the Gristmill, and also Longfellow's Wayside Inn history and recipes—a combination history and cookbook in one. It has some absolutely splendid color photographs showing some of the typical dishes they serve here, including their special recipe for meatloaf. By the way, baked beans should always contain molasses and curry powder. As I looked through this book before dinner I became even hungrier.

There were also some recordings of tunes reminiscent of the Wayside Inn, performed by the Sudbury Ancient Fife and Drum Company, which created such a stir a few years ago when we had a *Country Inns and Back Roads* meeting here.

Two of the guest rooms, which escaped damage by a fire in 1955, are over the original inn and are most Colonial in flavor, with wood paneling, exposed beams, and wide floorboards, and are reached by narrow, twisty stairs. The other, later, guest rooms are comfortably and attractively furnished in more of a country Victorian style.

I believe that the Longfellow's Wayside experience is particularly enhanced by the fact that the building and grounds and the atmosphere have been so well taken care of. Even though this is one of the most popular places in North America for lunches and dinners, and there are literally thousands of people coming here every year, it has a wonderful set-apart feeling about it, as if it's been waiting for you to arrive.

LONGFELLOW'S WAYSIDE INN, Wayside Inn Rd., off Rte. 20, South Sudbury, MA 01776; 617-443-8846. A 10-guestroom historic landmark inn, midway between Boston and Worcester. European plan. Lunch and dinner served daily except Christmas. Breakfast served to overnight guests. Within a short distance of Concord, Lexington, and other famous Revolutionary War landmarks. Francis Koppeis, Innkeeper.

Directions: From the west, take Exit 11A from Mass. Tpke., and proceed north on Rte. 495 to Rte. 20. Follow Rte. 20, 7 mi. east to inn. From the east, take Exit 49 from Rte. 128. Follow Rte. 20 west 11 mi. to inn.

HAWTHORNE INN
Concord, Massachusetts

There are two marvelous maple trees right next to the Hawthorne Inn that spread their wonderful, generous branches over a little terrace area and gardens, which immediately attract all of the guests. There's also a little fountain with some lily pads in it. The whole area has a very lovely, natural feeling, with many different kinds of bushes, ferns, and plants, and the grounds around it have been carefully nurtured by Gregory and Marilyn for the past few years. It's a lovely place to walk around and perhaps to peek across the road at Nathaniel Hawthorne's House, called "The Wayside."

In many ways, the somewhat conservative, austere lines of the Hawthorne Inn are a reflection of the lifestyle of the owners. It's yellow stucco with black shutters and has a sort of no-nonsense feeling. At the rear of the house, there is a small orchard, a carefully tended garden, and several footpaths leading down into a copse. There are also several beehives.

The town of Concord is unique because it has three famous periods in its history, any one of which would be a sufficient claim to distinction. The first began more than three hundred years ago, when the early Puritans made it the first Massachusetts settlement away from the Tidewater. Concord was the scene of the first battle of the Revolutionary War and, finally, in the 19th century, it was the home of Emerson, Alcott, Thoreau, and Hawthorne, the great authors of the period known as the "flowering of New England."

The inn is located on land that once belonged to Ralph Waldo Emerson, as well as the Alcotts and Hawthorne. Bronson Alcott planted

his fruit trees and made pathways to the mill brook, and the Alcott family tended their crops of vegetables and herbs here. Two of the original trees are still standing and can be seen on the west side of the inn. The Alcotts' Orchard House is just next door, and the Concord grape was developed at Grapevine Cottage, adjacent to the inn.

The guest rooms have antique furnishings, handmade quilts, and oriental and rag rugs. There are original art works, both ancient and modern, antique Japanese Ukiyoye prints, and sculpture by Gregory. There are floor-to-ceiling bookshelves in the Common Room, which is warmed by a cozy fire in the chilly season.

The doors of the nine bedrooms have name-plaques and scented wreaths. There are dried flowers in the rooms, AM-FM clock radios, fresh fruit, poetry books, and herbal sachets. Guests are offered tea or coffee as they check in.

Breakfast is taken in the Common Room and features home-baked breads, fruit juice, a selection of teas or a special blend of freshly ground coffee. In season, there are fruits from the gardens and vines of the inn, and honey from the inn's own beehives.

I believe that the generous and warm atmosphere at the Hawthorne Inn would be a marvelous experience in any setting, but when we add all of the ambience of Concord, Lexington, South Sudbury, and the other eastern Massachusetts communities, it becomes an exceptional opportunity to experience some of the best of America's past.

HAWTHORNE INN, 462 Lexington Road, Concord, MA 01742; 617-369-5610. A 9-guestroom (7 with private baths) bed-and-breakfast village inn approx. 19 mi. from Boston. Breakfast to houseguests is the only meal served. Closed Mar. 1 to April 19. Within walking distance of all of the historic and literary points of interest in Concord. Limited facilities for young children, but ideal for young people who have an appreciation for history and literature. No pets. No credit cards. Gregory Burch, Marilyn Mudry, Innkeepers.

Directions: The Hawthorne Inn is in the historic zone of Concord, ¾ of a mi. east of the town center. From Rte. 128-95 take Exit 45 west for 3 mi. Bear right at the single blinking light. The inn is 1 mi. farther on the left (south side), directly across from the Wayside (home of Hawthorne and Alcott).

COUNTRY INN AT PRINCETON
Princeton, Massachusetts

It was an absolutely magnificent day at the height of the fall foliage season. After parking my car, I walked around the north end of the Country Inn at Princeton out onto the lawn, which I shared with some pigeons and blue jays, and just stood on the terrace for a moment looking over the rolling northern Massachusetts countryside. The autumn colors of rust, yellow, and orange blended with the high hills in the far distance and were complemented by the perfect blue of the sky. I walked across the terrace, with its handsome white outdoor furniture and glass-topped tables, and onto the porch, lush with hanging flowers. Then I stepped through the unusually large orange door into the reception area.

Later, enjoying iced tea on the sunny porch, I asked Don about the obvious coordination between the furnishings and decorations of the inn and the menu offerings.

"We offer country products of New England, and the game and wild fowl are not only very popular on our menu, but we are using them as artifacts and decorative pieces around the inn. You see, we have bird collections and wood carvings everywhere. This feeling of natural freshness is carried into both of our dining rooms and is perpetuated by our logo, which has a rose."

"Flowers and floral motifs are essential to us," Maxine declared. "I spend a great deal of time gathering and arranging the flowers, and we have expanded our own garden tremendously."

Interestingly enough, this decorative theme is continued in the Washburn dining room with arrangements of pheasants and with wall mountings of boar heads, deer heads, and others. Mr. Washburn, the original builder, was apparently a good friend of Theodore Roosevelt's and they hunted wild game together.

There are six guest rooms—some are spacious parlor-size suites—each uniquely decorated with authentic antiques and attractive bedroom furniture, and with views of the countryside or forest. Two of them are the largest bedrooms I have ever seen in a real country inn. Since breakfast is served in the privacy of the guest rooms, all have small tables for dining.

Maxine and Don further explained the interesting cross-reference to decorative theme and menu: "Our five-star chef is Frank McClelland, who came to us from Boston's famed L'Espalier. He is serving such interesting menu items as glazed quail with walnuts and blueberries; crabmeat with wild mushroom raviolis; warm ragout of crayfish, shrimp, and mussels with fresh mango; farm-raised pheasant with cabbage and currant moussette; pork tenderloin pistachio; and beef tenderloin with caramelized endive. All menu ingredients are purchased, prepared, and

served fresh. Nothing is frozen. We don't own a microwave.

"Our most exciting innovation is the Private Gourmet Dinner Party evenings. Approximately every six weeks or so we close the inn to all general public dining on a Thursday night. Invitations have been extended to all guests who visit and dine here and they arrive about seven o'clock for social greetings and introductions. Remember, they all have demonstrated one thing in common: the willingness to explore the *un*common since the entire evening's bill-of-fare has not been disclosed in advance. This dinner is a seven-course meal with wines, and the entire purpose is to provide a social culinary evening for those of our guests whose dining experience and love of adventure make them want to explore an even higher elevation of refined dining."

Put all these factors together in such a romantic setting and one might have what one guest describes in the guest book as "a perfect country inn."

COUNTRY INN AT PRINCETON, 30 Mountain Rd., Princeton, MA 01541; 617-464-2030. A 6-guestroom late-Victorian mansion, 50 mi. from Boston and 14 mi. north of Worcester. Open all year except Christmas. Dinner reservations Wed. thru Sun. evenings. Sun. brunch. Closed Mon. and Tues. Near Wachusett Ski Resort, Audubon and Wildlife Society, Mt. Wachusett State Reservation. Tennis, swimming, fishing, hiking, nature trails nearby. Downhill and xc skiing 3 mi. Lodging for couples only, no accommodations for children. Sorry, no pets. Don and Maxine Plumridge, Innkeepers.

Directions: From Boston, follow Rte. 2 west to Rte. 31 south. From Conn. and Mass. Tpke. (90), follow Rte. 290 north to Rte. 190; then take Exit 5 and continue on Rte. 140. At Rte. 62 turn left 4 mi., and turn right at post office and flashing light. With the town common on your left, the inn is 200 yards up Mountain Rd. on right.

COLONEL EBENEZER CRAFTS INN
Sturbridge, Massachusetts

If you're traveling on the Massachusetts Turnpike there are two reasons to stop off in Sturbridge. One is to take advantage of the really exceptional lodgings at the Colonel Ebenezer Crafts Inn and to enjoy dinner or lunch at the Publick House.

The other is to pay a serious visit to Sturbridge Village, a restored 19th-century environment. Such a visit would take at least two and a half hours to skim it and longer to really recognize its significance and appreciate all the work that has gone into it.

The village covers over 200 acres with farms, shops, a tavern, a blacksmith shop, and a working gristmill. All of the nearly forty buildings were moved here from throughout New England and then restored and authentically furnished. Year-round, costumed men and women demonstrate skills that have almost disappeared today.

To get to the Publick House, where one must check in for the Colonel Ebenezer Crafts Inn, if you're coming to Sturbridge from the Massachusetts Turnpike be sure to take the first exit to the right, marked "Route 20 West." Follow that to Route 131, turn left, and you're on your way not to old Sturbridge Village, but to today's contemporary Sturbridge Village. On the way you'll pass the Sturbridge Town Hall, the Federated Church, the library, the village green, and the Publick House on your right.

On the June day I arrived at Colonel Ebenezer Crafts Inn, the apple trees on the ridge had shed their blossoms and the small green apples gave promise of good things to come in future months. The lawn was neatly mowed to the edge of the woods and the birds almost seemed to signal my arrival with a pleasant welcome. I walked up the stone steps to the porch with its long deacon's bench and rang the bell. I was greeted by the hostess, Pat Bibeau.

Each of the guest rooms has its own bath and shower, and there's almost always a bowl of apples in each room for guests to enjoy. Pat commented that she frequently turns down the beds in the evening and also leaves cookies. Both of these are nice country inn touches. There is a comfortable terrycloth robe provided for the use of each guest at the poolside or after a shower.

The rooms are very light and airy and are furnished either in antiques or good reproductions. There were a number of chenille bedspreads, including one called "The Pride of Sturbridge."

The living room really invites guests to get acquainted, and I was delighted to find a generously supplied bookcase and also stacks of the *National Geographic*, which makes wonderful bedtime reading.

The exterior landscaping for the inn includes a beautiful brick patio where guests may have morning breakfast or afternoon tea, surrounded by plants and an herb garden. A stone stairway leads from the patio to the pool area, and shrubbery has been planted to form a live sundial around the flagpole.

Because guests at the Colonel Ebenezer Crafts Inn take a great many of their meals at the nearby Publick House, it is of interest to know that luncheons and dinners there include excellent New England clam chowder, as well as New England dishes such as lobster pie, broiled native scallops, double-thick lamb chops, deep dish apple pie—à la mode or with cheddar cheese—and indian pudding served with vanilla ice cream.

COLONEL EBENEZER CRAFTS INN, c/o Publick House, Box 187, Sturbridge, MA 01566; 617-347-3313. A 10-guestroom bed-and-breakfast inn in a historic village, 18 mi. from Worcester. Old Sturbridge Village nearby. Lodging rates include continental breakfast and afternoon tea. (Lunch and dinner available at nearby Publick House.) Open year-round. Swimming pool on grounds. Tennis nearby. Buddy Adler, Innkeeper.

Directions: From Mass. Tpke. take Exit 9; follow signs to Sturbridge on Rte. 131. From Hartford follow I-84, which becomes I-86. Take Exit 3.

"European plan" means that rates for rooms and meals are separate. "American plan" means that meals are included in the cost of the room. "Modified American plan" means that breakfast and dinner are included in the cost of the room. The rates at some inns include a continental breakfast with the lodging.

PEIRSON PLACE
Richmond, Massachusetts

"The number of guests researching their family trees is truly gratifying," said Margaret Kingman. "Two couples were pleasantly surprised to find the name Richmond, Massachusetts, in *CIBR*. Their ancestors were buried here, but they could not find the town on the map. Two Cogswell families recognized their coat of arms on the Cogswell sign, drove in, and stayed. This is a good place to trace family backgrounds with the assets of the Berkshire Atheneum and the Lenox and Stockbridge libraries, and also those of the Mormon Microfilm Center and the Albany Public Library, only a short drive away."

Margaret and I strolled around the grounds of Peirson Place and she mentioned that the Cogswell House was built in 1762 by Joseph Cogswell, and a few years later a tannery was built on the land by Nathan Peirson, starting a connection through a later marriage between the Cogswells and the Peirsons.

Peirson Place is really very unusual, and Margaret and her son, Lou, have created an intimate country inn that is markedly different from other accommodations in the Berkshires, and, in fact, from most other places. She has many guests who have been returning each year because they enjoy the shaded quiet of the Victorian gazebo, the tranquility of the woods, and the quietude of the pond.

Bird watchers have myriad feathered friends to observe, and guests also enjoy riding bicycles and swimming and the use of the sauna.

Peirson Place is open year around, and during the winter it provides very warm and cozy quarters to accommodate cross-country skiers, who actually do not have to leave the grounds to enjoy that favorite outdoor sport. A good point for me to mention is that lunches and dinners are available on weekends at all times; however, special arrangements can be made for midweek repasts with advance notice.

Speaking of those lunches and dinners, I discovered that many people prefer the dinners at Peirson Place, particularly during the summer, and most particularly on the Friday evenings of Tanglewood. For example, the fare might include a chilled fruit soup, chicken, pasta, a fresh vegetable salad, and melon for dessert. Another menu might be minestrone, fetuccini Alfredo, and strawberry shortcake. Still a third might be cream of broccoli soup, a scallop casserole, and dutch apple pie. Each menu has three courses: soup, an entrée, and dessert. By the way, this combination lunch/dinner is served all afternoon; as Margaret says, "People seem to want to eat all day long."

Breakfasts are also rather special, and include whole-grain cereals with honey, maple syrup, milk or cream, raisin bran, various cheeses, toast, muffins, and pastries.

As we continued walking around the grounds, stopping at the grape arbor—a favorite place for weddings—she told me that many guests are fascinated by the fact that her great-grandfather, her mother, and she were all born in the same room in the Peirson house, which has very sumptuous rooms. It has been in the family since the 18th century.

Although Peirson Place is sometimes referred to as an "obscure inn," Margaret insists that she and the guests enjoy the obscurity.

PEIRSON PLACE, Richmond, MA 01254; 413-698-2750. A 10-guestroom (private and shared baths) country house 6 mi. from Pittsfield on Rte. 41. Open year-round. Minimum stay of 2 nights during Tanglewood season and holiday weekends. Complimentary breakfast. Near all the scenic attractions of the Berkshire Hills, including Tanglewood, Hancock Shaker Village, and marvelous backroading in 3 states. Pond, sauna, badminton, darts, boating on grounds. Tennis, golf, horseback riding, etc., nearby. No facilities to amuse children under 12. No pets. The Kingman Family, Innkeepers.

Directions: From Boston: Take Mass. Tpke. to Exit 1. Follow Rte. 41 north through Richmond. Peirson Place is on left-hand side. From New York: Leave Taconic State Pkwy. at Rte. 295 and continue east to Rte. 41. Turn left. From Albany: New York Thruway (Berkshire Spur) to State Line Exit; left on Rte. 22 to Rte. 295; right on Rte. 295 to Rte. 41. Turn left.

THE VILLAGE INN
Lenox, Massachusetts

It was a lovely, bright and shiny Thanksgiving day in Lenox and I was on my way to the Village Inn for Thanksgiving dinner. I passed the entrance to Tanglewood and continued to the center of the village

The bright carved sign in the front, showing a booted Berkshireman being greeted by the innkeeper, seemed even a little brighter and more inviting than usual, and the American flag was whipping away in the November breeze. I passed through the door on the porch and into the main reception area.

Now Cliff Rudisill greeted me in his usual hearty manner, and I barely had time to catch my breath, when he took my arm and guided me into the side parlor. "Just look at this. These are pieces of my grandmother's furniture!" "From Texas?" I asked. "Yes, from Texas." "Looks like New England furniture to me," I declared. "Well, most of it is from New England," he said. "It was carried down to Texas and now I've brought it back to New England."

I must say that it all fitted in very well in this room, with the many handsome paintings and the piano at one end, and with the atmosphere at the Village Inn.

We were joined by Cliff's partner, Ray Wilson, also a Texan, and we passed back into the main reception area, which, like many others I have visited in Europe, had the check-in desk at the bar. Cliff pointed out a beautiful English grandfather's clock made about 1750. "The works are from Paisley, Scotland, and the cabinet is English."

The Village Inn is a two-and-a-half-story yellow clapboard building with a basic Federal design that has been adapted to meet various needs over many years. Built in 1771, it became an inn in 1775, and has been one ever since. Two rear wings were once well-constructed barns, forming an L-shaped sheltered terrace with a lawn on which there are a number of beautiful maples. Plantings of iris, daffodils, petunias, roses, and tulips brighten the picture during the warmer weather, and the interior of the inn is enhanced by flowers throughout all months of the year.

Rather than share my Thanksgiving menu with you, I will say that some of the entrées that appear on the menu many months of the year include New Orleans pecan-breaded breast of chicken, fresh poached salmon in a gingered hollandaise sauce, prime rib of beef with James River spoon bread, and roasted Long Island duckling with a maple glaze. Breakfast includes johnnycakes and Belgian waffles.

Even in their short tenure, Cliff and Ray have already established some traditions, including regular chamber music concerts throughout the year and the serving of tea every afternoon with homemade scones and a special clotted cream. The inn has also been acquiring some very handsome paintings, particularly those from the Hudson River school, and the newest addition is a splendid watercolor of a Berkshire scene by Gifford Beal.

On the floors above, authentic New England rooms and suites are available for overnight guests or for those with longer stays in mind. Many of the guest rooms have four-poster beds, and some have working fireplaces.

Thanksgiving Day or any day is a lovely experience at the Village Inn.

THE VILLAGE INN, Church St., Lenox, MA 01240; 413-637-0020. A 27-guestroom inn in a historic Berkshire town, 4 mi. from Stockbridge, 8 mi. from Pittsfield, and 1 mi. from Tanglewood. Breakfast and afternoon tea served daily to travelers. Dinner served Wed. thru Sun. Open every day of the year. Lenox is located in the heart of the Berkshires with many historical, cultural, and recreational features. Swimming in pleasant nearby lakes. All seasonal sports, including xc and downhill skiing available nearby. Well-behaved children over 4 welcome. No pets. Personal checks accepted. Cliff Rudisill and Ray Wilson, Innkeepers.

Directions: After approaching Lenox on Rte. 7, one of the principal north-south routes in New England, exit onto Rte. 7A to reach the village center and Church St. When approaching from the Mass. Tpke. (Exit 2) use Rte. 20W about 4 mi. and turn left onto Rte. 183 to center of town.

THE WEATHERVANE INN
South Egremont, Massachusetts

"Good evening, folks, how are you? I'm the innkeeper, Vince Murphy." While I was having a welcome cup of tea in front of the very cozy fireplace at the Weathervane Inn on a midwinter afternoon, Vincent Murphy excused himself at least four times to welcome new guests. Vince is a man who has the knack for making people feel welcome immediately.

Among the things that I look for in an inn are qualities of memorability. Besides innkeeper Murphy, who is, as he says, "a private investigator from the streets of New York," there are many other memorable features.

For example, there's Anne Murphy with the laughing eyes and a most pleasant manner with all of the guests. Then there's Patricia (or Trish), Anne and Vince's daughter, who had just returned from a Florida vacation at the time of my visit and must have knocked them dead on the beaches, because she had a super suntan to go with her Irish good looks.

The Weathervane Inn, listed in the National Register of Historic Places, is a small cluster of buildings set off the highway, with sections dating back to 1785. It is located in the lovely little village of South Egremont in the Berkshires, where there are many pre-1800 houses and a graceful church. Replete with wide-board floors, beautiful moldings, and an original fireplace that served as a heating and cooking unit with a beehive oven, the inn has a comfortable, warm atmosphere.

There are eight very attractively furnished country inn guest rooms, all with private baths, enhanced by Anne's eye for design and her needlework. Antique maple high double beds and some king-sized beds, all with coordinated linens, along with Anne's handmade pierced lampshades, all combine to make each room distinctive. There are many dried flower arrangements, ball fringe curtains, books and magazines, and good reading lamps.

I talked to Anne about the menu at the Weathervane. "Well," she said, "the kitchen is my domain and I'm very proud of the response that our guests have had to our entrées. Our specialties have been Cornish hens with kiwi sauce, veal Dijonnaise, pork tenderloin Normandy, duckling with black cherries, seafood Mornay, and soups like split pea, New England chowders, and a hearty borscht. We've had to print our recipe for celery seed dressing because so many of our diners requested it."

Vince came cruising by and decided to make his contribution: "Let me tell you about our desserts—Trish is the pastry chef par excellence! The best homemade pies with the best crust. All kinds of fresh fruit combinations—blueberry-peach, strawberry-blueberry, peach-nectarine, and pear-blueberry. And her cheesecake and chocolate chip walnut pie get nothing but raves!"

There are two dining areas, including a new dining room overlooking the garden and the swimming pool, with a glimpse of the antique shop in a barn that has a feeling somewhat akin to the Sturbridge Village buildings. The shop specializes in early quilts and folk furniture, and inn guests often wander back there to browse.

Eventually, we all sat down in front of the fireplace, next to a sort of little pub corner, and for an hour and a half I was beguiled by the various members of the Murphy family. Vince really *is* a private investigator, but he takes all of the "Mike Hammer" jokes with exceptionally good grace and even adds a few of his own. "I did that for many years in the city," he said, "and I still go in about one day a week, but all of us have taken up this new life here in the country. As a matter of fact, I'm even a member of the South Egremont Volunteer Fire Department!"

THE WEATHERVANE INN, Rte. 23, South Egremont, MA 01258; 413-528-9580. An 8-guestroom village inn in the Berkshire foothills. Modified American plan in summer; in winter, modified American plan, Thurs. through Sun. Breakfast served to houseguests. Dinner served to travelers Fri. and Sat. Open year-round. Swimming pool on grounds. Golf, tennis, bicycling, backroading, hiking, horseback riding, fishing, downhill and xc skiing nearby. Tanglewood, Jacob's Pillow, Berkshire Playhouse, Norman Rockwell Museum, and great antique shops all nearby. No pets. Vincent, Anne, and Patricia Murphy, Innkeepers.

Directions; From New York City follow Sawmill River Pkwy. to Taconic Pkwy. to Rte. 23 east. South Egremont and the inn are about 2 mi. past the Catamount Ski area.

THE RED LION INN
Stockbridge, Massachusetts

The Red Lion Inn is over 200 years old. At least there has been an inn on this site for over 200 years. There have been some changes in the various buildings—just as the methods of reaching Stockbridge have changed. At first, it was only by horseback. Then the Springfield–Albany stage came through. Railroads used to run dozens of trains to Stockbridge and the Red Lion buggies met guests at the Stanford White-designed railroad station. Now it is about two-and-a-half hours from New York and Boston by auto.

I was having dinner outdoors in the flower-laden courtyard at the Red Lion with owners Jack and Jane Fitzpatrick and innkeeper Betsy Holtzinger. It was a soft, fine evening and the lanterns on the trees swayed in the gentle breeze.

We were talking about how Stockbridge has changed through the years from an 18th-century Indian village, discovered by missionaries, to a secluded retreat for prominent artists, musicians, and writers in the 19th century, and how, today, Tanglewood, the Berkshire Theatre Festival, and Jacob's Pillow attract people from everywhere.

"Don't forget we have the Corner House with Norman Rockwell's original paintings, Chesterwood, the Mission House, and Naumkeag as well," Jane observed.

Speaking of Norman Rockwell, almost every guest room in the inn has a print of a Norman Rockwell painting. There is a generous sprinkling of Rockwell's Huckleberry Finn lithographs in the hallways.

"We know that for many people the Red Lion is their first country inn experience," Betsy commented, "and for that reason we take a special care in seeing to it that everything is as authentically 'country inn' as possible. Mrs. Fitzpatrick is very particular about details and I believe the inn certainly shows the results of the love and interest that both she and the Senator have taken in it during these years. (Jack Fitzpatrick was at one time our state senator.)

As often as I have walked through the lobby and parlors of this community-minded village inn, I am always impressed by the beautiful collection of antiques, which includes tables, cabinets, highboys, clocks, paintings, and prints that seem to be very much at home in the low-ceilinged setting. A collection of teapots was actually started in the middle of the 19th century by a Mrs. Plumb, who owned the inn.

Stockbridge has five seasons. Summer, autumn, winter, spring, and "fall foliage." I see many visitors who are guests at the Red Lion as they pass the window of my office on Pine Street, enjoying a quiet New England town with fresh air, lots of trees, and friendly people, many of whom have migrated here from the city themselves.

The four of us ended up, as most people do, in rocking chairs on the broad front porch. We waved and called out to our Stockbridge neighbors who were passing in front of the broad porch on an early September evening promenade.

The Red Lion hosted the twentieth annual meeting of *CIBR* innkeepers, which included some from England and Europe, in November, 1985. It was a smashing success with over 250 innkeepers attending.

THE RED LION INN, Stockbridge, MA 01262; 413-298-5545. A 95-guestroom historic village inn, dating back to 1773, in the Berkshire hills. European plan. Breakfast, lunch, and dinner. Open year-round. Adjacent to Tanglewood, Norman Rockwell's Old Corner House Museum, the Berkshire Playhouse, Jacob's Pillow, Chesterwood Gallery, Mission House, and major ski areas. Outdoor pool. Tennis, golf, boating, fishing, hiking, mountain climbing, and xc skiing nearby. Jack and Jane Fitzpatrick, Owners; Betsy Holtzinger, Innkeeper.

Directions: From the Taconic State Pkwy., take Exit 23 (N.Y. Rte. 23) to Mass. Rte. 7. Proceed north to Stockbridge. From the Mass. Tpke., Exit 2 at Lee, and follow Rte. 102 to Stockbridge.

THE INN AT STOCKBRIDGE
Stockbridge, Massachusetts

What a wonderful, gorgeous Berkshire afternoon! The last forty-five minutes of an October sun was streaming across the meadows, lighting up the swaying trees and the two-story columns of the Inn at Stockbridge with a wondrous golden light. I pulled around the circular driveway and stood for a moment on the steps drinking in the entire scene, almost reluctant to join Lee Weitz and other guests for the usual afternoon wine and cheese.

Anticipating my mood, Lee opened the front door of the inn and said, "Oh, I know how you feel, it's so wonderful that you almost hate to come inside. But come on in, because we're all having such a good time in here!" Lee introduced me to some of the guests, all of whom had enjoyed a wonderful afternoon walking or driving in the Berkshires.

I trailed off into the library, another very large room furnished in a most comfortable way, quite reminiscent of an English country house with deep chintz-covered sofas and another big fireplace. Then I crossed over to the other side of the house to see the fourteen-place Chippendale dining room table, where I have had breakfast quite a few times myself. You see, I live about a mile away from the Inn at Stockbridge.

I returned and sank down on a sofa, immediately becoming engrossed in conversation with a couple from California who were traveling with CIBR. "We love it here," they said. "It's our third time and it's like coming home again. What we particularly remember is the good time around the breakfast table, when people are so stimulating and fascinating."

Lee came and spirited me upstairs to look at some of the beautiful guest rooms. These are all most attractively furnished and decorated, and all have interesting names. "I like to furnish every room entirely differently," Lee commented, as we moved from room to room. "Fortunately, this was a lovely, spacious private house for many years and so most of the bedrooms are unusually large. All of them have views of the countryside."

Each of them has some little hidden things, such as candy or little flower arrangements or something special to make the room more distinctive.

Some rooms have a view of a spacious patio where, during the warm weather, the tables are set with pink tablecloths and napkins and fresh flowers. It's all very festive. Beyond the patio is a graceful, secluded swimming pool.

As we rejoined the group in the living room I asked Lee about dinners. "We serve a lighter main course instead of roast prime ribs of beef or heavy cuts of steak," she remarked. "There are light things like fish, chicken, salads, soup, good wholesome homemade bread, and desserts that are appealing but lower in calories. We serve the evening meal in the dining room or out on the patio. There's one menu for dinner; we post it in the morning and the guests can make a reservation that day. When they call off-season we will ask them if they want dinner, which is always served at a set time. I have to tell you," she went on, "that people in the summertime love the breakfast out on the patio. Many of them take pictures because the setting is so pretty. Breakfast might include a soufflé or eggs Benedict or a thick slice of french toast with whipped Grand Marnier butter. This makes it taste like crêpes Suzette, but even better. There's also fresh fruit, blueberry pancakes, herbed eggs with cheese and mushrooms, and many other things. We make our own coffee with a French roast blend."

Yes indeed, there was much more to say about the Inn at Stockbridge. It is a most pleasant, intimate inn experience.

THE INN AT STOCKBRIDGE, Rte. 7, Box 618, Stockbridge, MA 01262; 413-298-3337. A 7-guestroom (5 with private bath) country house about 1 mi. north of the center of Stockbridge. Closed during winter months. Lodgings include a full breakfast. Dinner available by request and advance reservation. Convenient to all of the Berkshire cultural and recreational attractions. A summer swimming pool on grounds. No facilities for children under 10. No pets. Lee and Don Weitz, Innkeepers.

Directions: From N.Y.C.: take any of the main highways north to Stockbridge, and continue north on Rte. 7 for 1.2 mi. Look for small sign on the right after passing under the Mass. Tpke. Inn cannot be seen from the road. From Mass. Tpke: exit at Lee, take Rte. 102 to Stockbridge and turn right on Rte. 7 going north for 1.2 mi. as above.

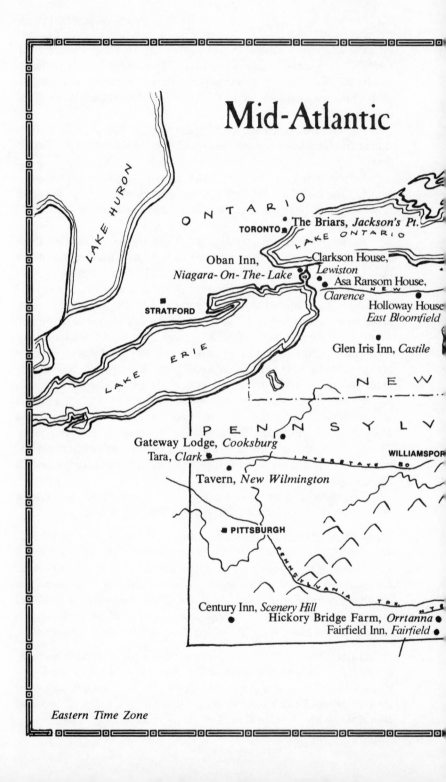

Mid-Atlantic

LAKE HURON

O N T A R I O

LAKE ONTARIO

TORONTO ● The Briars, *Jackson's Pt.*

Oban Inn, Clarkson House,
Niagara-On-The-Lake *Lewiston*
● Asa Ransom House,
Clarence

N E W

STRATFORD ■

Holloway House
East Bloomfield

LAKE ERIE

Glen Iris Inn, *Castile*

N E W

P E N N S Y L V

Gateway Lodge, *Cooksburg* ●
Tara, *Clark* ●
WILLIAMSPOR

INTERSTATE 80

Tavern, *New Wilmington*

PITTSBURGH ■

PENNSYLVANIA TPK.

MTS

Century Inn, *Scenery Hill*
● Hickory Bridge Farm, *Orrtanna* ●
Fairfield Inn, *Fairfield* ●

Eastern Time Zone

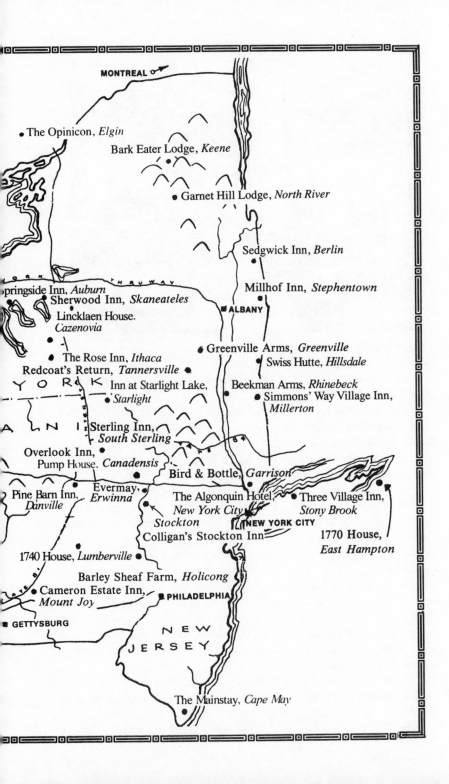

MONTREAL

The Opinicon, *Elgin*

Bark Eater Lodge, *Keene*

Garnet Hill Lodge, *North River*

Sedgwick Inn, *Berlin*

Millhof Inn, *Stephentown*

pringside Inn, *Auburn*

Sherwood Inn, *Skaneateles*

Lincklaen House. *Cazenovia*

ALBANY

Greenville Arms, *Greenville*

Swiss Hutte, *Hillsdale*

The Rose Inn, *Ithaca*

Redcoat's Return, *Tannersville*

Inn at Starlight Lake, *Starlight*

Beekman Arms, *Rhinebeck*

Simmons' Way Village Inn, *Millerton*

YORK

Sterling Inn, *South Sterling*

Overlook Inn, Pump House. *Canadensis*

Bird & Bottle, *Garrison*

Evermay, *Erwinna*

Pine Barn Inn, *Danville*

The Algonquin Hotel, *New York City*

Three Village Inn, *Stony Brook*

Stockton

Colligan's Stockton Inn

NEW YORK CITY

1770 House, *East Hampton*

1740 House, *Lumberville*

Barley Sheaf Farm, *Holicong*

Cameron Estate Inn, *Mount Joy*

PHILADELPHIA

GETTYSBURG

NEW JERSEY

The Mainstay, *Cape May*

ALGONQUIN HOTEL
New York, New York

I have always had a great deal of fun writing about my experiences at the Hotel Algonquin in New York City.

The first time I mentioned it was in the 1971 edition, when it had come to my attention that many people following *Country Inns and Back Roads* felt the need of a place to stay in New York City. Someone recommended the Algonquin, and after a long visit, I agreed that it was the closest thing to a country inn I'd yet found in New York.

In the 1972 edition I spoke about seeing a well-known French movie actor having tea in the lobby, and about riding up in the elevator with a famous stage actress who announced in the glorious tones of a French horn, "Fifth floor, please."

Andy Anspach, the innkeeper, commented that people like actresses, diplomats, and internationally famous figures deserve a private life, and the Algonquin attempts to provide it while they are in New York. As he said, "We are terribly conservative by inclination. We've tried not to change too many things around here since the early 1920s, when it was famous as a meeting place for the Algonquin Round Table wits. People seem to enjoy our accommodations, which include oversized bathtubs and meticulous room service."

In 1974 I spoke at length about the friendliness of the staff and how guests are quite likely to be remembered even though the Algonquin is, in truth, a very busy place.

In 1975 I did a long piece on the late evening supper buffet where guests come in after the theater, the opera, the basketball or hockey games to enjoy Welsh rarebit, lobster Newburg, salad, fluffy cakes, apple pie, and ice cream.

(It is now possible to enjoy a delightful repast every evening of the week, including Sunday.)

In 1976 I luxuriated with breakfast in bed at the Algonquin, and described the browned corned beef hash with a poached egg, warm dutch coffee cake, and above all, the superb Algonquin hot chocolate.

Recent news from the Algonquin includes the fact that the story of the celebrated Algonquin Round Table was made into a one-hour documentary for National Public Television, and that a new book, charmingly titled *The Ten Year Lunch*, based on the two years of research that went into that TV project, has been published. It is the eighth book published about the Algonquin over the many decades since its doors opened in 1902.

Following a London summer that greatly enhanced his English following, Steve Ross is back at the piano in the Oak Room during supper hour from 9 p.m.

Redecorating is something that goes on in the Algonquin all the time, and the most recent is the new Playbill Suite, a living room, bedroom, and bath designed this year by Clare Fraser to commemorate the 100th anniversary of *Playbill Magazine*, given to every playgoer in every Broadway theater. The new suite is decorated with fifty-six fascinating *Playbill* covers spanning those hundred years, each one depicting a Broadway theatrical production in which celebrated Algonquin guests played major roles.

ALGONQUIN HOTEL, 59 W. 44th St., New York, NY 10036; 212-840-6800. A 200-guestroom quiet, conservative country inn in the heart of Manhattan. Convenient to business, theaters, and shopping. Breakfast, lunch served every day. Dinner is served Mon. through Sat., and a Sun. supper is served on Sun. from 5:30 p.m. The late supper buffet is offered Mon. through Sat. at 9:30 p.m. Open year-round. Very near bus, rail, and air transportation. Garage directly opposite entrance, with complimentary parking for weekend visitors arriving after 5 p.m. Fri. for minimum 2-night visit. No pets. Andrew Anspach, Innkeeper.

Directions: 44th St. is one-way from west to east; 43rd St., from east to west. Garage is accessible from either street.

ASA RANSOM HOUSE
Clarence, New York

I turned off the New York State Thruway at the Pembroke exit and turned west on Route 5. There were only a few rather pleasant country miles to the village of Clarence. It was mid-October and many of the trees, fields, and villages were carrying wonderful beige, russet, and orange hues. This is the western New York State of author Carl Carmer, and these are the broad flatlands with grains and orchards that beckoned early settlers, many of whom either worked on or used the Erie Canal. Many of them stayed on and prospered.

Now I was on the outskirts of Clarence, a quiet pleasant village that boasts one of the best-known village inns in the Northeast: the Asa Ransom House. The village was settled in 1808 and Asa Ransom was one of the town's most forward-looking citizens.

Each time I visit I seem to find something not only new but exceptional to share with my readers. In previous issues I have made mention of the Carpigiani ice cream maker that Bob and Judy Lenz, along with their young daughters, Abby and Jennie, have been using to delight their guests with homemade ice cream—fresh raspberry from their own berry patch, fresh peach, elderberry, and other delicious flavors.

This time I must say that I oohed and aahed over the herb garden. "There are over fifty-two herbs here," Judy said. "In the summertime when the herbs are really in full bloom and growing, we invite people to tour the garden before and after dinner. We have a chart that tells them the culinary and medicinal value of each herb. I think that there is a new awareness of using herbs."

The Asa Ransom House has two distinctly different dining rooms and four totally different guest rooms. Each has a name to suit its own personality. An 1825 cannonball double bed proudly presides in the Red Room. The larger Gold Room is outfitted with twin iron-and-brass beds with coordinated patchwork coverlets, and originally designed stenciling on the upper walls, whose theme is old-fashioned American hospitality. The Green Room has two double beds, a sitting area with a love seat, a bookcase, and a view of the herb garden.

Each of the two dining rooms has its own decorative theme, and one room is set aside for non-smokers.

The Asa Ransom House menu reflects the Lenzes' innovative flair, as well as some deep convictions about their life. For example, their religious persuasion prohibits serving pork and shellfish. As a pork substitute, "one of our favorite dishes," Bob comments, "is chicken breasts with raspberry sauce. This was discovered last winter on one of the gourmet nights held frequently during the winter season." Other pork substitutes are smoked corned beef with apple-raisin sauce. There are

also "country pies," including "Salmon Pond," a house specialty, chicken pot pie, and steak-and-kidney pie. In the kitchen of the inn they whip their own cream, use honey and natural raw-milk cheese from a local cheese factory, and never use any MSG. Three different kinds of butter are served.

Breakfast for houseguests consists of fresh fruit, muffins, and a beverage, as well as Judy's special breakfast egg pie.

The Asa Ransom House is closed on Fridays and Saturdays because of the religious beliefs of Bob and Judy, who are members of the Church of God. Friday provides them with the opportunity to spend time with their families or to set off with their daughters for some point in western New York or southern Ontario to enjoy many scenic attractions. As Bob says, "We frequently end the day with a fine dinner at an old favorite or sometimes discover some new country inn."

ASA RANSOM HOUSE, Rte. 5, Clarence, NY 14031; 716-759-2315. A 4-guestroom village inn approx. 15 mi. from Buffalo near the Albright Knox Art Gallery, the Studio Arena Theatre, the Art Park, and Niagara Falls. European plan. Dinner served on Mon. through Thurs., 4:00 to 8:30 p.m.; Sun., 12:00 to 8:00 p.m. Jackets required. Lunch is available on Wed. only. Closed Fri. and Sat. Tennis, golf, fishing, swimming nearby. Limited amusement for children under 12. No pets. No credit cards. Bob and Judy Lenz, Innkeepers.

Directions: From the New York Thruway traveling west, use Exit 48A-Pembroke. Turn right to Rte. 5 and proceed 11 mi. to Clarence. Traveling east on the N.Y. Thruway, use Exit 49; turn left on Rte. 78, go 1 mi. to Rte. 5 and continue 5 1/4 mi. Coming from the east via Rte. 20, just east of Lancaster, N.Y., turn on Ransom Rd., go to end and turn left.

BARK EATER LODGE
Keene, New York

The most welcome comment I can receive about this book is, "The inn was exactly the way you wrote about it." I try to do that in every inn-stance (little play on words, there). In this case, I'm going to let Joe-Pete Wilson and Harley McDevitt describe Bark Eater themselves.

"The lodge is a modest, 150-year-old farmhouse, preserved to give the guest a true feeling of 'life back when.' We offer good home cooking, sometimes done on our wood stove, informal family-style meals, and relaxed evenings with good conversation around the fireplace. Occasionally, we schedule talks and advice on ski waxing, mountain safety, or skiing technique.

"We maintain several miles of cross-country ski trails; some to entice the beginner, others to challenge the expert. We have certified instruction, tours, and rentals or sales from our own ski shop. We also have moonlight tours, citizen races, and guided picnic trips into the wilderness.

"In summer, we switch to exploring the great outdoors on foot, mountain or rock climbing, or just strolling around nearby country roads or trails. There is great trout fishing nearby and plenty of opportunity for swimming, canoeing, sailing, tennis, golf, horseback riding, and other sports.

"We have fifteen horses and we offer picnic trips, trail rides, and lessons. Our horses range from good-looking easy trail horses to well-trained English riding horses.

"A visit during the Adirondack autumn, with its spectacular colors, is unbelievable."

Bark Eater Lodge is a year-round country inn specializing in cross-country skiing in the winter, and enjoyment of the outdoors in all seasons of the year. It is situated on sixty acres of beautiful rolling meadow with a delightful pond, in the High Peaks region of the Adirondacks.

It is homey and informal, and at the same time, eclectic. The magazines and newspapers include the *New York Times, Architectural Digest, Natural History, Backpacker,* and *Gourmet,* to name a few. There are stacks of books on a wide diversity of subjects. I've always been able to tell a great many things about an inn by the nature of the books that are available to the guests.

The kitchen is wide open for everyone to enjoy. There are a couple of old-fashioned stoves and modern ones, as well. Guests are welcome to sit down at the table and talk with Harley while dinner is being prepared. By the way, these dinners are a feature of the inn and, because of the great outdoor activities, are often very hearty. Everybody sits down about seven o'clock in the evening around the big table.

Guest rooms have rocking chairs, many old-fashioned wash stands, double and single beds, over and under bunks, wooden chests, and a wonderful old-fashioned feeling.

Bark Eater is on a special "inn-to-inn" program, described in a special folder, that begins with the Greenville Arms in the Catskills and continues north to Garnet Hill Lodge in the Adirondacks. All three of these inns are in *CIBR*, and full details are available at any inn.

To illustrate just how "up country" Bark Eater is, if you don't succeed in making a telephone connection on the first try, keep trying. It's a real country telephone system.

When you visit Bark Eater Lodge, bring a great sense of expectancy.

BARK EATER LODGE, Alstead Mill Rd., Keene, NY 12942; 518-576-2221. A 12-guestroom (shared baths) rustic mountain inn in the Adirondacks. Rates include a full country breakfast. Open all year, but check in advance during April. Dinners served. A wide variety of mountain recreation available at the inn or nearby, including High Peaks climbing, Hudson River Gorge whitewater rafting, and self-guided hiking tours. Horseback riding, swimming, tennis, golf, canoeing, sailing available nearby. Children welcome. No credit cards. Joe-Pete Wilson and Harley McDevitt, Innkeepers.

Directions: From the Northway take exit 30, follow Rte. 73 for 1 mi. past the village of Keene and turn right on Alstead Mill Rd. Inn is ½ mi. beyond.

BEEKMAN ARMS
Rhinebeck, New York

Chuck LaForge, proprietor at the Beekman Arms, claims that this is the "oldest hotel in America." Since Francis Koppeis of Longfellow's Wayside Inn in South Sudbury, Massachusetts, makes the same claim for his establishment, this has created a great deal of friendly rivalry between the two inns.

By 1769, the Beekman Arms, which started from rather humble beginnings in 1700, had increased in size to two full stories with a roomy attic that later became a ballroom. When trouble arose with the Indians in the area, the entire community would take refuge within the inn's walls.

During the Revolution, George Washington and his staff enjoyed the fare of the inn, and the window from which he watched for his couriers is still in place. Those were anxious days also for Lafayette, Schuyler, Arnold, and Hamilton, who spent many hours at the inn. In fact, over the years hundreds of men who have helped fashion the destiny of our nation partook of the inn's hospitality.

Recently, on an early December evening I enjoyed dinner in the low-ceilinged Tap Room. The light from the flickering candles was reflected in the varnished tabletops and in the overhead beams. The walls were hung with ancient documents and prints, many of them dating back to the Revolution.

The first thing brought to the table was a loaf of freshly baked bread. The waitress, dressed in a red costume, suggested that I might enjoy the rack of lamb, the special that day. It was delicious.

While earlier Colonial Beekman Arms menus probably included such items as roast beef, venison, bear steak, pheasant, quail, and turkey, tonight, chef Bruce Harm's menu had varieties of boned roast duckling (raspberry sauce or hunter's style), fresh seafood, scrumptious veal preparations, as well as a few select recipes from other inns featured in *CIBR*. Casual but elegant country dining is the fare.

During most of the last twenty years, I have visited the Beekman Arms in anticipation of sharing some of Chuck LaForge's newest ideas. These have included the construction of additional rooms in a small building in the back of the main inn, the creation of a new greenhouse-dining area on the front of the building, and the opening of the Delameter House nearby.

Now he suggested that we take a stroll to the Delameter House to see all of the recent developments. "This is the Delameter courtyard," he commented, as we walked into an open-ended square area. There were buildings on three sides, including one that had been there earlier and a Federal house of batten-and-board design similar to the original Delameter House, which had been moved from another point in the village.

The guest rooms in this section are furnished with a very pleasant restraint; all have four-poster beds and a fireplace, and there is split wood for the fire. Each of them has its own little refrigerator. There are thirty-one rooms in this complex.

"I think that these rooms add a completely new dimension to what we offer at the Beekman Arms," Chuck declared, as we walked back through the courtyard past the Carriage House, which also has some attractive guest rooms. "The house was designed in 1844 by Alexander Jackson Davis, one of the foremost designers of his time. We have attempted to emulate him as much as possible."

So we see that the Beekman Arms today is more than a historic inn where thousands of guests enjoy its fascinating and authentic Colonial decor and menu; like many other country and village inns, it is still the community meeting place. Decisions great and small have been made within its walls for almost three hundred years.

It is a living link to America's past.

BEEKMAN ARMS, Rhinebeck, NY 12572; 914-876-7077. A 12-guestroom village inn with an additional 24 rooms and 2 suites in nearby guest houses. European plan. Breakfast, lunch, and dinner served to travelers daily. Open year-round. One mile from Amtrak station at Rhinecliff (2-hr. train ride from Grand Central Station). Short drive to Hyde Park with F.D.R. home and library, Rhinebeck World War I Aerodrome, and Culinary Institute of America. Golf, tennis, swimming nearby. No amusements for young children. Bob Hansen, Innkeeper.

Directions: From N.Y. Thruway, take Exit 19, cross Rhinecliff Bridge and pick up Rte. 199 south to Rte. 9. Proceed south on Rte. 9 to middle of village. From Taconic Pkwy., exit at Rhinebeck and follow Rte. 199 west 11 mi. to Rte. 308 into village.

BIRD AND BOTTLE INN
Garrison, New York

I had awakened to the joyous sound of the birds and had lingered under the covers at the Bird and Bottle for just a few more minutes, noting with appreciation the handsome overhead beams made of mellowed, weathered barnboard and the rest of the furnishings in my room in one of the outbuildings of the inn. Out the window I could see the high spreading branches of one of the huge old trees against the blue spring sky, with just a wisp of a white cloud.

There was much to do that day, so a few minutes later I ambled over the red brick walk to the main building of the inn for breakfast. Some birds flew overhead and one of them landed on the chimney of this yellow clapboard house that has played host to so many travelers and guests over the years. I opened the Dutch door with its heavy cast-iron hardware and stepped into the main reception area where the polished, wide pine floorboards seemed almost to reflect an oil portrait of a young lady dressed in Colonial costume.

To my right was the low-ceilinged dining room, where the previous night there had been gleaming white napery with candles and many diners seated side by side—a very romantic idea, indeed. The menu on the blackboard had announced that there was ratatouille au froid, also smoked trout, french onion soup, and then a supreme of chicken, roast duckling Bigarade, and rognon de veau moutarde. Dinners are *prix fixe*.

For breakfast, innkeeper Ira Boyar suggested the small dining room with a crackling fire against the chill of the early spring morning. There were fresh flowers on the table.

I had selected my breakfast order the night before from a menu that included all kinds of eggs, sausage, and fruit juice. I chose scrambled eggs and sausage and noticed some other houseguests were having beautiful french toast served with syrup or honey. We soon began to talk with one another because it's that kind of atmosphere.

Breakfast completed, I leaned for a moment on the window overlooking a little terrace and stream, where a light spring rain was making punctuation points in the small puddles. The trees were in early bud and I could well imagine what magic the entire scene would reveal in another two or three weeks.

Ira suggested that I might like to see more of the bedrooms in the main building, and as I walked up the stairs I realized that I was looking at the same Colonial wallpaper that I have in my own dining room. However, it seemed much more appropriate in this setting, here on the second floor where the floorboards creaked a little and were slightly aslant.

All of the bedrooms are furnished in Early American antiques and

have either a canopy or a four-poster bed. All have private baths and woodburning fireplaces. There are two double rooms and a suite which includes a cozy sitting room.

The Bird and Bottle goes back to the mid-1700s, when it was a stagecoach stop on the New York to Albany route. Its nearness to West Point undoubtedly made it a meeting place for Benedict Arnold's emissaries to the British, prior to his defection.

Today, the Colonial atmosphere is preserved with narrow clapboards (quite unusual), low ceilings, and rich paneling. The inn is beautifully decorated with many duck decoys, period wallpaper, pewter, old paintings, and many wooden accessories. It is indeed like stepping back into an earlier time.

BIRD AND BOTTLE INN, Garrison, NY 10524; 914-424-3000. A 4-guest-room country inn, rich in antiquity, located on Rte. 9, a few miles north of Peekskill, N.Y. MAP rates include both a full breakfast and dinner. From April 1 to Nov. 1 lunch and dinner served daily. From Nov. 1 to April 1 dinner served Wed. thru Sun. Sunday brunch served year-round. A short distance from Boscobel Restoration, U.S. Military Academy at West Point, and Sleepy Hollow Restorations. Ira Boyar, Innkeeper.

Directions: From NYC: cross Geo. Washington Bridge and follow Palisades Pkwy. north to Bear Mtn. Bridge. Cross bridge and travel on Rte. 9D north 4½ mi. to Rte. 403. Proceed on Rte. 403 to Rte. 9, then north 4 mi. to inn. From I-84, take Exit 13 and follow Rte. 9 south for 8 mi.

GARNET HILL LODGE
North River, New York

Spring was in the air, but snow was on the ground as I turned off Route 28 to 13th Lake Road in North River, heading ever upward into the Adirondacks toward Garnet Hill Lodge.

I followed the inn signs on the ascending roads through the woods and soon arrived at the Log House, where innkeeper George Heim greeted me, saying, "This is one of my favorite times of the year. It's wonderful to see the woods come to life as a few birds are returning and some early flowers are peeking their way up through the snow."

Garnet Hill Lodge, overlooking 13th Lake, is an all-seasons resort-inn. The Log House was built in 1936, and it is a true rustic lodge, with a big, combination dining/living room of varnished Adirondack white pine in a post-and-beam construction— the bark has been left on in many cases. Guests gather around the big fireplace for some good conversation and fun.

George pointed out some of the latest renovations, which included new balconies with full glass doors for six of the guest rooms, affording spectacular views. All of the rooms in the Log House have private baths and are finished in a nice mixture of original pine paneling and wallpaper. Cut flowers are a pleasing touch throughout the lodge.

The Big Shanty, a beautiful old manor house nearby, also has guest rooms; and most recently, the Birches, just a few steps from the Log House, has four additional guest rooms.

Among the many outdoor activities available on the grounds or nearby are whitewater rafting trips on the upper Hudson River through a fifteen-mile gorge, with some of the most spectacular rapids and scenery in the Adirondacks.

"Fishing is a big thing here," George said. "We have land-locked salmon and brook trout right here on 13th Lake, and the nearby lakes and streams have lake trout, rainbows, brownies, bass, walleyes, and pickerel.

"The foliage is absolutely spectacular, and it's a wonderful time for hiking to the abandoned Garnet Mine or one of the distant ponds. On a morning walk down to the beaver pond we might see anything from deer to blue herons.

"And in the winter," he continued, "the Adirondacks offer some of the best snow in the East. We get over 125 inches here, and there is downhill skiing at Gore, Whiteface, and Lake Placid. We're very much into cross-country skiing here, with over forty kilometers of scenic groomed trails. We have a well-equipped ski shop with an experienced staff for lessons and tours."

Garnet Hill, along with Greenville Arms and Bark Eater Lodge, has a special inn-to-inn lodging program.

Mary Heim's home-style cooking always gets a rousing hand, with such entrées as pot roast, chicken, and baked fish, and a wonderful smorgasbord on frosty Saturday nights during ski season. The breads and desserts are all freshly made by Mary and her helpers.

GARNET HILL LODGE, 13th Lake Rd., North River, NY 12856; 518-251-2821. A 20-guestroom rustic resort-inn high in the Adirondacks, 32 mi. from Warrensburg. Open year-round except 2 wks. in June and Nov. Mod. American and European plans available. Breakfast, lunch, and dinner served to travelers. Swimming, boating, hiking, fishing, and xc skiing on grounds. Downhill skiing, long distance hikes, Hudson River whitewater rafting trips, and beautiful Adirondack drives nearby. The area has many museums, arts and crafts centers, and historical points. No pets. No credit cards. Taxi service provided to bus stop 30 mi. away. George and Mary Heim, Innkeepers.

Directions: From the Northway (I-87) take Exit 23 and follow Rte. 8 north 4 mi. Take left fork (Rte. 28) 22 mi. to North River. Take second left (13th Lake Rd.) 5 mi. to lodge. For more explicit directions, write for brochure.

I do not include lodging rates in the descriptions, for the very nature of an inn means that there are lodgings of various sizes, with and without baths, in and out of season, and with plain and fancy decoration. Travelers should call ahead and inquire about the availability and rates of the many different types of rooms.

GLEN IRIS INN
Castile, New York

Cora and Peter Pizzutelli and I were leaning over the stone wall gazing at the 107-foot Middle Falls of the Genessee River in front of the Glen Iris Inn. The wonderful lyrical sound of the river is ever present, and the nearest point from which to view the falls is a terrace about 25 steps from the front of the inn.

"Our guests have always enjoyed the beauty and majesty of Letchworth Park," Cora said, "and there are many animals that are seen in great abundance, including deer, raccoons, chipmunks, ground hogs, foxes, wild turkeys, quail, grouse, and pheasants. Lots of people enjoy the great variety of wild flowers."

"Letchworth State Park is about eighteen miles long and about two miles wide," said Peter. "It follows the course of the Genesee River in what is best described as a miniature Grand Canyon. The full length is traversed by an auto road. There are several different turn-off points with spectacular views carved out by the river through the land on its way north to Lake Ontario. There is not a single bit of commercialism to mar this enchanting experience."

The inn was the former home of William Pryor Letchworth, first built in the early 1800s. The bedrooms are very comfortably furnished and are reached by a twisting, turning staircase of dark chestnut wood that leads all the way to the third floor. Instead of having room numbers, the rooms have the names of trees found in the park. All are funished in

the 19th-century style. A modern motel unit is located in a nearby grove for additional overnight guests.

Cora and Peter Pizzutelli, sensitive, nature-loving people, are the innkeepers. Each is deeply devoted to this beautiful inn. The feeling has run in the family, because both their son, Peter, Jr., and their daughter, Paula, grew up in the inn.

Peter is a chef with years of experience, and the many different dishes that come out of the kitchen are always prepared under his watchful eye.

Cora's area of interest is the ever-growing gift shop within the inn.

The unusual combination of a beautiful country inn located next to a spectacular waterfall in a totally protected state park in a historical section of western New York State attracts large numbers of visitors to the area and to the Glen Iris Inn. Consequently, I cannot emphasize too strongly the advisability of having reservations in advance for breakfast, lunch, or dinner, and also for lodgings. Cora tells me that every summer they regretfully have to tell people that there is no room in their inn.

My dear friends from Grand Rapids, Clare and Lucy Dee Dee, wrote me that they had a wonderful lunch at the Glen Iris recently, and Clare was enthusiastic about the London broil and also the cinnamon parfait.

Just as I was leaving the Glen Iris, I got one of the biggest thrills that I've had in more than ten years of visiting: a freight train rumbled over the great railroad bridge that spans the Genesee River just above the inn, and it was a thrilling sight to see the locomotive and the cars chugging their way high above the riverbed. The engineer obliged with a few blasts on the whistle to top it off.

GLEN IRIS INN, Castile, NY 14427; 716-493-2622. A 20-guestroom country inn located at the Middle Falls of the Genesee River in Letchworth State Park. European plan. Breakfast, lunch, dinner served to travelers daily. Open from Easter Sun. through first Sun. in Nov. Footpaths, swimming, and bicycles nearby. Historical sites in park and spectacular views within walking distance. Peter, Cora, and Paula Pizzutelli, Innkeepers.

Directions: Inn is located off Rte. 436, 19A, and 39 in Letchworth State Park, 55 mi. from Buffalo and Rochester.

GREENVILLE ARMS
Greenville, New York

To me one of the most exciting things about my visits to country inns for the past twenty-one years is the spirit of innovation expressed at many inns. This is particularly true at the Greenville Arms in the northern Catskills. Besides having a family tradition of innkeeping extending at least forty years into the past, for the past few summers the inn has been hosting special painting workshops, which I'll discuss in just a moment.

A Victorian country mansion with several interestingly fashioned porches, cupolas, gables, and corners, the inn is well shaded with tall trees and beautifully landscaped with bushes and shrubs. Throughout, the atmosphere could best be described as "homey and inviting."

Another dimension to be found at the Greenville Arms is its role as a very comfortable resort-inn. Behind the main house, with its several

bedrooms with private and shared baths, is the Carriage House, where there are more contemporary rooms, all with private baths. There is a large, beautiful lawn with shuffleboard, ping-pong, horseshoes, badminton, lawn bowling, and a swimming pool.

The innkeepers at Greenville Arms are two sisters, Barbara and Laura Stevens. They are carrying on the family tradition, since Greenville Arms was originally owned by their mother; their aunt and grandmother still own inns in the Catskill Mountains.

The main house at the Greenville Arms was built in 1889 and has the feeling of being almost frozen in time, with the same type of furniture, decorations, and lifestyle. There are even button switches for some of the lights. One of the most delightful things for me was the many different types of bedspreads. Off the second floor is a porch that you always wanted and never had.

Dinner is single entrée and is really typical Catskill Mountain home-cooking with lots of turkey, baked ham, roasts, and fresh vegetables from the garden.

Greenville Arms is located in a region rich in history and resplendent with natural beauty. The northern Catskill Mountains, the Hudson River, and the rural farmland in the valleys between have attracted travelers and inspired artists for generations. This is the land of Thomas Cole, Frederick Church, and the renowned Hudson River school of art.

I had the opportunity to attend for a brief time one of the art classes being conducted by Sygmund Jankowski. While I didn't have the opportunity to take any lessons, I talked to some of the students, all of whom were most enthusiastic about not only the instructor but the opportunity to take advantage of the limitless subject matter in the area and to work one-on-one with such a splendid communicator. As one student told me, "He said, 'I'll walk with you along every step of the way.' And he did. He just sat with me and talked about drawing and shapes, and I found it fascinating to be doing something new and different and interesting."

For a special brochure with all the details, call either Laura or Barbara. I have seen the schedule for 1986, and also the list of the artist-instructors and, believe me, nothing would give me more pleasure than to be able to take an entire week and participate myself.

One other note: the Greenville Arms has joined with Garnet Hill Lodge and the Bark Eater Lodge, both *CIBR* inns located in the Adirondacks, in a special "inn-to-inn" program.

GREENVILLE ARMS, Greenville, NY 12083; 518- 966-5219. A 20-guest-room Victorian country inn in the foothills of the northern Catskill Mountains, 25 mi. south of Albany, 120 mi. north of New York City. Modified American plan rates include a hearty breakfast and a specially prepared single-entrée country dinner. Bed-and-breakfast rates also available. Open mid- April to mid-Nov. Pool and lawn sports on grounds. Antiquing, country auctions, historic sites, horseback riding, golf, tennis nearby. Children are welcome. Pets accommodated in nearby kennels. No credit cards. Laura and Barbara Stevens, Innkeepers.

Directions: Exit N.Y. State Thruway at 21B (Coxsackie–New Baltimore). Turn left on 9-W south 2 mi. to traffic light. Turn right on 81 west, 13 mi. to Greenville. Turn left at traffic light on 32S. You will see Greenville Arms on the right. Via Taconic Pkwy.: Exit at Ancram on Rte. 82W, over Rip Van Winkle Bridge and follow Rte. 23W to Cairo. Turn right on 32N, 9 mi. to Greenville.

LINCKLAEN HOUSE
Cazenovia, New York

Innkeeper Helen Tobin, whom I have known for almost as many years as this book has been published, and I were having dinner at the Lincklaen House. She was bringing me up to date on all the special events that took place in 1985.

"We set aside June 9 to celebrate our 150th anniversary. The inn was built in 1835 as a luxurious stopover. It has hosted such well-known persons as President and Mrs. Grover Cleveland, John D. Rockefeller, and many other prominent figures throughout the years. The village also was celebrating other local historic events, and our summer was filled with festivals, fairs, and other good times."

If an old-time stagecoach driver were to pull up his team in front of the Lincklaen House today, he would find the hotel looking almost the same as it did in 1835, at least outwardly. The locally made brick, the fine chimneys, the broad front steps, and the columns flanking the doorway

were built to last—and they have. Twenty or more stagecoaches passed through Cazenovia each day traveling over the Third Great Western Turnpike, and the snap of the drivers' whips was a familiar sound. The stages carried the mail and as many as fourteen passengers, and the Lincklaen House must have been a welcome respite from hours spent in those lumbering horse-drawn conveyances.

Guests staying at the Lincklaen House and meeting Helen for the first time frequently say, "Oh, I feel as if I have known you for a long time." This is because Helen has genuine warmth and consideration, and the Lincklaen House reflects this feeling. She insists on fresh flowers, crisp vegetables, hot popovers, hearty portions, lots of bath towels and, above all, a feeling of rapport with her guests.

"I try to visit with everyone while they're here," she said. "Many become good friends and stop off many times. We always get lots of Christmas cards from them.

"We have been working over the past years repainting and stenciling as many guest rooms as possible. We've also refurbished the front of the building with fresh paint. As a matter of fact, I think we'll look quite 'spiffy.'"

The Lincklaen House has been called one of the best examples of early 19th-century architecture in central New York State. Its Greek Revival lines are in harmony with other buildings in this college town. The inn was named after the founder of the village, and over the years, many famous guests have enjoyed its hospitality.

Cazenovia is one of the attractive towns along Route 20 in central New York State. This road, by the way, is a very interesting alternative to traveling across the state entirely on the Thruway, just a few miles to the north.

"Cazenovia is getting to be a very special-event-minded community," Helen remarked. "We have the winter festival every February; the Lorenzo needlework exhibit the whole month of June; arts and crafts on our village green; plus a parade and fireworks over the 4th of July; the Lorenzo driving competition, which takes place in July; the Franklin car reunion each year in August and our own events here at the Lincklaen House at Christmastime.

"We serve afternoon tea here every day and it's the one time of the day that I make every effort to be back here to meet my guests and introduce them to each other. It's one of the nicest times of the day at the Lincklaen House, when we are all sitting around the fire or in the courtyard."

LINCKLAEN HOUSE, Cazenovia, NY 13035; 315-655-3461. A 27-guestroom village inn, 20 mi. east of Syracuse. European plan. Modified American plan upon request. Breakfast, lunch, and dinner served to travelers daily. Open year-round. Near several state parks, the Erie Canal Museum, and the Canal Trail. Tennis, golf, bicycles, alpine and xc skiing nearby. Helen Tobin, Innkeeper.

Directions: From west on NY Thruway, take Exit 34A, follow Rte. 481 south, take Exit 3E and follow Rte. 92 east to Cazenovia. From east on NY Thruway, take Exit 34 and follow Rte. 13 south to Cazenovia. From Rte. 81, take Exit 15 (Lafayette) and follow Rte. 20 east, 18 mi. to inn.

MILLHOF INN
Stephentown, New York

I was speeding across Richmond Mountain in Massachusetts headed toward Route 22 in New York State to make my annual visit to the Millhof Inn and the Tallet family.

I'd been looking forward to this twenty-mile trip from Stockbridge to Stephentown, because I knew there are always some new and exciting things to share with Ronnie and Frank, and with their three rapidly-growing-up children. Debbie has now graduated from college with a degree in hotel management and tourism; Lisa is in her second year at college; and

young Gregory, with whom I have toured the Millhof several times in the past, is growing like a weed and is looking forward to the day when he can wait on tables.

The word "millhof" really means millhouse, and this building was actually used as a sawmill for many years. Frank and Ronnie have made numerous alterations and additions, but the basic structure remains the same. It is the colorfully decorated, handcarved railings and window shutters that make it similar to many European inns I have visited.

Frank is from a French background and Ronnie was born in Yugoslavia. Many of the furnishings and decorations are from the old country. Ronnie is quite an accomplished artist and has done a number of the paintings displayed at the inn.

The European alpine theme extends throughout the inn and particularly to the lodging rooms, each one of which is individually decorated and furnished with plants, books, fresh flowers, and magazines. Frank has done almost all of the decorating and redesigning, and he also constructed the very attractive garden deck where breakfast is served in the summertime.

"Guests love our breakfasts," Ronnie said. "There is always homemade jam, oatmeal, sunflower seed home-baked bread, and, your favorite, blueberry wheat pancakes." Afternoon tea is served at the Millhof and this is especially appreciated by guests who arrive after a long drive.

Frank's most recent project has been to make a second very lovely suite with a fireplace. Ronnie says that the two suites are their most frequently asked-for accommodations.

The Millhof has what I consider to be a most commendable policy that restricts smoking to the downstairs common area. "This seems to be sufficient for almost all of the smokers," she said.

The ever-growing and increasing gardens are a most engaging feature at the Millhof, including the rock garden by the swimming pool, where there are some gorgeous day lilies and clumps of lavender. This pool area is particularly popular with guests at the end of the day.

"We're attracting people who want a quiet place, a place to relax," is the way Ronnie summed up the pleasant evolution of the Millhof Inn. "We try to make things as comfortable and as pleasant as possible, and the result is that guests are coming for longer stays. One couple actually got married here.

"These have been wonderful years for us. Although we are quite close to Tanglewood, where the Boston Symphony plays every summer, and Williamstown, with its summer theater, many of our guests find the atmosphere of rest and relaxation very pleasing."

MILLHOF INN, Route 43, Stephentown, NY 12168; 518-733-5606. A 10-guestroom middle-European-style country inn, 14 mi. from Pittsfield and 12 mi. from Williamstown. A pleasant drive from both Tanglewood in the summer, and Jiminy Peak and Brodie Mountain in the winter. European plan. Full breakfast menu served daily. Afternoon tea served to guests. Many fine restaurants nearby. Open every day from May 26 through March 31. Swimming pool on grounds. Hiking, skiing, back-roading, and all of the famous Berkshire recreational and cultural attractions nearby. No pets. Frank and Ronnie Tallet, Innkeepers.

Directions: From New York: exit the Taconic Pkwy. on Rte. 295. Travel east to Rte. 22, making a left turn and continuing north to Rte. 43. Turn east (right) on Rte. 43 toward Williamstown. The inn is 1 mi. on the left. From Boston: exit Mass. Tpke. at New Lebanon. North on Rte. 22 to Rte. 43, as above.

A number of inns have nearby airports where private airplanes may land. An airplane symbol at the end of the inn directions indicates that there is an airport nearby. Consult inn for further information.

THE REDCOAT'S RETURN
Tannersville, New York

What a lovely day to visit Redcoat's Return! It was mid-June, and I realized that it was the first time I'd been here on a summer day for quite some years. On the walk from the parking area there were wooden tubs with pansies and geraniums and other spring flowers, and a wonderful old wooden wheelbarrow filled with pansies. There were hanging baskets of impatiens hung between the posts on the front porch. Then I saw a peculiar piece of sculpture on the lawn that I noted I would have to ask Peggy Wright about. I walked around the porch to the opposite side, and there was the croquet lawn and a wonderful gazebo and a terribly tempting hammock. Meanwhile, I could hear the sounds of carpenters carpenting and sawyers sawing and I was sure that in just a few moments Peggy and Tom would be telling me about some good things that were happening. The big Belgian sheep dog went lipperty-lopperty over the lawn and into the high grass.

By this time, I'm sure that many of our readers are acquainted with Tom and Peggy Wright's story. Tom was with the Cunard Line as a chef for a number of years and on the *Queen Mary*. He was brought up in England and apprenticed at the Dorchester Hotel in London. He does all of the cooking, and some of his dishes include prime ribs with Yorkshire pudding, poached fillet of sole, roast duck in orange sauce, steak-and-kidney pie, and English-style fish and chips.

The Wrights were looking for a country inn to buy and came up to the Catskills a number of years ago. "As soon as we saw it, we knew this just had to be the place," Peggy said. "We're 2,000 feet high here, and this section of the Catskills has some beautiful old homes and a private park nearby. When we saw the building and realized its potential, we all agreed we would leave the city and become country innkeepers."

There are twelve guest rooms in the inn, all with wash basins, and several with private baths. Rooms with shared baths are furnished with terrycloth bathrobes. "We've tried to preserve the best of what is really appropriate for the building," Tom said, "and have made a few major changes that will provide more bathrooms." These guest rooms are rather small and cozy and definitely of the country inn variety.

At the first opportunity I asked about the renovation activity, and Tom and Peggy explained that they are adding an additional section to the dining room with beautiful big windows overlooking the impressive Catskills. "The room faces west so we're looking for some beautiful sunsets. We will not be adding any more tables to the dining area, but will change part of the present dining room into a residents' lounge and common room."

Did I mention earlier the strange sculpture on the lawn? Well, Tom and Peggy said they've had a great deal of fun with it. Actually, it's a fiberglass black figure with no insides, done by Marina Karella, titled "Humpty Empty." It has to be seen to be believed. It looks like a pair of black unbuttoned long johns with no head.

The Redcoat's Return and Tom and Peggy were featured in a recent edition of a British hospitality-field trade journal. The article points out that the Redcoat's Return was one of the earliest country inns in the Catskills.

A visit to the Redcoat's Return is always great fun for me, and this was no exception.

THE REDCOAT'S RETURN, Dale Lane, Elka Park, NY 12427; 518-589-6379. A 12-guestroom English inn approx. 4 mi. from Tannersville, N.Y. in the heart of the Catskill Mts. European plan. Lodgings include breakfast. Dinner served daily except Thurs.; no lunches served. Open from Memorial Day to Easter. Closed 1 wk. in early Nov. Please call for details. Within a short drive of several ski areas and state hiking trails. Nature walks, trout fishing, croquet, skiing, swimming, ice skating, riding, tennis nearby. No pets. Tom and Peggy Wright, Innkeepers.

Directions: From the New York Thruway, going north, use Exit 20; going south, use Exit 21. Find Rte. 23A on your map and follow it to Tannersville; turn left at traffic light onto County Rd. 16. Follow signs to Police Center, 4½ mi. Turn right on Dale Lane.

THE ROSE INN
Ithaca, New York

I was born in the Southern Tier country of New York State—in fact, not very far from the town of Ithaca. We used to take Sunday drives around the beautiful Finger Lakes country, with its gorgeous stretches of farmland and hills. It was always great fun to buy apples there.

Perhaps it is because I am so attuned to the characteristics of the region that the flat-topped cupola of the Rose Inn attracted my eye. Many 19th-century New York State homes have such cupolas. I was driving north from Ithaca along the shore of Cayuga Lake, and there on top of a small hill was a gorgeous mansion with the easily recognizable, graceful lines of a mid-19th-century Italianate home.

It was a very special day for me; I'd spoken at a seminar on country innkeeping at Cornell University, and had been promised a tour of the inn, along with dinner, by Sherry and Charles Rosemann, the innkeepers. Charles met me as I was parking the car, and together we started on this lovely experience.

About the first thing I learned is that the Rose Inn is known locally as "the house with the circular staircase."

As Charles explained, "The house is a gem of woodcraft, built of heavy timbers with large, heavy handcut doors of oak. The floors are laid with quarter-sawed oak, inlaid in parquet fashion. It was built and completed in 1851, with the exception of a center staircase that would have led to the cupola. No one capable of completing it could be found. Hundreds of feet of priceless Honduras mahogany were stored for over half a century. In 1922 a master craftsman appeared, and he worked for two years building a circular staircase of that solid mahogany, which extended from the main hall through two stories to the cupola."

The inn displays the ambience of its period. High ceilings, the warm glow of woods from indigenous American trees long gone, marble fireplaces, and period antiques provide an elegant but surprisingly comfortable setting. Sherry Rosemann said, "Telephone callers sometimes ask us what the atmosphere of the inn is like, and we tell them that we have an elegant country mansion that is at the same time intimate and relaxed. To illustrate the point, guests feel as comfortable coming down for dinner casually dressed as they do in formal attire."

Because I have a space limitation, please take my word for it that all of the guest rooms are done in the same beautiful but comfortable fashion.

Dinner is something special. Sterling silver settings and candlelight set the mood for such four-course, single-entrée dinners as rack of lamb with an herbed sauce or scampi Mediterranean, cooked in a light curry and cream sauce. For larger parties there is Chateaubriand grilled over charcoals. Eclectic and ethnic meals are also available, and since dinners

are served only with advance reservations the innkeepers have a chance to create something quite different.

My visit was true to form and I was delighted. At breakfast (Sherry cooks the evening meal and Charles cooks breakfast), Charles explained, "We like to give our guests a good start, and so we have full breakfasts, including hand-squeezed orange juice, our own blend of coffee, homemade jams and jellies, along with fresh fruits, German apple pancakes, french toast, or eggs Benedict."

There are many, many more things to share about the Rose Inn, but I think the best way for such sharing is a visit to the inn itself. It may be known as the inn with the circular staircase, but I think the second most wonderful thing is that Sherry and Charles Rosemann appeared on the scene—just the right people to maintain this beautiful building and permit those of us who love inns to enjoy its hospitality.

THE ROSE INN, 813 Auburn Rd., Rte. 34—P.O. Box 6576, Ithaca, NY 14851; 607-533-4202. A 5-guestroom elegant New York State mansion just a few moments from Cornell University. Breakfast included in room rate; dinner offered by advance reservation. Open all year. Conveniently situated to enjoy the beautiful Finger Lakes scenery and attractions, including Cayuga Lake, wineries, and college campuses. No facilities for children under 10. Arrangements can be made for pets. Charles and Sherry Rosemann, Innkeepers.

Directions: From N.Y. State Thruway take Exit 40 and Rte. 34 south about 36 mi. The inn will be on your left before arriving in Ithaca. From I-81 use Exit 11 (Cortland) to Rte. 13 to Ithaca. Take No. Triphammer Rd. right, 7.4 mi. to inn.

SEDGWICK INN
Berlin, New York

Mr. Currier and Mr. Ives would have loved the Sedgwick Inn. It has the beckoning windows framed by wooden shutters and the traditional white clapboard walls reminiscent of homey farmhouses and buildings seen so often in Currier and Ives colored prints. Although the central part of the building was constructed in 1791 during the Colonial period, the principal architecture is Victorian.

On a moonlit night, as I approached the Sedgwick Inn, I was struck by the feeling of brightness and vitality. The windows of the Coach Room Tavern revealed a scene resembling a Dickens party. The low-ceilinged room, with its antique chairs and tables, was filled with diners. The candles, flickering in their solid brass holders, created a warm, intimate glow. From the animated conversations between the tables, it was evident that many of these patrons were acquainted with one another.

When I mentioned this to innkeeper Bob Evans, he explained that for the most part this was the "Friday night crowd," many of whom were on their way from the city to their weekend or vacation homes. "I think they began to use the Sedgwick as a 'switchover' point," Bob said, "where they were able to change from being city people to being country people. I don't know how it happened," he said. "But everyone seems to have a good time."

Maybe "having a good time" was part of the motivation for Bob and his sculptor-wife, Edie, a most attractive woman from Vienna, when they left their careers in the psychiatric field and became innkeepers. "We had it in mind for some time, and after searching several different areas, decided it was almost providential that this lovely piece of property, which had been a restaurant for many years, became available." It is on Route 22, one of the main roads between New York and Montreal.

Today, Bob and Edie have added considerable dimension to the establishment. They have created some excellent Victorian country inn guest rooms in the main house, and an antique shop in a beautiful one-room building, designed in the neo-classic style of the early 19th century and used, I understand, during the Civil War as a recruiting station. An old carriage house has been converted into an art gallery where old prints, modern paintings, stained glass, and sculpture (including some by Edie) are for sale.

The dinner menus at the Sedgwick Inn are really quite simple, with three entrées and a menu change twice weekly. Menus feature such fare as filet mignon, beef carbonnade, Yankee pot roast, and sole Veronique. Lunch is also served.

After dinner, I had a chance to chat with Edie in the beautifully furnished living room about the transition from being a sculptor to being the cook. "Oh," she laughed, "sculpting was always a hobby with me. Actually, I was a psychiatric social worker and took up sculpting at the Silvermine School of Art in Norwalk, Connecticut, as a diversion. Bob was the director of a children's psychiatric facility on Long Island. I enjoy the fact that every once in a while I have a chance to pick up my chisels and files and return to my studio for an hour or two. I love to create polished figures from the rough stone."

And so the many fascinating elements that make up the Sedgwick Inn—its previous history as a stagecoach stop, a summer house for a prominent New York City family, Edie's Viennese background, and the wonderful enthusiasm that both Bob and Edie bring to innkeeping—have come together. It makes a wonderful mix.

THE SEDGWICK INN, Rte. 22, Berlin, NY 12022; 518-658-2334. A 5-guestroom (private baths) country inn almost midway between Tanglewood, Shaker Village, and Williamstown. European plan. Breakfast, lunch, and dinner served daily, except Mon. Open all year. Conveniently located to enjoy all of the recreational and cultural activities of the Berkshires. Motel accommodations also available. Bob and Edie Evans, Innkeepers.

Directions: The inn is located on Rte. 22 between Petersburg and Stephentown, New York.

1770 HOUSE
East Hampton, Long Island, New York

"Acquiring the 1770 House was part of a longtime dream for us," recounted Sid Perle. "We spent many months searching outer Long Island for just the right place for the ideal country inn." Sid and I were seated in the main living room of the inn, where some of the most recently acquired pieces are from the old Easthampton Post Office. They have been used very cleverly. There was one window labeled, "General Delivery." Another one for money orders now has a tiny television set that disappears completely, if necessary.

We were joined momentarily by Miriam Perle, who is the chef at the inn. She formerly ran a cooking school in Great Neck for twelve years and studied earlier at the Cordon Bleu in Paris.

The menu changes weekly and, with the exception of desserts, it is a complete meal. There are such appetizers as spaghettini with a robust fresh tomato sauce, fresh poached salmon served with three sauces, stuffed artichoke Siciliano, crabcake Edna Lewis—lump crabmeat cake sautéed in a butter and mustard dressing. The salads are different every week, as are the salad dressings.

I asked Miriam about the main dishes. "Well, as you know, we're here on the end of Long Island, where there is lots of fresh fish available. So, our entrées very frequently include stuffed fresh swordfish, lobster creole, and other fish dishes. Tonight, we also have stuffed filet mignon, rack of lamb, roast loin of pork with a lemon-garlic marinade, and your favorite, roast duck with a lingonberry glaze." She knows my great love of roast duckling and knew that she had, indeed, made a conquest.

Downstairs in the Tap Room there is a beautiful beehive fireplace, and many old trivets and other artifacts on the wall. The atmosphere is quite similar to an English pub.

"Your readers might be interested in the fact that on Thanksgiving we have hors d'oeuvres and soup in the Tap Room, then everyone goes upstairs to the main dining room for dinner, and dessert is offered in the library—but not until we have all had a walk in the village!"

The bedrooms are delightful. Several of them have canopied beds and combinations of French and American Victorian antiques, including several bedside tables with marble tops. They are all very romantic, and one in particular on the ground floor overlooking the garden struck my fancy as being an ideal honeymoon suite.

Incidentally, guests at the 1770 House can also be booked at the Mill Garth in Amagansett, just a short distance away. It has fetching rustic cottages, some of which have their own cooking conveniences.

Sid said there have been several references to my quotation from Owen Meredith, which is occasionally used on their menus:

We may live without friends, we may live without books, but civilized man cannot live without cooks.

Sid put an arm around Miriam. "I always tell them that I'm the luckiest guy in the world because I'm married to one of the world's great cooks."

1770 HOUSE, 143 Main St., East Hampton, Long Island, NY 11937; 516-324-1770. A 6-guestroom elegant village inn near the eastern end of Long Island. Open all year. Dinner served Friday through Tuesday during the summer months. During the off-summer months, dinner served Saturday only. During July and August, weekend reservations made for 4 days only and mid-week reservations for 3 days only. Convenient to many cultural and recreational diversions, including antiquing and back-roading. Not comfortable for children under 14. No pets. The Perle Family, Innkeepers.

Directions: From New York City, take the Long Island Expressway to Exit 70, and then turn south to Rte. 27 East, the main street of East Hampton. The inn is located diagonally across the street from Guild Hall.

THE SHERWOOD INN
Skaneateles, New York

Skaneateles is a pleasant village oriented to the lake of the same name, with several impressive old buildings whose integrity has been preserved, although the town has been modernized. The center of activity is undoubtedly the Sherwood Inn.

Talk about a clear day! I stood on the front steps of the Sherwood, looking as far down the lake as I could see. There were a few early-morning fishermen and, even as I watched, a couple of swimmers came to the beach, right in front of the inn.

On this trip something new and rather exciting has been added: a beautifully restored 26-foot mahogany Chris Craft was moored just a few paces from the front of the inn. Known to owner Bill Eberhardt, as well as to the staff of the inn, as the "The Boat," it is the newest of the amenities offered at the Sherwood, and is available for rides on the lake.

This morning I returned to the lobby to find a very unusual display of crafts all made by craftspeople from Skaneateles and the vicinity. For example, there was a display of wooden blocks put together to form a small village. This is part of the Sherwood's continuing effort to bring area crafts and arts to the attention of the traveling public.

In one corner of the lobby, the continental breakfast for inn guests was laid out with orange juice, some tempting sweet rolls, and pots of coffee. On the piano, a print of the inn was displayed.

Many of the sixteen lodging rooms and three apartments have a view of the lake, and almost all of them were completely redecorated within the past year. A community open house was held to show off these rooms and over 350 people attended! Skaneateles is certainly proud of its inn, which is now sporting a new coat of exterior paint.

Like many other New York State hostelries, the Sherwood Inn started its life as a stagecoach tavern and, after several ups and downs, has finally achieved an even greater reputation as a village inn and vacation destination.

Christmas is very colorful and rewarding here. The town itself has more than the usual display of colored lights and wreaths and the inn is ablaze with a joyous Christmas spirit. It so happens that the lobby lends itself very well to an unusually tall Christmas tree that, along with three others, creates a very festive setting for the many community activities and Christmas parties held at the inn. During the holiday season out-of-town guests think they are in some kind of make-believe village.

A recent edition of *Travel and Leisure* featured the village of Skaneateles. The Sherwood Inn received prominent coverage, with particular attention to the inn's Federal-period antiques, oriental rugs, peg-board pine floors, and a special mention of the antique dollhouse and the

fireplaces that send a warm glow into the lobby during the late fall and winter.

Skaneateles is in the heart of New York State's scenic Finger Lakes area, and the inn makes an ideal touring center for a stay of several days while visiting the many other lakes in the area, as well as the nearby vineyards and other western New York places of interest, such as Ithaca, the home of Cornell University.

THE SHERWOOD INN, 26 West Genessee St., Skaneateles, NY 13152; 315-685-3405. A 16-guestroom village inn on the shore of Lake Skaneateles in the Finger Lakes district of New York State. Continental breakfast included in room tariff. Lunch and dinner served daily to travelers. Open every day except Christmas. Tennis, swimming, golf, and indoor winter ice skating available nearby. Near Everson Museum, Barrow Art Gallery, and William Seward House. William and Joy Eberhardt, Owners; Ellen Seymour, Innkeeper.

Directions: From New York State Thruway use Weedsport exit and follow Rte. 34 south to Auburn (6 mi.). Turn east on Rte. 20, 7 mi. to Skaneateles. From the south use Rte. 81 to Cortland, then Rte. 41 to Skaneateles, turning left on Rte. 20 for about 1 mi.

I do not include lodging rates in the descriptions, for the very nature of an inn means that there are lodgings of various sizes, with and without baths, in and out of season, and with plain and fancy decoration. Travelers should call ahead and inquire about the availability and rates of the many different types of rooms.

SIMMONS' WAY VILLAGE INN
Millerton, New York

"We are actually only two hours from Manhattan! Just take the Sawmill River Parkway to Route 684, then Route 22, and on up to Millerton, and here we are."

Robert and Carol Sadlon and I were seated in wicker chairs around one of the round tables on the broad porch of the Simmons' Way Village Inn. A broad lawn swept down to the village street, and there were some old-fashioned street lamps along the driveway. The inn sits right next to a church, sharing some gorgeous trees.

The inn, a comfortable old majestic Victorian, is highly photographable, with a porte cochere, a third floor, and several balconies and porches.

The inn's interior, almost completely renovated, has been done over with great *panache*.

The front doorway leads into a center hall, and on the left is a very cozy parlor with a fireplace and twin couches. In this room, as in all of the other public rooms and guest rooms, the finish has been taken down to the original wood, resulting in some most remarkable colors and hues. The Sadlons' interest in art is reflected throughout the inn with handsome prints and paintings.

Access to the guest rooms is up a twisty little paneled-oak staircase that has two stained-glass windows. In the guest rooms there are spool beds, brass beds, four-poster beds, beds with draped canopies, down pillows, plush linens, handsome wardrobes, beautifully refinished tables and chests of drawers. There are sitting areas and some fireplaces, and each room has a private bath. It is a most romantic environment with a traditional European touch. Each of the guest rooms has its own distinctive color and a wonderful light, airy feeling.

Dinner is also special. The starters include a scallop mousse with chilled prawns, baked Camembert in phylo with honey and almonds; and a ribbon pasta in a light basil cream with walnuts. Some main dishes are grilled Norwegian salmon in a honey ginger butter; breast of duck sautéed with seasonal fruits, grains, and wild rice in an apple brandy sauce; and veal medallions sautéed with wild mushrooms and a morel sauce. These are just part of the seasonally changing menu.

Mention has to be made of the fact that the Sadlons are also the proprietors of the Movie House, right across the street from the inn. There are actually two cinemas available: one on the first floor shows more-or-less conventional films, and a second-floor cinema offers foreign and art films. Cappuccino and light refreshments are offered in the second-floor art gallery. Actually, the Movie House is well patronized by inn guests as well as by local people. As Carol says, "We introduced cappuccino to

Millerton four years ago, and our little café has become an important social endeavor in the village today."

For me one of the memorable things about the Simmons' Way Village Inn is that it is indeed a *village* inn. Millerton is a very pleasant and peaceful little community and the inn is the center of social activity there. Furthermore, it is in a perfect place for parents to make private school visits with their children, since there are at least a half-dozen private schools within a very short distance.

And all of this just two hours from Manhattan!

SIMMONS' WAY VILLAGE INN, Main St., Rte. 44, Millerton, NY 12546; 518-789-6235. An 11-guestroom village inn in a pleasant rural community on the Conn./N.Y. border. Open year-round. Dinner is served Wed. thru Sun. during the winter. Sunday brunch. Starting in April lunch and dinner served every day and afternoon tea on weekends. Convenient for much recreational and cultural activity including the Sharon Playhouse, Music Mountain, Lime Rock Race Track, Rudd Pond State Park with walking trails, antiquing and shopping. Just a few miles from the mansions along the Hudson River. Robert and Carol Sadlon, Innkeepers.

Directions: From New York City take Henry Hudson Pkwy. to Sawmill River Pkwy. to Rte. 684 north and follow Rte. 22 to Millerton.

SPRINGSIDE INN
Auburn, New York

Once again the familiar red clapboards of the Springside Inn, with beautiful hanging flowers on the front porch and more hanging flowers on the little lamps flanking the graceful drive that circles the broad lawns, came into view. It occurred to me that with all of these flowers, plus those in the windowboxes, in the gardens, and in the various dining rooms, this could be known as "the inn of the flowers."

I had driven across New York State on Route 20, after a short visit with Helen Tobin at the Lincklaen House in Cazenovia and Bill Eberhardt at the Sherwood Inn in Skaneateles. Nearing the center of town, I kept my eye out and turned left on Route 38, proceeding to the traffic circle and then down the west shore of Owasco Lake.

Many years ago when I was about eight years old, my father and mother drove from where we lived in Elmira, New York, to this very spot on the shore of the lake, where there was a wonderful amusement park. What a great day that was to ride the then world-famous roller coaster. The park is no longer in existence and I must say I really haven't enjoyed roller coasters since.

Bill Dove, who said he had been keeping a weather eye cocked for me, was waiting on the porch and suggested that it would be time to have some "breakfast in a basket," fruit and homemade muffins, offered to every Springside Inn guest as a part of the room rate. "The first person down plugs in the coffee pot," he said with a smile. "Norm, you'd be surprised at how many guests send us thank-you notes for this breakfast."

Springside Inn is in the heart of New York State's Finger Lakes District. I've been visiting it for many years and each time Bill has some more news for me about activities at the inn.

"Before Barbara passed away in 1983, both she and I had always been interested in the theater," he remarked, "so it seemed like a wonderful idea to combine good food and good theater. Our dinner theater, begun at least fourteen years ago, has been increasingly popular every year. The current production is *George M.*"

"I'll tell you who's been doing a wonderful job here, and that's Abe Eberhardt, my daughter Missy's husband. He is a real 'jack-of-all-trades' and is a great asset to the inn. He can fix everything from leaky faucets to refrigeration units. During the busy summer months, he works in the kitchen behind the broiler. We're going to have a couple of new guest rooms probably in 1985, and he is responsible for most of the work."

Our breakfast completed, we walked inside and up the red-carpeted stairway to the second floor to look at several of the guest rooms. Each of them is decorated to give a different feeling; one is in shades of pink, with a pink bedspread and matching curtains. There are friendly rocking chairs in front of the window overlooking the small pond and the lake beyond. Still another guest room has twin beds, Victorian furniture, and lamps with red bows. By way of contrast, the room on the top floor is done in shades of beige and yellow with formal valances on the windows, a Tiffany-type lamp, hooked rugs, and twin beds.

I noticed that there were small baskets of cheese and Finger Lakes wine in each of the guest rooms.

We wandered into the main dining room, the Surrey Room, and from my first visit I remember the authentic turn-of-the-century lamps that lend a pleasant feminine elegance to what otherwise might be considered a masculine room. By the way, the Sunday brunch and the family dinner, served for many years at the inn, still continue to be real culinary treats.

"You know, Norm, I'm always surprised and happy to see so many of our guests from Canada. Many of them come from Toronto and Montreal, and some have been coming back for years."

SPRINGSIDE INN, 41 West Lake Rd., Auburn, NY 13021; 315-252-7247. A 7-guestroom (some shared baths) country inn, 1 mi. south of Auburn with a view of Owasco Lake, in the heart of the historical Finger Lakes. Lodgings include continental breakfast. Open every day; however, may be closed during the month of Jan. Boating, swimming, bicycling on grounds. Golf, riding, alpine and xc skiing nearby. The Dove Family, Innkeepers.

Directions: From N.Y. Thruway, take Exit 40 and follow Rte. 34 south through downtown Auburn to Rte. 38. Follow Rte. 38 south to traffic circle at lake and take 2nd exit right at west shore of Owasco Lake. Drive ¼ mi. to inn.

SWISS HUTTE
Hillsdale, New York

Tom and Linda Breen are people of many enthusiasms. Happily enough, most of them can be found here at this alpine country inn located in the southwest corner of the Berkshires in a valley formed by mountains reminiscent of the Bavarian Alps, where Linda was born. (I am happy to say I had a very pleasant visit with her brother in Munich a few years ago.)

Nestled among the firs and hemlocks, the inn's architecture has a distinctly alpine feel that impresses first-time guests almost without fail. Dinner guests, as well as those enjoying overnight accommodations,

Catamount ski area

have the pleasure of an unobstructed view of Catamount Ski Area, very spectacular in the wintertime, and equally so during the other seasons. The uphill lifts and the start of the cross-country ski trails are literally within walking distance of the inn's front door.

On a lovely July afternoon I took the short drive from Stockbridge to Great Barrington and then bore west on Route 23 toward New York State. After turning at the Swiss Hutte sign, I followed the road down a gentle slope past the swimming pool, the tennis courts, and the putting green to the swift-running brook where masses of flowers caught my eye.

Flowers are one of Tom's enthusiasms. He has not only a beautiful rose garden, but a perennial garden with over 150 different plants providing a serene country atmosphere. Many's the time I've found Tom in his chef's whites attending his beloved flowers, and at the same time keeping a watchful eye on preparations for the evening meal in his spotless kitchen.

A very attractive gazebo on the bank of the pond creates an almost

Japanese effect. Large boulders placed around the shoreline are interspersed with plantings, and after night falls there are gay colored lights illuminating the trees.

Accommodations at the Swiss Hutte are in the main inn where there are country inn-type rooms, and in chalet-type motel units, each with its own balcony and an excellent view of the mountains.

Apart from the natural beauty, perhaps the inn is best known for its food, another great enthusiasm shared by Linda and Tom. Both lunch and dinner are leisurely affairs with individually prepared dishes. Since the time of my first visit in early 1970, I have always enjoyed many of the mid-European specialties, such as Wiener schnitzel; however, among other menu items are french pancakes filled with chicken, sweetbreads in Béarnaise sauce, sauerbraten, and veal chops Normande. The French and Swiss specialties have received many awards.

Linda is very particular about the salads. "We feel that they must be fresh and cool and we try to have a perfect combination of oil and vinegar along with the condiments," she said. "They are delicious when they are eaten with fresh, hot french bread."

Among the desserts, which are included in the price of the main dish, are crème caramel, french apple torte cheesecake, and a super-delicious raspberry cream pie.

Other diversions to be enjoyed at the Swiss Hutte include tennis, swimming, hiking, downhill and cross-country skiing, and many other seasonal attractions. In summer, Tanglewood, Jacob's Pillow, and the Berkshire Playhouse are just a few miles away. The Berkshire and nearby New York State backroading is exceptional with dirt roads that lead through the forest.

SWISS HUTTE, Hillsdale, NY 12529; 518-325-3333. A 21-guestroom alpine country inn overlooking Catamount ski area, 6 mi. from Gt. Barrington, MA. MAP (omits lunch) required on weekends; MAP or European plan during week. Breakfast, lunch and dinner served to travelers daily. Closed April and Nov. 15 to Dec. 15. Pool, tennis, putting green, alpine and xc skiing on grounds. Tom and Linda Breen, Innkeepers.

Directions: From Boston, travel on Mass. Tpke. and take Exit 2. Follow Rte. 102 to Rte. 7. Proceed on Rte. 7 to Rte. 23. From New York City, follow Taconic Pkwy. and Rte. 23. From Albany, follow N.Y. Thruway and Taconic Pkwy. Inn is 10 mi. east of Pkwy. on Rte. 23.

THREE VILLAGE INN
Stony Brook, Long Island, New York

On a fresh August morning, I was sitting in one of the beach chairs under a tree on the terrace in front of my cottage at the Three Village Inn. Seagulls circled over the scene, which included the broad lawn leading down to the marina, with its many sailboats and cruisers, to the marshes beyond and the low cliffs on the northern shore of Long Island in the distance. A friendly robin lighted on the rustic fence and began poking his way through the entangled rambler roses.

The previous afternoon, I had taken the ferry from Bridgeport, Connecticut, to Port Jefferson, Long Island, a trip that took an hour and thirty minutes, and then followed Route 25A through one or two villages, arriving at Stony Brook just about six-thirty in the evening. Once again it

was Whitney Roberts, who has literally grown up in this inn, who greeted me with the news that his mother and father, Monda and Nelson, along with his brother, Larry, would be joining me for dinner a little later on.

The Three Village Inn is, at all odds, a Long Island institution and tradition in one of the most interesting and well-preserved towns on Long Island. The Roberts family has a background of innkeeping which began with Whitney's grandfather, who came from Rockland, Maine, and opened a restaurant called "The Maine Maid" in nearby Jericho, Long Island.

Originally, accommodations were found only in the main house of the inn, but since 1971, the year of my first visit, several cottages have been refurbished or built to accommodate guests, some of which face the yacht club and marina. These are furnished with Colonial reproductions, and some have fireplaces. Monda Roberts says that they are quite a favorite with honeymooners.

From my very first visit I realized that Nelson (he's the head chef) and Monda Roberts have placed great emphasis on the food. They are very particular about some things, including not using foil for baked potatoes, and baking them in rotation through the evening. Vegetables are fresh whenever they are available. The menu is quite extensive and includes a great deal of beef, pork, veal, and lamb, as well as the fresh seafood. The extra touch of serving sherbet with the main meal is something I have always enjoyed. Desserts include such things as apple crisp, homemade cakes, indian pudding, and delicious fruit pies and tarts. They are all made in the inn's kitchen.

In addition to walking along the sandy beach behind the inn and watching the boats from the marina, there are many things to do on the north shore of Long Island, which is rich in Colonial history. There's quite a gathering at twelve o'clock noon each day at the Stony Brook post office where an enormous carved wooden eagle with a twenty-foot wingspread slowly flaps its wings.

"In the off-season we have a lot of people from Manhattan come out for a restful weekend, because everyone is working at such a pace these days," Monda told me. "During the week visitors to SUNY at Stony Brook are frequent guests. By the way, it is possible to come from Kennedy Airport to the Three Village Inn by limousine for a relatively reasonable rate. We can make arrangements." The inn is about sixty miles from New York City.

Nelson and Monda Roberts and their sons have been at the Three Village Inn since 1946, and since 1978 they have been the innkeeper/owners. It's given me a great deal of pleasure to be visiting it since 1971.

THREE VILLAGE INN, 150 Main St., Stony Brook, L.I., NY 11790; 516-751-0555. A 9-room village inn with 23 adjacent cottage motel accommodations, 5 mi. from Port Jefferson, on Long Island's historic north shore. European plan. Lunch and dinner served to travelers daily. Closed Christmas. Near the museums of Stony Brook. Golf, swimming, and boating nearby. Special attention given to handicapped persons. No pets. Nelson and Monda Roberts, Innkeepers.

Directions: From L.I. Expressway, take Exit 62 and travel north on Nichols Rd. to Rte. 25A. Turn left on Rte. 25A and proceed to next light. Turn right onto Main St. and travel straight ahead to inn. Available from New England via L.I. ferries from Bridgeport during the summer. Ferry reservations advisable. (N.Y.: 516-473-0286; Conn.: 203-367-8571.)

THE HOLLOWAY HOUSE RESTAURANT
East Bloomfield, New York

Doreen Wayne's letter was most welcome and filled with interesting news. "It's hard to believe that this is our twenty-fifth year at the Holloway House. What a lot has happened in that time. Our children have grown up and married, and we have all worked hard at maintaining and improving Holloway House.

"We are still doing all the things that are our specialties—Steve's wife, Dawn, is baking our Sally Lunn bread and rolls and pies; the summer Friday night buffet is popular and we've increased the number of our Sunday guests by offering a variety of lighter, full-course dinners."

Other entrées at the Holloway House include chicken, ham, lamb, steaks, scallops, flounder, and prime rib on a Saturday evening.

Holloway House is a real family adventure.

THE HOLLOWAY HOUSE RESTAURANT, Rtes. 5 & 20, East Bloomfield, NY 14443; 716-657-7120. A country restaurant 8 mi. west of Canandaigua, N.Y. No lodgings. Lunch served daily 12 to 2 p.m.; dinner—5:30 to 8:30 p.m., Sunday—12 to 7:30 p.m. Closed Mon. Open April 1 thru Thanksgiving. Sonnenberg Gardens, golf courses, and Finger Lake Racetrack nearby. Fred, Doreen, and Mildred Wayne, Innkeepers.

Directions: From N.Y. State Thruway, take Exit 45. Follow Rte. 96S 3 mi. to Victor, N.Y. At the third traffic light go south on Maple Ave., 5 mi. to Holcomb. Turn right at light and then take second left to Rte. 5 and 20.

CLARKSON HOUSE RESTAURANT
Lewiston, New York

Just a few minutes from Niagara Falls, the Clarkson House is very popular with regular diners who live in the area. Roast prime ribs of beef, New York strip sirloin, live Maine lobsters, fabulous baked potatoes, Cherries Jubilee, Baked Alaska, and a puff pastry stuffed with ice cream and topped with hot fudge sauce are some of the menu treats to consider. Special children's items are available

On the walls of the dining room there is a collection of tools and gadgets used more than one hundred years ago. "They haven't discovered the use for some of them!" said Marilyn Clarkson. There are old-fashioned kerosene lamps on the tables, and the walls have several good paintings interspersed with wall lamps.

Of great interest is the lobster tank that holds up to 200 lobsters in artificial sea water.

THE CLARKSON HOUSE RESTAURANT, 810 Center St., Lewiston, NY 14092; 716-754-4544. A country restaurant, 7 mi. from Niagara Falls and Olde Fort Niagara. No lodgings. Dinner served daily except Mon. Closed Christmas. Bob and Marilyn Clarkson, Innkeepers.

Directions: From I-190, exit at Lewiston and follow Rte. 104E for 1½ mi. Turn right on Rte. 18F and travel 2 blocks west to restaurant.

Favorite Back Roads

Our very favorite back road is one that we have shared with many, many guests. The destination is a small historic village nestled in the Helderberg Mountains. The eleven-mile drive is truly scenic, with lovely Catskill Mountain views all the way. The village itself was once a prosperous milling community. The beautiful homes and churches are a true find for anyone with an interest in 18th- or 19th-century architecture. My favorite reason for visiting the village is the State Preserve, located just at the end of town. The Preserve is like a well-kept secret! There are trails to walk leading to a quiet, peaceful lake, and an absolutely gorgeous waterfall that's perfect for walking under and up in the summertime! We like to direct people on alternate routes going and returning. Both routes offer antique shops and country stores that shouldn't be missed. One country store boasts an inventory of over 1,000 items—anything anyone could possibly want from fresh cut flowers to new snow tires!

Barbara and Laura Stevens
Greenville Arms
Greenville, New York

COLLIGAN'S STOCKTON INN
Stockton, New Jersey

Coming across the bridge from Pennsylvania to New Jersey, you can see the double outside gallery of Colligan's Stockton Inn. There are old stones, white pillars, and the mansard roof on the third floor.

Evidently, there's been an accommodation here on this site since about 1710, although the present building, or most of it, dates back about 150 years. The stone walls have the wonderful weathered look that comes with Pennsylvania–New Jersey stone.

I paid Colligan's a surprise visit early in March just to see what Todd Drucquer might be up to these days. Taking the rear entrance, past the famous wishing well, named after the song by Rodgers and Hart, I noticed a little blackboard saying that Easter would be celebrated at Stockton's Inn with a special family menu, and the week of April 11 to 17 would be Chocolate Week. Lunchers were in the rather gay gardenlike room in the back.

The five dining rooms have the narrow windows typical of their time, set into the thick walls. Five fireplaces bring a cheery atmosphere to the low ceilings and random-width floors.

As I wandered through the front dining room with the wonderful murals, my good friend of many years, Todd Drucquer, came bounding in, and I was caught up by his wonderful ebullience as we started on a tour of the inn.

I exclaimed over the truly unusual murals that have been there for years. "These were painted a number of years ago on the plaster walls and they depict the countryside as it was during the early part of the 19th century," he said. "As you see, we've been carefully restoring some of them, but it's a very painstaking process. These murals are one of the reasons Penny and I fell in love with this place."

About the tavern section he commented, "This has been here for the entire life of the inn. It's where the local townspeople come at the end of the day. It belongs to the town, and like an Englishman's pub it's 'their' place."

We continued into a large dining room with glass on two sides. "Actually there are three areas in the inn," he told me. "There's the old inn building itself, then this room with its open feeling, and we have entertainment here. Outside, we have the Old World Garden with waterfalls, hanging plants, two trout pools that supply fresh trout for our table, and lots of *gemütlichkeit*. As you see, it's an open garden with a roof overhead, and we're open for lunch and dinner from Memorial Day until Labor Day." The atmosphere here reminded me very much of surburban Vienna restaurants.

We returned to the main dining room and I asked Todd about the menu. "We serve such dishes as boneless roast duckling, rainbow trout, sirloin steak Roquefort, rack of lamb Persille, and Colligan's deviled crab cake. Our Lobster Night and our Roast Beef Night on Monday and Wednesday are very popular. We serve a full luncheon every day, designed for people who want a light lunch or something a little more substantial; it seems to work out rather well."

Guest rooms are attractively furnished, with the modern addition of air conditioning and color TV. The Colligan and Stockton suites each have two rooms with a fireplace and period antiques. A few steps away is the Carriage House, and a bit farther down the block is a handsome house, newly restored and decorated, with more guest rooms.

There's a wonderful bustle about Colligan's Stockton Inn. Part of it is perhaps a throwback to the days when Stockton itself was a port and shipping point for farmers, where the Delaware River traffic stopped off.

COLLIGAN'S STOCKTON INN, Route 29, Stockton, NJ 08559; 609-397-1250. An 11-guestroom (some suites) traditional inn in a Delaware River village. Lunch and dinner served every day. Open all year except Christmas Day. All of the scenic, historic, and cultural attractions of nearby Bucks County, Pa., and New Jersey are within a very short distance. No pets. Todd and Penny Drucquer, Innkeepers.

Directions: From New York City: Take New Jersey Tpke. south to Exit 10, then follow I-287 north of Somerville, exiting to Rte. 22 west. Go 2 ½ mi. and then take Rte. 202 south, past Flemington to the Delaware River. Use the last exit in New Jersey, marked "Rte. 29, Lambertville and Stockton." Go 3 mi. north on 29 to Stockton. From Philadelphia: Follow I-95 north to the Delaware River. Cross the Delaware to the first exit in New Jersey, marked "29 Trenton/Lambertville." Follow 29 north through Lambertville, approx. 17 mi. to Stockton.

THE MAINSTAY INN & COTTAGE
Cape May, New Jersey

"What is Renaissance Revival?" I inquired of Tom and Sue Carroll as we were sitting on the side porch of the Mainstay Inn having a cup of tea in the afternoon.

"It's interesting that you should mention that," remarked Sue, "because our furniture here is almost all Renaissance Revival. It's flowing to the eye with graceful curves. Walnut was used extensively during the 1870s, and there are very tall mirrors, tall headboards and wardrobes. They're a shock compared to things today. I think the fun of staying here is that you are seeing furniture that would probably never go in your house, and it can be very exciting."

In a community that has gained a great reputation for Victorian restoration and revival, the Mainstay Inn is an outstanding example. It was built in 1856 by wealthy Southern planters as an elegant gambling club. The first operator of the club, a Mississippi showboat minstrel,

employed a lady to rock on the front porch, watching for the police. If she rocked violently, the gamblers inside would quickly stash their evidence, and when the police arrived, they would be having a harmless musicale.

After such a flamboyant beginning, in 1896 the house was sold, quixotically enough, to a sedate Philadelphia family, who added the back wing and entertained some of the great and near-great of Philadelphia society during the many years that followed.

Today, the Mainstay is a lovely guest house in one of the most unusual remaining Victorian environments: the town of Cape May, New Jersey. Tom Carroll had pointed out to me that there are over 600 Victorian buildings in Cape May in various stages of restoration and preservation.

The drawing room has Victorian wallpaper, which can be seen in the Bradbury & Bradbury wallpaper catalog and also in some of their advertising. This is a carefully researched, authentic Victorian reproduction.

Since my last visit, Tom and Sue have created one of the most dramatic Victorian hallways in the country, with ceiling decorations, stenciling, oriental carpeting with brass rods on the staircase, gold cording as a rail. They've been refinishing floors, repairing wood, and finding old brass hinges, among other things. John Burrows, who is extremely talented in this field, stayed at the Mainstay and has done the intricate work. He is becoming recognized as an expert in Victorian decoration.

Upstairs, the guest rooms have such dramatic furnishings as ten-foot mirrors, ornately carved headboards, and marble-top dressers. Under some of the beds are chamber pots that roll out on wooden trays, and other beds have the original mosquito nets, attached to small pulleys in the ceilings.

The only meal served at the Mainstay is breakfast, offered in warm weather on the broad veranda, and on cool mornings in the Grand Dining Room. The house tour is conducted every day at 3:30 p.m. for both houseguests and interested visitors. Everyone is invited for tea after the tour.

Tom and Sue have renovated the beautiful old house next to the Mainstay, and now provide a total of twelve guest rooms in the two houses. They are all decorated in the Victorian manner and named for famous Americans who visited Cape May.

It's been quite some time since my very first visit to meet Tom and Sue, who at that time had another Victorian cottage also called the Mainstay. They moved to their present location a number of years ago, and it's been continual progress ever since.

THE MAINSTAY INN & COTTAGE, 635 Columbia Ave., Cape May, NJ 08204; 609-884-8690. A 12-guestroom inn in a well-preserved Victorian village just one block from the ocean. Breakfast served to houseguests. Open every day from Apr. thru Oct.; weekends in Nov. Open Sat. in Dec. for Christmas house tours. Boating, swimming, fishing, bicycles, riding, golf, tennis, and hiking nearby. Not suitable for small children. No pets. No credit cards; personal checks accepted. Tom and Sue Carroll, Innkeepers.

Directions: From Philadelphia take the Walt Whitman Bridge to the Atlantic City Expy. Follow the Atlantic City Expy. to exit for Garden State Pkwy., south. Go south on the Pkwy., which ends in Cape May. The Pkwy. becomes Lafayette St.; turn left at first light onto Madison. Proceed 3 blocks and turn right onto Columbia. Proceed 3 blocks to inn on right side.

BARLEY SHEAF FARM
Holicong, Pennsylvania

Ann Mills told me that I should not miss the pair of Canada geese who herd their four goslings in and out of the pond every morning. "The mother and father arrive every spring and stay long enough to produce the eggs and guide the family, and then a few weeks later they all fly away. The parents come back again every year."

Rather than disturb them, I sat on the terrace of Barley Sheaf Farm looking down across the lawns over the old stone fence, bordered by gorgeous spring flowers and covered with vines, into what could best be described as the next lower level of lawn, where the geese, the pond, and the swimming pool were.

Earlier that morning, lying abed in my room, which had been fashioned out of one of the original outbuildings of the farm, I became aware of the fact that Barley Sheaf was a series of foregrounds and backgrounds. For example, on the walls and window sills beside my brass bed there were several country artifacts. Then out of one of the windows, I could look over the red brick walks and farm fence in the foreground across the fields to the line of trees in the background. The

other window provided a wonderful view of the old barn on the property. This handsome building, which saw service on this property for most of the 19th century, if not longer, has the recognizable earmarks of an early Pennsylvania antiquity. The stone pillars and walls support the second and third floors, constructed of long plank siding. Meanwhile, the sounds of the mourning doves and busy birds filled the Bucks County morning air with their anticipation of another busy day.

Located in the heart of Bucks County, north of Philadelphia, Barley Sheaf Farm has been designated a National Historic Site; the original part of the farm dates back to 1740. There are chickens and horned Dorsets on the property, and the eggs that are eaten for breakfast are often straight from the nest. There are also beehives, and the wildflower honey they yield is often taken home by the guests. Almost everything comes from the farm and the bread is baked fresh every day.

The emphasis of Barley Sheaf Farm is more on hospitality than on farming. The living rooms and reception areas are adorned with impressive Early American oils and prints, and there's a decided interest by all the Mills family in Early American antiques.

Guest rooms indicate a continuous labor of love, as country antiques abound and personal touches, such as the international doll collection in one of the bedrooms, provide a homey feeling. Each room has its own distinct character and flavor; one has a mahogany sleigh bed with a Hitchcock dresser and still another has an antique iron bed with a very handsome quilt. There's an antique brass bed and a fireplace in the master bedroom suite, with a lovely view of the terrace.

The latest news from Don and Ann Mills is that the barn I mentioned a little earlier is being renovated and four suites will be added to the ten rooms, plus an apartment for Don Jr., and his family and one for Don and Ann. The barn will have lovely views of the horse farm next to the property. There will be an exciting large living room and in the future some other great possibilities because the barn is roomy.

Now, what about my Canada geese? I hadn't seen them yet. Could they have indeed flown off on the very morning of my arrival? Ah, I could now see a long graceful neck among the grasses along the edge of the pond and, sure enough, a four-gosling flotilla was heading out across the placid waters. Whatever else might happen today, the geese would be at Barley Sheaf Farm.

BARLEY SHEAF FARM, Box 10, Holicong, PA 18928; 215-794-5104. A 14-guestroom bed-and-breakfast inn, 8 mi. from Doylestown and New Hope, Pa. A full breakfast is the only meal served. Open Valentine's Day thru weekend prior to Christmas. Minimum 2-night stay on weekends; 3-night minimum on holiday weekends. Near Delaware River, Bucks County Playhouse, George Washington's Crossing. Croquet, badminton, swimming pool, farm animals on grounds. Tennis, boating, canoeing, and horseback riding nearby. Near all of the natural and historical attractions of Bucks County, Pa. Recommended for children over 8. No credit cards. Don and Ann Mills, and Don Mills, Jr., Innkeepers.

Directions: Barley Sheaf Farm is on Rte. 202 between Doylestown and Lahaska.

CAMERON ESTATE INN
Mount Joy, Pennsylvania

Betty Groff was telling me about the history of the Donegal Presbyterian Church, which adjoins the Cameron Estate Inn property. We had been wandering around the parklike grounds of the inn and quite naturally gravitated toward this historic spot.

"Founded by Irish settlers prior to 1721, this is the church with the famous Witness Tree. On a Sunday morning in September, 1777, an express rider came to the church with the news that the British Army under Lord Howe had left New York to invade Pennsylvania. Challenged to show proof of their patriotism, they joined hands around the historic tree and declared their loyalty to the new cause of liberty and to the founding of a new nation."

As we walked beside a woodland stream, she pointed out the many trout darting about in it. "We stock this stream with trout, which our guests may fish for," she said. Standing for a moment on an old stone bridge, she continued the narrative. "As you know, Abe and I live right here in Mount Joy and we've been operating the Groff Farm Restaurant for quite a few years. But we've always wanted to own an inn and we had our envious eye for a long time on this estate."

Agreeing to meet for dinner later on, Betty and I separated at the front door of the inn, a most impressive red brick mansion, built in 1805, with attractive dormer windows on the third floor. I speculated mentally that the broad veranda running around three sides of the inn probably had been added later in the 19th century.

Stepping inside, I found the interior to be exactly what one would have expected in a mansion: large living rooms, a library, generous-sized bedrooms, some with canopy beds and a great many with fireplaces. There are many oriental rugs and period furnishings chosen by Abe and Betty to define the historical significance of the inn. These are fitting complements to the fine paneling and marble embellishments.

Dinner that evening in the main dining room was another baronial experience, with excellent service, delicate china, and fine silverware against pristine napery. The menu included roast Long Island duckling with a mandarin orange sauce; chicken sauté "Simon Cameron" served with ham and complemented by a wine-and-cheese sauce, and white asparagus; and a succulent Steak Diane. These are an interesting contrast to the dinners offered at nearby Groff's Farm Restaurant, which specializes in Pennsylvania Dutch food. Many inn guests also eat there.

Betty Groff is the author of two best-selling cookbooks: *Good Earth Country Cooking* and *Betty Groff's Country Goodness Cookbook*. She's also been seen on many TV programs and featured in magazine articles.

CAMERON ESTATE INN, R.D. #1, Box 305, Donegal Springs Rd., Mount Joy, PA 17552; 717-653-1773. An 18-guestroom (16 with private baths) elegant inn in a former mansion, 4½ mi. from Mt. Joy and Elizabethtown. Complimentary continental breakfast. Lunch and dinner served every day except Sun. and Christmas. Open year-round. Convenient to all of the attractions in the Pennsylvania Dutch Amish country, as well as the Hershey and Lancaster museums, art galleries, crafts shops, and theaters; halfway between Gettysburg and Valley Forge. No children under 12. No pets. Abram and Betty Groff, Innkeepers.

Directions: The inn is situated in the heart of the triangle formed by Harrisburg, York, and Lancaster. Traveling west on Pennsylvania Tpke. take Exit 21. Follow Rte. 222 S to Rte. 30 W to Rte. 283 W. Follow Rte. 283 W to Rte. 230 (the first Mt. Joy exit). Follow Rte. 230 through Mt. Joy to the 4th traffic light. Turn left onto Angle St. At first crossroads, turn right onto Donegal Springs Rd. Go to the stop sign. Turn left onto Colebrook Rd. Go just a short distance over a small bridge. Turn right, back onto Donegal Springs Rd. Follow signs to inn—about ½ mi. on the right. Traveling east on the Pa. Tpke. take Rte. 72 at Lebanon Exit to the Square in Manheim. Turn right on W. High St. This becomes the Manheim–Mt. Joy Rd. Follow directly into Mt. Joy. At the first traffic light, turn right onto Main St. Follow Main St. to the next traffic light. At light turn left onto Angle St. Follow above directions from Angle St.

THE CENTURY INN
Scenery Hill, Pennsylvania

Her name was Julia and she was one of the guests at the Century Inn. She said that she and her husband had been on a two-week inn tour and she thought that this was certainly by far the most authentic of all the inns that they had visited.

According to Webster, the word "authentic" means "genuine; free from admixture, adulteration, sham, etc." With this in mind, there's no doubt that about 90% of the Century Inn is authentic, because almost every piece of furniture is indeed an antique and almost every print or painting has a true authenticity.

Julia and I continued down the hallway and looked in on Room 5, which will probably never be occupied because it is jampacked with the most marvelous collection of dolls and doll clothing and doll carriages and small dollhouses. The inn has a sort of continuing collection of Americana—everything from Colonial to Norman Rockwell. Its seasonal decorations, especially those for Halloween, are always fun.

I had arrived the day before in the brisk dusk of a late October evening. I walked up the front walk past the pillars on the stone-paved porch and through the front door. The beautiful antique-blessed interior and front sitting room with the Whiskey Rebellion flag is just as it was during the time of my first visit many years before, when I met innkeepers Gordon and Mary Harrington. We talked all through dinner and far into the night of the things that inn-seekers enjoy so much: history, music, art, the lovely countryside, and, of course, the newest addition, George Franklin Harrington III.

The Century Inn remains what it has been for so many years: the pride of the community and a place sought out by true lovers of country

inns. They've been coming for many years to enjoy stuffed pork chops, roast turkey, seafood, whipped potatoes, sweet potatoes, absolutely scrumptious cole slaw, and homemade pies. Lately, new dishes have been added—beef burgundy, filet mignon, and breaded shrimp.

Today, my new-found inn-friend, Julia, and I were looking through all of the dining rooms and bedrooms that reflect the true passion for collecting that was really started by Gordon's mother and father. Now there are even more things than ever being proudly shown.

The inn was decorated for Halloween with many arrangements of cornstalks and colorful autumn leaves. A very fierce pumpkin glared at me from one of the tables. We peeked into the kitchen where a few of the ladies of the village who have been employed at the inn for many years were preparing the Saturday evening meal. We continued on into the Keeping Room with its huge fireplace and truly astonishing collection of old tools and artifacts hung around the mantel. This is a cozy dining room of the inn and many a lovely meal have I enjoyed in this pleasant atmosphere.

The Century Inn was built before 1794 and is the oldest continuously operating tavern on the National Pike, most of which is today's U.S. 40. Consequently, the inn has played an important role in the history of southwest Pennsylvania. General Lafayette stopped here on May 26, 1825, and Andrew Jackson was a guest twice, once on his way to his inauguration as President of the United States.

Knowing how much of themselves Gordon and Mary Harrington have put into this inn, Julia and I agreed that they must be very pleased that Gordon Franklin Harrington III, was already off to a good start as a third-generation innkeeper.

THE CENTURY INN, Scenery Hill, PA 15360; 412-945-6600 or 5180. A 10-guestroom village inn on Rte. 40, 12 mi. east of Washington, Pa., 35 mi. south of Pittsburgh. European plan. Breakfast served to houseguests only. Lunch and dinner served to travelers daily. Closed approx. mid-Dec. to mid-March. Contact inn for exact opening and closing dates. No pets. No credit cards. Personal checks welcome. Meggin and Gordon Harrington, Jr., Innkeepers.

Directions: From the east, exit the Pa. Tpke. at New Stanton. Take I-70W to Rte. 917S (Bentleyville exit) to Rte. 40E and go 1 mi. east to inn. From the north, take Rte. 19S to Rte. 519S to Rte. 40E and go 5 mi. east to inn or take I-79S to Rte. 40E and go 9 mi. east to inn. From the west, take I-70E to I-79S to Rte. 40E and go 9 mi. east to inn.

EVERMAY-ON-THE-DELAWARE
Erwinna, Pennsylvania

It was six o'clock in the morning at Evermay-on-the-Delaware. The sun was coming up over the river and the geese were heralding the first streaks of daylight.

I had a grandstand seat to the first act of the new day from the window of my third-floor bedroom. It had a very intimate feeling and was furnished with Victorian furniture and an oriental rug, as were the other third-floor rooms.

I raised the window, more easily to hear the first sounds of the happy birds as they swooped from tree to tree along the banks of the Delaware River, building nests and lifting paeans of praise to morning. At that early hour there were very few cars on the river road and I felt very much as if I were in my own private world. What music would best accompany such a scene? I decided that Grieg's "Morning" from the *Peer Gynt Suite* would be best.

Long before Ron Strouse and Fred Cresson, former innkeepers of the Sign of the Sorrel Horse in nearby Quakertown, discovered and explored the full potential of this lovely property, Evermay had existed as an accommodation as far back as 1871. The original part of the house was built in 1700 by a prominent family in the valley. A 1905 photograph in the parlor of the inn shows that it has hardly been changed since that date.

A great deal of work has been done restoring the woodland garden, cutting wider paths, trimming back the evergreens, and planting five hundred daffodils, narcissus, and tulip bulbs.

A fenced-in pasture is complete, and they moved their sheep, goats, and geese from Quakertown to Erwinna. Ron tells me that Rosebud, Jenny-Rebecca, and Greta should have kids in the spring, and Shelba and

Mary Elizabeth Alexandra should have lambs. They've invited me down when it's time to milk the goats. A proper pen, complete with a lattice roof, has also been constructed for the peacocks. Animals are an important part of Ron's life, and flowers and plants are important to Fred, so I'm sure that future guests will always find something exciting and unusual in both departments.

Beside the snug rooms on the top floor, Evermay also has larger, second-floor, master-sized bedrooms, many with fireplaces. The views from the front of the inn include the Delaware River, but I find that the views from the rear are equally inviting. These include the meadows and gardens that Ron and Fred have developed, as well as the hills beyond. Additional bedrooms are now available in the recently remodeled carriage barn.

One of the reasons for the inn's immediate popularity undoubtedly is the cuisine. Dinner is prix fixe, usually five courses and a choice of two or three entrées. Ron and Fred request that gentlemen wear coats and ties in the dining room and since there is only one seating at 7:30 p.m., reservations are necessary.

At Evermay, the price of the room includes breakfast and also afternoon tea. "Many of our guests arrive late afternoon after driving from New York or Philadelphia," Fred said, "and we serve a proper tea that will hold them until dinner."

Besides all of the enjoyable but hard work that is being done on the grounds, Fred and Ron have now converted the Dusty Dove House into an antique and gift shop.

EVERMAY-ON-THE-DELAWARE, Erwinna, PA 18920; 215-294-9100. A 16-guestroom riverside inn in upper Bucks County. Breakfast and afternoon tea included in the room tariff. Box lunches available for houseguests. Dinner served Fri., Sat., Sun., and holidays at 7:30 p.m. by reservation. Open every day for lodging except Dec. 24. Convenient to all of the Bucks County natural and historical attractions, including handsome mansions, museums, and amusements for small children. No pets. Ron Strouse and Fred Cresson, Innkeepers.

Directions: From New York City, take Rte. 22 to Clinton; Rte. 31 to Flemington; Rte. 12 to Frenchtown. Cross river and turn south on Rte. 32 for 2 mi. From Philadelphia, follow I-95 north to Yardley exit and Rte. 32 north to Erwinna. There are several other routes also.

FAIRFIELD INN AND GUEST HOUSE
Fairfield, Pennsylvania

"No matter how many other suggestions we make on our menu, guests continue to ask for our chicken and biscuits."

David Thomas, Gerry Milsom, and I were having dinner in the low-ceilinged main dining room at the Fairfield Inn, where the combination of rough stone walls, wide, shining, old floorboards, and country furniture, with a generous collection of plants and flowers, make it a most rewarding dining experience. The fact that Gerry is an innkeeper at one of our *CIBR* English inns made the evening even more lively.

The Fairfield Inn is one of the most "country" inns in *CIBR*. It is the only inn that serves dinner in the middle of the day and supper at night. This is a definite offshoot of the predominantly agricultural nature of Fairfield Village and Adams County; those are the terms used by farm families to describe the two meals of the day.

Just to add further to the country feeling, my bedroom in the main inn (there are four more in the guest house just a few paces across the street) had ball-fringe curtains, a bed with a macramé canopy, fresh roses, and a growing fern. The shiny, varied-width floorboards have found a fitting complement in a beautiful oriental rug.

The main building of the Fairfield Inn is an impressive three-story Pennsylvania stone building with wood balconies on the front. Further country influences are the window boxes found in great profusion everywhere. The inn is famous not only for having extremely enjoyable country food and pleasant service, but also for being in every sense of the

word a meeting place and a center of the social activity for the region. The new Country Squire Gift Shop in their loft is drawing both local visitors and travelers.

The building began its long career as the plantation home of the Miller family, who settled here in 1755. The rear portion of the building dates from 1757, and the front stone section was built about the same time that Squire William Miller laid out the town.

The four bedrooms in the guest house across the village street are furnished mostly with original antiques. Some of the rooms look out over the village scene and others in the rear have a view of the mountains.

In response to a question from Gerry, David explained that the inn is a setting for many events throughout the year, including the Festival of Christmas. "This is held on four weekends in December. Reservations are open the first Monday in November and are filled almost within hours."

The inn and the village are also the scene of the "Pippinfest," held on an autumn weekend, usually in September. This is a real apple harvest celebration, with cider pressing, apple butter, square dancing, an antique car display, an apple dessert baking contest, bonfires, old movies, and block parties.

Besides the specialty of chicken and biscuits, the menu of the Fairfield Inn also has country ham steak, which David describes as "the salty kind," scallops in wine sauce, roast prime ribs of beef, and baked seafood pie. The honey for the homemade biscuits comes from their own beehives.

Bean soup is always on the menu, because it commemorates the occasion when the townswomen made bean soup in iron kettles to feed the starving soldiers after the battle of Gettysburg.

Speaking of Gettysburg, Fairfield is just eight miles west of Gettysburg and is an excellent place to stay during visits to the battlefield. Jeb Stuart is said to have stolen 700 horses from the valley to further the Confederate cause in 1862.

Yes, the Fairfield Inn is real "country," but David Thomas has added a few very sophisticated touches as well.

FAIRFIELD INN AND GUEST HOUSE, Main St., Fairfield, PA 17320; 717-642-5410. A 6-guestroom (shared baths) country inn and restaurant near Gettysburg. Breakfast, lunch, and dinner served daily. Closed on major holidays, Sun., and first week in Sept. and Feb. Dinner reservations advised. Nearby region is rich in history, including Gettysburg Battlefield, Caledonia State Park, and Totem Pole Playhouse; 3 mi. from Ski Liberty. No pets. David W. Thomas, Innkeeper.

Directions: Fairfield is 8 mi. west of Gettysburg on Rte. 116.

GATEWAY LODGE
Cooksburg, Pennsylvania

Linda and Joe Burney were telling me about black bears. "Well," quoth Linda, "we always seem to have bears around, but everybody loved our mother bear with two cubs who was here last year. At one time the two cubs were in the tree and she was down at the bottom keeping her eye on them. They looked so cute and cuddly up there—those little black furry creatures."

Joe took a more pragmatic view. "Actually, we tell our guests to keep their distance from the bears, and *never* to get between the mother bear and her cubs. There's never been any problem. I think part of the reason that our guests return is the opportunity to see some of the forest animals, including raccoons, chipmunks, porcupines, and foxes. The deer come right up to the porch of the lodge and the guests feed them lettuce leaves and vegetables."

Gateway Lodge is a rustic country inn in Cook Forest, where the pine and hemlock may be seen in all their majesty, towering 200 and more feet above the pine-needle-carpeted forest. Hundreds of years of growth, untouched by human progress, has preserved for us some of the most magnificent forest scenery east of the Rocky Mountains. The pine and hemlock logs of the lodge suggest the ruggedness of our pioneer forebears.

The big living room of the main lodge has log walls and a beautiful big fireplace, with lots of deep, comfortable chairs gathered around it. The guest rooms have beds with chestnut headboards, and all have comforters and dust ruffles. Most rooms with baths "down the hall" also provide fluffy robes for the trip.

In addition to the rustic guest rooms in the main lodge, there are six cabins across the road in the forest, which require a minimum two-night stay. These cabins have kitchen conveniences, porches, and fireplaces, and are very snug with lots of firewood. Some guests decide to return to these for longer stays.

The Cook Forest really serves as the recreational motivation to visit this rustic hideaway. It has twenty-seven miles of hiking and over seventeen well-marked trails for good cross-country skiing. It's possible to fish for trout and warm-water fish in the Clarion River, and there are over ninety species of birds that have been identified in the park. Canoeing and inner-tubing can also be enjoyed, as well as golf, horseback riding, swimming, superb backroading, and there's even a summer theater nearby.

The newest and most exciting addition is the indoor swimming pool, which is especially nice in the winter for the cross-country skiers. It is available to lodge guests only.

With all of this vigorous outdoor activity, one can imagine that truly gigantic appetites are the order of the day, and Linda is very fussy about food, especially the evening meal. "There are three choices on the menu each evening, including chicken and biscuits. Our system is still the same; the first person who calls for a reservation each day can set the menu. Today, we are having stuffed steak, but we are also serving stuffed pork chops and country-style spareribs. The second person who calls can set the second choice on the menu for that evening."

Linda made a sign to me and put her finger to her lips. She pointed down the forest road to where three deer were crossing. "It happens all the time," she whispered, "but it always gives me a big thrill."

GATEWAY LODGE, Rte. 36, Cooksburg, PA 16217; 814-744-8017. An 8-guestroom (some private baths) rustic lodge in the heart of Cook Forest in western Pa. Cabins require 2-night minimum stay. Open year-round, except Wed., Thurs., and Fri. of Thanksgiving week and from Dec. 22 to 25. Indoor swimming pool. Beautiful backroading and many trails in forest. All types of seasonal outdoor recreation available. The Burney Family, Innkeepers.

Directions: Because Cooksburg is accessible from all four directions, locate Cook Forest State Park on your map of Pa., and find Rte. 36. The lodge is on Rte. 36, 15 min. north of I-80.

HICKORY BRIDGE FARM
Orrtanna, Pennsylvania

Once again I was taking the road from Fairfield to Orrtanna and Hickory Bridge Farm. It is one of my most favorite back roads. This time I was accompanied by Gerry Milsom, a visiting English *CIBR* innkeeper.

The road had great cornfields on one side and apple orchards on the other and, in the midst of all, a large farmstand with a wonderful collection of pumpkins out in front, and every imaginable type of the fresh farm produce that is abundant in this highly agricultural area.

We turned at the inn sign, passed over the railroad track, and were in sight of Nancy Jean and Doctor Jim Hammett's Hickory Bridge Farm. There were the big red barn, the many flower gardens, the old farmhouse, and the ever-growing collection of old farm machinery and carts. The newest addition was a natural swimming pond with a diving platform. All of this was set against the background of beautiful, swaying trees, which in late September were beginning to take on their autumnal colors.

Walking through the gate, we were greeted with open arms by Nancy Jean. Introductions completed, we stepped into the house, where there was a beautiful, welcome fire in the huge stone fireplace, over which a musket was hung. Nancy Jean proudly pointed out the decorations in the dining room, done by her son David, who has completed his studies at the Gettysburg Seminary and now has full-time charge at a church just east of Gettysburg. Breakfast was well in progress, and on the sideboard was a selection of dry cereals, some hot oatmeal, granola, and orange juice.

As usual, Nancy Jean was overflowing with energy and exuberance. "The apple butter is made right here on the farm," she said. "The vegetables are from our garden, and the peaches, from our neighbor's orchard. We have honeydew melons and cantaloupes from our own farm, too."

The bedrooms in the main house are Pennsylvania farm bedrooms. Many have washstands and one even has an old-fashioned radio on the shelf. There are many additional touches, such as good country-type fixtures on the walls, that make the bedrooms very pleasant, including a rocking chair for two in one room.

The guests take breakfast out on the deck, overlooking the island and the covered bridge over the creek. "Sometimes they stay out here so long I have to shoo them out so that we can get the breakfast dishes done," Nancy Jean said. "This is a wonderful place for birders, and guests come out with their spyglasses."

We took a little tour around the grounds, ably assisted by one of the eight grandchildren. One of the points of interest is a country store museum, where there is penny candy, molasses, sarsaparilla, and apple

butter for sale. However, it is basically a museum store, with an old post office money window, and it provides a great deal of amusement for guests.

Hickory Bridge Farm has additional accommodations in two cottages beside the brook in the woods.

The sequel to this particular visit is that in August of 1985 Nancy Jean and Doctor Jim made a seventeen-day trip to Great Britain, and their first stop was to visit Gerry Milsom at Maison Talbooth, his beautiful country house hotel in Dedham. Her note said that everything was simply perfect and it was wonderful to see Gerry once again.

HICKORY BRIDGE FARM, Orrtanna, PA 17353; 717-642-5261. A 7-guestroom (private baths) country inn on a farm (with cottages) 3 mi. from Fairfield and 8 mi. west of Gettysburg. Open year-round except Dec. 20 thru Jan. 10. Ten-day advance deposit required. Full breakfast included in rates. Dinner served to public on Sat. evenings by reservation. Near Gettysburg Battlefield Natl. Park, Caledonia State Park, and Totem Pole Playhouse. Hiking, biking, hayrides, fishing, swimming, hunting, and country store museum on grounds. Golf available nearby. The Hammett Family, Innkeepers.

Directions: From Gettysburg take Rte. 116 west to Fairfield and follow signs 3 mi. north to Orrtanna.

THE INN AT STARLIGHT LAKE
Starlight, Pennsylvania

The orchestra was playing "Moonglow." The peepers were peeping and the sunset afterglow was lighting the western sky. I had wandered out on the front porch of the Inn at Starlight, speaking, as everyone else did, to the mother cat and her two brand-new kittens. I wandered down the steps through the little grove of trees next to the lake and out onto the long dock, off of which were moored boats and sailboats.

I turned around to look at the lights of the inn and could hear the voices of some of my innkeeping friends from Pennsylvania and New York, who had gathered here to enjoy the opportunity to exchange experiences, tell good stories, and perhaps lend encouragement and counsel to each other. The trees along the shore created lacy silhouettes against the darkening blue sky. Then I noticed that several other innkeepers had decided to take a walk along the shore of the lake to help digest the wonderful evening meal. The small orchestra changed to a bit more up-tempo with "String of Pearls."

My evening meanderings also brought me within sight and earshot of four ducks who had taken up residence in the lake near the inn. Three of them were feathered in beautiful hues and the fourth was an ordinary white barnyard duck. They all had names and, as Judy McMahon explained, they had "just sort of all arrived and never left. They are busy morning and night rooting in the lush green grass at the edge of the lake for some succulent tidbits, and then cruising energetically this end of the lake, occasionally diving down into the depths of the lake after some elusive fish."

This inn is on a back road, overlooking beautiful Starlight Lake. It is a rambling, old-fashioned, comfortable place with an accumulation of furniture from over the years. The combination lobby/living room has a

fireplace in one corner, and there are reminders that the McMahons are originally from "show business." Besides the piano and the guitar, books of plays or sheet music may be found on the tables or on the bookshelves.

Guest rooms are in the main building and also in adjacent cottages that have been redecorated and winterized. The inn is on the modified American plan, meaning that dinner and breakfast are included in the room rate. Lunch is offered every day at an additional charge.

There's a TV room, a game room in the main house, and lots of outdoor activity, from canoeing, sailing, swimming, and bicycling to ice skating on the forty-five-acre lake and cross-country skiing on eighteen miles of marked trails. There is a very pleasant lakeside play area, and many lovely walks and dirt roads for backroading in the picturesque woods. By the way, the McMahons have a fabulous collection of old films.

Some of my favorite reading is country inn menus and this one is particularly extensive. There are several different beef dishes including filet medallions Bordelaise and sirloin steak au poivre. One of several veal dishes is a really tasty Wiener schnitzel. Roast duckling always makes a hit with me, and there are a few seafood dishes as well.

Now I could hear Jack McMahon's high tenor voice wafting out from the living room and I knew it was time to go back for a very pleasant evening at the Inn at Starlight Lake. It's always a pleasure to visit.

THE INN AT STARLIGHT LAKE, Starlight, PA 18461; 717-798-2519. A 30-guestroom resort-inn, 5 mi. from Hancock, NY. Modified American plan. Breakfast, lunch, and dinner served daily between May 15 and April 1. Closed April 1 through April 15. Swimming, boating, canoeing, sailing, fishing, hunting, tennis, hiking, bicycling, xc skiing, and lawn sports on grounds. Golf nearby. No pets. Judy and Jack McMahon, Innkeepers.

Directions: From N.Y. Rte. 17, exit at Hancock, N.Y. Take Rte. 191S over Delaware River to Rte. 370. Turn right, proceed 3½ mi.; turn right, 1 mi. to inn. From I-81, take Exit 62 at Tompkinsville. Follow Rte. 107 east 4 mi. to Rte. 247N and Forest City. Turn left on Rte. 171 (the main street), and continue 10 mi. north to Rte. 370. Turn right and go 13 mi. east to Starlight. Turn left, 1 mi. to inn.

"European Plan" means that rates for rooms and meals are separate. "American Plan" means that meals are included in the cost of the room. "Modified American Plan" means that breakfast and dinner are included in the cost of the room. The rates at some inns include a continental breakfast with the lodging.

THE OVERLOOK INN
Canadensis, Pennsylvania

It was cookies-and-lemonade time at the Overlook Inn. Ann Mills from Barley Sheaf Farm and I had driven down from the Inn at Starlight Lake, and waiting for us on the front porch was some iced tea, lemonade, and freshly made cookies as well as scones and lemon curd. Lolly Tupper observed that hot mulled cider is a big favorite in the fall.

If Overlook had nothing else, the entrance into the inn itself would be worth a visit. It is through a handsome porte cochere, over which is a large covered porch. This is a most interesting way to arrive at a country inn.

The porch itself is a most engaging feature, with one piece after another of absolutely splendid white wicker furniture. It's a nice broad porch where one can sit when it's raining and not get wet. All around are wonderful woods of evergreens interspersed with apple trees, and there is a beautiful red maple right in front.

And birds. We were there in the middle of spring, and what is a happier sound than birds chattering and chirping, while caring for another bumper crop of birdlings! There's also a salt block for deer within sight of the porch. It's such a wonderful experience to see these wild creatures.

The Overlook Inn, kept by Bob and Lolly Tupper, is high in the Pocono Mountains in northeastern Pennsylvania. The fragrant pine, blue spruce, and locust forests stretch out in all directions, and the robins, cardinals, and quail find them as inviting as the rhododendron and mountain laurel.

The Tuppers have been here since the late 1970s, when I first paid them a visit. Bob is a big man with a wonderful sense of humor and a booming laugh. Lolly is quiet and has the knack of making guests feel as if they really are in a very special place.

"Country inn guests seem to be nicer and more interesting than ever," says Lolly, "and they come in all sizes and ages. The guests are really the best reason to be an innkeeper; they keep the machinery going!"

Incidentally, I always receive several telephone calls and letters in the late fall from people who are looking for a place to spend the Christmas holidays. I am happy to recommend the Overlook, which is open every day of the year. At Christmas they put a big evergreen covered with Christmas lights on the porte cochere, and it's a merry beacon to arriving guests.

Food at the Overlook is, for the most part, American cooking and includes several seafood entrées, including shrimp Royale, broiled lobster, brook trout, clams Casino, and oysters Rockefeller. Escargots are also offered, and there are some surprise specials almost every evening.

I mustn't forget the selection of homemade desserts, including several flavors of fresh ice cream, made right out in the kitchen.

The country inn bedrooms are all cozy and warm, the food is delicious, the fireplace crackly and beckoning, but ultimately, what sets the Overlook apart are Bob and Lolly themselves. They have a keen understanding and rapport with their guests, and this is the thing that is mentioned most frequently in letters I receive about the Overlook Inn.

THE OVERLOOK INN, Dutch Hill Rd., Canadensis, PA 18325; 717-595-7519. A 21-guestroom resort-inn in the heart of the Poconos, 15 mi. from Stroudsburg, Pa. Mod. American plan. Dinners served to travelers; jackets requested. Open year-round. Pool, shuffleboard, bocci, horseshoes, hiking on grounds; golf, tennis, antiquing, backroading, summer theater, downhill and xc skiing nearby. No children under 12. No pets. Bob and Lolly Tupper, Innkeepers.

Directions: From the north, exit from I-84 and to Rte. 390 south thru "Promised Land" about 12 mi. to traffic light in Canadensis. Make right-hand turn on Rte. 447 north—go ⅓ mi. to Dutch Hill Rd. and turn right—inn is 1½ mi. up hill. Look for sign on right. From New York City take Geo. Washington Bridge to I-80 west. Turn off at Pa. Exit 52. Follow Rte. 447 north—straight through Canadensis traffic light— about ⅓ mi. past light to Dutch Hill Rd. Follow above directions from Dutch Hill Rd. From Phila., Pa. Tpke. to Northeast Extension to Exit 35. Follow I-80 East to 380 West to Mt. Pocono Exit 8. Turn right on Rte. 940 to dead end. Make right and quick left; you're still on 940. Follow 390. Make left. Follow 390 to traffic light in Canadensis. Make left ¼ mi. to Dutch Hill Rd. Turn right 1½ mi. up hill.

THE PINE BARN INN
Danville, Pennsylvania

From the very first edition of *Country Inns and Back Roads*, which I wrote in 1966, I've maintained that innkeepers and their growing families were every bit as important to me as the changes and developments in the inns themselves.

The Pine Barn Inn is a case in point. I've been visiting and writing about it now for many years and I've seen some interesting developments—originally in the concepts and new ideas shared by innkeepers Shube and Marty Walzer. Later on, as Shube more or less retired to Florida, Barbara Walzer entered the picture, saving Marty from complete dissolution by marrying him a few years ago.

The inn began life in the 1870s as a wonderful Pennsylvania barn and later served for a long time as a riding stable, and then as a private home. It was transformed in 1950 into the Pine Barn Inn, and in 1967 it was purchased by the Walzers, father and son. Today, it is an inn and restaurant of considerable reputation.

The residents of that area of Pennsylvania think most kindly of the Pine Barn as a restaurant, with its menu that includes roast beef and roast leg of lamb, as well as homemade pies, breads, and rolls. Travelers speak highly of the accommodations. Even though they are somewhat "motel" in style, the rooms are furnished with attractive cherry reproductions and have many thoughtful touches that I always enjoy finding in a country inn, such as plants and magazines and books for guests to read in each guest room.

I have shared Marty's yearly letter with readers for the past few years in which he brings us up to date on son Christopher: "I'm going to make a serious attempt not to dwell on the progress of a certain 4½-year-old. We must not bore the reader, although after last year's edition, every time Christopher comes in for breakfast it seems everyone knows him and greets him by name. This, of course, pleases him no end and encourages him to become the dining room cut-up. Yesterday, we came in for breakfast and he stood in the middle of the dining room yelling, 'Where's the beef?' The Pine Barn is really his second home, and it is a marvelous atmosphere for him.

"Barb finished redecorating one of our private dining and conference rooms with a library theme. Oak paneling and oak floor-to-ceiling bookshelves, with reproductions of old photographs of Danville, have given the room an all-new look and it's excellent for private parties.

"The inn looks wonderful even if we can't brag of any great additions. We're taking a breather right now and looking at our priorities. Flowers adorned the grounds despite my entire ignorance of horticulture. Craig, who heads our maintenance department and who Christopher says can fix anything, managed to keep everything seeded, watered, and growing.

"Chef Ralph Richardson with the able assistance of Larry Horne and Scott Smith has kept the menu varied and fresh. I am also ready to put forward to the scientific world a new law of physics, which is: 'No one can possibly lose weight as long as they are a patron of Rose's soups or Polly's pies.'

"Sue Dressler, my assistant, continues to do the work of ten. She is the 'Betsy Holtzinger' (Red Lion Inn) of the Pine Barn and I don't know what I'd do if she made a career change at this point. She was born to be in the hospitality business."

And now, dear reader, thus endeth the yearly report on the Pine Barn Inn. I will mention one more thing: when you visit ask Marty to tell you about the time he swam against Johnny Weissmuller.

THE PINE BARN INN, Danville, PA 17821; 717-275-2071. A picturesque country restaurant with 45 attractive motel rooms in central Pennsylvania. European plan. Breakfast, lunch, and dinner served daily except Christmas, July 4, and Memorial Day. Near several colleges and historic sites. Golf, tennis, waterskiing, sailing, and canoeing nearby. Pets allowed in some rooms. Martin and Barbara Walzer, Innkeepers.

Directions: From Exit 33 of I-80, go south 3 mi. to Danville. Take a left at the first traffic light. Proceed 10 blocks and follow signs to Geisinger Medical Center. Pine Barn adjoins the Center.

PUMP HOUSE INN
Canadensis, Pennsylvania

I love to read menus; in fact, I read menus the way some people read mystery stories. I have a stack of them on the table next to my bed, and on some nights when I might wake up with a little too much on my mind, I reach over and enjoy myself by deciding what I'm going to order the next time I visit a particular inn.

In this case, I was looking at the summer menu for the Pump House Inn, high up in the Poconos of eastern Pennsylvania. John Keeney, the innkeeper, had sent along several different samples, and I was having a wonderful time just checking off some of the dishes.

For example, among the starters on the summer menu are smoked trout with horseradish cream sauce; shrimps in beer batter and a pungent fruit sauce (a perennial favorite at the Pump House); poached oysters with spinach, served with tomato fennel butter; smoked cold rare tenderloin in a tarragon and horseradish cream sauce; goat cheese baked in phylo pastry and served with a bourbon sauce; mussels marinated with lemon, capers, and olive oil; and tortellini with a lobster cream sauce.

Now I moved into second gear with the entrées, which include prime rib, served every day; chicken breasts with lobster stuffing and sherry cream sauce; rack of lamb roasted with Dijon mustard and herbed bread crumbs; duck of the day, with a different sauce for every day of the week; sautéed bay scallops served in white wine and a ginger lime sauce; twin lobster tails with crab stuffing in a basil cream sauce; grilled pork chops with sliced apples in an apple brandy sauce.

Even the salads have an innovative flare, and they include smoked duck with spinach and mushrooms served with hot walnut sherry vinaigrette, and shrimp and scallops tossed with boston lettuce, dill, and scallion dressing.

The winter menu has some of the summer favorites, including shrimps in beer batter, but also has chilled poached Norwegian salmon, and poached leek wrapped in prosciutto and mozzarella, and encased in a puff pastry. The main dishes for the cooler weather include some of those summer favorites that guests have come to appreciate.

The Pump House also has an equally impressive Sunday dinner menu.

John Keeney points out that the chef is Jeffrey Lang, who has been at the Pump House for a few years.

In the midst of all this ambrosial eating, it is well to mention that the Pump House maintains some very pleasant country inn-style guest rooms for the convenience of guests who not only enjoy the cuisine, but also the wonderful back roads and vistas that are a part of the Pocono Mountains experience.

By the way, friends of Todd Drucquer will be happy to know that Todd and Penny and the family are carrying on at Colligan's Stockton Inn in nearby New Jersey and are delighted to see old friends.

Now, I'm wondering how many of our readers also share my penchant for poring over menus—certainly the Pump House is a wonderful place to start.

PUMP HOUSE INN, Sky Top Rd., Rte. 390, Canadensis, PA 18325; 717-595-7501. A 7-guestroom country inn, with a separate guest cottage, high in the Poconos, 1½ mi. north of Canadensis village and 16 mi. northeast of Stroudsburg. European plan. Restaurant open daily from mid-June to mid-Sept; Tues. thru Sun., mid-Mar. to mid-June; Wed. thru Sun., Oct. thru Dec.; and weekends only Jan. to mid-Mar. Downhill and xc skiing and golf nearby. John Keeney, Innkeeper.

Directions: From the north, follow I-84 to Rte. 390 south. Inn is located 13 mi. south on Rte. 390. From the south, follow I-80 to Rte. 191. Travel north on Rte. 191 to Rte. 390 north. Follow signs to Canadensis. Inn is 1½ mi. north from traffic light to Canadensis.

1740 HOUSE
Lumberville, Pennsylvania

As often as I have driven up the so-called River Road, in reality Route 32, on the Pennsylvania side of the Delaware, it never ceases to wonder me (as our Pennsylvania Dutch friends would say) just how beautiful it is. Especially visible before the trees are in leaf, are the hills sloping up from the road on one side, and on the other, the canal and long stretches of the Delaware River. The road has a roller coaster quality, lifting up to the top of the hills, and dropping down beside the river. The laurel is green and welcome at all seasons, and here and there in April I could see errant tufts of grass that enjoyed a little more sunshine than others beginning to push up along the river bank.

It is a small wonder that many years ago, my friend Harry Nessler, the innkeeper at the 1740 House, came to this section of Pennsylvania and saw the possibilities of opening what at that time was a rather remarkable phenomenon, a country inn in the cluster of barns and other farm outbuildings. Each of the bedrooms at the 1740 House has either a balcony or a terrace with a full view of the canal and the Delaware River beyond. The inn abounds with bushes, shrubs, flowers, trees, and birds. A portion of the building is covered with beautiful green ivy.

There is a sort of natural division between the buildings, separated by a very small swimming pool. As Harry has said, "It's just enough to get wet."

A typical menu at the 1740 House includes a choice of three appetizers—things like mushroom soup, herring in cream sauce, and fettucini Alfredo. Typical entrées are filet mignon, chicken Marsala, crab Imperial, broiled scallops, and a baked fish. Desserts usually include crème caramel and always ice cream. Although there are several restaurants in the area, many of the returning guests have found it most convenient and

quite enjoyable to have a quiet dinner at the 1740 House. It is most necessary to make reservations for that dinner in advance.

There is a bridge over the river in Lumberville—a single-passenger bridge—and it's possible to go across to New Jersey on the other side. There is also a preserved canal lock, which shows exactly how boats were assisted through the canals in the old days.

Of course, backroading is one of the favorite pastimes of visitors to Bucks County. The back roads here not only have a great deal of history connected with them, but they have the historic old buildings, homes, barns, and sheds that make it even more enjoyable. There is something about the quarried stone in this part of Pennsylvania that mellows and weathers in a most handsome way.

Harry pointed out that one of the additional sports guests may enjoy is canoeing and tubing on the river, and there are places where canoes and inner tubes are available for this purpose. "The Delaware during the time when the water would be warmest is a relatively placid experience," he said, "with none of the hair-raising elements that we hear about on other rivers."

1740 HOUSE, River Rd., Lumberville, PA 18933; 215-297-5661. A 24-guestroom riverside inn, 6½ mi. north of New Hope, in the heart of historic Bucks County. Lodgings include breakfast, served to houseguests daily; dinner served daily except Sun. and Mon. by reservation only. Open year-round. Weekend reservations must include 2 nights. Pool and boating on grounds. Golf and tennis nearby. Superb backroading in an area rich in American history. Harry Nessler, Innkeeper.

Directions: From N.Y.C., travel south on N.J. Tpke., and take Exit 10. Follow Rte. 287 north to another Exit 10. Proceed west on Rte. 22 to Flemington, then Rte. 202 south over Delaware Toll Bridge. After an immediate right U-turn onto Rte. 32N, drive 5 mi. to inn. From Pa. Tpke., exit at Willow Grove and proceed north on Rte. 611 to Rte. 202. Follow Rte. 202 north to Rte. 32 and turn north to inn. From Phila., take I-95 to Yardley–New Hope Exit, follow 32N through New Hope and 7 mi. to inn.

I do not include lodging rates in the descriptions, for the very nature of an inn means that there are lodgings of various sizes, with and without baths, in and out of season, and with plain and fancy decoration. Travelers should call ahead and inquire about the availability and rates of the many different types of rooms.

STERLING INN
South Sterling, Pennsylvania

I could not resist it any longer—I had been listening to the gurgling waters of the Wallenpaupack Creek for about twenty minutes on a warm, lazy afternoon. I was sitting on a lawn chair about fifty paces from the back of the Sterling Inn, just two feet from the bank of the creek. The smell of the freshly-cut lawn mingled with the scent of the forest on the other side of the water.

I kicked off my shoes, rolled up my pants, and waded out to stand on the flat, smooth shelf of rock in the middle of the creek. The water was clean and cool. There was a little pool about twenty-five feet away, deep enough for someone to sit in and have the water come up to his chest. A flash of red and another of blue signaled a cardinal and a bluejay darting into the woods, deep in the Pocono Mountains of Pennsylvania.

I climbed back on the bank and was drying my feet, when one of the other guests came and plunked down on a nearby chair. "I think this is one of the best-kept, neatest places that I have ever visited," she said. "It's as American as apple pie and fresh vegetables. The rooms are so comfortable, and I'm very glad I came. Don't you just love it here?"

Even if her enthusiasm hadn't been catching, I would have had to agree.

This was the friendly and unpretentious atmosphere that Alice Julian had in mind over a half-century ago when she acquired the Sterling Inn. That is the way her daughter and son-in-law, Carmen and Henry Arneberg, kept it, and the same way that the present owners, Ron and Mary Kay Logan are keeping it today.

The Sterling Inn is on a back road in the Poconos. There are enticing hiking and walking trails on the inn property and nearby. One of them,

Ron told me, leads to a waterfall on the ridge behind the inn. There is a very pleasant nine-hole putting green, a swimming area with a sandy beach, and a little pond with willow trees and a few ducks.

Guest rooms are to be found in several very attractive buildings in the parklike atmosphere. The Wayside, Lodge, Meadowlark, Spruce, and Spring Run are all beautifully situated with extremely attractive rooms, all with private baths.

The menu includes such entrées as roast lamb, pot roast, and standing rib roast because, Mary Kay Logan says, "This is the kind of food that people serve only when they are having guests for dinner." All the baking is done in the warm, friendly kitchen.

In many ways this Pocono Mountain inn personifies the things that I find most delightful in country inns. For example, fresh flowers are on the dining room tables at all times, and there are books and magazines in all parlors and sitting rooms. When guests advise the inn of their arrival time, the inn automobile will meet buses and airplanes. Special diets can also be accommodated.

The inn is open year-round, and the setting is like a picture postcard. Winter activities include cross-country skiing and lessons, ice skating, sledding, winter hikes, and roasting chestnuts or marshmallows by the open fire. Major ski areas are within a short drive from the inn.

In the blaze of autumn colors there are incredibly beautiful nature walks along Wallenpaupack Creek and hikes on woodland trails. Spring and summer at the Sterling Inn, of course, offer all sorts of outdoor enjoyment.

STERLING INN, Rte. 191, South Sterling, PA 18460; 717-676-3311. From Ct., N.Y., N.J., Md., Del., Wash., D.C.: 800-523-8200. A 60-guestroom secluded country inn-resort in the Pocono Mountains, 8 mi. from I-84 and 12 mi. from I-380. American plan. Reservation and check-in offices close at 10 p.m. Breakfast, lunch, and dinner served to travelers daily. Jackets required for dinner. Open year-round. Swimming, putting green, shuffleboard, all-weather tennis court, scenic hiking trails, xc skiing and lessons, ice skating, and sledding on grounds. Golf courses, horseback riding, major ski areas nearby. Gift shop and print gallery. No pets. Ron and Mary Kay Logan, Innkeepers.

Directions: From I-80, follow I-380 to Rte. 940 to Mount Pocono. At light, cross Rte. 611 and proceed on Rte. 196 north to Rte. 423. Drive north on Rte. 423 to Rte. 191 and travel ½ mi. north to inn. From I-84, follow Rte. 507 south through Greentown and Newfoundland. In Newfoundland, pick up Rte. 191 and travel 4 mi. south to inn.

TARA
Clark, Pennsylvania

Inspired by the world's most renowned movie, *Gone With the Wind,* Jim and Donna Winner restored a beautiful antebellum mansion located midway between Cleveland, Ohio, and Pittsburgh, Pennsylvania. They named it "Tara."

As Donna described it to me, "When you first see Tara from the rolling highways of western Pennsylvania you might wonder if magically you've been transported in time to the Old South of the early 1800s—the era before the Civil War, when grace and grandeur, honor, fine clothes, plantations, and Southern hospitality were the lifestyle."

She went on to tell me that the house was built in 1854 and is one of western Pennsylvania's most famous historic landmarks. The mansion, with its two-story Grecian columns, overlooks 4,000-acre Lake Shenango surrounded by rolling hills of maple and pine.

Incurable romantics, Jim and Donna knew from the first time they saw what was to become Tara that it should definitely be a country inn. They have made it their home and have lavishly displayed their entire collection of antiques, art, rare china, and crystal throughout, including crystal chandeliers from Austria and a hand-painted Dresden chandelier from Germany. An antique brass chandelier featuring Steuben shades graces the circular stairwell.

There are fifteen guest rooms, most with working fireplaces. Each room has been carefully decorated to reflect the personality of a character from the book. For example, "Miss Melanie's" room is all feminine and fluffy in yellow and pink, with bows and wicker furniture. Overlooking the lake, it boasts one of the best views in the house. "Rhett's" room is

masculine and strong. Its focal point is a center-island bed with a canopy that rises to the nine-foot ceiling. The "Katie O'Hara" room has an 18th-century hand-carved bed and a hand-painted ivy floor. The "old maid's" stairwell descends to the lovely antique private bath below.

There are two main dining rooms plus a patio café for outdoor dining in clement weather. "Ashley's" is for formal dining, with such offerings as rack of lamb, an array of tantalizing desserts, and special gourmet coffees, all served on antique tables, one of which belonged to President James Buchanan and was used in the White House during his administration, just before the Civil War. The "Old South" room is a true-to-life Southern-style dining room, serving fried chicken, smoked ham, grits, cornbread, and other Dixie favorites, all served family-style.

Tara is just fun to browse through. There is an authentic, primitive slave kitchen, a primitive bedroom with a genuine rope bed, and a collection of antiques that date back to 1760. The library itself is most impressive, with both old and new books, and one can read on the veranda or in "Miss Pittypat's Parlor."

If it's outdoor fun you're looking for, Jim and Donna have thought of just about everything, with croquet or bocci, carriage rides or sleigh rides, bicycles, and all the water-related sports on the lake.

The day after Thanksgiving, Tara is transformed into a festive showplace, with thousands of lights outdoors and gaily decorated Christmas trees everywhere. Bows and holly adorn the crystal chandeliers, and the costumes are all in red and green. Talk about being transported back in time! I could almost hear Scarlett saying, "I won't think about that until tomorrow. . ."

TARA, 3665 Valley View Rd., Box 475, Rte. 18, Clark, PA 16113; 412-962-2992. A 15-guestroom mansion, 8 hrs. west of New York and 8 hrs. east of Chicago. Breakfast, lunch, and dinner served. Croquet, bocci, boating, fishing, swimming, carriage rides, bicycling, backroading, xc skiing, and golf. Not suitable for children. No pets. Jim and Donna Winner, Innkeepers.

Directions: Just inside the Pa. border on I-80 take Exit 1N and follow Rte. 18 north for 8 mi. Tara is located on the east side overlooking Lake Shenango.

THE TAVERN RESTAURANT
New Wilmington, Pennsylvania

Mrs. Ernst Durrast has kept this exceptional restaurant for more than forty-five years. The luncheon menu alone has twenty-seven main dishes. This is real country fare, including creamed chicken on a biscuit, cabbage rolls, grilled smoked pork chops, ham steaks, and cheese soufflé with creamed chicken. Two warm honey buns with whipped butter are always served.

Dinners include most of the luncheon offerings, plus about twelve other main dishes. Often, there is the most unusual combination of the white meat of chicken and lobster tail served in a special sherry sauce.

New Wilmington is just a few minutes from I-80, the east-west highway that traverses northern Pennsylvania. It's about 240 miles from the Poconos.

THE TAVERN RESTAURANT, Box 153, New Wilmington, PA 16142; 412-946-2020. A bustling country restaurant on the town square with 5 sleeping rooms in a lodge directly across the street. European plan. Lunch and dinner served daily except Tues. Reservations required. Closed Thanksgiving and Christmas. Sports and cultural events at Westminister College nearby. No credit cards. No diversions for small children. Mrs. Ernst Durrast, Innkeeper.

Directions: From I-80, take Exit 1-S, and follow Rte. 18 south to Rte. 208. Proceed east on 208 to town square. From I-79, follow Rte. 208 west for 14 mi. to New Wilmington.

Favorite Back Roads

It is true that all roads leading to the Inn at Starlight Lake are back roads. It's impossible to get here without finding yourself on some little-traveled, curving, up-and-down-road. Pointing out a few: Coming from New York City or the northern New Jersey area, one can approach Hancock from NY Route 97, which snakes along the Delaware and passes the replica of Old Fort Delaware. The Delaware River is one of our national treasures. In its upper portion it has changed little, scenically, since the last century. The upper Delaware branches into two parts at Hancock and forms some wonderful areas to travel by. You could really arrive by canoe with a little planning.

Coming from the south through Pennsylvania, one could drive through Honesdale, a charming 19th-century county seat with several historic points of interest, and take either Route 191 N, or Route 670-247 N to Route 370 through miles of . . . well . . . just COUNTRY.

Coming from the north, one can take Route 92 S (NY) to Route 171 (Pa.), and, at Lanesboro, see a national engineering landmark, the Starrucca Viaduct, built in 1848, the oldest train bridge still in use in America. The area is filled with railroad lore for the true railroad enthusiast and the casual observer— Honesdale, site of the first steam engine and gravity railroad, and Susquehanna, site of the first railroad depot and hotel combined in America, now a restaurant. While people are here, we are always pleased to give them hand-out maps and route them along these byways. The roads, by the way, are great for cyclists, too.

Judy and Jack McMahon
The Inn at Starlight Lake
Starlight, Pennsylvania

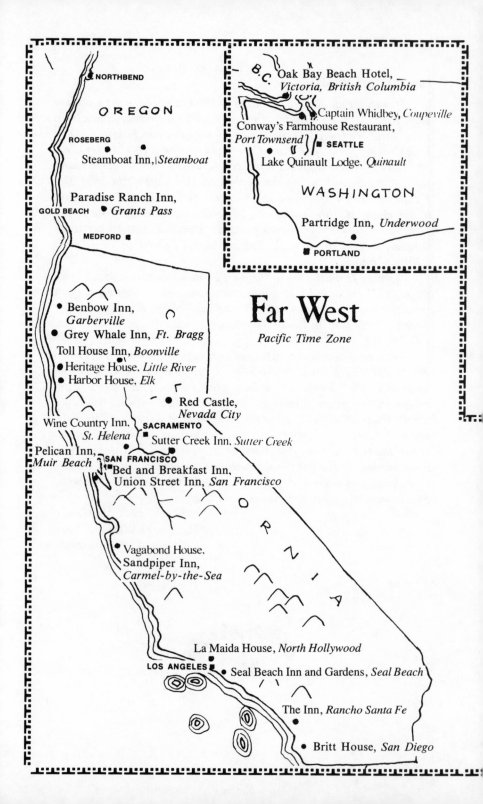

NORTHBEND

OREGON

ROSEBERG

Steamboat Inn, *Steamboat*

Paradise Ranch Inn,
GOLD BEACH ● *Grants Pass*

MEDFORD ■

B.C. Oak Bay Beach Hotel,
Victoria, British Columbia

Captain Whidbey, *Coupeville*
Conway's Farmhouse Restaurant,
Port Townsend ■ SEATTLE

Lake Quinault Lodge, *Quinault*

WASHINGTON

Partridge Inn, *Underwood*

■ PORTLAND

Far West

Pacific Time Zone

● Benbow Inn,
 Garberville
● Grey Whale Inn, *Ft. Bragg*
Toll House Inn, *Boonville*
● Heritage House, *Little River*
● Harbor House, *Elk*

● Red Castle,
 Nevada City

Wine Country Inn,
 St. Helena   SACRAMENTO
Sutter Creek Inn, *Sutter Creek*

Pelican Inn,
Muir Beach   SAN FRANCISCO
Bed and Breakfast Inn,
Union Street Inn, *San Francisco*

CALIFORNIA

● Vagabond House,
Sandpiper Inn,
Carmel-by-the-Sea

La Maida House, *North Hollywood*

LOS ANGELES ● Seal Beach Inn and Gardens, *Seal Beach*

The Inn, *Rancho Santa Fe*

● Britt House, *San Diego*

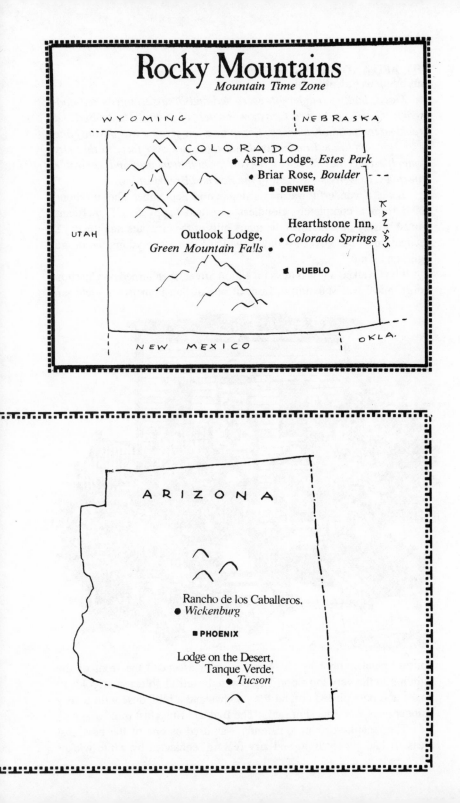

THE BED AND BREAKFAST INN
San Francisco, California

Good, bad, or indifferent, every bed-and-breakfast inn or bed-and-breakfast home on the West Coast owes a debt of gratitude to the Bed and Breakfast Inn in San Francisco. For quite a few years it was the only one of its kind, and now I understand that there are over forty in that city alone. It's a pity they did not all borrow the high standards and admirable objectives, as well as the idea, of the Bed and Breakfast Inn.

It was a wonderful warm morning in mid-September. The sun shone down from a completely cloudless sky, and happy San Franciscans moved briskly up and down the many hills of the city pursuing the day's occupations—the kind of a day in which I knew everything would go right, and it did.

I had walked a few blocks on Union Street, then turned on Charlton Court, and I was standing in front of one of San Francisco's Victorian

houses, painted light green; wooden stairs ascended the front of the building to the very top floor. There were beautiful golden marigolds in boxes and pots placed around the porches and a birdhouse with a very chipper occupant. The sign said, "The Bed and Breakfast Inn."

The reception room apparently was used as one of the breakfast areas. It had a very light and airy feeling, enhanced by white wicker furniture, many flower arrangements, and light touches everywhere. The enticing aroma of fresh coffee filled the room, and some guests were just finishing delicious-looking croissants.

There followed in delightful order my first meeting with Marily Kavanaugh and her husband, Bob; a tour of all the rooms in the inn, and a leisurely chat on the garden deck.

First the lodging rooms: some of them are named after various parts of London. There's Covent Garden, Chelsea, Green Park, and Kensington Garden. Other rooms are called The Library, Autumn Sun, The Willows, Mandalay, and The Celebration. A new accommodation, "The Mayfair Flat," has been created in the Kavanaughs' former duplex apartment on the top floor. It has a spiral staircase to a bedroom loft, a double tub, a kitchen, and a view of the Golden Gate Bridge.

Each room provides an entirely different experience. For example, many have completely different sets of sheets, pillowcases, and towels. There are all varieties of beds, including traditional shiny brass bedsteads. There are flowers everywhere, thermos jugs of ice-water, many books, baskets of fruit, electric clocks with an alarm, down pillows, and gorgeous coverlets and spreads. Five of the bedrooms have their own bathrooms, and the others share. Four rooms have the garden view. I saw old-fashioned British ceiling fans in some of the rooms.

The location of the Bed and Breakfast is another virtue. Charlton Court is a little dead-end street off Union, between Buchanan and Laguna. It's within easy walking distance of Fisherman's Wharf. In fact, San Francisco is such a "walking place" that it's convenient to everything. The nicest part of it is that when people get tired of walking, they can always take the cable cars!

THE BED AND BREAKFAST INN, Four Charlton Court, San Francisco, CA 94123; 415-921-9784. A 9-guestroom European-style pension in the Union Street district of San Franciso. Convenient to all of the Bay area recreational, cultural, and gustatory attractions. Continental breakfast is the only meal offered. Open daily year-round. Not comfortable for children. No pets. No credit cards. Robert and Marily Kavanaugh, Innkeepers.

Directions: Take the Van Ness Exit from Rte. 101 and proceed to Union Street. Charlton Court is a small courtyard street halfway between Laguna and Buchanan, off Union.

BENBOW INN
Garberville, California

I first visited the Benbow Inn in 1973 and was immediately intrigued not only with its location in the glorious redwood country of northern California, but also with its design, which shows definite influences of the Art Deco style of the early 1920s. There are also some touches of an English Tudor manor house found in the half-timbers, carved dark wood paneling, solid oak furniture, bookcases, hardwood floors, handsome oriental rugs, and truly massive fireplace in the main living room.

Some guest rooms are on the terrace and garden levels with private patios. With four-poster beds, antiques, and country fabrics, their decor is most attractive. Three of them have fireplaces. Other guest rooms in the main inn had also been handsomely redecorated, and my own room, Number 313, was on the top floor and looked out over the gardens and a wonderful changing panorama of clouds.

The owners-innkeepers of the Benbow are Patsy and Chuck Watts, whom I have known for many years. The one outstanding quality that each of them has in such marvelous abundance is enthusiasm, and all of the improvements and additions to this truly unusual northern California inn have been undertaken by them with great joy and love.

"Ever since Day One," said Chuck, "we have been very happy and have had a really tremendous time. It's a continuing challenge and we've gotten a great deal accomplished, but I like the idea that the future is big with plans."

"We feel that we are a destination resort-inn, able to accommodate and provide amusement and diversion for all our guests of any age," chimed in Patsy. "We have acquired some fabulous antique pieces, most

particularly a magnificent carved buffet for the dining room. We have added a beautiful carved mantel for the fireplace in the lobby and have installed an antique mantel and a fireplace in the lounge.

"We will be having our wine tasting in November, and this has now become a semi-annual affair, with about fifteen of the California boutique wineries represented."

The Benbow is, indeed, a destination resort-inn—in addition to swimming, it offers tennis on two tennis courts nearby, a good golf course within walking distance, hiking, and magnificent backroading. By the way, it's very accessible by public transportation since the Route 101 buses stop almost at the front door.

At Christmastime there's a twelve-foot tree with teddy bears playing drums hanging from every branch. Under the tree there are Patsy's very special antique, oversized toys. An antique sleigh is on the front porch filled with presents and wreaths. Holly and masses of decorations are all over the inn.

On Christmas Day there is a special two-seatings Christmas dinner and everyone has a wonderful time.

Incidentally, in the fall and all through the holidays, English tea and scones are served in the lobby. Chuck's mother, Marie, is the tea lady.

The Benbow also has a film library with over seventy-five classic films. These are shown every evening. On one of my visits I cheered and wept a little at James Cagney's great portrayal of George M. Cohan in *Yankee Doodle Dandy.*

Patsy, Chuck, and Muffin (their gorgeous Afghan hound, the most photographed canine in northern California) are having a wonderful time greeting guests, sharing their enthusiasm, and providing their own bubbling brand of warmth and hospitality. In short, they're model innkeepers. I'm glad they and the Benbow Inn found each other.

BENBOW INN, 445 Lake Benbow Dr., Garberville, CA 95440; 707-923-2124. A 55-guestroom English Tudor inn in the redwood country of northern California. On Rte. 101 near the Benbow State Park. European plan. Breakfast, lunch, and dinner served to travelers daily. Open mid-Apr. to Nov. 28; re-open Dec. 17 for holiday season. Swimming on grounds; golf, tennis adjacent. Hiking and magnificent backroading. Chuck, Patsy, and Muffin Watts, Innkeepers.

Directions: From San Francisco follow Rte. 101 north 200 mi. and exit at Benbow.

BRITT HOUSE
San Diego, California

Lying abed in the morning in this exquisitely and lovingly furnished bedroom of the Britt House, I couldn't help thinking that Daun Martin and Robert Hostick, with their attention to important details, have placed their truly valued guests in an atmosphere of at least ninety years ago with authentic furniture, wallpaper designs, lighting fixtures, and other significant features.

True, to begin with, they have a most remarkable Victorian house, as you can see from the Jan Lindstrom drawing. A marvelous stained glass window flanking the stairwell is a truly magnificent work. The preservation of the handcarved doorways and moldings and the interior make it an almost living museum.

My mind drifted back to my arrival on the previous afternoon when Daun had shown me to the Camphor Tree Room, a quiet, intimate bedroom done in forest green, teal, and peach, with a carved oak dresser and a matching headboard for the queen-sized bed. True to its name, it has a thrilling view of the eighty-year-old camphor tree surrounded by ferns and flowers, and also has its own balcony where breakfast can be taken. This is typical of other rooms, all of which are done with an abundance of lace curtains, velvet swags, beautiful woods, oversized couches, and marble-top dressers.

The Britt House's answer to "down the hall" bathrooms is to provide their guests with terry cloth bathrobes. It's wonderful to slip into one of these after a shower or a bath.

Daun's affection for animals has created an additional special feature at the Britt House. Not only are there some very nice kitty cats and a couple of amusing dogs on the premises, there is also a collection of stuffed animals of all kinds to be found in every bedroom. Usually they hold a welcoming note, personally addressed to each guest. Some of the animals are even taken out to dinner by guests. (I know you won't believe this, but it's true. They sit them at the table, and everybody has lots of fun.)

Because it's the only meal served, Britt House breakfasts are quite special. Freshly squeezed orange juice, hard- or soft-cooked eggs, freshly baked yeast breads, sweet butter and honey, and European coffee, prepared filter-drip style, or tea are provided on the individual trays taken to each room. On Sunday morning, Robert creates an elegant fresh fruit salad as a special treat.

There are four bathrooms, two on each floor, and one has handsome twin antique bathtubs and bubble bath. The bathroom next to the billiard room offers a luxurious Finnish sauna that is available to all guests.

The newest addition is the cottage, with its own private bath, just a

few steps from the handsome camphor tree. Decorated in cheerful blue and yellow, it has a romantically cozy bed-nook with a canopy, a full-sized bed, a kitchen, and a porch that faces the main house and the beautiful gardens.

These gardens have a remarkably tall hedge that protects the house, and provides excellent privacy. Regardless of what time of year I visit the Britt House, there always seems to be a profusion of flowers in bloom.

BRITT HOUSE, 406 Maple St., San Diego, CA 92103; 714-234-2926. An 11-guestroom bed-and-breakfast inn (private and shared baths) a short distance from Balboa Park with its world-famous zoo, Museum of Art, Man and Natural History, Reuben H. Fleet Space Theater, and the beaches, desert country, and Mexico (13 mi.). Breakfast only meal served (special dinners can be arranged with advance notice). Open all year. Sauna on grounds; jogging, biking, skating, bicycles nearby. No pets. Not particularly suitable for young children. Daun Martin and Robert Hostick, Innkeepers.

Directions: Take Airport-Sassafrass turnoff coming south on Hwy. 5. Proceed on Kettner. Turn left on Laurel; left on Third; right on Nutmeg; right on Fourth St., and come down one block to the corner of Fourth and Maple.

THE GREY WHALE INN
Fort Bragg, California

Ever since the first edition of this book in 1966, I have visited inns that were formerly gristmills, poorhouses, majestic mansions, carriage houses, stagecoach taverns, farmhouses, and log cabins. However, the Grey Whale is the first inn that began life as a hospital!

"The building was constructed in 1915," explained John Bailey, who with his wife, Colette, acquired it in 1978. "It was the Redwood Coast Hospital before it was transformed into an inn in 1974."

John, Colette, and I were browsing through the thirteen guest rooms, eleven of which have private baths. Its early life as a hospital creates a distinct advantage for present-day inn guests, because the rooms are quite large, with many generous windows.

The Grey Whale features an unusual variety of textures and colors, ranging from the marvelous weather-beaten exterior boards to the brilliant colors of the interior carpeting and the wide selection of original contemporary paintings. The guest rooms have comforters with matching pillow covers, bright decorator sheets, and one has a working fireplace.

Each room contains a folder describing all of the sights and attractions of Fort Bragg and the Mendocino Coast, including the redwood forest, art galleries, the Botanical Gardens, the beautiful Pacific Ocean beaches, the Skunk Railroad, and a brief summary of some of the restaurants. (The Grey Whale offers bed and breakfast.)

When we passed through the second-floor dining room, Colette explained that she bakes all the breads and coffee cakes that are served on

the continental breakfast. "These can be enjoyed right here, or the tray may be taken to the bedroom. Many guests like to eat breakfast in bed," she said.

Colette received two blue ribbons at the Mendocino County Fair and Apple Show—her apricot-prune coffee cake and the lemon-yogurt bread were winners, and St. Timothy's coffee cake won a third prize. John said, "Competition was keen, but no match for the specialties that we serve our guests at the Grey Whale Inn."

Motorists passing through Fort Bragg on Highway 1 just can't miss the Grey Whale, because it stands at the north end of town surrounded by a large grass and turf area with some very colorful plantings of marguerite, California poppies, amaryllis, African daisies, and geraniums.

"Whale watching is one of our great pastimes," said John. "The whale watch starts in mid-December and from then on through March there are programs planned at various points along the coast."

Along with the whale-watching programs, there is a whale festival that includes a whale art exhibit, held last year for the first time with great success. Many nationally known marine artists will be coming to Fort Bragg again this year for the concurrent whale art exhibits at the Grey Whale Inn and the Wildlife Gallery in nearby Mendocino.

It was from John that I learned of the many activities and attractions in this section of northern California. "We have theater, crafts shows, scuba diving, fishing, hiking, and many museums," he reported. "We appeal to the art buff, the whale-watcher, the beachcomber, and anyone who wants to have some unhurried hours away from pressures."

Whether the traveler is headed north or south along the Mendocino coast, or bent on staying a few days, the Grey Whale provides a unique country inn experience.

THE GREY WHALE INN, 615 No. Main St., Fort Bragg, CA 95437; 707-964-0640. (California toll-free reservations: 800-382-7244.) A 13-guestroom inn located on Hwy. 1 at the north end of Fort Bragg. Continental breakfast included in room rates. (Only meal served.) Open every day in the year. Advance reservations important. Many natural, historic, and recreational attractions within a short distance. Beachcombing, scuba diving, fishing, and hiking nearby. Available by Greyhound Bus and Skunk Train. John and Colette Bailey, Innkeepers.

Directions: From the south, follow Hwy. 101 to Cloverdale, take Rte. 128 west to Hwy. 1, and follow north to Fort Bragg. Alternate route: Exit Hwy. 101 at Willits, then west on Rte. 20 to Fort Bragg. Driving time from San Francisco, 4 hrs. Another alternative: Hwy. 1 along the coast. Driving time from San Francisco: 6 hrs.

HARBOR HOUSE
Elk, California

Every so often I happen upon a letter that describes an inn-going experience so convincingly that I feel compelled to share it. Such a letter describes a visit to Harbor House in Elk, perched on a high cliff overlooking a truly unusual rock formation in the Pacific Ocean.

The inn is constructed entirely of redwood taken from nearby forests. Four of the five rooms have fireplaces, and there are four additional cottages on the south side, all with private baths.

Well, that's enough of the preliminaries—let's turn to the letter:

"We had the good fortune to discover your inn while visiting friends in California. We had planned to drive to the coast and spend a night by ourselves as a romantic break. Since we hadn't made reservations in advance, we were prepared to take pot luck.

"We finally got through to you and were able to reserve cottage 4. We were told we wouldn't really have an ocean view, and that dinner was at seven.

"The moment I stepped into the main house to register, I became aware of peace all around me. Though dinner was being prepared in the kitchen with its accompanying cheery noises, the impression I had was one of quiet. The evening sun glinted off the silverware, and I sensed a respect for the pervading silence.

"My first glimpse of our room made me smile, as I kept doing all during our magic stay at the Harbor House. A wood stove—how romantic—with wood piled and ready, a private porch, nice furniture—and there was a plant in the room! And clean, everything clean. And there was a view of the ocean, even though we had been told there was none.

"The whole experience of your inn was like that: surprise after tasteful surprise. Matching cloth tablecloths and napkins, wooden tables, real silverware, vegetables from the garden, a candle at our table when it got dark.

"Our dinner was the nice, slow, mellow kind I love and get so rarely. Such pleasant, unhurried service. We were free to be alone together or speak to the others if we wished. A wonderful blend of solitude and society. How have you produced this atmosphere?

"Incredibly, more surprises followed. We had been told about your beach path and wanted to say good night to the ocean. We asked if this was feasible in the dark, and during our brief discussion were presented with a huge flashlight and a key to the main house 'in case we needed to get in for any reason.'

"The ocean was beautiful by night. I felt really adventurous des´ ending that steep path by flashlight. The cove was just as beautiful the next morning when we made our pre-breakfast visit. I could see the little grotto and waterfall better in the morning light.

"I was also astounded when I arrived at breakfast. In addition to eggs baked with avocado and topped with cheese (who else has ever served such a breakfast?), a tiny flower appeared on the canteloupe slice on my plate.

"We got wonderful pictures of all the colorful flowers and scenery in your little spot. Beautiful as the pictures are, though, they do not capture what it was like to be there, or explain why I felt homesick when I had to leave."

HARBOR HOUSE, 5600 S. Hwy. #1, Box 369, Elk, CA 95432; 707-877-3203. A seaside inn with 5 guestrooms in the inn and 4 cottages, 16 mi. south of Mendocino, overlooking the Pacific. Modified American plan omits lunch. Breakfast and dinner served daily to houseguests. Open year-round. Ocean wading, abalone and shell hunting, fishing, and hiking on grounds. Golf, biking, boating, ocean white-water tours, deep-sea fishing, and canoeing nearby. Unsuitable for children or pets. No credit cards. Dean and Helen Turner, Innkeepers.

Directions: Take Rte. 128 from I-101 to Coast. Turn south on Hwy #1, 6 mi. to Harbor House.

"European plan" means that rates for rooms and meals are separate. "American plan" means that meals are included in the cost of the room. "Modified American plan" means that breakfast and dinner are included in the cost of the room. The rates at some inns include a continental breakfast with the lodging.

HERITAGE HOUSE
Little River, California

It might have been the Maine coast. The sixty-foot cliffs looked out over an ocean sparkling in the sun. The sloping lawn led to an ivy-covered white Colonial that could have graced Kennebunkport. Behind it was a low hill covered with evergreens that reminded me of Bar Harbor or Camden. Taken all together, the guest houses looked like a village near Bucksport, seventy-five years ago. Even the names have the flavor: "Firehouse," "Schoolhouse," "Chart Room," "Ice Cream Parlor," Apple House," "Barber Pole," and "Stable."

However, I was sitting in a rustic chair on the edge of the Pacific at Heritage House in Little River, California.

"There's good reason for you to feel as if you're in Maine," declared innkeeper Don Dennen. "Many 'down easters' came out here over 130 years ago, lured by the big timber. Naturally, the homes they built were similar to those they left behind. There are many along the Mendocino coast."

The guest houses at Heritage House were inspired by the early-day buildings. Mine was the "Country Store," and like most of the others it had many antiques and its own fireplace.

Although the New England influence is quite strong in this lovely little seaside inn, I believe the Dennens have blended the best of both coasts, because there is a reaching out for new ideas, a willingness to try new things that is typical of California.

This is reflected in the menu and the service as well. To illustrate: this is the only place where I was asked how crisp I wanted my breakfast bacon, or where I could make my own toast at the breakfast table, and where for dinner I've had corned beef spiced with ginger (the recipe for which is in the *CIBR Cookbook*). And while I was out having breakfast, someone was cleverly making my bed and freshening my room. "We think that our guests should return to a civilized-looking room," Don explained. Later in the day, there is a complete cleaning.

My eye was drawn inescapably to the continuous action of the Pacific Ocean as it thundered up against the rocks and cliffs just below. I asked Don what his guests enjoyed most about the area.

"We've never known a guest to be bored here on the Mendocino coast," he said. "Sometimes the days are crystal clear with the Pacific a deep blue, frothed with white. Sometimes sea, sky, and land are all of a color, broken only by the misty greens of pines, eucalyptus, and redwood and the carpeting of a hundred kinds of tiny plants. Nearby are things to explore and enjoy, but sometimes our guests just want to do what we are doing, sitting here and listening to the soothing sounds of the waves."

Heritage House is different. It has a pleasant, intimate atmosphere without room telephones or television. There are no planned activities. There are beautiful drives and walks along the ocean and in the forests and mountains and valleys nearby.

Guests are provided with ample information about circle tours along the coast and into the great woods. There are no amusements or special entertainment for children.

Each time I have visited the Heritage House since my original visit in 1970 I have found something that I've missed on previous trips or something that has been added. Don and I have had many a laugh over the first time I wrote about Heritage House and I referred to the "sun rising over the Pacific." Somehow or other I had gotten myself completely turned around.

Anyone planning a visit for a weekend should reserve months in advance. It might be a little easier in the middle of the week, but even then, reservations should be made.

From San Francisco, 140 miles distant, I believe the fastest way to Little River is via Route 101 to Cloverdale and then Route 128 west to the sea. Coastal Highway 1 through Bodega Bay, Jenner, and Point Arena sometimes seems to hang by its fingernails on the cliffs over the ocean.

HERITAGE HOUSE, Little River, CA 95456; 707-937-5885. A 52-guest-room elegant oceanside inn on Coast Highway 1, 144 mi. north of San Francisco, 6 mi. south of Mendocino. Modified American plan omits lunch. Breakfast and dinner served to travelers daily by reservation. Open from Feb. thru Nov. No amusements or special facilities for children. No pets. No credit cards. Don Dennen, Innkeeper.

Directions: From San Francisco (a 3-hr. drive) follow Rte. 101 to Cloverdale then Rte. 128 to Coast Highway 1. Inn is 5 mi. north of this junction on Hwy. 1.

THE INN
Rancho Santa Fe, California

The town of Rancho Sante Fe, California, is one of the most attractively designed that I have ever visited. It has been well described as a "civilized planned community." The homes and estates have been created in perfect harmony with nature's generous endowment of climate and scenery. One of the dominating factors is the presence of the gigantic eucalyptus trees.

Innkeeper Dan Royce told me the story. "It's hard to imagine this place without these great trees, but back in 1906 it was nothing but an area of sand and occasional low trees and brush. At that time the Santa Fe Railroad purchased the land for the purpose of growing eucalyptus trees for railroad ties. About three million seedlings were planted, but the project failed when it was discovered that the wood was not suitable. Fortunately, the trees were left to flourish and today we have glorious shade and beauty. They provide homes for literally thousands of birds.

"The first building of the Inn was constructed in 1923 and is now a part of the main building of today's inn. Beginning in 1941 it was expanded into a quiet resort where guests could enjoy the truly beautiful surroundings.

"In 1958, my father, Steve, acquired the property and it's been a family operation ever since."

At this mention of Steve Royce, who was dean of southern California hotelmen for many years, I was reminded of my first visit to Rancho Santa Fe.

Steve had given me the pleasure of a tour of the entire community with its beautiful homes and orange groves. When I mentioned this to Danny, he smiled and said, "Yes, my father certainly made a great contribution to innkeeping. One thing I learned from him that will never leave me is to make a point of meeting personally every guest in the Inn during his or her stay. I think in the true definition of the word dad was a real innkeeper."

The "family" feeling is extended even further when guests learn that the stunning framed needlepoints very much in evidence through the main lobby and living rooms of the Inn have been done by Danny's mother. For example, there is one very large, extremely handsome piece showing a large eucalyptus tree. It has become the symbol of the Inn and is found on all the stationery. My favorite is a needlepoint clock on one wall of the cathedral-ceilinged living room.

Cottages are scattered among the towering trees, and there's recreation for everyone here, including the younger set. The Inn has membership in nearby private 18-hole golf courses, and there are three tennis courts and a croquet green on the grounds. The swimming pool has an outdoor terrace where luncheons and refreshments are available. Also, the Inn has a beach cottage at nearby Del Mar for use during the summer months.

One of the most useful and gratifying amenities at the Inn is a map showing many short motor trips to points fifty miles away, including Lake Elsinore to the north and Tijuana, Mexico, to the south. I am personally acquainted with the rolling ranch and orchard country to the east as far away as Julian. All of these trips make a stay at the Inn worth several extra days.

Part of the pleasure of staying at the Inn is the opportunity to visit the shops in the village. They are all designed to be attractive, but unobtrusive. I stood in front of one building for three minutes without realizing that it was a supermarket!

All of this is happening today at Rancho Santa Fe because eucalyptus trees could not be used for railroad ties!

THE INN, Rancho Santa Fe, CA 92067; 714-756-1131. A 75-guestroom resort-inn, 27 mi. north of San Diego Freeway 5, 5 mi. inland from Solana Beach, Del Mar. European plan. Breakfast, lunch, and dinner served to travelers daily. Open year-round. Pool, tennis, and 6-wicket croquet course on grounds. Golf and ocean nearby. Daniel Royce, Innkeeper.

Directions: From I-5, take Exit S8 and drive inland about 6 mi.

LA MAIDA HOUSE
North Hollywood, California

Among the guidelines I have for selecting an inn for this book is the condition that it should have been in business at least one year, preferably longer. On my first visit to this old-world villa, set in a quiet residential neighborhood of North Hollywood, innkeeper Megan Timothy and her mother had not fulfilled this requirement, so I came back almost a year later and was absolutely enchanted by it.

I must confess that I found Megan equally as enchanting as the house. She was born in Rhodesia; however, she has lived in California for the past twenty years. She is an artist, working in stained glass as well as tiles. In fact, there are many articles in a large scrapbook, either about Megan or written by her on these subjects.

She explained to me that she also works in stone, silks, and fabrics as well as clay, and there are several examples of her crafts throughout the inn.

The entrance is through an old iron gate and the doorway is set within graceful Moorish arches. The living room is simple, with a very open feeling and a wonderful Italian marble fireplace. The main dining room has a lovely crystal chandelier, and another smaller dining room with a glass-topped table opens into an atrium where there are beautiful hanging plants. There is much leaded glass in evidence.

The stairway to the second floor takes a graceful turn, past one of Megan's great stained glass windows, and there is a tiny balcony looking out over a garden with an antique Italian fountain and massive magnolia trees, where breakfast may be taken. The hallway walls are adorned with photographs of Africa, many of them showing Megan as a horsewoman.

Bedrooms are large, light, airy, and inviting, and they have oriental rugs and primitive art gathered during Megan's worldwide travels.

Megan feels about cooking the same way she does about her other art: "We don't have any written menu and we try to adjust each menu to the preferences of our guests. We determine what they like and don't like. We do all ethnic cuisines, including, Indian, Indonesian, African, and Moroccan. Actually, there are about 2,000 different dishes that I can prepare.

"We get up early for breakfast, because we make all of our breads fresh, with a different bread every morning. We make our own fruit juices fresh. When we hear the guests coming down we make the juice immediately. There are seventeen different kinds of fruits in our own gardens." And, I might add, a great profusion of flowers, including daffodils that start blooming around January or February.

Besides guest rooms in the main house, there are additional accommodations in a series of little bungalows, just a short distance away,

which I found very pleasant indeed. One cottage had a bedroom and a garden and another has two bedrooms and a full kitchen. Incidentally, there is bottled spring water available for everybody. All of the guest rooms have terrycloth bathrobes. Megan pointed out the swimming pool, available to La Maida guests.

I never thought that I would find such a delicious inn in the Los Angeles area, but I did.

LA MAIDA HOUSE, 11159 La Maida St., North Hollywood, CA 91601; 818-769-3857. A 4-guestroom villa-like inn in a quiet residential area of North Hollywood. Additional bungalows nearby. Open year-round. Breakfast included in room rate. Dinner served on advance request. Conveniently located for Hollywood and Los Angeles. No smoking. Not suitable for children. No pets. No credit cards. Megan Timothy, Innkeeper.

Directions: From north or south on Hollywood Fwy., exit at Magnolia, turn east at first light; turn right on Tujunga Blvd., continue to next light; left on Camarillo St., 3 blocks to Bellflower. Turn left 1 block to La Maida and Bellflower.

I do not include lodging rates in the descriptions, for the very nature of an inn means that there are lodgings of various sizes, with and without baths, in and out of season, and with plain and fancy decoration. Travelers should call ahead and inquire about the availability and rates of the many different types of rooms.

THE PELICAN INN
Muir Beach, California

"Saturday sounds just fine. We really do lay on a first-rate Saturday lunch."

I almost had to pinch myself to make sure I wasn't in Surrey or Sussex, but on the telephone in Palo Alto, California, talking with the archetype of all British innkeepers, Charles Felix of the Pelican Inn. I had just made arrangements for Karen and Denny Levett and myself to drive up to Muir Beach the next day.

Charles Felix is, as he proudly announces, "the son of a publican." He cuts a most stylish figure, frequently wearing tweed coats, grey flannel trousers, and suede shoes. His distinctive white hair and mustache are further accentuated by a rich California tan, because Charles and Brenda, although British, have made California their home for many years.

Leaving San Francisco, Karen, Denny, and I turned off Route 101 at Mill Valley and followed Route 1 toward Muir Beach. The scenery on the way over to the ocean is in itself well worth the trip. Soon the white, half-timbered Pelican Inn, set amongst the trees, came into view and we had arrived. There were several other guests arriving for Saturday lunch, too.

Charles saw us as soon as we stepped inside the heavy wooden door and said, "Let me get you something from the pub." We sat for awhile in a low-ceilinged room with its heavy posts and beams and beautiful old tables, hutches, and sideboards. Charles explained that many of the furnishings had been sent over from England and many were over 200 years old. We wandered around a bit and admired the Inglenook fireplace and then took our places at a table on the outside patio.

Brenda Felix sat with us for a while, even though it was a very busy day of the week. "I do hope you will be able to return sometime when we have our 'players' here. They do excerpts from Shakespeare's plays with some variations, playing amongst the tables and often involving the audience. It's really wonderful. They also did *Beyond The Fringe* recently and everybody laughed themselves silly."

The menu that Saturday included baked beans, sausage rolls, chicken, zucchini soup, various cold meats, marinated chicken wings, salads, a quiche, french bread, and several different desserts. Karen said the shepherd's pie was absolutely divine, as were the little round goodies made with sausage and served with hot mustard.

Meanwhile, patrons were coming through the front door with great expectation, and soon it was very much like such scenes I have enjoyed in England at a Saturday or Sunday pub lunch.

Our trip also included a tour of the Tudor-style guest rooms with

heavy exposed beams and white plaster walls. There are Hogarth prints and English countryside scenes adorning the walls. Many rooms have half-tester beds, and all have a profusion of fresh flowers. Charles explained that the morning paper and a hearty English breakfast are part of the tariff. Hanging over one of the beds was a stone with a hole in it to "prevent rickets in case of pregnancy." Witches and the little folk are all kept at bay, which, as Charles says, "makes the Pelican a haven from the evil eye."

A discreet card is found in each room with the legend, "It is humbly requested that your breakfast be consumed between 8:15 and 10:00 a.m., since the management is intimidated by a ferocious cook who commences luncheon preparations at that time. It is further requested that your departure be completed by noon to allow the harried chambermaid to attend to the rooms."

Following lunch, we walked down to Muir Beach and then strolled back just in time for afternoon tea.

I think Karen summed up our trip beautifully with the remark, "It is all that I expected and much, much more."

THE PELICAN INN, Muir Beach, CA 94965; 415-383-6000. A 6-guest-room (private baths) English inn on the northern California coast, 8 mi. from the Golden Gate Bridge. Price of lodgings includes breakfast. Breakfast, lunch, and dinner served daily. Swimming, tennis, backroading, walking, and all San Francisco attractions nearby. Charles Felix, Innkeeper.

Directions: From Golden Gate Bridge follow Rte. 101 north to Mill Valley exit, turn left at traffic lights and follow Hwy. 1 to Muir Beach.

RED CASTLE INN
Nevada City, California

"We are, I believe, one of the prime examples of Gothic Revival architecture in California." Jerry Ames, Chris Dickman, and I were seated in the pleasant garden of the Red Castle Inn, high above Nevada City, discussing the history and other fascinating features of the inn. Chris, who is extremely knowledgeable about such things, asserted that, as far as he knows, the Red Castle is one of two examples of genuine Gothic Revival design on the West Coast, and this should not be confused with "Carpenter Gothic," which is quite common. "It's particularly identifiable by the arched windows on the top floor and the double brick walls. The house has never been altered since it was built in 1860 by Judge John Williams, a mine owner and civic leader, who with his family crossed the plains in 1849.

"In near-ruins, the house was restored by James W. Scharr in 1963. I think it stands today as a proud reminder of the part that the 'Argonauts' played in the heritage of California. It's a registered point of historical interest and recognized as such by the Daughters of the Golden West."

The house tour included one fascinating feature after another.

On that particularly warm day, I was delightfully impressed by the fact that the temperature inside the house was at least twenty degrees cooler than it was outdoors. Jerry said that was because of the double brick walls. I saw all eight bedrooms, five of which have private baths, and all are furnished with very handsome antiques. Each one has its own individuality. "By the time we bought it, the house had been through several different careers," commented Chris. "Fortunately, it has never been altered, which is wonderful because some of these old buildings have been butchered over the years." Chris proved to be rather adamant on the subject of preservation, undoubtedly because of his background in interior design.

We started from the very top floor and worked our way down, and it was on the small balcony way up in the treetops that I learned about one of the early inhabitants, Judge William's son, and his penchant for playing the cornet from this vantage point. I believe it had something to do with communicating with the ladies of the town. There's a photograph of him in the hallway sporting a very fierce mustache.

Throughout the house there are wonderful collections of wall hangings and such decorative pieces as beautiful fans and theatrical masks from all over the world, including a Japanese *No* mask made about 1870 and signed by the actors. I've never seen an inn with a collection of masks before. Much interesting reading is available, with a wide selection of magazines and books.

We tarried for awhile in the main living room where I felt the sense of buoyancy that fresh flowers give to a room. On an antique desk there was an old-fashioned brass telephone with a separate earpiece, as well as stereoscopic photographs and a special viewer. Fascinating bric-a-brac filled almost every corner. "We've tried to keep everything as authentically 'period' as possible," Jerry said.

In Nevada City, California, where gold strikes were a way of life a hundred years ago, I found one of my own: the Red Castle Inn.

RED CASTLE INN, 109 Prospect St., Nevada City, CA 95959; 916-265-5135. An 8-guestroom inn on a hill overlooking one of the great gold rush communities in the foothills of the Sierra Nevada Mountains at approx. 2800-ft. altitude. Lodgings include continental breakfast (the only meal served). Open year-round. There are numerous historic, cultural, and recreational attractions, all within a very short distance. No recreation on grounds. Hiking, golf, xc skiing nearby. No diversions for small children. German and Spanish are spoken. Jerry Ames and Chris Dickman, Innkeepers.

Directions: Nevada City is on Rte. 49, the Gold Rush Highway. Eastbound: When arriving in town, take Broad St. turnoff. Turn right, and then right again up the hill to the Exxon station. Take a hard left into Prospect St. Westbound: Take Coyote St. turnoff. Turn left down the hill, and left on Broad St., right on Sacramento; up the hill to the Exxon station and a hard left into Prospect.

THE SANDPIPER INN
Carmel-by-the-Sea, California

It was a very stimulating morning at the Sandpiper because it had rained during the night in Carmel, and all of the flowers and bushes in the gardens in front of the inn were glistening with water, and birds were twittering merrily, going about from branch to branch. Inside, in the impressive cathedral living room, a good fire was burning and at the far end there were guests enjoying breakfast and reading the morning papers. In the reception area there was the pleasant hustle and bustle of departing guests promising to meet again next year.

Graeme and Irene Mackenzie, looking as bright and fresh as the morning, were moving from guest to guest making arrangements, expressing concern and hospitality in their clipped British accents. I happened to hear Graeme explaining what I took to be the inherent nature of Carmel to one of the guests.

"We who live here think that Carmel is a city of serendipity," he said. "We have houses and cottages with sunny balconies and courtyards, and I'm sure you've experienced the collection of small streets." I might add that Carmel's white beaches, narrow cypresses and magnificent seascapes are further rewards for the visitor.

"We're a kind of sleepy village." he continued. "There are no street lights, no sidewalks in residential districts, no street numbers, and, I guess most important, no neon signs."

I drifted over to another group where Irene was carrying on a lively conversation in French. She is quite at home with many other languages as well.

Each time I visit I'm impressed with the resemblance of this inn to an English country house hotel. Irene and Graeme fit beautifully into this ambience because they are both Scottish, so one might say that they blend right into the English and French antiques, flowered quilted bedspreads, wallpapered bathrooms, and freshly picked nosegays. Some of the bedrooms have wood-burning fireplaces, but there are no TVs or telephones in the rooms, ensuring peace and quiet.

The inn itself is about seventy yards from the beach with sweeping views across Carmel Bay to Pebble Beach. The wide beach has white sand and is a marvelous place for sunning and picnicking. Both Irene and Graeme are very much interested in outdoor sports, including golf, tennis, and racquet ball, and are happy to introduce their houseguests to some of the clubs on the peninsula in which they have membership. There are also excellent back roads, as well as a tour of wineries in the area. The new Aquarium on Cannery Row is well worth a three-hour visit.

Later, after things had calmed down a bit and guests had gone off to play golf, walk the beach, or just sit in a quiet corner reading a book, I asked Graeme how an inn happened to be in this section of Carmel, where I had noted there were only private homes.

"The original guest house was built in 1930," he explained. "It came into existence before the very stringent zoning laws went into effect; hence our guests have the advantage of being in a very quiet section of the village and still only a few steps from the beach."

THE SANDPIPER INN at-the-Beach, 2408 Bayview Ave. at Martin St., Carmel-by-the-Sea, CA 93923; 408-624-6433. A 15-guestroom bed-and-breakfast inn and cottages near the Pacific Ocean. Breakfast only meal offered. Open all year. Carmel and Stuarts Cove beaches, Old Carmel Mission, Point Lobos State Park, 17-Mile Drive, and Big Sur State Park nearby. Ten-speed bicycles available; jogging and walking on beach. Arrangements can be made to play at nearby private golf and tennis clubs with pools and hot tubs. Children over 12 welcome. Please, no pets. Graeme and Irene Mackenzie, Innkeepers.

Directions: From Hwy. 1 turn right at Ocean Ave., through Carmel Village, and turn left on Scenic Dr. (next to Ocean). Proceed to end of beach to Martin St. and turn left.

I do not include lodging rates in the descriptions, for the very nature of an inn means that there are lodgings of various sizes, with and without baths, in and out of season, and with plain and fancy decoration. Travelers should call ahead and inquire about the availability and rates of the many different types of rooms.

THE SEAL BEACH INN AND GARDENS
Seal Beach, California

The best way for all of us to keep as up-to-date as possible with Marjorie Bettenhausen at the Seal Beach Inn is for me to share portions of her recent correspondence:

"The decision to build a state-of-the-art kitchen and hire Kay Trepp, a two-star chef, has opened up all kinds of wonderful possibilities, from room service to elegant dining, from picnic lunches to high teas and what finer setting than in our lovely gardens.

"Not too long ago seventeen crates of artwork from France arrived. Two of them contained a wonderful 17th-century fountain that once sat in a village center and now graces our poolside gardens. We had to hire a huge crane just to place the treasure. Another piece we enjoy immensely

is a marble cherub. Guests photograph themselves with him. Many other beautiful pieces found their home throughout the property. We're gathering quite a notable antique garden art collection, and Jack and I really enjoyed those shopping trips to France.

"I'm also happy to say that your friend Jens Deikmann has added us to the limited number of Romantik Hotels in North America. We're very proud.

"We're still doing Sunday afternoon chamber music concerts. It's been such a pleasant way to please the guests and have the community join us.

"We've always considered ourselves a romantic hideaway, and now have even more reason to believe so. Just five blocks away our guests can avail themselves of a romantic gondola ride through the canals of Naples. This becomes an attractive part of a honeymoon package."

When I first visited the Seal Beach Inn it was little more than a motel from the 1920s, but Marjorie and Jack Bettenhausen with talent, enthusiasm, and boundless energy have converted it into a fairyland of brick courtyards, old ornate street lights, blue canopies, objets d'art, fountains, shuttered windows, window boxes, and vines.

The French Mediterranean appearance is enhanced by the marvelous gardens. All of the lodging rooms are named after flowers, including fuchsia, gardenia, and camellia. The full-time gardener keeps the flowers blooming even in winter. There are rare vines, climbing vines, flowering bushes, sweet-smelling bushes, deciduous trees, evergreen pear trees, and a wonderful variety of cascading willowy tree that looks like a weeping willow, but really isn't. It stays green all year.

The entrance to the inn from the street is through a three-sided square, around which the guest rooms are situated, and which becomes a flower-filled courtyard, lit by street lamps that were rescued from the scrap pile at nearby Long Beach. There is a red English telephone booth in one corner; a kiosk that would be quite at home in Nice has notices of all the nearby attractions. Breakfast is served in a small, cozy, French-style tearoom, presided over by a cheerful hostess.

Marjorie maintains that it takes many years to establish an inn *par excellence* and declares that "we finally are reaching the end of inn adolescence and moving into golden maturity. We want to be the best inn in the state, not just in beauty but in the warmth and love in which we serve."

THE SEAL BEACH INN AND GARDENS, 212 5th St., Seal Beach, CA 90740; 213-493-2416 or 213-430-3915. A 22-guestroom village inn located in a quiet residential area of an attractive town, 300 yds. from beach. Breakfast only meal served. Open all year. Near Disneyland, Knott's Berry Farm, Lion Country Safari, Catalina Island (20 mi. offshore), and California mountains and lakes 2 hrs. away. Long Beach Playhouse, Long Beach Music Center nearby. Swimming pool on grounds. Tennis, beach, biking, skating, golf nearby. No pets. Marjorie and Jack Bettenhausen, Innkeepers.

Directions: From Los Angeles Airport take Hwy. 405 Freeway south to Seal Beach Blvd. exit. Turn left toward the beach, right on the Pacific Coast Hwy., left on 5th St. in Seal Beach, which is the first stoplight after main street. Inn is on the left, 2 blocks toward the beach on 5th St.

SUTTER CREEK INN
Sutter Creek, California

It was 1967 when I first flew to the West Coast in search of country inns. I had been persuaded by Jane Way at the Sutter Creek Inn to visit the gold fields of California. She was sure that I would love it. Well, Jane was right, and I have been visiting California and writing about the Sutter Creek Inn ever since.

It is, in fact, an inn with its New Hampshire heritage much in evidence in the porches and high, pointed roof. There are grape vines, tomato plants, gardenias, trumpet vines, Virginia creepers, hollyhocks, chrysanthemums, gooseberries, zinnias, and roses in abundance.

On that first visit and every time since, at the end of the day, I have joined the other guests on the porch to watch the huge, old white owls that live in the barn circle over the backyard and fly off to the redwood trees to spend the rest of the night.

The only meal served at this inn is breakfast, but it is really an experience. When the bell rings at 9 a.m., everyone sits at long, family-style tables. "Our breakfasts are big and hearty," says Jane. "It's a good basis for a full day of exploring the mother lode country."

Ten of the several bedrooms of the inn have fireplaces and four have swinging beds that hang from the ceiling on chains. These, by the way, can be stabilized. Jane fell in love with the idea while traveling in the tropics. They are the most popular rooms at the inn. "Very romantic, indeed," says Jane.

I should caution our readers that reservations in advance are almost always necessary in order to avoid disappointments. There is a two-day minimum stay on weekends, either Friday and Saturday or Saturday and

Sunday. "Sometimes," said Jane, "we do have last-minute cancellations." With this in mind, a telephone call to Jane on a Thursday might provide a very pleasant surprise.

"You might also point out to your readers," Jane added, "that we are rather small, so children are not encouraged as guests. In addition, pets and cigar smoking are a 'no-no.'"

At the Sutter Creek Inn, deep in the mother lode country, fireplaces blaze in cold weather and there are warm lazy summer days to be spent in hammocks, or out exploring the gold rush country. Sutter Creek, Volcano, Murphy's, Angel's Camp and Sonora are all part of the great living legend of gold in California and they are all on or near Route 49, which runs along the foothills of the Sierras.

For many of her guests, Jane Way and the Sutter Creek Inn are the "first" country inn experience. "People frequently ask me," she said, "about the essential qualities for successful country innkeeping.

"I reply that the most important is unlimited love for people."

SUTTER CREEK INN, 75 Main St., Box 385, Sutter Creek, CA 95685; 209-267-5606. A 19-guestroom New England village inn on the main street of a historic mother lode town, 35 mi. from Sacramento. Lodgings include breakfast. No meals served to travelers. Open all year. Water skiing, riding, fishing, and boating nearby. No children under 10. No pets. Mrs. Jane Way, Innkeeper.

Directions: From Sacramento, travel on the Freeway (50) toward Placerville and exit at Power Inn Rd. Turn right and drive one block; note signs for Rte. 16 and Jackson. Turn left on Fulsom Rd., approx. ¼ mi.; follow Rte. 16 signs to right for Jackson. Rte. 16 joins Rte. 49. Turn right to Sutter Creek. From San Francisco, follow Freeway (80) to Sacramento and take previous directions or drive via Stockton to Rte. 49.

I do not include lodging rates in the descriptions, for the very nature of an inn means that there are lodgings of various sizes, with and without baths, in and out of season, and with plain and fancy decoration. Travelers should call ahead and inquire about the availability and rates of the many different types of rooms.

TOLL HOUSE INN
Boonville, California

"How in the world did this place get its name?" I asked. "I didn't realize that there were toll roads in this part of California; in fact, I didn't realize that there were *any* toll roads in California."

Beverly Nesbitt and I were seated on a terrace in the rear of Toll House, looking out over the gently rolling landscape of this valley, midway between Route 101 and the Mendocino coast.

"At one time," she recounted, "this house served as the main head-quarters for the Miller family's vast sheep-grazing and hop-growing holdings. The family maintained this road and extracted a toll from the muleskinners who hauled redwood logs to the inland mills; hence, the name Toll House. Actually, the Miller ranch was here much earlier in the 19th century and is a part of the pioneer history of early California."

Our chat was preceded by a walk through the little inn, where there are four guest rooms. The library on the first floor has a queen-sized Murphy bed, as well as a sofa, fireplace, and private bath. It also has its own solarium, which is wonderful for watching the sunset.

Upstairs, Mollie's Room, named for Beverly's granddaughter, has very feminine colors and a most comfortable air. Kathy's Room, named for Beverly's eldest daughter, also has a queen-sized bed, daybed, and lounges. A very pleasant surprise is the Blue Room, with a larger-than-life bathroom and its own fireplace. Everything is countrified, but at the same time has a pleasant, sophisticated feeling about it.

I noticed that Beverly had installed a hot tub on the terrace, and had added an extra little feature that she called a foot warmer. "After you get out of the hot tub, you put your feet in this place and it keeps them warm."

It was the spring of the year and the fruit trees were in bloom, including a handsome flowering cherry. "The garden was planted in 1915," she remarked. "So you can see that it's all fully matured. Those are European cut-leaf birches, which are very unusual for California."

Dinner is offered to inn guests on advance request; however, there is no public dining room. "We have either a three-course country supper or a five-course formal dinner," she explained. "Tonight, we are doing a Middle Eastern lamb stew with apricots. We do lots of roasts—roast beef, roast pork, and so forth. We really do what our guests want and then build the menu around it. When they make reservations, we find out their preferences as far as main courses are concerned.

"Breakfast of course is always a wonderful time and everybody enjoys our breakfasts of freshly squeezed orange juice, fresh fruits, pancakes, waffles, and homemade breads. We like to send our guests out for a day on the coast or in the great redwood forests with something substantial."

I asked Beverly how guests occupy themselves when they come here for two or three days. She replied, "Ask them."

So I did.

"Well, we eat very well," was the reply, "and the last time we were here we went over to Mendocino and had a very pleasant ride back. There are very many interesting things to do, including touring the wineries and bird watching, and the backroading is wonderful."

Beverly's latest news is that a cozy little room with twin brass beds has been created in the garden.

One final point. Highway 253 is no longer a toll road.

TOLL HOUSE INN, P.O. Box 268, Hwy. 253, Boonville, CA 95415; 707-895-3630. A 5-guestroom (2 with private bath and fireplace) former ranch house in the secluded Bell Valley and the Mendocino wine country of northern Calif. Full breakfast included. Open all year. Dinner available by prior arrangement. Hot tub, sundeck, garden, bird watching on grounds. Wineries, Mendocino, the Skunk Railway, and Fort Bragg nearby. No children under 10. No pets. No credit cards. Smoking discouraged. Beverly Nesbitt, Innkeeper.

Directions: From the north on U.S. 101, exit Rte. 253 south of Ukiah. Watch for inn on your right about 6 mi. north of Boonville. From the south on U.S. 101, exit Rte. 128 on the northern outskirts of Cloverdale. Upon reaching Boonville, turn right on Rte. 253 and the inn will be on your left after 6 mi.

UNION STREET INN
San Francisco, California

"We are Edwardian, not Victorian."

Helen Stewart and I were having breakfast, seated in the sunny garden at the rear of the Union Street Inn. The fragrance of lilacs, camellias, and violets filled the air, and an occasional hummingbird darted from blossom to blossom. Some guests were enjoying breakfast on the spacious deck overlooking the garden, and there was the unmistakable aroma of fresh coffee and croissants. In this quiet retreat it was difficult to realize that we were in the heart of one of San Francisco's most attractive shopping and entertainment areas.

"I say Edwardian," Helen continued, "because we're rather proud of the fact that in a city that has so much Victoriana, we are a bit different. The Edwardians, already into the 20th century, were less ostentatious than their elders. Their ornamentation was tempered by a new conservatism, and we like to feel that many of our decorations and furnishings are understatements."

Helen is a former San Francisco schoolteacher, who found herself involved in a mid-life career change. She restored and remodeled this handsome turn-of-the-century building, using tones and textures that are not only in the period, but also increase the feeling of hospitality.

The five bedrooms have such intriguing names as Wildrose, Holly, Golden Gate, and English Garden. Two have private bathrooms, and the others have running water in the rooms and share two bathrooms.

Two of the bedrooms have queen-sized beds with canopies, two have gleaming brass beds; all have really impressive, carefully chosen antiques. The brochure of the inn explains the different color schemes for each room. "If reservations are made sufficiently in advance, and the guests can anticipate a mood, these can all be coordinated." Helen made this comment with the faint suggestion of a twinkle.

My room had one of the queen-sized beds with very pleasant dark green wallpaper and matching draperies, which were most helpful in keeping the sun from intruding too early. The walls were adorned with two of the well-known Degas prints of ballet dancers. I thought they were quite appropriate, remembering King Edward's fondness for pretty women.

One end of the room had been turned into an alcove containing a rather elegantly decorated wash basin with mirrors and generous, fluffy towels. A very handsome antique mahogany dressing table had a three-way oval mirror. This is typical of the appointments of the other bedrooms, and I found many welcome living plants in all of the bedrooms.

Helen has converted the old carriage house at the bottom of the garden into a very fetching accommodation, with a large bay window

overlooking the garden, and its own jacuzzi. The garden has been remodeled, and a Victorian-looking curved fence with a lovely old-fashioned gate has been added. It truly does resemble an English garden.

A glance at the comments from the guest book told me the story: "Happiness is staying here!" "What a refreshing change from typical hotel stays." "Like returning to visit an old 'friend.' " "We'll be back for a second honeymoon."

"How far are you from Fisherman's Wharf?" I asked, helping myself to another tasty croissant. "Oh, we're just minutes away," she said. "Our guests walk to Ghirardelli Square, the Cannery, and Pier 39. It's possible to take streetcars and cable cars to almost every point of interest in San Francisco."

UNION STREET HOTEL, 2229 Union St., San Francisco, CA 94123; 415-346-0424. A 5-guestroom (3 rooms share 2 baths) bed-and-breakfast inn. Convenient to all of the San Francisco attractions, including the cable car line. Breakfast only meal served. Open every day except Christmas and New Year's. Unable to accommodate children under 12. No pets. Helen Stewart, Innkeeper.

Directions: Take the Van Ness exit from Rte. 101 to Union St.; turn left. The inn is between Fillmore and Steiner on the left side of the street.

VAGABOND HOUSE
Carmel-by-the-Sea, California

I had joined a group of other Vagabond House guests in the parlor, where we were all enjoying a continental breakfast. The conversation turned to the squirrels who were knocking on the windows and disporting themselves in the trees and the gardens. Manager Bruce Indorato explained that they consume about thirty pounds of peanuts a week, and so saying, he opened up the window just enough to put some more peanuts on the outer ledge. "Every once in a while one gets inside," he said, "and then it's hilarious. Of course, they are very tame and they really do know how to find their way out again, but it's fun while it lasts."

I'll have to explain next that the breakfast we were enjoying was a *true* continental breakfast, with fresh pastries, cheese, hard-boiled eggs, and lots of coffee and tea. One of the guests remarked that it was like the continental breakfasts he had come to enjoy while traveling in Europe.

The Vagabond House is a delightful experience that begins when guests walk up the stone steps and enter an atmosphere that seems almost magical. There is a three-sided courtyard enhanced by many trees, including mock orange, magnolia, and live oaks. The plantings include camellias, primroses, tulips, and daffodils in great profusion, along with impatiens, rhododendrons, fuchsias, and many other varieties of flowers.

Accommodations are in eleven completely different cottage rooms or suites, many of which have their own woodburning fireplaces. The rooms are large and pleasingly furnished with Early American maple furniture, quilted bedspreads, and antique clocks; some have kitchens. Most rooms are supplied with coffeepots and fresh ground coffee for brewing.

Actually, reservations for three different inns may be arranged through the Vagabond House, and each provides a different kind of atmosphere. The Vagabond House itself is the best known and most popular of the three.

The other two are equally interesting in their own way. The San Antonio House, somewhat European in nature, is a smaller building in a very quiet residential section. Each large room has its own fireplace.

On the other hand, Lincoln Green, in another residential section of Carmel, is particularly adaptable for children, with much more space for running about. The four little dwellings, called Maid Marian, Robin Hood, Little John, and Friar Tuck, offer a total of four suites, each with a living room and bedroom able to accommodate four people comfortably. In each living room is a stone fireplace and a sofa that turns into a bed.

Carmel is justly famous for its shopping and galleries, and a walk along Ocean Avenue will afford the chance to browse on the way down to the spectacular beachscape.

Another point of interest in the area is Point Lobos, just south of Carmel. Its six-mile-long, unbroken coastline encompasses many spectacular views, as does the 17-Mile Drive. Incidentally, the main road south through Big Sur is now open, after being closed by mudslides.

Golf is one of the main reasons to come to this part of the world, and during the annual Bing Crosby tournament, many of the touring pros have reserved for years in advance at the Vagabond House.

VAGABOND HOUSE, Fourth & Dolores Streets, P.O.Box 2747, Carmel-by-the-Sea, CA 93921; 408-624-7738 or 408-624-7403. An 11-guestroom village inn serving a European continental breakfast to houseguests only. No other meals served. Open every day of the year. Bike renting, golf, natural beauty, enchanting shops nearby. Not ideal for children. Attended, leashed pets allowed. Dennis and Karen Levett, Owners; Bruce Indorato and Jewell Brown, Innkeepers.

Directions: Turn off Hwy. 1 onto Ocean Ave.; turn right from Ocean Ave. onto Dolores, continue 2½ blocks. Parking provided for guests.

I do not include lodging rates in the descriptions, for the very nature of an inn means that there are lodgings of various sizes, with and without baths, in and out of season, and with plain and fancy decoration. Travelers should call ahead and inquire about the availability and rates of the many different types of rooms.

THE WINE COUNTRY INN
St. Helena, California

Once again, Jim Smith of the Wine Country and I were taking a short walk after dinner following a meeting of the West Coast innkeepers in *CIBR*. This time, however, it was in the spring of the year at the Benbow Inn in Garberville. Jim reminded me of our previous stroll several years earlier at the Heritage House.

"Well, we've made a good deal of progress since then," he commented. "I think at the Wine Country Inn a great deal of our emphasis in recent years has been in landscape designing and garden planting, and fortunately Marge and Ned are enthusiastic gardeners."

Marge and Ned Smith (Jim's mother and father) visited me in Stockbridge, Massachusetts, back in the early 1970s. They were looking for ideas, furniture, and inspiration to create what was the first and for many years the only country inn in the Napa Valley.

After visiting about fifteen New England inns they returned to California, found a perfect site, and the whole family began to work on building their inn.

I first visited them in 1975 and, believe it or not, as I drove down Lodi Lane there was a muscular young man I later learned was Jim Smith, putting up the new sign that announced "The Wine Country Inn." He and I have had many a laugh over that day ever since.

"The inn was a family project right from the start. We tried to arrange for every room to have a view," Jim recounted. "Some have intimate balconies and others have patios leading to the lawn. The natural wild mustard, lupines, poppies, and live oak trees blended with plantings of oleanders, petunias, and Chinese pistachios to accent the scenery."

Well, Ned and Marge picked up quite a few antiques on that first trip to New England, but there have been many other trips since, so today each bedroom is individually decorated with country antique furnishings, refinished and reconstructed by everyone in the family. Many of the rooms have fireplaces, canopy beds, tufted bedspreads, and handmade quilts. There are no televisons or radios, but a generous supply of magazines and books, and big, comfortable, fluffy pillows encourage what I continually refer to as the lost art of reading.

Jim and I continued our stroll along a branch of the North Eel River, flowing beside the Benbow Inn. "My plans for a swimming pool and spa are coming right along," he said, "and I expect our guests to be using and enjoying them in the summer of '86."

Visitors in the Napa Valley enjoy visits to the many wineries, as well as to mineral baths, geysers, a petrified forest, and several Robert Louis Stevenson memorial sites. There are a number of antique shops in the area and the manicured agricultural beauty of the valley contrasts with the

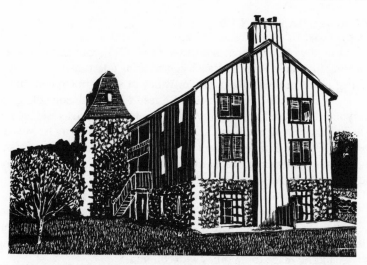

rugged, tree-covered hills surrounding it. It is dotted with century-old stone bridges, pump houses, barns, and stone buildings, all of which are a delight to both painter and photographer.

On a more personal note I have to say that becoming acquainted with people like Ned and Marge Smith and their sons, Jim and Jeff, and watching the progress of such families over the years has always been a great source of satisfaction for me. I think other innkeepers in California are fortunate to have such a model inn after which to fashion themselves. The care and consideration that have gone into the designing, and the result, prove that a country inn doesn't have to be old to be legendary.

It's the spirit that matters.

THE WINE COUNTRY INN, 1152 Lodi Lane, St. Helena, CA 94574; 707-963-7077. A 25-room country inn in the Napa wine valley of California, about 70 mi. from San Francisco. Continental breakfast served to houseguests, no other meals served. Open daily except Dec. 22-27. This inn is within driving distance of a great many wineries and also the Robert Louis Stevenson Museum. Swimming pool and spa on grounds. Golf and tennis nearby. No children. No pets. Jim Smith, Innkeeper.

Directions: From San Francisco take the Oakland Bay Bridge to Hwy. 80. Travel north to the Napa cutoff. Stay on Hwy. 29 through the town of St. Helena, for 1¾ mi. north to Lodi Lane, then turn east ¼ mi. to inn.

PARADISE RANCH INN
Grants Pass, Oregon

Once a working ranch, homesteaded in 1913, with cattle, horses, and other livestock, Paradise Ranch began taking guests many years ago. Nestled in the beautiful Rogue River Valley of southern Oregon, in the last few years it has become more of a resort-inn, with something for everyone. There are lighted, all-weather tennis courts and a resident pro, a heated swimming pool and spa, jogging and bicycle trails, several ponds stocked with rainbow trout and other fish, a lake with swans and ducks, a chip-and-putt green, horses and trails, and whitewater rafting on the Rogue River. As if that weren't enough, there is also a recreation barn where any number of activities and special events take place.

Mattie and Oliver Raymond have been here for nineteen years and they run the ranch with the help of other family members, extending their friendly hospitality to their many guests. I find it particularly appealing as a wonderful place for families with children.

The white rambling ranch house, white fences, and neat outbuildings set against the backdrop of rolling, green meadows make a fetching picture, indeed. The guest rooms are all comfortably and individually furnished with flowered wallpaper, beamed ceilings, double and queen-sized beds, and, something I appreciate, extra pillows.

Mattie is justly proud of their chef, Billy Dunn, whom she describes as "one of the finest chefs in southern Oregon. He is classically trained and has worked at distinguished restaurants throughout this country. Actually, he was born here in Grants Pass, but ventured out into the world to learn cuisine. He emphasizes natural ingredients, and all of the breads and desserts are prepared daily in our kitchen." His menu is eclectic, with such dishes as chicken teriyaki, fresh fish in season, veal scaloppini à la Marsala, scampi Milanese, porterhouse steak smothered in onions and mushrooms, and a vegetarian plate. His hors d'oeuvres include escargot,

sweet and sour chicken wings, and french-fried zucchini. The dining room has windows on three sides and overlooks the lake, with breathtaking views of the Cascade Mountains.

I noticed a little folder entitled "Fishing Guide" that has everything you need to know about fishing in the three stocked ponds. Prospective fishermen are cautioned about not fishing in the Garden Pond, which is reserved for their pet fish—they get fed, not caught. All the paraphernalia necessary for fishing may be obtained at the ranch. "We use barbless hooks," Ollie told me, "because the fish are so plentiful we feel it is not very sporting otherwise." You can catch a fish for your dinner if you like and Billy Dunn will cook it for you, in which case, you pay for your dinner, but not the fishing fee.

The game room of the barn has three pool tables, a beautiful ping-pong table, and shuffleboard. There's also a piano, and on cool days, a cheery fire burns in the fireplace.

So, whether it's action in a whitewater raft on the Rogue River or helping with a cattle roundup or simply relaxing under a tree, Paradise Ranch Inn offers an attractive vacation.

PARADISE RANCH INN, 7000 Monument Dr., Grants Pass, OR 97526; 503-479-4333. A 16-guestroom ranch-inn nestled in the beautiful mountains of the Rogue River Valley. Open year-round. Restaurant open to public; closed Mon. and Tues. Heated swimming pool, hot tub, lighted all-weather tennis courts, fishing, surrey rides, hayrides, trail rides, cattle roundup, square dancing, recreational center, and children-watching available on grounds. Spectacular Rogue River raft trips and all-day horseback riding, Shakespearean Festival, Crater Lake, and Oregon caves nearby. Children most welcome. Mattie and Ollie Raymond, Innkeepers.

Directions: From the Bay Area follow Rte. 101 north to Crescent City and then Rte. 199 to Grants Pass; turn north on Rte. 5 and exit at Merlin. Go under Rte. 5, turn right on Monument Mountain Dr. for 2½ mi. Ranch is on left.

A number of inns have nearby airports where private airplanes may land. An airplane symbol at the end of the inn directions indicates that there is an airport nearby. Consult inn for further information.

STEAMBOAT INN
Steamboat, Oregon

I was on the Umpqua Highway (Route 138) on my way for a visit with Jim and Sharon Van Loan at the Steamboat Inn, a country inn that is a steelhead fisherman's dream.

This is the heartland of Oregon, and after a pleasant trip from Crescent City and Eureka, California, up Routes 101 and 199, I thrilled to the scenery on I-5 from Grants Pass to Roseburg.

Now, having left the Interstate and turning east, I was getting the feeling of what inland Oregon is really like. There were many cattle farms and fruit orchards gradually giving way to the beautiful upland country, and soon the road was running parallel to the North Umpqua River.

The road was getting steeper and the river more rambunctious. I remembered that Jim and Sharon had suggested in their inn folder that even though it's a challenge, they discouraged guests from trying canoe or boat trips on this river.

This idyllic trip along the river ended as I arrived at the Steamboat Inn and was immediately taken in tow again by both Jim and Sharon, who are two very friendly people, quite suited to innkeeping.

I was shown to one of the eight original rustic cabins, all of which are joined by a deck that extends out over the river, and soon I was enveloped in the euphoria created by the melodious, ever-present sounds of the water rushing by on its way to the Pacific Ocean.

I joined the other guests on the new back porch of the lodge in time to be well introduced by Jim and Sharon and to admire the original paintings that line the walls. After hors d'oeuvres we were all invited to sit down around the great harvest table in the dining area and enjoy the main course. Sharon explained that a typical dinner includes several vegetables, homemade bread or pasta, and a selected entrée of the evening. On this particular evening it was a lamb roast. There is one main dish at each meal but, as Jim said, "Even if you're here for three weeks you will not have the same evening meal twice. Sharon even keeps a record of the entrées guests were served on previous visits to make sure they will have a different main dish each time."

Dinner is generally served a half-hour after dark every night during summer months and around seven during the winter.

Following dinner, I had a chance to talk with Jim and Sharon about how they came to be located here. "Originally, we came because of Jim's enthusiasm for fly-fishing," Sharon responded. "Then it occurred almost simultaneously to all of us that this would be a wonderful place to raise a family, and it seemed like a viable way of involving everyone and still being able to make financial progress. It's worked out wonderfully and all of our children are involved."

Jim continued, "Although fishing is a big activity here about three months of the year, the rest of the time there are many non-fishing guests who arrive with the intention of remaining for one night and who extend their stay for two or three. It's an excellent place for families, because the cabins can accommodate up to four people quite comfortably, and we have another new building that can accommodate even more."

"Our guests enjoy the wonderful presence of the river," Sharon commented. "They can explore the waterfalls, swim in the creek, and

return at night to put their feet up on the porch railing and read a good book. We also have frequent cooking classes that many of our guests enjoy. Information about classes is included in our brochure."

So we see the Steamboat Inn is a combination of a great many things, but the real, compelling attraction is the river—its sound, color, and ever-changing textures.

STEAMBOAT INN, Steamboat, OR 97447; 503-496-3495 or 503-498-2411. An 8-guestroom rustic riverside inn in one of Oregon's most spectacular nature areas. Open all year. Breakfast, lunch, and dinner served daily; breakfast is not included in the room rate. Dinner ½ hr. after sundown in summer, 7 p.m. in winter. Fishing, backpacking, and hiking in abundance. Sharon and Jim Van Loan, Innkeepers.

Directions: From Roseburg drive 38 mi. east on Rte. 138.

THE CAPTAIN WHIDBEY INN
Coupeville, Washington

I'm going to share with you the contents of a very interesting letter written by John Stone, the innkeeper of the Captain Whidbey Inn. I think it shows that country inns are in reality continually adjusting and changing to meet the preferences and needs of their guests.

First, just a word about the Captain Whidbey. It's an old-fashioned New England inn, way up in the northwest corner of the state of Washington. The New England part of it comes quite naturally because the original owners were Steve and Shirley Stone. Steve is a native of Nantucket Island, off the coast of Massachusetts in the East, and a good example of the old saying, "You can take the boy out of Nantucket, but you can't take Nantucket out of the boy"; the tweedy look, the unmistakable accent, and the corncob pipe are all there. John refers to his father as the "Innkeeper Emeritus."

The exterior of the inn, built in 1907, is of the distinctly regional peeled madrona logs, a shiny, red-hued wood, a large relative of the manzanitas. It remains just about the same as it has always been, with highly polished log walls decorated with antiques and bric-a-brac.

The natural center of the inn is the living room, with a very big fireplace made of round stones. Here, everybody—houseguests and dinner guests alike—sits around talking and leafing through the dozens of magazines.

Some of the guest rooms are upstairs in the main house, and an additional number of rustic lodges, called Lagoon Rooms, were built in the woods across the road from the main house a few years ago, and they overlook their own private lake. The guest rooms are tastefully furnished with antiques, and those in the main house have down comforters and feather beds. A nice area for general relaxing has been set aside for houseguests on the second floor, with floor-to-ceiling bookshelves jam-packed with books.

Now, to John's letter: "We've had a couple of interesting events over the course of the year. One was a luncheon for the Western Australian Tourism Commission (they're the ones who have the America's Cup), who were sponsoring one of the days of Whidbey Island Race Week. We had to lengthen the pier forty-eight feet for them to accommodate the twenty-five travel agents they were hosting, who were coming by a fifty-four-foot yacht at an extremely minus tide. We accomplished this with the help of Peter Jefferds, our local mussel farmer, who lent us four of his mussel floats, which we were able to put together to extend the pier.

"This year, in addition to our Oktoberfest and Dickens Dinner (our traditional English Christmas dinner), we are adding a Northwest Harvest Festival, featuring the bounty of the Northwest, as well as a mussel

festival in January. (The world's best mussels are grown in Penn Cove, not a mile from the Captain Whidbey.)" (I might add that John and Geoff also throw a Summer Solstice party, complete with croquet, volleyball, and a bonfire.)

"Our best addition, however, is our new chef/restaurant manager, Lorren Garlichs, a graduate of the Institute of Culinary Arts in Hyde Park, who has a great interest in serving the freshest and best food, using local items. We look forward to a long and rewarding relationship with him."

The Captain Whidbey, located on the shore of Penn Cove, with the Cascades to the east dominated by Mount Baker at more than 10,000 feet and Mount Olympus on the west at almost 8,000 feet, provides a most unusual and scenic country-inn adventure.

THE CAPTAIN WHIDBEY INN, Rte. 1, Box 32, Coupeville, WA 98239; 206-678-4097. A 25-guestroom (4 cottages) (private and shared baths) country inn, on protected Penn Cove off Puget Sound, 50 mi. north of Seattle, 3 mi. north of Coupeville. European plan. Breakfast, lunch, and dinner served daily to travelers. Open year-round. Boating and fishing on grounds. Golf nearby. Pets allowed in cottages only. The Stone Family, Innkeepers.

Directions: Whidbey Island is reached year-round from the south by the Columbia Beach–Mukilteo Ferry, and during the summer and on weekends by the Port Townsend–Keystone Ferry. From the north (Vancouver, B.C., and Bellingham), take the Deception Pass Bridge to Whidbey Island.

LAKE QUINAULT LODGE
Quinault, Washington

It was ten o'clock on a summer evening and the big living room of the Lake Quinault Lodge was filled with a number of guests reading, talking, doing puzzles, and playing bridge. In one corner some people were singing softly to the accompaniment of a guitar. The moon had risen over the lake and a light breeze was stirring the leaves of the great trees on the mountains.

One of the guests who had been there about a week, dropped a couple of aromatic birch bark logs on the fire. Although it was a mild night, a small fire was quite welcome.

"Well," he asked me, "what did you do all afternoon?"

I replied that I spent most of the time just walking in the woods getting the feel of the great trees. "Yes," he replied, "I think that's what almost every newcomer does. It takes time to get used to these two- and three-hundred-foot giants that surround us."

This is indeed big tree country with cedars, redwoods, spruces, Douglas firs, hemlocks, and pines in profusion. My afternoon walk in the woods was an inspiring experience.

"It's interesting to watch people come into this relaxing atmosphere for the first time," my new friend continued. "They arrive tired and tight from city living and I can see them unwind. Finally, they're sitting around like all of us without a worry in the world. I think that the saunas, jacuzzi, and indoor swimming pool help out a great deal, too," he added.

In 1890, two brothers of the pioneer Olson family built a crude log hotel, which served as the only haven for travelers coming to Quinault. Another temporary structure was built to provide additional shelter for travelers in 1923, and finally, in 1926, the site for Quinault Lodge was selected in a natural clearing, and the lodge was constructed with great care and the finest materials.

The present innkeepers, Marge and Larry Lesley, have worked very hard to preserve the best of the old and, of course, to incorporate some of the improvements of today's conveniences. The result is a growing lodge in which many of the rooms look out over the lake and command an excellent view of the mountains.

The Lesleys are also the owners of Kalaloch Lodge, overlooking the beautiful Pacific Ocean, a few miles north on Route 101.

The Lake Quinault Lodge is a year-round resort-inn about three hours from Seattle and Tacoma. Frankly, I feel totally inadequate to describe the tremendous scope of the trees and the entire forest, mountain, and lake experience.

Everything about the lodge is homelike and comfortable, and is clearly a source of pleasure to the many families staying there. The irrepressible younger set spends many an enjoyable evening in the dandy recreation room with its variety of games.

With so much time spent out of doors, it is easy to see why the dining room is an important part of the inn experience. I found homemade baked bread, Yankee pot roast of beef, and many other typical country inn items interspersed with things that are found only in the Northwest, like alder-smoked Quinault salmon.

As the evening moved on, I strolled over to the corner where the people were singing to a guitar and joined the widening circle. About

thirty minutes later, the great old grandfather's clock in the corner tolled eleven. With this, the group started to break up and say good night, all of them headed for another deep sleep here in the woods.

LAKE QUINAULT LODGE, Southshore Rd., Quinault, WA 98575; 206-288-2571. A 55-guestroom resort-inn in the Olympic National Forest of the State of Washington, about 40 mi. from Aberdeen. European plan. Breakfast, lunch, and dinner served daily to travelers. Open every day of the year. Indoor swimming pool, chipping green on grounds. Hiking, mountain climbing, fishing, nature walks nearby. Fee for pets; must be attended. Marge and Larry Lesley, Innkeepers.

Directions: Use Quinault exit from Rte. 101. Proceed 2 mi. on south shore of Lake Quinault to inn.

CONWAY'S FARMHOUSE RESTAURANT
Port Townsend, Washington

My life is considerably enriched not only for my visits to Dorothy and John Ashby Conway at their restaurant in Port Townsend on the Straits of Juan de Fuca, but for the lively and entertaining correspondence I have enjoyed with them over the years. Their yearly newsletter (available on request) also has flashes of John's literary hors d'oeuvres, sometimes as spicy as his Greek and Hungarian dishes.

Monthly ethnic specialties are served at Conway's Farmhouse from February to May and from September through November. Single entrée dinners are served during the summer from Thursday through Sunday. Reservations are absolutely essential, and full details of the menu may be obtained from John Ashby Conway at the same time. He was the recipient of the Holiday Travel Magazine Award for Distinctive Dining, and is a member of the Associated Master Chefs of the United States.

CONWAY'S FARMHOUSE RESTAURANT, North Beach, Port Townsend, WA 98368; 206-385-1411. A unique gourmet country restaurant, 50 mi. from Seattle. Meals by reservation only. Dinner served Thurs. thru Sun. in June, July, and Aug.; dinner served Fri., Sat., and Sun. from Sept. thru May. Closed Dec. and Jan. No lodgings available. Dorothy and John Ashby Conway, Innkeepers.

Directions: From Seattle take the ferry for Winslow from Colman Dock. Follow signs to Floating Bridge; Poulsbo; cross bridge and follow main road to turnoff for Port Townsend. Call inn from Port Townsend for further directions. From Vancouver, B.C., take the Whidbey Island ferry to Kingston. From Victoria, B.C., take ferry to Port Angeles.

THE PARTRIDGE INN RESTAURANT
Underwood, Washington

After running the Partridge Inn for many years, my good friends Nora and Jacque Moyse have turned the inn over to Nora's son, Peter McNab, who often worked with his mother. Many of the same items that created the Partridge's reputation are being carried on by Peter, including Cornish game hen barbecued with a zesty sauce, country-style ribs, chicken tarragon, medallions of pork, and a special casserole with shrimp, scallops, and sole.

THE PARTRIDGE INN RESTAURANT, Box 100, Underwood, WA 98651; 509-493-2381. A country restaurant with an excellent view of the Columbia River Gorge, 60 mi. east of Portland, Ore., or Vancouver, Wash. Dinners by reservation. Open year-round: 5-9, Wed. thru Sat.; 12-7, Sun. No lodging rooms. Hiking trails and camping, logging flume and falls nearby. Pears and apples for sale most of the year. No credit cards. Peter McNab, Innkeeper.

Directions: On Washington Hwy. 14, 60 mi. east of Ft. Vancouver, turn left onto Cook-Underwood Rd. at the confluence of the Columbia and White Salmon Rivers. (This road has 2 ends; do not turn off at Cook.) Follow yellow line up the hill for 2 mi. When the Columbia River is on the left begin to look for inn sign on the right. Coming from the Oregon side along I-84N, 60 mi. east of Portland, cross the interstate bridge at the town of Hood River. Turn left and drive 2 mi. to Cook-Underwood Rd. directly after crossing the White Salmon River. Follow directions up the hill as above. From coastal region take any highway leading to Portland, Ore., then pick up 84N going east

OAK BAY BEACH HOTEL
Victoria, British Columbia

"It was the custom in English pubs of the past to have one room reserved for those patrons who, for social or other reasons, did not wish to be seen in the public bar. This room was known as the 'snug' and the clientele could include the local 'bobby,' who would nip in for a quiet pint, or the vicar, to count the house. Our Snug here at the Oak Bay Beach Hotel retains all of the old comfort and atmosphere, and cheery friendliness is the order of the day."

Bruce Walker, the genial owner of the Oak Bay Beach Hotel, was describing some of the more British features of this very pleasant seaside hotel in Victoria, British Columbia, to a group of *CIBR* innkeepers from Canada and the Northwest, who were having a short meeting there.

Bruce's son, Kevin, who is the manager of the hotel, chimed in. "We serve afternoon high tea in the lounge and also on the patio in the gardens. We're very proud of our real Devonshire clotted cream, which is very frequently a topic of conversation."

For me, Victoria is the most English of all Canadian cities, and the Oak Bay Beach Hotel is like a visit to the North Devon shore or Cornwall in England. Like the Mermaid in Rye, it also has the handsome Tudor-style half-timbers.

The English theme is carried out in the guest rooms, and in fact the third floor has the same white plaster and Tudor half-timber finish as the exterior of the building. The rooms and suites, all furnished in handsome antiques, have such names as Samuel Pepys, Prince Albert, and Queen Anne. The rooms in the back of the house overlook the Straits of Haro,

with a view of Discovery Island and the San Juan Islands. Mount Baker rises ten thousand magnificent feet in the distance.

Lest I be carried away by the English atmosphere, let me say that British Columbia is a wonderful place to visit. There are impressive water and mountain views everywhere and all types of outdoor recreation. I might add that it's an ideal place for a honeymoon.

There are pleasant walks in the hotel's gardens and along the pathway down to the sea, as well as through the surrounding residential streets with their attractive houses and the shops of Oak Bay Village. The Oak Bay golf course is a ten-minute walk away, and the hotel will arrange charter-boat fishing. Killer whales, seals, and salmon are often spotted off-shore.

Christmas is celebrated in a big way, with sing-alongs, "city-lights" tours, and a gala buffet extravaganza on Christmas Eve. Hotel guests are invited to enjoy a sumptuous complimentary breakfast on Christmas morning, and they may also avail themselves of a Christmas Day brunch and a five-course Christmas dinner.

There are two pieces of exciting news from Oak Bay, and I'm delighted to say that Kevin Walker and his wife, Shawna Dee, now have a new baby girl called Brooklyn Rae, who arrived on May 20.

The other news is that the hotel now has sightseeing and fishing cruises aboard a forty-one-foot custom yacht. It departs four times a day from the hotel's own wharf, and offers a delightful sightseeing excursion on the beautiful Oak Bay waters and along the coast of Victoria's Inner Harbor. The return trip to the hotel is approximately two hours, and each cruise includes a light meal appropriate to the time of day (i.e., breakfast, lunch, late afternoon or evening snack). Extended fishing trips may also be made on the Oak Bay waters.

OAK BAY BEACH HOTEL, 1175 Beach Dr., Victoria, B.C. V8S 2N2 Canada; 604-598-4556. A 48-guestroom seaside inn located in one of the quiet suburbs of Victoria. European plan. Breakfast, lunch, and dinner served to travelers. Open every day in the year. A short distance from the spectacular scenery and recreational resources of British Columbia. Swimming on grounds. Daily yacht cruises. Golf, tennis, fishing, sailing, and Butchart Gardens nearby. No pets. Bruce R. Walker, Innkeeper.

Directions: Take Johnson St. or Fort St. from downtown Victoria, east to Oak Bay Ave., which leads into Newport Ave. Turn left into Windsor Ave. to Beach Dr. Turn right and continue to 1175 Beach Dr. If arriving by air at Victoria Airport, I suggest you take public transportation to the center of the city and then take a taxi to the hotel.

THE LODGE ON THE DESERT
Tucson, Arizona

The slanting rays of the western sun, providing spectacular back-lighting for the great banks of clouds that seemed to skim the jagged peaks of the Santa Catalina Mountains, streamed through the casement window and lit up the interior of my spacious studio bedroom at the Lodge on the Desert.

Even though the afternoon temperature in September reached 85 degrees, I knew that later that evening I would want a fire in my fireplace to ease the chill of the cool desert night.

My bedroom was really most impressive, with three windows on two sides and a patio facing north. The two double beds had rich bedspreads that complemented the orange curtains, and an armful of freshly picked flowers lent an air of gaiety to the dark tones of the carved

wooden tables and chests. The full-sized closet reminded me that many people come here to spend weeks at a time, enjoying the benefits of a friendly climate in both summer and winter, plus the many opportunities for outdoor recreation, as well as the pursuit of the arts.

Tucson is one of the most sophisticated cities in the Southwest, with many fine homes and attractive shops in the downtown area. The University of Arizona is an active cultural center with a continuing program of music, drama, and arts and crafts exhibitions.

"My father built the Lodge on the Desert outside Tucson in 1936," commented Schuyler Lininger, the *patron grande* of this resort-inn. "Now the city has grown up around us; fortunately, we have no tall buildings to disrupt our guests' view of the mountains, and yet we are set apart by the hedges around the property. However, many of our guests find nearness to the center of things in the city most desirable, even though it seems we are way out in the country."

Here in the Southwest desert, during the outdoor weather, everybody gathers around the swimming pool, and here is where many conversations and lasting friendships start.

For cooler days, the Lodge has a very spacious and inviting living room with lots of books, which guests are free to take to their rooms, a chess game, a jigsaw puzzle, and many opportunities just to sit and relax.

The guest rooms of the inn have been designed after the manner of Pueblo Indian farmhouses, the beige adobe color frequently relieved by very colorful Mexican tiles.

Although the dining room features many dishes of the Southwest, I found there were also such favorites as Chateaubriand for two, roast rack of lamb, and several veal dishes. Schuyler explained that he and Helen have gone to great lengths to bring milk-fed Wisconsin veal to the table in different versions. Incidentally, one of the most popular features of the inn is breakfast served on the patios of the guest rooms in the beautiful early-morning sunshine.

I believe another guest succinctly summed up my feelings about the Lodge on the Desert while we were both taking advantage of that bright September sun to get a few more degrees of tan.

"What I like about it here," she said, "is the really endless variety of things that are going on in Tucson—the Art Center, the many different theaters, the new museum, the exhibition of Indian arts, the opera company, the ballet, the Tucson Symphony, the golf courses, the racetrack, and all kinds of sports events—it's so *civilized!*"

THE LODGE ON THE DESERT, 306 N. Alvernon Way, Tucson, AZ 85733; 602-325-3366. A 40-guestroom luxury inn within the city limits. American and European plans available in winter; European plan in summer. Continental breakfast included in European plan. Breakfast, lunch, and dinner served to travelers every day of the year. Near several historic, cultural, and recreational attractions. Swimming pool and lawn games on grounds. Tennis and golf 1 mi. Attended, leashed pets allowed. Schuyler and Helen Lininger, Innkeepers.

Directions: Take Speedway exit from I-10. Travel about 5 mi. east to Alvernon Way, turn right (south) onto Alvernon (¾ mi.). Lodge is on left side between 5th St. and Broadway. ◣

RANCHO DE LOS CABALLEROS
Wickenburg, Arizona

It was the late afternoon cookout ride at Los Caballeros and we were all strung out on the ascending trail of the high desert behind the ranch, headed toward Vulture Peak, where rumor has it that a prospector named Wickenburg discovered by accident (is there any other way?) the richest gold mine in Arizona. We were certainly an assorted group, consisting of almost 100 innkeepers who are included in this book, enjoying our three-day annual conference. There were also innkeepers from England and Europe, and although none of us was really an experienced rider, we were all having a wonderful time.

Just before the ride we all gathered at the corral where Buford Giles, the head wrangler, had given us all some excellent instructions as to how to use good horse sense and trail etiquette—noting, among other things, that the horse is an animal weighing over a half-ton with a mind of its own. "Our horses are gentle, but you will have to urge him along with a little kick now and again. He cannot run all the time as he will tire quickly. To conserve horsepower, rides are controlled for the horse's sake as well as the rider's. Always keep in mind that if he is spooked by a blowing newspaper, falling hat, or something unexpected, he is capable of shying or moving very quickly in most any direction. Each of the groups of 12 or 15 will have a wrangler who will lead the rides and see to it that it's at a pace that is comfortable for all."

As we walked along, picking our way among the rocks and small hummocks, I thought about the many other times I have visited Los Caballeros. Certainly they were all enjoyable, but because I was here this time with so many good friends, this promised to be a really memorable occasion. I have some photographs of all of us in various groups just before this trailride started, and they bring back happy memories.

As is almost always the case at Los Caballeros, on our first morning we had a sun-drenched breakfast in the dining room overlooking the swimming pool, and some of our members had the morning off to play golf or tennis and others went skeet shooting. A program of planned activities for younger people is one of the reasons this ranch experience is so popular with families.

Rancho de los Caballeros is an elegant ranch-inn. Many of the lodging rooms and suites are built around a carefully planned cactus garden and oversized putting green. They are decorated in Arizona desert colors with harmonizing hues of tan, yellow, and brown. Each suite or "casita" has a private patio and many of them have fireplaces.

With Buford leading the way and the rest of us following, we arrived at the rendezvous point for our cookout, where some of our non-riding members had been transported by the ranch truck. The steaks never tasted

so good and the joshing and good-natured kidding went on. We all drew closer to the fire as the sun set and a pleasant early December chill descended upon us. There was informal music and soon all of us were joining in singing led by one of our Scottish guests who was an excellent tenor. It was during this very pleasant evening that Gerald Milsom, one of our innkeeping friends from England, remarked on his surprise that there were no television sets or telephones in the bedrooms. Rusty Gant, the owner of the ranch, explained that it was part of the "get away from it all" atmosphere most guests seem to appreciate very much.

All of us, the North American innkeepers as well as our new friends from Britain and Europe, had such a wonderful time at Los Caballeros that we made a firm date to return for another three-day conference in 1987. Like the other guests we came away with beautiful tans, lower golf scores, improved forehands, and an appreciation for the pommel on the western saddle.

RANCHO DE LOS CABALLEROS, Wickenburg, AZ 85358; 602-684-5484. A 73-guestroom luxury ranch-resort, 60 mi. from Phoenix in the sunny, dry desert. American plan. Breakfast, lunch, dinner served to travelers daily. Open from mid-Oct. to early May. Swimming pool, horseback riding, hiking, skeet shooting, putting green, tennis, and 18-hole championship golf course on grounds. Special children's program. No pets. No credit cards. Dallas C. Gant, Jr., Innkeeper.

Directions: Rtes. 60, 89, and 93 lead to Wickenburg. Ranch is 2 mi. west of town on Rte. 60 and 2 mi. south on Vulture Mine Road.

TANQUE VERDE
Tucson, Arizona

The postmark on the letter was "Caldwell, New Jersey." It said in part: "We've been reading about your last visit to Tanque Verde Ranch, just outside of Tucson. It sounds very intriguing. My wife and I are enthusiastic about the prospect of a new vacation experience in the desert country. The idea of staying at a ranch that may have even survived Indian raids, and your description of steak over mesquite fires and bird watching, are most inviting. However, it is a long way for us to go, and neither of us has ever been astride a horse. We're both about fifty years old and we'd like a little more advice as to whether we should venture forth on this trip."

Until my first visit to Tanque Verde in 1969, horseback riding for me consisted of a couple short hauls on a Tennessee walking horse and one or two rides on the gentlest nag in my local livery stable. When I went out to Tanque Verde, I talked this over with the head wrangler, and he picked out a horse that he thought was the right size for my weight and had enough experience to guide me.

On that ride (the first of many during subsequent visits), I met a husband and wife from the Boston area, who were at a Western ranch for the first time and out on their first morning trail ride. We left the corral in single file and rode out into the desert. The entire experience was so exhilarating that by the time we got back to the ranch my Massachusetts neighbors were inquiring as to whether they could have more active horses and go for a longer ride the next day.

By the end of the week, these people had purchased some blue jeans, western shirts, cowboy hats, and boots, and knew all the horses by their first names.

Tanque Verde is a completely different type of country inn. There are many diversions, including both indoor and outdoor pools and an active tennis program. I spent one New Year's Eve there and had a great time with all the parents and children who had been there since Christmas.

In Tanque Verde's 100-year-old history as one of Arizona's pioneer guest cattle ranches, there are even stories of Indian raids. The ranch is set back in a semicircle of mountains, about a thirty-minute drive from downtown Tucson and the airport. The accommodations are in almost luxurious individual *casitas,* all of which have their own Spanish-style corner fireplaces. Everyone eats at long tables in the vaulted dining room, and there's nothing like the desert air to encourage big appetites.

One further point: Tanque Verde is open throughout the entire year, and during the summer there are many guests from Europe and Asia enjoying the full holiday in the desert. As innkeeper Bob Cote says, "We have so many guests speaking different languages, we could almost advertise that it's a good place for children to get some language tutoring."

TANQUE VERDE RANCH, Box 66, Rte. 8, Tucson, AZ 85710; 602-296-6275. A 65-guestroom ranch-inn, 10 mi. from Tucson. American plan. Breakfast, lunch, and dinner served to travelers by reservation. Open year-round. Riding, indoor and outdoor pool, tennis, sauna, exercise room, and whirlpool bath on grounds. Robert Cote, Innkeeper.

Directions: From U.S. 10, exit at Speedway Blvd. and travel east to dead end.

"European Plan" means that rates for rooms and meals are separate. "American Plan" means that meals are included in the cost of the room. "Modified American Plan" means that breakfast and dinner are included in the cost of the room. The rates at some inns include a continental breakfast with the lodging.

I do not include lodging rates in the descriptions, for the very nature of an inn means that there are lodgings of various sizes, with and without baths, in and out of season, and with plain and fancy decoration. Travelers should call ahead and inquire about the availability and rates of the many different types of rooms.

ASPEN LODGE AND GUEST RANCH
Estes Park, Colorado

"I think the best way to describe us is 'truly Colorado,'" Buddy Surles declared. "We feel this is a real Colorado experience and we've tried to make it as authentic as possible with Colorado materials. All of our designs are built around the Colorado mountains, which of course are visible on all sides. Our upholstery has an Indian design and our furniture—beds, chairs, tables, and chests of drawers—are crafted right over in Steamboat Springs."

The main lodge, shown in the accompanying sketch, has a wonderful open feeling with splendid views of the great mountains that dominate the scene. A cathedral window in the dining room offers even more of a vista. There are various types of guest rooms and suites in the main lodge, in cottages, and in an annex.

As I hinted in the last edition, the Aspen Lodge has considerably widened its horizons since my last visit. Now it has ample opportunities for recreation in both summer and winter. "During the summertime we're going to continue to be a wonderful mountain experience for everyone,

with a special emphasis on families," Buddy explained. "However, with the first snowfall, we put on a slightly different face between Monday and Friday and offer conference and seminar facilities. On the weekends, once again, we'll revert back to being a family resort."

This family atmosphere is one feature that I find most attractive. There are shared activities for everyone to enjoy, including horseback riding and hiking. There is a summertime children's counselor, who takes charge of the young people, introducing them to the many farm animals, as well as helping them to learn about the riding horses and wild animals that abound in the area. It's a little gold mine of experiences here, because trails range from a short after-dinner hike to the climbing of majestic Long's Peak. There are also horse-drawn hayrides, jeep trips, wildlife drives, good fishing, and lighted tennis courts.

Winter activities include cross-country skiing, snowmobiling, sleigh rides, tobogganing, ice skating, and ice fishing. The sports center is open year around with an enclosed swimming pool, sauna, hot tub, and racquet ball.

Now Buddy, speaking in his soft Texas accent, said, "I've got something really unusual to show you." He pointed to the mountain that provides a backdrop for Aspen Lodge. "We're going to drive around to almost the exact opposite side." Thereupon unfolded a really unusual adventure. We went on a dirt road in a four-wheel-drive vehicle to a hidden valley, crossing through gates and over cattle grids, and finally came to a sign that said, "Elk Park Ranch, operated by Aspen Lodge." It was just like a John Wayne movie, with wonderful mountains, cattle grazing, real ranch fences, and, at the end of the valley, a movie-set ranch house.

"Our guests can now enjoy horseback riding, hayrides in the evening, cattle roundups, pack trips, fishing, and all of the real ranch-life experiences. We are completely removed from the main lodge, and lodge guests can get a wonderful insight into what ranch life is really like. There's even a real working corral."

Indeed, Aspen Lodge has enlarged its borders, and "truly Colorado" is a wonderful, two-word description.

ASPEN LODGE AND GUEST RANCH, Long's Peak Route (Hwy. 7), Estes Park, CO 80517; 303-586-8133. A 56-guestroom Rocky Mountain resort-inn. Accommodations in main lodge and adjacent cottages. Full American plan (3 meals) available June 4 to Labor Day; daily cottage rental and restaurant service available all year. Weekly and daily rates available year-round. Horseback riding, fishing, hunting, nature trails, heated enclosed pool, jacuzzi, racquet ball, health club, ice skating, xc and downhill skiing, tobogganing, back-country hiking, sleigh rides, and tennis. Golf, whitewater rafting nearby. In the summer, a complete children's program is available. No pets. The Surles Family, Innkeepers.

Directions: From Denver take I-25 north; turn west on Rte. 66, and follow Hwy. 7 to Aspen Lodge. Public bus transportation from Denver to Estes Park, where pick-up service to lodge can be arranged.

BRIAR ROSE BED & BREAKFAST
Boulder, Colorado

I'm going to share a part of a sparkling letter I received from Emily Hunter, the innkeeper at the Briar Rose:

"Briar Rose is filled with people who have come to see the CU–Ohio football game. There is a bouquet of autumn leaves in the Briar Rose window seat, screening the bird feeder from the activity at the dining room table. A flock of grosbeaks has taken up residence in the lilac bushes and lost all hesitations, sitting for hours, sharing pounds of sunflower seeds with Rusty the squirrel.

"We built the first fire of the season yesterday. The big poplar out front is turning that great marigold yellow that I look forward to every year. The fire alarms are all checked, the firewood ordered and to be split next week, and the down puffs go back on the beds tonight. It feels like all the appropriate gestures have been made to stave off the cold and dark and snow for a few more months."

The ground floor exterior of the inn is a beautiful rose-colored brick, with Queen Anne shingles on the second story. I noticed several other small houses in Boulder that featured some of the same basic design.

The Briar Rose has also undergone some extensive redecorating in the public rooms, dining rooms, and some of the bedrooms in a small building immediately adjacent. Almost all of the furnishings are Regency Victorian, and there are splendid additional touches, such as roses in the guest rooms, baskets of fruit on the nightstands, and the aforementioned down puffs on the beds.

More as an accommodation to the guest than anything else, the Briar Rose offers a modest dinner consisting of a single entrée of different types of casseroles with puff-pastry tops. There's usually a choice of beef with onion, wine, and mushrooms or turkey with cream, onions, and carrots. This is augmented by a simple dessert that goes along with dinner.

As Emily says, "Boulder is a great restaurant town, and there are good restaurants within walking distance, but we want to be able to offer dinner to those guests who are arriving really tired from a long trip and who don't want to take the trouble to go out for dinner. This is particularly true of businessmen, and if they want to have dinner in front of the fire or at the table—or even on the back porch in the summertime—they can take their tray and enjoy it wherever they like."

During the past few years Emily has gained a considerable reputation for conducting conferences and seminars whose basic subject is "how to open a bed-and-breakfast inn." These are held several times a year and I'd suggest contacting her to find out all of the details.

Emily's letter went on: "We have an ideal climate here in Boulder with four distinct and wonderful seasons. There are over 300 sunny days a year and many things for visitors to enjoy, both recreational and artistic. Of course, the mountains offer everything, including climbing, hiking, cross-country skiing. Some people say that the powder snow offers the best downhill skiing in the world. Biking is also very popular here in this part of Colorado and there are bicyclists everywhere, as well as joggers and runners."

Emily's letter continues: "At this moment my dining room here at home is filled with six-foot-long cardboard boxes, in turn filled with dried whole roses that I dried in my attic. A friend, who is a floral

designer, has begun just this week to market 'Briar Rose Potpourri.' A friend gave me a plastic pink flamingo that now resides hidden in the water lilies of the fish pond. Only the most observant guest is treated to the sight of our own 'Loch Ness Flamingo.' "

BRIAR ROSE BED & BREAKFAST, 2151 Arapahoe Ave., Boulder, CO 80302; 303-442-3007. A 12-guestroom (some shared baths) inn located in a quiet section of a pleasant, conservative Colorado city, approx. 1 hr. from Denver. Open all year. Breakfast included in lodging rate. Evening meal available upon request. Afternoon tea served. Convenient for all of the many recreational, cultural, and historic attractions nearby. Limousine service available to and from Denver airport. Emily Hunter, Innkeeper.

Directions: From Denver, follow I-25 north and Rte. 36 to Boulder. Turn left on Arapahoe Ave. Briar Rose is on the right on the corner of 22nd St.

HEARTHSTONE INN
Colorado Springs, Colorado

Many of my *CIBR* innkeepers are multitalented and quite a few have a distinctly literary bent. Such is the case with Dot Williams, who with Ruth Williams (not related) is the innkeeper at the Hearthstone Inn, one of the most outstanding Victorian restorations and preservations I have ever seen.

By way of further exposition on the Hearthstone, let me quote extensively from a recent letter: "Many of our guests are people who've been coming to the Hearthstone for two, three, or four years, and some of them have been visiting us yearly since we opened almost seven years ago. We continue to have lots of contact with parents and other family members who are here to visit their children at both the Air Force Academy and Colorado College. It's gratifying to meet some of these fine people at parents' weekend in the first year and then to see them two and three times a year until graduation—and occasionally to be invited to either the graduation or a wedding soon thereafter!

"Our July 4th ice cream social was lots of fun. This year we made vanilla (superb), strawberry (delicious), and butter pecan (too sweet— need to work on this recipe some more!). Everyone enjoyed croquet or cranking the ice cream.

"The Colorado Springs Hot Air Balloon Classic, on all three days of the Labor Day weekend, was spectacular. Sixty-four hot air balloons rose into the clear Colorado sky through a rainbow on one of the days!

"Our month-long Christmas celebration is always a joy to be a part of—from the trimming of the tree on December 1 to the Special Day itself. The crunch of fresh snow, the smell of special Christmas baking, homemade gingerbread cookies hanging on the tree, cross-country ski tracks in the park directly behind the inn—all beckoning one to relax in memories with a cup of cider or coffee in front of the crackling fire.

"We sponsored a contest at the state fair this year called 'Breaking the Fast.' It was for breakfast eaters and fixers! The grand prize was a night at the Hearthstone, and the winner was a whole family—dad, mom, daughter, and son all entered different breakfast meals and prepared them in front of us all.

"We now pack picnic lunches for people who are on the go. In the guest rooms are picnic forms, and the guest drops the form off at the desk in the evening and their picnic is ready to go in the morning. For those escaping to the mountains for the day, walking down to the park behind the inn, or even those driving long distances toward another destination, it has been a nice choice.

"Our newest project, Sheltering Pines, fifteen minutes into the foothills west of Colorado Springs, is now ready for occupancy. So far, it has been especially popular with family reunion groups and small business training seminars. In the summer, suites are rented only by the week, but the rest of the year they are available with a 2-day minimum."

Thank you, Dot and Ruth, and I hope you don't mind my sharing your letter with our readers. After all, *sharing* is what innkeeping is all about, isn't it?

THE HEARTHSTONE INN, 506 N. Cascade Ave., Colorado Springs, CO 80903; 303-473-4413. A 26-guestroom bed-and-breakfast inn within sight of Pike's Peak, in the residential section of Colorado Springs. A full breakfast is included in the price of the room; only meal served. Open every day all year. Convenient to spectacular Colorado mountain scenery as well as Air Force Academy, Garden of the Gods, Cave of the Winds, the McAllister House Museum, Fine Arts Center, and Broadmoor Resort. Golf, tennis, swimming, hiking, backroading, and Pike's Peak ski area nearby. Check innkeepers for pet policy. Dorothy Williams and Ruth Williams, Innkeepers.

Directions: From I-25 (the major north/south hwy.) use Exit 143 (Uintah St.); travel east (opposite direction from mountains) to third stop light (Cascade Ave.). Turn right for 7 blocks. The inn will be on the right at the corner of St. Vrain and Cascade—a big Victorian house, tan with lilac trim.

OUTLOOK LODGE
Green Mountain Falls, Colorado

Sometimes letters from our readers pick up the spirit of an inn better than anything I could say. For instance here is one from a reader in New York City—let's join her as she describes Outlook Lodge:

"We felt we were in an inn in the truest sense of the word...that is, a place that serves not just as a residence, but as a warm, inviting gathering place where guests get to know one another and enrich each other's visits.

"In the morning, drawn by Impy Ahern's delicious homemade breads and muffins and a good hot cup of coffee, we sat around the dining room tables, eagerly sharing ideas for places to visit in the Colorado

Springs and Pike's Peak area. In the afternoon, some of us would sit on the porch overlooking the green hills, discussing the day's experiences, and at night those who were not out sightseeing felt free to lounge around the dining and living rooms, playing cards, talking, and joking.

"It was fascinating getting to know people from Kansas, Texas, and Wisconsin, as well as other Easterners. Many of us exchanged names and addresses for the future.

"The atmosphere at Outlook Lodge was very special—even those who were initially shy, relaxed and made themselves at home. This warmth and cordiality I believe had most to do with the proprietress Impy Ahern. She showed a genuine interest in each of her guests and her friendliness and enthusiasm filled the air.

"Thank you for recommending Outlook Lodge. It was a wonderful home base for our travels and made our visit a memorable one."

I think that letter has caught the true essence of Impy and Outlook

Lodge. However, since essence alone isn't enough, let me say that this is a country Victorian inn with twelve lodging rooms located literally on the lower slopes of Pike's Peak. It's only fifteen miles from Colorado Springs, but worlds apart in a great many other ways. The village is located at an altitude of almost 8,000 feet and the inn is located next to the historic "Church in the Wildwood."

Lodgings include a complimentary continental breakfast featuring homemade breads. There are kitchen facilities for guests who would care to prepare an occasional meal at the inn themselves.

As the letter hints, everything is geared towards family enjoyment and in addition to sing-a-longs, often with Impy leading the way, the dining room becomes a guest playroom and there are lots of games that can amuse children of all ages.

Besides all of the nostalgia and the really homelike feeling, the Outlook Lodge is also very convenient to an awesome collection of sightseeing opportunities during all seasons of the year. Those that come readily to my mind are Pike's Peak, the Cog Railway that runs to the top, the old gold-mining town of Cripple Creek, and the Air Force Academy. Energetic guests can go horseback riding or hiking, and enjoy tennis, swimming, or other vigorous pursuits. The back roads have magnificent pine-scented views of the impressive mountain scenery.

It's worth noting that Outlook Lodge may be open for a few days during the winter in the future to accommodate skiers who are visiting the new Pike's Peak Ski area. Better check ahead to make sure.

OUTLOOK LODGE, 6975 Howard, Green Mountain Falls, CO 80819; 303-684-2303. A 12-guestroom (private and shared baths) rustic lodge on the slopes of Pike's Peak, 15 mi. from Colorado Springs. European plan. All lodgings include continental breakfast. No other meals served. Open from June 1 thru Labor Day weekend. Immediately adjacent to all the copious mountain recreational activities as well as the U.S. Air Force Academy; Colorado Springs Fine Arts Center; Cripple Creek Gold Camp. Tennis, swimming, horseback riding, hiking, backroading, all nearby. Impy Ahern, Innkeeper.

Directions: Green Mountain Falls is 15 mi. west of Colorado Springs on U.S. 24. Outlook Lodge is located next to the historic Church in the Wildwood.

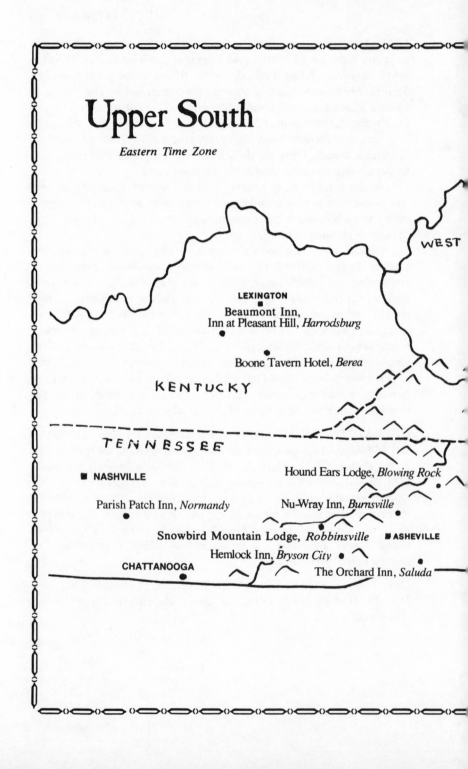

Upper South

Eastern Time Zone

WEST

LEXINGTON
Beaumont Inn,
Inn at Pleasant Hill, *Harrodsburg*

Boone Tavern Hotel, *Berea*

KENTUCKY

TENNESSEE

■ NASHVILLE

Hound Ears Lodge, *Blowing Rock*

Parish Patch Inn, *Normandy*

Nu-Wray Inn, *Burnsville*

Snowbird Mountain Lodge, *Robbinsville* ■ ASHEVILLE

Hemlock Inn, *Bryson City* ●

CHATTANOOGA

The Orchard Inn, *Saluda*

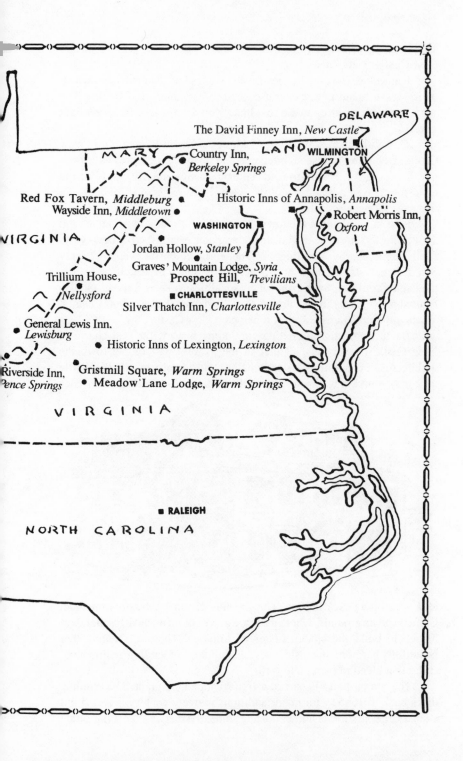

DELAWARE

The David Finney Inn, *New Castle*

MARY LAND WILMINGTON

Country Inn,
Berkeley Springs

Red Fox Tavern, *Middleburg* ●
Wayside Inn, *Middletown* ●

Historic Inns of Annapolis, *Annapolis*

Robert Morris Inn,
Oxford

VIRGINIA

WASHINGTON ■

Jordan Hollow, *Stanley*
●
Graves' Mountain Lodge, *Syria*
Prospect Hill, *Trevilians*

Trillium House,
●
/Nellysford

■ CHARLOTTESVILLE
Silver Thatch Inn, *Charlottesville*

General Lewis Inn,
● *Lewisburg*

● Historic Inns of Lexington, *Lexington*

Riverside Inn,
Pence Springs

Gristmill Square, *Warm Springs*
● Meadow Lane Lodge, *Warm Springs*

VIRGINIA

NORTH CAROLINA

■ RALEIGH

THE DAVID FINNEY INN
New Castle, Delaware

Jean Hatter took me by the arm and we walked over to a table where there was a brand-new, never-used-before, pristine guest book. "You see," she said, pointing to the first line, "you are our very first overnight guest!"

This all happened in April, 1985, at the David Finney Inn in New Castle, Delaware, whose architectural and historical treasures have been a well-kept secret. Thanks to Jean Hatter and a most impressive collection of historical observations about the town, I was to become immersed in this exceptional atmosphere.

First, a word about the town. The earliest settlement began around 1638, shortly after the Swedish government established a new-world foothold in nearby Wilmington. The early colonists were not only Swedish but also Finnish and Dutch adventurers in search of readily available farmland. Such colorful personalities as Peter Stuyvesant also figured prominently in the early history. He named the town Fort Casimir. When the English arrived, they renamed it New Castle.

Aside from this fascinating continuing history, the real charm of New Castle lies in the fact that in the historic part of the town the architecture and building design remains almost totally pre-1800. As trite as it may sound, a walk across the village green is indeed an experience

akin to stepping back in time. This green is dominated by the Immanuel Church and its grounds, where there are graves of men who in earlier days helped to build the United States of America. There are many other beautifully harmonizing residences and buildings of varying architectural styles that blend in extremely well.

The inn property is part of a 1650s Dutch land grant. The building dates back to 1685, with major additions in every century since. It has been a large, luxurious home, hosting some of America's most important people. At least three signers of the Declaration of Independence knew it well.

Furnished with antiques, it is an exceptionally fine restoration/renovation, featuring four two-room suites and thirteen double rooms, all with private baths. Breakfast, lunch, and dinner are served in the restaurant, and there is courtyard dining in season. Entertainment is offered in the tavern, where the nautical theme is heightened with museum-quality model ships.

The evening menu, which changes daily, includes charcoal-grilled swordfish steak with teriyaki butter, and grilled breast of duck with water chestnuts, snow peas, and ginger sauce. It's a little hard to pin the cuisine down because it reflects not only the area, but a Continental theme as well. Chef Lisa Scolaro, a graduate of the Culinary Institute of America, has already received many plaudits from the media for her offerings.

Five museums in the town display life as it was lived in the Dutch and English Colonial periods with guides to explain every detail. It is a delightful experience to walk along the Strand and other streets lined with antique homes, or to visit the marketplace and the village green.

Among the seasonal events and festivals in historic New Castle are "A Day in Old New Castle" on the third Saturday in May, which includes a tour of private homes, gardens, and public buildings; "May Market," the first weekend in May; "Separation Day," the first Saturday in June, celebrating the separation of Delaware from England. There are also numerous other art and antique shows and a Christmas candlelight tour.

There is history aplenty in New Castle, and fortunately for the enthusiastic country-inn-goer, the town and area is splendidly served by the David Finney Inn.

THE DAVID FINNEY INN, P.O. Box 207, 216 Delaware St., New Castle, DE 19720; 302-322-6367. A 17-guestroom (private baths) meticulously restored 18th-century inn in a historic riverfront village, 35 mi. south of Phila. Continental breakfast included in tariff. Breakfast, lunch, and dinner served every day of the year. Many historic, recreational, and cultural attractions in New Castle or nearby. Convenient off-street parking available. No entertainment facilities for children under 10. No pets. Tom and Louise Hagy, Owners; Skip and Jean Hatter, Innkeepers.

Directions: Coming south on the New Jersey Tpke., take the first exit after crossing the Delaware River Bridge and turn south on Rte. 9, which goes directly into New Castle. The inn is located in the historic section of Old New Castle.

HISTORIC INNS OF ANNAPOLIS (formerly Maryland Inn)
Annapolis, Maryland

Very exciting things have been happening in the beautiful city of Annapolis during the more than dozen years I have been visiting Paul Pearson, the proprietor of the Maryland Inn, and innkeeper Peg Bednarsky.

The Maryland Inn was built in the 1770s; however, it has gone through many additions and permutations since that date. Hospitality has been offered in its flatiron-shaped building for more than 200 years. The original innkeeper, Thomas Hyde, advertised it as "an elegant brick house in a dry and healthy part of the city...one of the first houses in the state for a house of entertainment."

For many years, guests in Annapolis, the home of the United States Naval Academy, were accommodated in this beautiful old building with a fourth-story mansard roof. They enjoyed wonderful meals in the many dining rooms, and in recent years, good jazz by the guitarist Charlie Byrd, and singers Ethel Ennis and Mose Allison. The Maryland Inn has always been a place for great holiday celebrations, with special happenings on Christmas, New Year's, Valentine's Day, the Fourth of July, and the like.

A new concept, called Historic Inns of Annapolis, has now changed and broadened the entire aspect of this historic property. Several different, impressively restored buildings in Annapolis, many of them dating back to before the American Revolution, will now provide more than 140 guest rooms.

These are actually a whole family of inns, each of which has its own innkeeper responsible for maintaining the comfort and well-being of each guest.

The Governor Calvert House, the oldest part of which was the home of the second provincial governor of Maryland in the very early eighteenth century, has been handsomely restored with a contemporary addition, resulting in a fifty-five-room inn and conference center nestled between lovely Colonial gardens on one side and the state capitol on the other. The Governor Calvert House provided a most accommodating center for a three-night meeting of *CIBR* inns.

The State House Inn is a nine-room bed-and-breakfast inn, also facing the state capitol. The Robert Johnson House, originally built in 1773, has been impressively restored along with two other adjoining historic homes as a thirty-room bed-and-breakfast inn. It is situated only half a block from the Maryland Inn, and directly across from both the governor's mansion and the state capitol garden.

The Reynolds Tavern, on Church Circle, includes the original tavern with its great fireplaces and brick floors, a fine restaurant with dining in the courtyard in season, and four distinctive guest rooms.

I am very much afraid that this explanation of the concept of Historic Inns of Annapolis has taken up a great deal of space, and I will wait till the next edition of this book to explain what a wonderful experience it is to visit Annapolis—actually "a museum without walls"— and at that time, I will delve into greater detail about the guided walking tours and the harbor cruises.

Suffice it to say at this time that the beauties of Annapolis are even much more accessible with the additional facilities offered by Historic Inns of Annapolis.

HISTORIC INNS OF ANNAPOLIS, Church Circle, Annapolis, MD 21401; 301-263-2641. (U.S reservations: 800-847-8882; within Md.: 800-638-8902.) A 142-guestroom complex of 5 separate inns in the heart of historic Annapolis, near the U.S. Naval Academy and Chesapeake Bay. Open year-round. Breakfast, lunch, and dinner served to travelers daily. Music nightly in the King of France Tavern, home to guitarist Charlie Byrd. Tours can be arranged to historic and scenic points of interest. Paul Pearson, Proprietor; Peg Bednarsky, Innkeeper.

Directions: From Baltimore, take Rte. 2 south to first directional turnoff "Washington/Annapolis." From Washington, take Rte. 50 east to "Annapolis Naval Academy/Rowe Blvd." Exit.

ROBERT MORRIS INN
Oxford, Maryland

This time I came from the north to Oxford via the Cape May–Lewes Ferry, which takes about seventy-five minutes and cuts off all of the trip through Baltimore and the Annapolis Bay Bridge. I found that it did take a bit of sharp navigating, because I had at least two old maps where the numbers did not match the road signs; however, after finding my way across both Delaware and the eastern shore of Maryland, I arrived in Easton to see clumps of forsythia already in bloom, even though the calendar said still one more week to go in March.

I continued out of Easton on the road to Oxford between the fertile fields, which, besides providing provender for hungry humans, are also a support link for the great Eastern Shore waterfowl population.

This time innkeepers Ken and Wendy Gibson had reserved one of the suites that have been converted from two small bedrooms into a sitting room and bedroom. I was very much impressed with all of the hard work that had been done by Wendy and her mother. Among the many kinds of interesting knickknacks and doodads that decorate the walls of the bedrooms are some very attractive tops of china serving dishes of many different designs. There are old-fashioned country coverlets and carpets as well.

As I pointed out in an earlier edition, there are four new river rooms (for non-smoking guests only) on the point beside the Sandaway Lodge. These have screened-in porches that look out over the Tred Avon. Each room has a four-poster, king-sized bed and a large Victorian-style bathroom, complete with a paddle fan, an Essex tub, and wooden floors. The mixture of antique pieces and nice furniture is aptly described by Wendy

Gibson as "country classy." Each of the guest rooms has an unobstructed view of the water.

Wendy told me that further renovations in the inn will create private baths for all the guest rooms. There will also be some sitting rooms and some non-smoking rooms.

The inn's location in the Chesapeake Bay area means that there is a considerable emphasis on seafood at lunch and dinner—crab cakes, baked seafood au gratin, lobster pie, seafood pot pie and fresh fish with a Robert Morris special sauce. Incidentally, their crab cakes earned a special mention in the *Washington Post* last summer: "The Robert Morris makes superlative crab cakes that manage the neat trick of being both creamy and light, just short of melting as you cut into them."

The inn starts taking reservations on the tenth of January for the current year, and accommodations should be reserved as early as possible, even for midweek stays.

Kent and Ben, twelve and fourteen, who have grown up in the inn, have developed a reputation for being exceptional "weeders"—a job they fit in around their baseball and tennis schedules.

Wendy and her mother continue to receive unlimited praise for their perennial flower bed, where something is blooming all the time.

ROBERT MORRIS INN, Oxford, MD 21654; 301-226-5111. A 28-guest-room waterside inn and lodge (private baths) in a secluded Colonial community on the Tred Avon, 10 mi. from Easton, MD. (Some rooms with private porches and some non-smoking rooms; two cottages only available for children). European plan. Breakfast, lunch, and dinner served to travelers and guests daily. Open year-round except Christmas. Tennis, golf, seasonal river swimming, sailing, fishing, and bicycles nearby. Recommended for children over 10. No pets. Kenneth and Wendy Gibson, Innkeepers.

Directions: From Delaware Memorial Bridge, follow Rte. 13 south to Rte. 301 and proceed south to Rte. 50, then east on Rte. 50 to Easton. From Chesapeake Bay Bridge, follow Rte. 50-301 to Rte. 50 and proceed east to Easton. From Chesapeake Bay Bridge Tunnel, follow Rte. 13 north to Rte. 50 and proceed west to Easton. From Easton, follow Rte. 322 to Rte. 333 to Oxford and inn.

HEMLOCK INN
Bryson City, North Carolina

I've always thought that I was "some punkins" as a shuffleboard player. You see, I've played shuffleboard in well over 100 places in North America. That's part of the advantage of traveling in search of inns. I thought I had the game down to a science, but I was wrong. Three gentlemen of consummate skill and infinite humor really put me in my place on a warm Wednesday afternoon in September at the Hemlock Inn.

I sat around like Paul Newman in *The Hustler,* waiting for them to invite me to play. They did and it was then I realized that they had actually hustled me, because as soon as the game started I knew I'd been taken. Of course, we weren't playing for money, we were playing for the fun of kidding the other guy. It was a laugh from start to finish.

Maybe that's the best way to put the Hemlock Inn in focus. It's a smile and warmth and consideration from the time a guest arrives until the time he regretfully leaves.

Take my case for example. I had driven considerably far that afternoon and Ella Jo Shell was instantly aware of the fact that what I needed most was probably a cold soft drink and a chance to just sit and look at the mountains. Oh boy, it certainly felt good to be back again. That's when the shuffleboard hustlers put the mark on me.

It was soon dinnertime, the event of the day at Hemlock. It is country inn food, like beef pie, country ham, baked apples, stuffed tomatoes, okra fritters, three or four kinds of delicious relish, homemade hot biscuits and country butter, all served country-style around big Lazy Susan tables. We talked and laughed and kidded and joked and ate.

We made plans to go out on the Great Smoky trails the next day. We challenged each other at checkers and promised to "come visit" each other in the winter.

But before all of this happened at dinnertime, we stood behind our chairs and joined John Shell in grace with the most sincere and heartfelt tones. He later said, "In times when there seems to be a shortage of a few things, I think we ought to be very grateful for the abundance we have."

John and Ella Jo love innkeeping; they're both from Marietta, Georgia. As she says, "It's more like fun or like having company all of the time." Two meals are served every day, breakfast and dinner. They both are served family-style, which certainly allows everybody to get acquainted.

Local ladies do the cooking and some of them have been at the inn for a long time. If I close my eyes now I can inhale the marvelous aromas of that delicious food.

There is no swimming pool, golf course, or television, but there is warmth, friendliness, and consideration. There are also the glorious Great Smokies all around.

Then there are those shuffleboard hustlers. Believe me, I'm going to practice up on my game.

I wrote the above account a few years ago, but I must say that it always gives me great pleasure to remember that day. More recently, a group of *CIBR* innkeepers from North Carolina had a wonderful dinner-meeting at the Hemlock Inn, and all of us came away just like all the other guests at Hemlock, with a feeling of being cared for.

The spring of 1986 will be the thirty-fifth season. Arthur Stupka will be back again in the early spring for the Wildflower Walks and Talks. As Ella Jo says, "We look forward to a nice season spent with old friends, the same excellent help, and new friends. How fortunate we are to live in an area where we are central to whatever people come to do in the Great Smoky Mountain National Park. It is the most visited one in our country."

HEMLOCK INN, Bryson City, NC 28713; 704-488-2885. A 25-guest-room Smoky Mountain inn, 4 mi. from Bryson City and 60 mi. from Asheville. Modified American plan omits lunch. Breakfast and dinner served to travelers by reservation only. Sunday dinner served at noontime. Open late April to early Nov. Near Fontana Dam, Cherokee, and Pisgah National Forest. Shuffleboard, skittles, ping-pong, hiking trails on grounds. Tubing, rafting, and tennis nearby. No pets. No credit cards. Ella Jo and John Shell, Innkeepers.

Directions: From 19-A (19 Bypass) take the Hyatt Creek Rd.–Ela exit. Bear right until you reach old Rte. 19. Turn left on Rte. 19 and continue for approx. 2 mi. Turn right at inn sign. Take paved road to top of mountain.

HOUND EARS LODGE
Blowing Rock, North Carolina

There are very few sights more inspiring to the golfer in me than to look over the golf course on a pleasant June morning from the balcony of Hound Ears Lodge. In the foreground is a lake fed by a small mountain stream that winds its way through the valley. This lake also serves as a hazard for the final hole and a very good 9-iron shot to the green is necessary to stay out of trouble.

The fairways that stretch out in the distance toward Grandfather Mountain are being watered by great fountains sent forth by the automatic watering system. When this is completed and the mist burns off, there is revealed a ring of mountains around the entire area. However, in the meantime, the greenskeepers are busy sweeping off the moisture that has accumulated overnight and the head greenskeeper can be seen tootling about in his golf cart, making sure that everything is ready for another day's play.

I had arrived at Hound Ears early in June, just at the time when the special golf packages, in effect since April, were being replaced by the regular social season. It was a good opportunity for me to have a pleasant visit with David Blust, the assistant manager at Hound Ears, who actually started as a bellboy a number of years ago. It's hard to imagine a more enthusiastic devotee of not only Hound Ears, but of golf and of North Carolina. We enjoyed a few moments of listening to Gene Fleri, who plays piano in the pleasant lounge before dinner and in the dining room during dinner. It is said that he can play any song that anyone can name.

Hound Ears is a golf- and ski-oriented country inn, but is somewhat different in atmosphere than the other *CIBR* inns in North Carolina. It is a luxurious, modified American plan resort-inn and the rates reflect the additional services and elegance. In the many, many years that I have been revisiting Hound Ears I've always found a very gratifying number of *CIBR* guests.

Among the many amenities offered are turn-down service each evening, the *Charlotte Observer* at the door every morning, fresh towels supplied to the rooms while guests enjoy dinner, and a careful monitoring of guests at the main gate by courteous custodians. Advance reservations are to be preferred; however, occasionally there are some guest rooms available.

The property surrounding Hound Ears has been purchased by home-owners who have built attractive, luxurious vacation homes, and who are very much involved in the future and welfare of the entire resort complex.

A great many of the guests are from Florida, and during the warm weather they escape to this very high mountain area to enjoy all of the relative coolness, as well as the golf.

During the winter, in addition to being near several downhill ski areas aided by snowmaking, Hound Ears also has its own beginners' and intermediate slopes, providing enjoyment for those of us who are looking for a less vigorous downhill experience.

The staff at Hound Ears is made up for the most part of students from nearby Appalachia College in Boone. These are very pleasant, alert young people who have grown up in the area, for whom Hound Ears is a source of pride.

The furnishings, appointments, interiors, and exteriors are carefully harmonized. For example, my room was done in complementary shades of brown and yellow. All of the buildings are set among the rhododen-drons and evergreens, and in many places huge handsome boulders were allowed to remain where they rested. The road was built around them, curving and twisting and climbing.

Nearby Grandfather Mountain is a place where the Scottish clan gathering is held during the second week in July. Scotsmen gather from all over the globe to take part in athletic competitions, dances, and piping. There are also a great deal of other cultural and recreational events held at the same time.

HOUND EARS LODGE AND CLUB, P.O. Box 188, Blowing Rock, NC 28605; 704-963-4321. A luxurious 25-guestroom resort-inn on Rte. 105, 6 mi. from Boone. Near natural attractions. American plan. Meals served to houseguests only. Open year-round. Tennis, 18-hole golf course, swimming, and skiing on grounds. David Blust, Innkeeper.

Directions: From Winston-Salem, follow Rte. 421 west to Boone, then travel south on Rte. 105 to inn. From Asheville, follow Rtes. I-40 east to Marion then Rte. 221 north to Linville and Rte. 105 north to inn. From Bristol, Va., and I-81, follow Rte. 58 east to Damascus, Va., then Rte. 91 to Mountain City, Tenn., and Rte. 421 to Boone, and Rte. 104 south to inn (5 mi.)

THE NU-WRAY INN
Burnsville, North Carolina

The drive from Hound Ears Lodge in Blowing Rock to the Nu-Wray Inn in Burnsville, North Carolina, on a sunny morning in June is most enjoyable. It provides an overview of the various intriguing altitudes in this part of North Carolina, which has the highest mountains east of the Rockies. Traveling next to Grandfathers Mountain, we start out literally in the high clouds and drop through various layers of mists to reach a more fertile farming country.

The Nu-Wray Inn provides an interesting contrast to the Hound Ears, a sophisticated, somewhat elegant country club resort. The Nu-Wray is a North Carolina inn that has been in existence since the 19th century and has remained much the same, thanks to the members of the Wray family who have carefully preserved some of the best of the past.

On the village square in Burnsville, the Nu-Wray now enjoys a well-deserved recognition for its venerability and individuality, especially in light of the proliferation of inns in North Carolina. My first visit goes back quite a few years when I met the late innkeeper emeritus,

Rush Wray, and spent the better part of the evening listening to his fascinating accounts of history and literature in North Carolina. It was also my introduction to the distinctive regional cooking at the Nu-Wray, characterized by the fried chicken and wonderful country hams.

At a bountiful breakfast on one of my later trips, after introducing everybody seated at the long harvest tables, Rush went into particulars about dinner:

"On Monday, Wednesday, and Friday we have fried chicken; Tuesday, Thursday, and Saturday we have baked country ham. The vegetables and desserts vary each day according to what's fresh from the various farms in the area. We have corn on the cob, fresh tomatoes, beans, carrots, and similar vegetables. One of the things we've been serving is homemade scalloped potatoes. We have found that a great many of our guests have sort of forgotten about scalloped potatoes and many have asked for our recipe."

The inn is really a very old building and the hallway walls are made of tongue-in-groove paneling, which in some cases is painted. Different sections of the building obviously have been put together at various times during the past 100 or more years, so that there are some interesting variations in interior design. It has been on the National Register of Historic Places for many years.

There is an assortment of bedrooms at the Nu-Wray. Those on the top floor are a bit smaller and in a lower price range. The inn also has an assortment of parlors and sitting rooms including one on the second floor with an old A.B. Gate & Co. piano of beautiful wood and several hand-some antique tables and a chest of drawers.

Almost all the letters I get about the Nu-Wray say that it's different. Almost everyone mentions the rousing bells rung at 8:00 and 8:30 a.m. to announce breakfast. It's good to get an early start here in this part of North Carolina, because the flora and the fauna and the back roads provide a most rewarding vacation experience.

A word about my dear friend, Rush Wray, who passed away in July of 1985. Rush was really a one-of-a-kind individual, giving freely of himself to friends and strangers alike. I'll miss the long talks and good-natured joshing that we both enjoyed. He was a true innkeeper.

However, I'm sure that Howard and Betty Wray Souders, who have been the working innkeepers in recent years, will carry on his tradition of warm hospitality and friendliness.

THE NU-WRAY INN, Burnsville, NC 28714; 704-682-2329. A 35-guest-room village inn on town square on Rte. 19E, 38 mi. north of Asheville. Breakfast and dinner served every weekday to travelers. Noon dinner served on Sun. only. Open daily May to Dec. 1. Golf, swimming, hiking, and skiing nearby. A few miles from Mt. Mitchell. Howard and Betty Souders, Innkeepers.

Directions: From Asheville, go north on Rte. 19-23 for 18 mi., then continue on 19. Five miles from Burnsville, Rte. 19 becomes 19E. From the north via Bristol or Johnson City, Tenn., take Rte. 19-23 to Unicoi. Turn left on 107 to N.C. State Line. Take Rte. 226 and turn right on Rte. 197 at Red Hill to Burnsville.

THE ORCHARD INN
Saluda, North Carolina

Because I spend so much time in an automobile, I have invented a little game of my own. I call it "Inn Word Association." I think of an inn and then I think of words I associate most readily with it.

In the case of the Orchard Inn there are many words that come to my mind—flowers, paintings, music, sculpture, the view, cordiality, intellectual curiosity, good conversation, mountain tranquility, and the changing tones and colors as they are affected by the mists off the mountains at various times of the day.

On my first visit to this mountaintop inn in Saluda a few years ago, innkeeper Ken Hough and I picked our way over all kinds of building paraphernalia that was scattered around both the interior and exterior of the inn. At that time he and Ann, his wife, were busy restoring this building, which has had a most interesting history as a vacation retreat for Southern Railway employees. Now the work has been done, the workmen are finished, and the results are worthy of their toil.

This restoration (by the way, I think this is the Houghs' seventeenth) combines country farmhouse warmth with many touches of southern plantation elegance. The inn reflects not only Ken and Ann's love of restoration, but also their passion for collecting. It has oriental rugs, original artwork, baskets, quilts, and Flow Blue china, which Ann has been collecting for some time.

With an extensive background in interior design, Ann has exercised a splendid restraint in decorating the ten guest rooms with antiques, including some with iron and brass beds and hand-woven rag rugs.

This inn has one of the most interesting second-floor hallways I have ever seen. Several bookshelves are loaded with books and magazines, including very old but readable ones. There are all kinds of unusual curios, dolls, childrens' toys, a dollhouse, and contemporary drawings, watercolors, and prints from the French Impressionists.

Perhaps most surprising of all is an art gallery on the ground floor, where the work of Jane Armstrong, an outstanding sculptor, is on permanent display.

Outside, there's a path that leads down through the woods, past a couple of beehives and many, many flowers, both wild and cultivated. The inn takes its name from the many orchards nearby, and much of their fresh fruit comes from those orchards.

Ken, who is the chef, has a background as a headmaster at a college preparatory school in Charleston and also as an operatic tenor. He has created such things as chilled peach soup, creamed seafood over rice, and chicken Madras. Broiled fresh mountain trout is a specialty. The desserts include apple crumble, blackberry cobbler, and pecan pie from a special New Orleans recipe.

The dining room is in the wonderful, long, glassed-in porch overlooking the splendid, rolling mountains of the Warrior Mountain Range. It was really quite magical after dusk had fallen—every table was candlelit and the strains of Schumann, Mozart, and Scarlatti wafted out into the gathering night.

I'm sure that when you visit the Orchard Inn, you'll have an even longer list of words to associate with it. We welcome it to *CIBR*.

THE ORCHARD INN, Box 725, Saluda, NC 28773; 704-749-5471. A 10-guestroom mountaintop (2500 feet) inn a short distance from Tryon in western North Carolina. Open year-round. Breakfast included with room rate. Lunch and dinner available. Antiquing, hiking, wild flower collecting, bird watching, and superb country roads abound. No pets. No credit cards. Ann and Ken Hough, Innkeepers.

Directions: From Atlanta, come north on I-85 to Hwy. 5. Inn is 2 mi. off I-26. From Asheville, take I-26 south.

"European plan" means that rates for rooms and meals are separate. "American plan" means that meals are included in the cost of the room. "Modified American plan" means that breakfast and dinner are included in the cost of the room. The rates at some inns include a continental breakfast with the lodging.

SNOWBIRD MOUNTAIN LODGE
Robbinsville, North Carolina

Bob and Connie Rhudy and I were seated where everyone sits at Snowbird Mountain Lodge—on the terrace that almost hangs over Lake Santeetlah, at least 1,000 feet below. Gazing over the railing we could see a tiny automobile on the thin, winding sliver of road climbing the adjacent mountain. Directly in front of us, almost close enough to touch, were at least fifteen majestic peaks with heights, from 4,000 to 5,000 feet.

Since my first visit to Snowbird quite a few years ago, I have always associated it with the increasing number of birds that make this area their habitat. I understand that some guests can identify as many as 110 different species. In the last couple of years wildflower walks have become extremely popular.

Connie and Bob were especially enthusiastic about the nature hikes led by several knowledgable guides in the past two years. "They have become enormously popular," Connie said. "There are wildflower, bird, and plant hikes, and our guides are acknowledged authorities in their fields. They are each here at different times during the spring and summer, and we have many reservations for next spring's adventures already."

Rustic Snowbird Mountain Lodge, built of chestnut logs and native stone, harmonizes beautifully with its mountain setting. Two huge stone fireplaces add beauty and warmth. (There is also steam heat for the cooler months.)

The main lounge is paneled in butternut, the dining room in cherry, and guest rooms are paneled in a variety of native woods with custom-made furniture to match. The comfortable beds have bright bedspreads.

The Rhudys have two excellent assistant innkeepers in their daughter, Becky, who will graduate from Robbinsville High School in June, 1986, and their son, Bobby, who will have completed his sophomore year at Furman University in the same month. All of the Rhudys have combined to make this mountaintop lodge a veritable haven for guests who enjoy the many outdoor activities in the area.

Boxed lunches are provided in lieu of lunch at the lodge, if guests prefer. Snowbird is on the full American plan.

"Last year we did something for the first time that we're going to continue," explained Bob. "We decided to add one final weekend to our season and call it 'Fall Finale at Snowbird.' Fresh hot coffee starts the Friday afternoon and then after the evening meal, which will have fresh mountain trout and homemade coconut cream pie, we'll gather in front of a roaring fire to enjoy music from some of our local musicians. After breakfast on Saturday morning, a packed lunch will be available for

anyone wishing to explore the Joyce Kilmer–Slickrock Wilderness Area. Following a dinner of Rock Cornish game hens we'll retire to our sitting room for another evening of reading, games, and swapping stories of the day's activities. The weekend closes on Sunday morning with a delicious breakfast of country sausage and blueberry pancakes."

Sounds like a wonderful way to wind up the autumn.

SNOWBIRD MOUNTAIN LODGE, Joyce Kilmer Forest Rd., Robbinsville, NC 28771; 704-479-3433. A 22-guestroom inn on top of the Great Smokies, 12 mi. from Robbinsville. American plan (room and 3 meals). Open from end of April to early Nov. Lunch and dinner served to travelers by reservation only. Shuffleboard, table tennis, archery, croquet, horseshoes, badminton on grounds. Swimming, fishing, hiking, backroading nearby. Guided walks for nature lovers by reservation. Not suitable for children under 12. No pets. The Rhudy Family, Innkeepers.

Directions: The inn is located at the western tip of No. Carolina, 10 mi. west of Robbinsville. Approaching from the northeast or south take U.S. 19 and 129; from the northwest take U.S. 129, then follow signs to Joyce Kilmer Memorial Forest.

A number of inns have nearby airports where private airplanes may land. An airplane symbol at the end of the inn directions indicates that there is an airport nearby. Consult inn for further information.

PARISH PATCH INN
Normandy, Tennessee

"Cortner Mill stayed with the same family from 1848 until the late 1950s. It was a working mill for that entire time. We've kept some of the original equipment right here, including the scale and some of the wonderful grain chutes."

Marty Ligon, the owner of Parish Patch Inn, and I were seated on the porch at Cortner Mill in Normandy, Tennessee. Here above the dam, the waters of the Duck River seem so placid until they drop over the dam and gather momentum from their fall. Upstream on both banks the branches of the trees hang out over the water, and one branch has a rope swing, where one could swing out over the river, let go, and splash right into the water just like a lad in a Norman Rockwell painting. The sound of the water has a wonderful soporific effect. It's the kind of place to sit and read a book, maybe take a nap in one of the beautiful ladder-back rockers, or possibly even *write* a book.

The Mill, which also has its own accommodations, is actually part and parcel of Parish Patch Inn, the main house being just a few moments away. The combination of the two places provides a most interesting contrast in a country inn experience. The Mill has a pleasant rustic elegance, with four different guest rooms, including one bunk room with seven twin beds. I think the most impressive feature, of course, is the presence of the river and the dam.

The main house of the Parish Patch presents an entirely different aspect. This is a lovely board-and-batten structure with comfortable rooms, private baths, fireplaces, patios, rose gardens, and a swimming pool with an attractive poolhouse. Fresh-cut flowers and homemade pumpkin bread are some of the extra touches that make it enjoyable. The guest rooms are not at all rustic, unless you count the beautifully varnished overhead beams. All have splendid views of the rolling Tennessee countryside, and the outdoors is immediately available, in some cases, through a sliding door onto a balcony. There's a mixture of natural woods, with some excellent antique pieces and well-designed lamps and other necessities. All of the guest rooms have two double beds and a television.

Dinner is served in a very pleasant dining room, for houseguests only, by reservation. I asked Marty what some of the entrées would be. "Well, we serve only one main dish," she replied, "and that could be meat loaf, fried chicken, chicken cordon bleu, roast beef, or stuffed pork chops. All of the breads, muffins, rolls, and coffee cakes are homemade right here. Mildred Kimbro is the cook, along with her daughter, Kay, and she is happy to take suggestions."

Parish Patch offers another unusual opportunity for guests to share the experience of being on a real working farm, because at times there may be many hundreds of beef cattle in the nearby pens.

Provisions are made for people traveling with children, with some outdoor swings, slides, bars, and other equipment. The house itself overlooks great cornfields on two sides, and the whole immediate area is surrounded by an old-fashioned Tennessee split-rail fence.

I'd like to suggest that readers making reservations at the Parish Patch Inn talk over their preferences with Marty or Phyllis Crosslin, the innkeeper, because there are a number of options.

Everything at both locations is beautifully maintained and cared for, and yet within just a few moments' walk you're in the beautiful Tennessee countryside.

PARISH PATCH INN, Normandy, TN 37360; 615- 857-3441. A 10-guest-room elegant inn in the verdant Tennessee countryside. European plan. Evening meals are served to houseguests only with advance reservation. Open all year. Closed Christmas Day. Swimming pool on grounds. Fishing, boating, canoeing, picnicking, bicycling, bird watching and backroading nearby. Personal checks accepted. Marty Ligon, Owner; Phyllis Crosslin, Innkeeper.

Directions: From Shelbyville continue south on 41-A for 7.2 mi. and look for a left turn at the sign for Normandy. Turn left onto Dement Rd. and follow signs to inn. From I-24, take Exit 97 (Beechgrove-Shelbyville-Hwy. 64 Exit). Take Hwy. 64 west to Wartrace. In Wartrace do not cross RR tracks. Take Hwy. 269 east. Pass shops and turn left at yellow light, up hill. Inn is 4 mi. from Wartrace.

BEAUMONT INN
Harrodsburg, Kentucky

"Oh, I wish you could have known Miss Pauline, she was here for so many years, and everybody loved her."

Mary Elizabeth Dedman and I had taken a few moments to talk about the history of the Beaumont Inn, and I found that not only was she a gold mine of wonderful, interesting anecdotes, but she had actually written a history of the inn and some of its furnishings, which is available to the guests.

The Beaumont, with its stately Grecian columns set against a dark red brick background, was built as a school for young ladies in 1845 and later became known as Daughter's College. Later on it was Beaumont College. In 1916, it was purchased by Mr. and Mrs. Glave Goddard and converted into the Beaumont Inn. The ownership and management passed from Mrs. Goddard to her daughter, Mrs. Dedman, and then to Mrs. Dedman's two sons. Today, Bud Dedman is the owner-manager, and his son, Chuck, following tradition, becomes the fourth generation to be trained here in the innkeeper's art. Moreover, Chuck has two children, one of whom is already showing great promise as an innkeeper of the future!

Each time I visit I find something I have not seen on my many previous visits. This time I discovered that Mary Elizabeth has a collection of saltcellars—handsome small dishes that were used everywhere before the saltshaker came into being. She must have at least one hundred or more in a glass case, and handsome they are indeed—many of glowing cut glass in various shapes and shades. It's just an example of the kind of memorabilia that is found throughout all of the public rooms, hallways, and guest rooms of the inn.

The decorations and furniture in all the parlors and guest rooms reflect American history. The hallways on the main floor have several cabinets with beautiful old china and silverware. The sitting rooms have elegant fireplaces and wallpaper decorated with roses.

The inn also has a very extensive gift shop, and some of the items that have the Beaumont Inn label are cornmeal batter-mix, brown sugar syrup, green tomato relish, sweet pickle relish, chicken-cheese casserole, creamed chicken, frozen fruit salad, soda biscuits with chopped country ham, and many different sauces. These are also served in the Beaumont Inn dining room, and besides that there is the famous Beaumont Inn cookbook with special recipes (also compiled by Mary Elizabeth), which was done many years ago and has been enlarged and revised, and is now in its second printing.

It's well worth noting that the traditions at the Beaumont also include a high interest in Kentucky horses, and it's just a short distance

to Keeneland, the Red Mile Harness Racing Track, and, of course, Churchill Downs, home of the Kentucky Derby.

A guest at the Beaumont is visiting the Dedman family, and there's always somebody named Dedman within earshot or at least just around the corner, and this includes Chuck and Helen's young son, Dickson, who is very much in evidence riding the tractors or in the kitchen or helping with the redecorating. In Kentucky, where families and relatives play such an important role in everyone's life, I'm sure it must be a source of great pride to Bud Dedman to see his grandson already shaking hands and greeting people like a good innkeeper should.

BEAUMONT INN, Harrodsburg, KY 40330; 606-734-3381. A 29-guest-room country inn in the heart of Kentucky's historic bluegrass country. European plan. Lunch and dinner served to travelers; all three meals to houseguests. Open every day from mid-March to mid-Dec. Tennis, swimming pool, shuffleboard on grounds. Golf courses and a wide range of recreational and historic attractions nearby. No pets. The Dedman Family, Innkeepers.

Directions: From Louisville: Exit 48 from east I-64. Go south on Ky. 151, to U.S. 127 south to Harrodsburg. From Lexington: U.S. 60 west, then west on Bluegrass Parkway to U.S. 127. From Nashville: Exit I-65 to Bluegrass Parkway near Elizabethtown, Ky., then east to U.S. 127.

Berea College Campus

BOONE TAVERN HOTEL
Berea, Kentucky

I was having lunch in the main dining room of Boone Tavern Hotel with the very attractive innkeeper, Miriam Pride. The high-ceilinged dining room, with affable and alert students of the Berea College Hotel School waiting on tables, created a most pleasant atmosphere.

The conversation with Miriam led quite naturally to the Boone Tavern menu, which has been famous for many, many years, using among other things some of the original recipes from former long-time manager, Dick Hougen.

"Oh yes," Miriam said, "we still use his recipes for southern peanut soup, plantation ham, Boone Tavern chicken pie, Georgian sweet potatoes, and Kentucky blackberry dumpling."

"What do you have on the menu that you can't take off, because it is so popular?" I asked. "Roast turkey most definitely is our most popular item. Fried chicken is another real winner, and chicken à la king in a bird's nest, which I believe is one of Mr. Hougen's recipes, is always popular."

I would suggest you telephone for lunch or dinner reservations in advance if you're on I-75. Their dress code permits casual attire for breakfast and lunch, Monday through Saturday, as well as Sunday breakfast. However, for Sunday noon and for all evening meals, coats are required for men, and dresses or pantsuits for women. Jackets are available for men. Incidentally, there is no smoking in the dining room.

I was astonished to learn that over 200,000 visitors stop at the inn each year for lodgings and meals.

At Berea, the college, the inn, and the town are all interlocked. It's impossible to speak of one without the other two. The college is a unique educational experience, because all students are expected to engage in a work program, and I'm happy to report that I have seen in the course of my many visits that it works.

I asked Miriam about the inn staff. "About ninety percent are students," she replied. "Most of them are majoring in hotel management. In fact, with the exception of the cooks and key personnel in the front office, students run the whole show."

To the promising young men and women from Appalachia (many of whom find here their only opportunity for college), Berea offers a liberal arts education of the highest academic standard.

Another entirely separate aspect of the school is the arts and crafts in which all students participate. There are student-conducted tours of the various workshops, including broom-making, weaving, woodcraft, pottery, lapidary arts, and several other crafts.

These are all sold in a shop located in the inn itself, which has expanded considerably since my last visit. The wooden products range from gorgeous tables that sell for as much as $2,500 to little carved animals, but the shop is a gay panoply of colors and textures.

The inn is comfortable and inviting, and has among other things a skittles game and chinese checkers set up in the lobby. These are manufactured in one of the college crafts shops and are sold commercially.

At the time of this particular visit many of the bedrooms were either fully redecorated or were in the process, and the rooms looked bright and cheerful, of course with furniture made in the college crafts shop.

I've toured the campus many times over the past eighteen years and, while I was in the library doing a little research on the background of the college, I discovered that one of the founders, Cassius M. Clay, had been converted to emancipation by a speech of the famous William Lloyd Garrison. This stand for racial freedom was a part of the original foundation of the college. Incidentally, the name Berea comes from the biblical town mentioned in Acts 18:10, "where men were openminded."

BOONE TAVERN HOTEL, Berea, KY 40403; 606-986-9341. A 60-guest-room village inn in a unique college community on I-75, 40 mi. south of Lexington, Ky., and 120 mi. from Cincinnati. European plan. Breakfast, lunch, dinner served daily to travelers by sittings only; reservations important. Dinner and Sun. noon, coats required for men; dresses or pantsuits for women. Open every day of the year. All campus activities open to guests; campus tours twice daily except Sat. and Sun. Tennis on grounds. Golf, pool, bicycles nearby. Berea is on Eastern time. Miriam Pride, Innkeeper.

Directions: Take Berea exit from I-75; 1 mi. north to hotel.

THE INN AT PLEASANT HILL
Shakertown, Kentucky

Betty Morris and I were driving down the twisty road that leads to the Shaker Landing on the Kentucky River, just a few moments from the Inn at Pleasant Hill. Soon, a handsome paddlewheel river boat, the "Dixie Belle," came into view, and already there were people waiting to board her for the morning cruise.

This cruise, very popular with the inn guests, follows the seventy-five mile course of the river, bordered by impressive 315-foot limestone cliffs. Betty who is manager of the Inn at Pleasant Hill, told me that a running history of the Kentucky River, including its importance to the economy of 100 years ago and the contributions made by the Shakers, is part of this cruise.

By an interesting coincidence, just as she pointed out the great railroad trestle that traverses the river, a freight train went by, right on cue.

The Inn at Pleasant Hill is located in a restored Shaker community in one of the most beautiful sections of central Kentucky. The Shakers were members of a religious sect, the United Society of Believers in Christ's Second Appearing. They were actually an offshoot of the Quakers. The founder was Mother Ann Lee, who brought her ideas to America late in the 18th century.

The Shakers held some advanced social ideas. They were hospitable to visitors and took in orphans and unwanted children. Their fundamental beliefs were in hard work and austere discipline that sought perfection. This sense of perfection was extended into the design of their furniture, and many people learn about Shakers for the first time as a result of being attracted by the beauty and simplicity of the functional Shaker designs.

The Shakers lived in communal dedication to their religious beliefs of celibacy, renunciation of worldliness, common ownership of property, and public confession of sins, which culminated in the frenetic dances that gave them the name of Shakers.

There were five "families" at Pleasant Hill, established in 1805. By 1820 it was a prosperous colony of five hundred persons. "Family" had a particular meaning, since the Shakers did not believe in marriage. Men and women, they maintained, could live more happily as brothers and sisters helping one another, but living personally apart.

The Civil War, plus 19th-century industrialism and worldliness, seeped into Pleasant Hill, and the celibacy rules prevented the natural increase in their numbers. In 1910 they were dissolved.

The reception area of the inn is located in the Trustees' House, one of twenty-five or more buildings clustered along the single country road. To construct buildings of enduring strength, some with walls three or four feet thick, the Shakers quarried limestone from the river bluffs and

hauled granite slabs a mile uphill from the river. Most of the buildings are of deep red brick or limestone.

The restaurant is on the first floor of the Trustees' House, and the guest rooms on the second and third floors are reached by two marvelous twin-spiraled staircases of matchless craftsmanship. There are many additional bedrooms on the second floor of restored Shaker shops.

The experience of sleeping in a Shaker room is most refreshing. In my room were two single beds, each with its own trundle bed underneath. The Shaker rockers were classic, and the extra chairs were hung by pegs on the walls.

Many of the tasty dishes served in the dining room are prepared from Shaker recipes. The young men and women on the staff all wear replicas of simple Shaker garb. Much of the produce has been raised on the fields of the restored community.

THE INN AT PLEASANT HILL, Shakertown, KY. P.O. address: Rte. 4, Harrodsburg, KY 40330; 606-734-5411. A 63-guestroom country inn in a restored Shaker village on Rte. 68, 7 mi. northeast of Harrodsburg, 25 mi. southwest of Lexington. European plan. Breakfast, lunch, dinner served daily to travelers. Open year-round. Suggest contacting inn about winter schedule. Closed Christmas Eve and Christmas Day. Ann Voris, Innkeeper.

Directions: From Lexington take Rte. 68 south toward Harrodsburg. From Louisville, take I-64 to Lawrenceburg and Graeffenburg exit (not numbered). Follow Rte. 127 south to Harrodsburg and Rte. 68 northeast to Shakertown.

GRAVES' MOUNTAIN LODGE
Syria, Virginia

Of all of the thousands of inn and hotel brochures that I have seen, none is more handsome, better designed, or more informative than "Mountain Hospitality," the booklet that describes literally five generations of innkeeping at Graves' Mountain Lodge.

For over 130 years, five generations of the Graves' family have been innkeepers in the shadow of the Blue Ridge Mountains near Syria, Virginia. In the early 1850s, Paschal Graves opened an "ordinary," or inn, along the Blue Ridge Turnpike on land now part of the Shenandoah National Park. The ordinary was a natural stopping point for travelers making the seventy-mile journey between Gordonsville and New Market. Here horses were changed to make the climb over the mountains, and farmers on foot herded their livestock to market along the turnpike or hauled wagonloads of bark and carts of apples, corn, and chestnuts.

Around 1857 the Graves family moved to their present location and for 100 years "took in" travelers and vacationers in their rambling farmhouse. Today's innkeeper is Jim Graves, and he can recall as a boy growing up the fun and work of having visitors arrive. Their cook fried chicken, baked hams and fresh fruit pies and cakes. Dinner was served family-style and people came from all around to have chicken. As he said, "When we had a lot of guests in the summer, our family moved out of the bedrooms and slept on the porch. We didn't mind because vacationers usually brought children for us to play with. We became friends with many of them and later some came back to work on the farm."

A lot of very exciting things have happened since Jim was a young boy. He met and married Rachel Lynn Norman, who shared his enthusiasm. Even during their courting days they drew sketches and developed ideas about a rustic but modern mountain resort. They discovered that they had the same pedigree; they are both descendants of Captain Thomas Graves, who sailed to Jamestown in 1608. Rachel's family stems from Thomas Graves' oldest son, born in England, and Jim's family is descended from a younger son, born in Virginia. Twelve generations later their marriage united two branches of a 375-year family tree. By the way, this tree is pictured in "Mountain Hospitality."

One of the most colorful figures connected with Graves' Mountain Lodge was Jim's father, "Mr. Jack," who was still on the scene during my first visit many years ago. It was a common sight to see him come to dinner fresh from his farm chores, but in clean overalls, to be on hand to meet all of the guests.

As I leafed through the pages of the booklet, I realized that very little has changed since the original concept of Graves' Mountain Lodge four generations ago. The new lodge is a unique collection of old and new buildings, each with a history all of its own. Over the years I have described the outbuildings that also serve as guest quarters. In recent years two additional buildings with tastefully furnished motel-type bedrooms enjoy a fantastic view of the great valley filled with cattle, sheep, farmland, and acres and acres of peach and apple trees.

What about the food at Graves' Mountain Lodge? Well, here is Suzanne Haney telling me, during a visit I made last November, about Sunday night supper at Graves' Mountain Lodge. "Sunday night dinner will be country ham, cold fried chicken, country-fried potatoes and onions, green beans, baked tomatoes, corn pudding, coleslaw, maybe one or two other vegetables, and probably spiced peaches or apples. Usually on Sunday night we have hot fudge cake for dessert.

"Tonight, we will have between 250 and 300 people. Last Sunday, we had about 700 people."

The original Graves family, including Mr. Jack, I'm sure, would be glad to know that everybody is served family-style inside the lodge and on the porch.

Although the lodge is operated on the American plan—three meals a day with lodging—those who want to stop by for a meal can call for a reservation and are always welcome.

GRAVES' MOUNTAIN LODGE, Syria, VA 22743; 703-923-4231. A 41-guestroom secluded, rustic resort-inn, including cottages and 2 motel units, on Rte. 670, off Rte. 321, 10 mi. north of Madison, Va., 38 mi. N.W. of Charlottesville, Va. American plan. Breakfast, lunch, dinner served to travelers by reservation only. Closed Dec. 1 to late Mar. Swimming, tennis, horseback riding, hunting, fishing, a special nature walk, rock hunting, and hiking on grounds. Golf nearby. Jim and Rachel Graves, Innkeepers.

Directions: Coming south from Wash. D.C., take I-66 to Gainsville. Follow Rte. 29 south to Madison, turn right onto Rte. 231 west, go 7 mi. to Banco, turn left onto Rte. 670 and follow 670 for 4½ mi. to lodge.

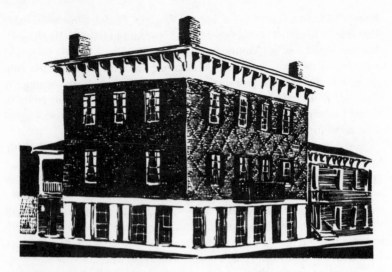

HISTORIC COUNTRY INNS OF LEXINGTON
Lexington, Virginia

A letter from the Meredith family in Lexington had some extremely exciting news:

"Our third inn, Maple Hall, is now open. It is located seven miles north of Lexington at the intersection of I-81 (Exit 53) and Route 11. It is a lovely old plantation home that was sadly in need of tender loving care, with a boxwood garden that had overgrown into a maze, and a beautiful view of the mountains and fifty-six acres of hilly woods and pasture."

The Peter Meredith family undertook the challenge and have created another inn to add to their two Historic Country Inns of Lexington, the Alexander-Withrow House and the McCampbell Inn.

Maple Hall was built on Maple Hill plantation around 1839 by Colonel John Gibson, CSA. About 1900 it was given the name Maple Hall, and John Gibson's descendants continued in residence there right up to 1984, when it was purchased by the Merediths.

Guest rooms have fireplaces and are furnished with antiques and modern conveniences. A gracious dining room serves the innkeeper's fare. The grounds feature a formal boxwood garden and walking trails.

So, now we've added a third inn to the complex of the Historic Country Inns of Lexington and it's possible to make reservations at all inns by using the telephone number in the closing paragraphs.

Each of these inns has the common denominator of real Lexington, Virginia, hospitality, but at the same time each has its own unique atmosphere. The Alexander Withrow House was built in 1789 with four corner chimneys, a most elaborate brickwork design known as "diapering," and a handsome Italianate roof. It is on the National Register of Historic Places. There are seven rooms or suites, all furnished with period antiques.

The McCampbell Inn, another historic house built as a residence in 1809, is right across the street from the Alexander-Withrow House. There are double porches along one side and the back, affording guests a place to relax in rocking chairs and a view of this lovely little town.

Dinner is now offered at Maple Hall to guests of both the Alexander-Withrow and the McCampbell Inn.

Other news from Lexington is that it has been chosen as the future site for the Virginia Horse Center. The first board meeting was held at the McCampbell Inn in August of 1985.

Lexington is one of the most interesting but off-the-beaten-path areas in the East. Besides the Military Institute and Washington and Lee University, it contains much memorabilia connected with Stonewall Jackson. Both Jackson and Robert E. Lee are buried in Lexington. The surrounding countryside is replete with some very impressive southwestern Virginia scenery, including the Natural Bridge, the Blue Ridge Parkway, Goshen Pass, and Cyrus McCormick's farm and workshop, where he invented the mechanized reaper.

There is always interesting news from the Meredith family and the Historic Country Inns of Lexington.

HISTORIC COUNTRY INNS OF LEXINGTON, 11 No. Main St., Lexington, VA 24450; 703-463-2044. Three historic houses offering 36 elegant suites and bedrooms. Lodgings and complimentary continental breakfast. Dinner is served. Advance reservations recommended. Open year-round. Within walking distance of Virginia Military Institute, Washington and Lee University, and the George C. Marshall Research Library. Natural Bridge, Blue Ridge Parkway nearby. Golf, hiking, Appalachian Trail, canoeing also available. No pets. Mr. and Mrs. Peter Meredith and Sons, Owners; Don Fredenburg, Innkeeper.

Directions: Take any Lexington exit from I-64 or I-81. Follow signs into Lexington. Check in at office in McCampbell Inn, 11 No. Main St.

THE INN AT GRISTMILL SQUARE
Warm Springs, Virginia

Bruce McWilliams was explaining the workings of the waterwheel at Gristmill Square:

"The waterwheel is known as an 'overshot wheel,'" he said. "It is driven by the weight of the water flowing into the buckets at the top of the wheel. It was manufactured in 1900 by the Fitz Waterwheel Company in Hanover, Pennsylvania, and operates from this little brook. There's been a mill on this site continuously since 1771, although the present mill building was erected in 1900."

Gristmill Square is built around a three-sided square, with a restaurant, a small antique shop, and a countrified store occupying the ground floors. Inn bedrooms are cleverly integrated on the floors above. Most of these are furnished with antiques and old prints, although some are done in a more contemporary style.

There are other bedrooms available in period buildings adjacent to the inn or across the village street from Gristmill Square. Both the Virginian Room and the Miss Jenny Payne Room, two rooms in the Steel House, have four-poster beds and fireplaces.

The Waterwheel Restaurant has been artfully fashioned from the grain mill, which was operated by the waterwheel. The heavenly aroma of the grain, the beige patina of the walls, and the geometric patterns created by the beams and posts make a most unusual setting for a candlelight dinner.

The menu features boneless Monterey mountain trout, barbecued baby spareribs in a special sauce, several veal specialties, and sautéed chicken "Simon Kenton" (named after an early settler), cooked in mushrooms and a tarragon cream sauce.

The McWilliams family has also provided additional amenities for guests who enjoy longer stays. The Bath and Tennis Club has a swimming pool and tennis courts that are playable for most of the year, and there is a sauna in the Steel House. In one of the golfing capitals of the world, the famous Cascades and Lower Cascades golf courses are a short drive away. The Warm Springs Pools are within walking distance.

There is horseback and carriage riding nearby as well as exceptional trout fishing, downhill and cross-country skiing, and some of the most beautiful backroading and hill-walking to be found west of Scotland.

Bath County is located in the west-central portion of Virginia. The 540-square-mile area is within one day's drive of half the population of the northeastern United States. The elevations range from 4,477 above sea level to 1,140 feet where the Cowpasture River flows into Allegheny County. Visitors began coming to the springs of Bath County as early as 1750 and it's been increasing in popularity every year since.

Jack and Janice McWilliams moved to this part of Virginia, becoming the innkeepers of the Inn at Gristmill Square a number of years ago. I am sorry to report to his many friends that Jack passed away in the summer of 1985; however, Bruce McWilliams has joined his mother, Janice, in taking over the innkeeping duties, and the inn continues to be in excellent hands.

THE INN AT GRISTMILL SQUARE, P.O. Box 359, Warm Springs, VA 24484; 703-839-2231. A 14-guestroom unusual restoration with a restaurant and many resort attractions in a small country town in the Allegheny Mtns., 19 mi. no. of Covington. European plan. Restaurant open for dinner daily Tues.—Sun., and Sun. lunch. Lunch served May 1 to Nov. 1, Tues.—Sun. Restaurant closed Mon. Suggest calling for details. Tennis courts, swimming pool, and sauna on grounds. Golf at nearby Cascades or Lower Cascades. Skiing at Snowshoe, West Va., about an hr. away. Skating, riding, hiking, fishing, hunting, antiquing, and backroading nearby. Children welcome. The McWilliams Family, Innkeepers.

Directions: From Staunton, Va. follow Rte. 254 to Buffalo Gap; Rte. 42 to Millboro Spring; Rte. 39 to Warm Springs. From Lexington, take Rte. 39 to Warm Springs. From Roanoke, take Rte. 220 to Warm Springs. From Lewisburg, W. Va., take I-64 to Covington; Rte. 220 north to Warm Springs. From northern W. Va. travel south to Rte. 39 east to Warm Springs. The inn is on Rte. 645. From Rte. 220 going north, turn left on Rte. 645 in Warm Springs. From Rte. 39W turn left on Rte. 692 and left again on Rte. 645 at Warm Springs.

JORDAN HOLLOW FARM INN
Stanley, Virginia

It has been recorded elsewhere in this book that I am not the Roy Rogers or John Wayne of the country inn set (see Rancho de Los Caballeros, Wickenburg, Arizona). However, I can wax poetic in the presence of beautiful horses and I love to visit the horse barns.

That's exactly what I was doing at Jordan Hollow Farm Inn, when Marley Beers joined me for a few moments before she had to exercise some of the horses at this Shenandoah Valley inn, which specializes in horseback riding.

"We are a working horse farm," she told me. "We raise German Holsteiner and thoroughbreds, as well as keeping pleasure horses for our guests. However, it's not necessary to be a horse rider to enjoy yourself here. Many of our guests who have never ridden in their lives and have come for the wonderful Shenandoah Valley mountain experience begin to feel at home with these beautiful animals, and we have persuaded them to try one of our beginners' rides. We never take out more than five or six people at a time and we have both English and Western saddles. There are some very quiet trail horses that are trustworthy for beginners and we have advanced horses for experienced riders.

"In most other places there is a walking trail ride and everyone goes in a long line. You see the scenery but you don't really have too much of an equestrian experience. We do things differently because we want everybody to enjoy as many experiences as possible."

Marley and her Dutch husband, Jetze (pronounced Yet-sah), purchased this former Colonial horse farm several years ago and began creating an inn for the enjoyment of their guests. Jetze speaks several different languages, and both of them have traveled widely and are sophisticated hosts. They met in Africa.

This African influence is mirrored in one of the three dining rooms with decorations from Africa. In many ways, they seemed quite in place with the rest of this wonderful atmosphere that is so removed from the hubbub of the city.

One of the engaging features of the inn is the front porch, where there are two swings and a conversational arrangement of chairs. In fact, conversation seems to happen frequently here. On the night of my most recent visit I sat up rather late with the innkeepers and another couple from Washington. I asked the gentleman what he enjoyed most about being here, and he said, "Just the peace and quiet and opportunity to read, take walks, and enjoy good food and good company."

This convivial atmosphere continues at dinner, when Marley and Jetze dine with their guests, and Rowe Baldwin, "resident grandma," seems to be everywhere at once. Marley describes the food as "country

French" style, with plenty of fresh fruits and vegetables, and homemade breads and desserts. She particularly recommends their roast quail and rib eye steaks.

In regard to the guest room furnishings, *Country Decorating Ideas* saw fit to photograph the interior of one of the bedrooms for a splendid feature in their magazine. The guest rooms are all furnished with comfortable cozy country-inn furniture with different types of beds and other pieces in each room, as well as dried flower arrangements, calico comforters, and wonderful, thick, fluffy towels.

On a guest's birthday, along with a birthday cake, Marley and Jetze have revived the old Virginia custom of buttering that person's nose, thus "helping him to slide through the next year without difficulty." One of the dinner guests received this special attention while I was there and everyone broke into gales of laughter.

JORDAN HOLLOW FARM INN, Rte. 2, Box 375, Stanley, VA 22851; 703-778-2285 or 2209. A 20-guestroom restored Colonial horse farm 6 mi. south of Luray in the northern Shenandoah Valley of Virginia. Open year-round. Breakfast, lunch, and dinner served daily to houseguests. Restaurant open to public Wed. thru Sun. The horse center is on the property with a wide variety of horses and lessons from beginner thru advanced. Scenic trail rides are planned for various levels of skill. Swimming, volleyball, ping-pong, board games, walking, and xc skiing on the premises. Hiking, canoeing, fishing, skiing, golf, tennis, auctions, museums, antiques, crafts shops nearby. Sorry, no pets; boarding kennel nearby. Marley and Jetze Beers, Innkeepers.

Directions: The inn is located 6 mi. south of Luray, Va.; 12 mi. from the Skyline Drive; and 19 mi. from I-81 at New Market. Go south from Luray 6 mi. on Rte. 340; turn left on Rte. 624; left on Rte. 689; and right on Rte. 626.

MEADOW LANE LODGE
Warm Springs, Virginia

I was wandering about in the great barn at Meadow Lane Lodge, located in Bath County, Virginia, a few minutes from the famous Cascades Golf Course in Warm Springs. Here, sheep and goats graze and gambol. Chickens, ducks, guinea fowl, geese, and turkeys inhabit the old horse stalls in the large stable and freely wander in the areas around them. Cats and kittens mingle, as do the farm dogs. No one hurts anyone and there is respect everywhere.

A few moments earlier I had reluctantly gotten up from a wonderful breakfast that featured a special recipe for scrambled eggs blended with some aromatic herbs, prepared by the innkeeper Philip Hirsh. Although Phip, as he is called, is a retired executive, he still takes great pride in occasionally doing the Meadow Lane breakfast.

In the beautiful Allegheny Mountains, Meadow Lane Lodge is an integral part of the Hirsh estate, comprised of 1,600 acres of woods, fields, and streams. In such an atmosphere, tranquility and relaxation are almost guaranteed.

Two suites and three double bedrooms are available in the main house, while Craig's Cottage, named for a Hirsh grandson, will accommodate two to four people. The cottage boasts a big stone fireplace in a lovely high-ceilinged bedroom with a large picture window looking over the meadows and mountains.

Cathy Hirsh took me off in one corner, saying, "Yesterday, Phip and I took a couple of hours off and with two of the dogs went up into the woods to walk around the horse exercise track, which was hewn out of the forest by Phip's father. We saw lady-slippers in bloom and lots of trillium and dwarf iris. Then we drove along the Jackson River to the trout ponds and the spring where the wild azalea and dogwood are flowering, and the watercress is a great patch of vivid green. Our river is one of Virginia's designated scenic rivers and two miles of it flow right through the farm.

"On cool spring and fall mornings and evenings the two fireplaces in the living rooms of the lodge are always in use. I'm sure you noticed that the upstairs rooms has screened-in porches with delightful views and breezes. Later on, our large front porch with its wicker furniture will be a scene for lots of relaxing and chatting with other inn guests."

Additional accommodations are offered in the center of the village of Warm Springs in the Francisco Cottage, which has been restored and furnished in the manner of the log house originally erected on the site, circa 1820. This cottage offers a very pleasantly furnished living room, porch, bedroom, kitchen, and bath, and an impressive view of the hillsides.

Starting in 1986, the Orvis Company of Manchester, Vermont, is going to have a series of seven fly-fishing courses at Meadow Lane Lodge. These are three-day courses, with the first one occurring early in May and the last at the end of October. For full details on what I'm sure is going to be an outstanding opportunity for fly-fishermen, please contact the inn directly.

MEADOW LANE LODGE, Star Route A, Box 110, Warm Springs, VA 24484; 703-839-5959. An 8-guestroom lodge-inn on a portion of a large estate about 10 min. from the center of Warm Springs and near the famous Cascades Golf Course. Guestrooms are in the main house and a cottage on the grounds and also in Francisco Cottage in Warm Springs. A full breakfast is the only meal served. Open Apr. 1 thru Jan. 31. Minimum stay in the lodge is 2 nights; in Francisco Cottage, 3 nights. Dinners are available at nearby restaurants. Tennis court, swimming, horseback riding, and excellent fishing on grounds. Also, miles of hiking and walking trails. Golf, skeet, and trap shooting nearby. Philip and Cathy Hirsh, Innkeepers.

Directions: From Staunton, Va., follow Rte. 254 west to Buffalo Gap; Rte. 42 south to Millboro Spring; Rte. 39 west to Warm Springs. From Lexington, take Rte. 39 west. From Roanoke, take Rte. 220 north to Warm Springs and Rte. 39 west to Meadow Lane Lodge.

PROSPECT HILL
Trevilians, Virginia

"Actually, all of this really started because a log cabin burned down!" Bill Sheehan, the innkeeper of Prospect Hill, and I were strolling around the extensive grounds and talking about the history of this plantation-cum-inn. "The Roger Thompson family owned it in 1732 and converted a barn on the property into their home after their log cabin burned.

"In 1840 a man named William Overton purchased the property and bought up other shares and quarters, and increased it all to 1,576 acres. He enlarged the original house by adding the two wings and the spiral staircase.

"The next chapter is a bit sad because after the War Between the States, the Overtons' son, William, returned to find everything in a completely run-down condition and, of course, the slaves were gone. It took quite an adjustment, so, among other things, they began to 'take in' guests from the city and, in 1880, additional bedrooms were added to the manor house and the slave quarters were enlarged to accommodate guests."

Today, guest rooms are in the main house as well as in three of the outbuildings, including Uncle Guy's House, with rooms both upstairs and down; the Overseer's cottage, with a suite; and the Boys' Cabin. It is to this building that Bill addressed himself more specifically. "The first half is early 18th century, having been built in the early 1730s as a cabin for the boys in Roger Thompson's family. It was later used as a slave cabin and spinner's cottage. As you see," he went on, "it's quite small inside, only twelve feet square. To the original fireplace, log walls, and pine flooring, we have added a new addition to the rear wall and called it '20th-century Californian,' because it has a very modern bath, complete with a whirlpool soaking tub and a deck for morning coffee."

When I mentioned the enticing aromas from the kitchen, Bill said, "There is one seating at eight o'clock, and I ring the bell to summon the guests to the dining room. We serve either a four- or five-course meal, prepared jointly by my wife, Mireille, and me. Mireille is French, and she and I try to visit France every year to pick up new ideas in French cuisine for Prospect Hill."

Because Prospect Hill's reputation as an excellent place to dine is spreading, let me share with you the bill of fare for one night. Among other things there is leek and potato soup, salade vinaigrette garnished with egg, veal sautéed in butter with a mushroom and wine sauce, and fresh asparagus and wild rice. For dessert, as Bill would say, "If you eat all your vegetables you get a strawberry cream tart." Bill is constantly in and out of the kitchen, exchanging *bon mots* with his guests and making certain that everything is exactly right.

Interestingly enough, because Bill and Mireille have traveled so widely in France the cuisine is patterned somewhat after that of the well-known French "Relais et Chateaux de Campagne" family-owned inns offering authentic French dining.

Now and then I receive letters from readers who tell me how much they enjoy Prospect Hill and how it really does preserve some of the best of the Old South, while at the same time taking a realistic look at country inn-goers of today, with such amenities as a bathroom with each bedroom. Some writers say they have a lot of fun trying to find it, and remembering my own very first trip (or even later ones), I agree that finding Prospect Hill is a lot of fun.

PROSPECT HILL, Route 613, Trevilians, VA 23170; 703-967-0844. A 7-guestroom country inn on a historic plantation 15 mi. east of Charlottesville, Va.; 90 mi. southwest of Washington, D.C. Bed and breakfast-in-bed Sun. thru Tues. Modified American plan with full breakfast-in-bed and full dinner Wed. thru Sat. Dinner served Wed. thru Sat. by reservation. Dining room closed Sun., Mon., and Tues. Breakfast always served to houseguests. Accommodations in manor house and restored slave quarters. Swimming pool. Near Monticello, Ashlawn (Pres. Monroe's home), Univ. of Virginia, Castle Hill, and Skyline Drive. Children welcome. No pets. Bill and Mireille Sheehan, Innkeepers.

Directions: From Washington, D.C.: Beltway to I-66 west to Warrenton. Follow Rte. 29 south to Culpeper, then Rte. 15 south thru Orange and Gordonsville to Zion Crossroads. Turn left on Rte. 250 east 1 mi. to Rte. 613. Turn left 3 mi. to inn on left. From Charlottesville or Richmond: take I-64 to Exit 27; Rte. 15 south ½ mi. to Zion Crossroads; turn left on Rte. 250 east 1 mi. to Rte. 613. Turn left 3 mi. to inn on left.

THE RED FOX INN AND TAVERN
Middleburg, Virginia

While I strolled with the chef through the immaculate kitchen at the Red Fox, he proudly announced, "We make all our own ice creams, all our own breads and desserts. We also make all our own sauces and soups, and bone our own meats. We are very adaptable in our cuisine, with some nouveau, some Italian, and some classic French things. We make all our own pasta and our own ravioli, and we use only sweet butter. You won't find preservatives or coloring in any of our food."

There are not many country inns in North America that have remained in the same building for more than 200 years; however, the Red Fox in Middleburg, Virginia, which started as a simple way station when the road to the west was known as "Ashby's Gap Turnpike," has passed the midway point of its third century and is an integral part of American history.

Joseph Chinn was the first proprietor and the inn became known as Chinn's Ordinary. His first cousin was George Washington, who was engaged by Lord Fairfax to survey the area around the tavern, which in turn became known as Chinn's Crossroads.

It's probably true that soldiers from both the American and British lines stopped at this local tavern during the war for American independence. During the War Between the States, Confederate General Jeb Stuart needed lodging for the night and chose the large rooms above the tavern. It was in these rooms that Colonel John Mosby and his Raiders had a celebrated meeting with Stuart, and it was downstairs in the tavern where many of the wounded received care. Among modern-day celebrities who have visited the Red Fox is President John F. Kennedy, who held a rare press conference in the pine-paneled Jeb Stuart Room.

The main entrance leads directly into one of the two low-ceilinged dining rooms where the thirty-inch-thick walls are appropriately decorated with fox-hunting regalia and sporting paintings. There are seven dining rooms in all. Cheery fires are always lit during the chilly months. A secluded terrace at the rear of the inn underneath the trees has an intimate outdoor feeling and is very popular during the clement weather.

Guest rooms in the Red Fox Inn and Tavern are carefully furnished in the 18th-century manner with period antiques and four-postered beds, most with canopies. Some of the rooms have original fireplaces, and all have private baths, direct-dial telephones, and central air conditioning. Fresh flowers, current issues of local country magazines, thick, cotton bathrobes, besides sweets and a *Washington Post* each morning, are some of the extras that make an overnight stay enjoyable.

In keeping with the tradition of naming rooms for famous local personalities, one is called the "Duffy Room" in memory of a colorful fox-hunting and steeplechasing personality, Louis Duffy.

Just a stone's throw from the Red Fox is the Stray Fox Inn, built as a private dwelling long before the Civil War. Guest rooms are carefully furnished with fabrics, furniture, wallcoverings and accessories in the 18th-century style. Stenciled floors and walls, hooked rugs and original wooden mantelpieces preserve the traditional character of the building. The McConnell House, the very latest addition, provides five more guest rooms.

An interesting gallery specializing in 19th-century animal sporting art has been opened in the old stables of the Stray Fox, and various oil paintings and watercolors, oriental rugs, and bronzes of that period are also featured.

THE RED FOX INN AND TAVERN, Middleburg, VA 22117; 703-687-6301. A 25-guestroom historic village inn (16 of the rooms in the Stray Fox) near the Blue Ridge Mountains, approx. 40 mi. from Washington, D.C. European plan. Breakfast, lunch, and dinner served to travelers. Open every day of the year. Near Manassas Battlefield, Oatlands, and Oak Hill (President Monroe's White House), Upperville Horse Show, Foxcroft School, and Nat'l Beagle Trials. Spectator sports such as polo and steeplechasing available nearby. No activities available for small children. Sorry, no pets. The Reuter Family, Innkeepers.

Directions: Leave the Washington D.C. Beltway (495) at Rte. 66 west, to Rte. 50 west. Follow Rte. 50 west for 22 mi. to Middleburg.

SILVER THATCH INN
Charlottesville, Virginia

It was Bill Sheehan, the innkeeper at Prospect Hill in nearby Trevilians, Virginia, who first suggested that I visit the Silver Thatch.

"It is really exceptional," he declared, "and Tim and Shelley Dwight are doing wonderful things at dinner as well."

Phil Hirsch from Meadow Lane Lodge also backed up Bill Sheehan's praise, so when I arrived to meet the Dwights and see the inn I was already prepared for something special. I certainly wasn't disappointed. The inn is a Colonial structure of much charm, dating back to 1780. I learned, with some amusement, that the original construction was per-

formed by Hessian soldiers who were taken prisoner during the battle at Saratoga, New York, and marched south to Charlottesville. The original two-story log cabin section of the building is now called the Hessian Room. Of course, there have been several additions through the years, including a recent one by the Dwights themselves.

The addition of the new guest wing, which is of course being constructed in the same Colonial architectural style, will now bring the total of guest rooms to eight, all with their own private baths and decorated with Colonial antiques and folk art and antique beds and country quilts, dressers, and armoires.

Tim, as maitre d', greets guests, and Shelley enjoys her cooking duties. The three dining rooms are elegantly appointed with white tablecloths, sparkling glassware, and soft candlelight. The menu, featuring Continental cuisine with emphasis on Southern specialties, changes every month. For instance, in October, there was Autumn Chicken, chicken breasts with apple brandy and fresh pears in a light cream sauce; Tangier Island duckling with peaches and cinnamon; redfish Provençal, sautéed with mushrooms, tomatoes, and olives in a white wine sauce;

filet mignon with a bleu cheese demi-glacé sauce; and veal Virginia, veal medallions in a brandied cream sauce with crabmeat and capers.

Tim and Shelley have found that being fifteen minutes from the Blue Ridge Mountains means that spring and fall are particularly busy times.

The nearby attractions are exceptional. The inn is located just eight miles from downtown Charlottesville and minutes away from the University of Virginia, the Skyline Drive, and the Blue Ridge Parkway. Thomas Jefferson's Monticello and James Monroe's Ash Lawn provide an interesting experience, as does a visit to Michie Tavern. The area also has fox hunting and steeplechase events.

Tim tells me that their swimming pool and tennis courts get quite a workout during the summer, while in the winter, after a day skiing or browsing in the many antique shops, everyone's favorite spot is in front of the fireplace in the cozy lounge.

So, with this edition we are happy to welcome the Silver Thatch Inn and we look forward to many happy years of revisits. It is a worthy entry to the already impressive Virginia inns in *Country Inns and Back Roads*.

SILVER THATCH INN, Off Rte. 29 at 3001 Hollymead Rd., Charlottesville, VA 22901; 804-978-4686. An 8-guestroom country inn on the outskirts of Charlottesville, 15 min. from the Blue Ridge Mtns. Lodgings include breakfast served to guests only. Dinner is served Tues. thru Sat. evenings. Open year-round. Closed last 2 wks of June and Christmas. Swimming and tennis on premises. Golf, horseback riding, hiking, skiing, biking, jogging, and wonderful back roads are all available nearby. Convenient to visit Monticello, Ash Lawn, and the University of Virginia. Not readily adaptable to children under 10. Tim and Shelley Dwight, Innkeepers.

Directions: The inn is 2 hrs. south of Washington, just off Va. Rte. 29. Turn east 1 mi. south of the airport road intersection onto Rte. 1520 and proceed ½ mi. to inn.

A number of inns have nearby airports where private airplanes may land. An airplane symbol at the end of the inn directions indicates that there is an airport nearby. Consult inn for further information.

I do not include lodging rates in the descriptions, for the very nature of an inn means that there are lodgings of various sizes, with and without baths, in and out of season, and with plain and fancy decoration. Travelers should call ahead and inquire about the availability and rates of the many different types of rooms.

TRILLIUM HOUSE
Wintergreen, Nellysford, Virginia

First, I'd better explain Wintergreen. This is a ten-thousand-acre residential community-cum-four-season resort on the slopes of the Blue Ridge Mountains, three hours southwest of Washington, D.C., and an hour from Charlottesville. Tucked away in the mountains is an 18-hole golf course, an extensive tennis compound, a sixteen-acre lake, landscaped swimming pools, an equestrian center, and ten ski slopes.

Now, Trillium House. A rambling cedar building with dormers and pitched roofs, this country inn at Wintergreen is named after one of the many species of wildflowers that grow in abundance in these mountains.

Rustic, but quite modern, the Trillium House makes an excellent first impression. After stopping at the gate, Trillium guests receive from the courteous gatekeepers a pass and directions upward through various clusters of condominiums to Trillium, on one of the highest points at Wintergreen. It happens to be directly across the road from the Wintergarden, a brand-new recreation complex with both indoor and outdoor swimming pools, exercise rooms, and a very attractive restaurant looking out on a splendid view of the Blue Ridge Mountains. It is just a short walk to one of the many ski lifts. Strange as it may seem to some northerners, this part of Virginia has first-rate cross-country and downhill skiing.

I stepped through the double entrance doors at ground level into the "great room" with a 22-foot cathedral ceiling and Jefferson sunburst window. A massive chimney with a woodburning stove dominates the room. Across the back of this room and up a short flight of steps stretches a balcony with a most impressive library, and on the other side of the fireplace is a big-screen TV-watching room and gathering place.

Hallways stretch out from both sides of this room, along which are guest rooms and suites, many of them containing heirlooms that Ed and Betty Dinwiddie have brought from their former homes.

The dining-room windows put the guest on almost intimate terms with the 17th fairway and green, and watching the chipmunks and squirrels and birds around the feeders provides entertainment at breakfast.

I would describe Trillium House as being basically informal. It is, after all, an area where one would come to enjoy all of the great outdoors, from walking and hiking to golf, tennis, and swimming. Gentlemen are comfortable with or without jackets at dinner, and Ed and Betty have a way of immediately making everyone feel very much at home.

Speaking of dinner, it is available every night with advance reservations. Talk it over with either Ed or Betty when you make your reservations. Betty says that she cooks the same kind of meals she has cooked for the twenty-five years she has been married, dishes that either family or friends have liked. "I do different things with shrimp and chicken and, of course, roasts. We always have a salad. It's a single entrée meal. I make almost all the desserts—lemon pie and chess pie, and dishes that most of our returning guests enjoy."

If by some chance you are arriving unannounced, it's necessary to have the gatekeeper phone ahead to Trillium House so that you can be introduced.

The Trillium House country inn experience is much greater than I can describe in one edition. The entire area—the beauty of the mountains, the vistas, and the splendid facilities are almost beyond my descriptive powers.

TRILLIUM HOUSE, Wintergreen, P.O. Box 280, Nellysford, VA 22958; 804-325-9126. A 12-guestroom country inn within the resort complex of Wintergreen. Breakfast included in room rate. Dinner served on request. Open year-round. Please call for reservations at times other than the dinner hour. Extensive four-season recreation available, including golf, tennis, swimming (indoor and outdoor pool), and downhill skiing, hiking, bird watching, and horseback riding. Ed and Betty Dinwiddie, Innkeepers.

Directions: From points north and east take the Crozet/Rte. 250 exit from I-64. Go west on Rte. 250 to Rte. 6 and turn left. Follow Rte. 151 south to Rte. 664; turn right on 664 to Wintergreen entrance. Check with inn for directions from other points.

WAYSIDE INN
Middletown, Virginia

Late in the summer of 1985, the Wayside Inn suffered a devastating fire that nearly destroyed the entire building. Complete restoration and repair of the inn was immediately started, and if all goes as planned, the inn will be ready to reopen its doors by the summer of 1986.

The Wayside Inn had begun its life in the Colonial period around 1797. Rescued and carefully restored in the 1960s by Leo Bernstein, a Washington lawyer and banker, the inn was an antique-lover's paradise. Its rooms were packed with a mind-boggling collection of fine period furnishings, paintings, and objets d'art.

I'm happy to say that nearly all of these priceless pieces were saved from the fire, and will continue to grace the rooms of the soon-to-be-restored Wayside Inn.

WAYSIDE INN, Middletown, VA 22645; 703-869-1797. A country inn in the Shenandoah Valley, about 1½ hrs. from Washington, D.C. European plan. Breakfast, lunch, and dinner served Mon. through Sat. Breakfast and dinner served on Sun. Open every day of the year. Professional Equity Theater, Belle Grove, Cedar Creek Battlefield, Blue Ridge Parkway, Crystal Caverns, Hotel Strasburg, Washington's Headquarters, Wayside Antique Warehouse, and Strasburg Antique Emporium nearby. Convenient to Apple Blossom Festival.

Directions: Take Exit 77 from I-81 to Rte. 11. Follow signs to inn.

Favorite Back Roads

Meadow Lane Lodge is located on a back road; one of the country's most beautiful and also one of the most historic. So historic, it has been named by the Virginia legislature as the "Charles Lewis and Andrew Lewis Memorial Highway." Those two gentlemen were two of the more famous colonists and Indian fighters, and were the heroes of the Battle of Point Pleasant in 1774, now known to be the opening battle of the Revolutionary War. Route 39, the official number for this fascinating road, runs from Lexington, Virginia, to the West Virginia line, passing through Goshen Pass, crossing the Cow Pasture and Jackson Rivers, headwater streams of the James River, and traversing the Allegheny Mountains as it winds its way west. The site of Fort Dinwiddie, one of George Washington's chain of forts during the French and Indian War period, is located just off Route 39 (a state historical sign marks the spot) on Meadow Lane property.

Philip and Catherine Hirsh
Meadow Lane Lodge
Warm Springs, Virginia

This eight-mile drive to Lake Moomaw from the inn is one of our very favorites.

Drive west on Route 39 about one mile. Turn left on Route 687. Down this road is the tiny village of Bacova. This entire town was purchased by one man in the 1960s. He restored each home and re-vitalized the town's only industry—a guild that uses a fiberglass and silk-screen process to craft mail boxes, ice buckets, and gift items.

Continue on Route 687 through the town to open meadows ringed by hills and mountains. After one mile, turn right on Route 603. This narrow two-lane gravel road gives instant shade from trees arching and touching overhead. On the left are laurel, maple trees, and boulders. To the right is the beautiful Jackson River. Stop and fish for trout (parts of the river are posted) or find a huge flat rock for a picnic. At the end of this 3½ mile stretch are open picnic areas at the base of Lake Moomaw—a 9-by-2 mile man-made lake headed by Gathright Dam. You can continue down the road along the lake to the visitors' center and the dam and return by way of Covington or return on the same road—just as nice the second time by.

Jack and Janice McWilliams
Gristmill Square
Warm Springs, Virginia

THE COUNTRY INN
Berkeley Springs, West Virginia

In the 1985 edition I noted that the big news at the Country Inn, where I've been visiting Jack and Adele Barker for more than half of the twenty-one years that I've been writing this book, is that the new building would be completed, giving the Country Inn thirty-six additional guest rooms. Each is of generous size with a private bath, Colonial decor, four-poster beds, and double-hung windows. Now let me share with you a portion of a letter from Jack Barker. It tells about the gala opening of "Country Inn West."

"The day started with a tour of the building, which has an old-world feeling very much in harmony with the old inn. Colored balloons marked the way. Girls in old-fashioned dresses were at each level to show off our rooms and to direct traffic. Free gifts included West Virginia apples, sample bottles of our well-known spring water and of course our famous buffet. Display rooms included the handicapped rooms, the Presidential Suite (where we invited President and Mrs. Reagan to spend a weekend at their convenience), the Honeymoon Suite with mannequins dressed as bride and groom, and finally a room in which George Washington was asleep in one of our poster beds with an open copy of *Country Inns and Back Roads* on his chest. I suppose he would read more when he awakened.

"When the guests finished their tour of the new facility they walked to the older building on a newly constructed, covered walkway."

I think perhaps this note adds an extra fillip, providing the reader with an insight into a country inn.

Quite interestingly, the nation's oldest health spa is adjacent to the inn, and among the early patrons was the aforementioned George Washington, along with a great many other notable people connected with the growth of our country. It's possible to enjoy a roman or a turkish bath followed by a relaxing massage, and the cost is surprisingly reasonable.

Jack Barker's interest in paintings and art has manifested itself in an impressive collection of prints and posters, found in all of the guest rooms and hallways of the inn. In fact, one entire living room has been set aside to display these well-chosen works of art for sale to the guests. Jack's taste is obviously eclectic, because he has reproductions of Italian, Flemish, French, and English masters as well as American primitives. In particular, there are excellent and reasonably priced reproductions of turn-of-the-century French theatrical posters.

Reflecting the fare of the countryside, the menu has country ham, smothered chicken, duckling with orange sauce, and homemade hot breads, besides some wonderful specialties.

This section of West Virginia, identified as the Potomac Highlands, offers boating and fishing as well as many, many antique shops and excellent backroading in every season. Guests come in the winter to enjoy the quiet peacefulness of the get-away weekend and now, with the opening of the new section, more and more people will be able to enjoy this truly country-inn hospitality.

THE COUNTRY INN, Berkeley Springs, WV 25411; 304-258-2210. A 72-guestroom resort inn on Rte. 522, 34 mi. from Winchester, Va. and 100 mi. from Washington, D.C., or Baltimore, Md. European plan. Most rooms with private baths. Breakfast, lunch, and dinner served to travelers. Open every day of the year. Berkeley Springs Spa adjoins the inn. Hunting, fishing, hiking, canoeing, antiquing, championship golf nearby. Jack and Adele Barker, Innkeepers; Bill North, General Manager.

Directions: Take I-70 to Hancock, Md. Inn is 6 mi. south on Rte. 522.

I do not include lodging rates in the descriptions, for the very nature of an inn means that there are lodgings of various sizes, with and without baths, in and out of season, and with plain and fancy decoration. Travelers should call ahead and inquire about the availability and rates of the many different types of rooms.

GENERAL LEWIS INN
Lewisburg, West Virginia

I had just returned from a walking tour of Lewisburg with its 19th-century residences and generous sprinkling of historic markers. I paused for just a moment at the bottom of the crescent-shaped drive that leads to the inn to read a marker that said, "Confederate troops under General Henry Heth on May 23, 1862, were repulsed by Colonel George Crook's Brigade."

As I settled into one of the rocking chairs on the long, shaded veranda, Mary Hock Morgan came out and joined me. "Well, what do you think of our little town?" she asked. I readily admitted that, as always, I was still completely captivated by Lewisburg.

"It was established in 1782 and is the third oldest town in the state," she said proudly. "It was named for General Andrew Lewis, who defeated the Indians at the first battle in the American Revolution in 1774.

"The old part of the inn, where the dining room is located, was built in 1798 as a private dwelling. My mother and father purchased the house in 1928 and hired a well-known architect, Walter Martens, who designed the West Virginia Governor's Mansion, to add on the section that embraces the lobby and the matching west wing. Care was taken to capture the feel of the early period, including the use of hand-hewn beams from the slave quarters in the dining room and lobby areas. Work was completed in 1929. It took my parents many years to collect all of these antiques, including the four-poster canopy bed you are going to sleep in tonight."

We were joined by innkeeper Rodney Fisher. "I make it a habit to pour coffee for our guests at breakfast." he declared. "This is a way that I can get to meet all of the guests personally and I'm particularly interested in meeting people traveling with *Country Inns and Back Roads.*"

The General Lewis Inn is like a permanent flashback to old West Virginia. It is furnished almost entirely in antiques. There is a sizable collection of old kitchen utensils, spinning wheels, churns, and other tools used many years ago, as well as an unusual collection of chinaware and old prints. The parlor has a friendly fireplace flanked by some of the many different types of rocking chairs that are scattered throughout the inn. The atmosphere is made even more cozy by the low-beamed ceilings.

The inn is surrounded by broad lawns, and in the rear there are fragrant flower gardens, tall swaying trees, and even a small rock garden.

The menu has many things that I associate with country cooking— pork chops with fried apples, pan-fried chicken, apple butter, country ham, and home-baked rolls and biscuits, to name a few. The entrée selection includes new specialties such as chicken Randolph, Coquille

St. Jacques, and a lean, smoky pork barbecue. The dessert menu, thanks to John's wife, Kim, includes many new mouthwatering items. Kim, not incidentally, won the blue ribbon for her cakes at the last two state fairs.

In fact, John told me their dining room has become so popular with local residents that houseguests have to make reservations to be sure of a table for dinner.

Dusk had fallen while we were talking, and the gaslights that illuminate the tree-lined streets began to dot the late twilight. Our talk turned to some of the famous golf courses here in the Greenbrier area, and we discussed some circle tours of the mountains that would include the fabulous scenery and a generous glimpse of rural West Virginia.

I have a letter from a recent guest who writes, "We returned to the General Lewis for our first anniversary, and our second stay was every bit as romantic and wonderful as the first. . ."

Small wonder that some call it "almost heaven."

GENERAL LEWIS INN, Lewisburg, WV 24901; 304-645-2600. A 30-guestroom (private baths) antique-laden village inn on Rte. 60, 90 mi. from Roanoke, Va. European plan. Breakfast, lunch, and dinner served daily. Dinner reservations necessary. Dining room closed Christmas Day. Famous golf courses nearby. Mary Hock Morgan, Proprietor; Rodney Fisher, Innkeeper.

Directions: Take Lewisburg exit from I-64. Follow Rte. 219 south to first traffic light. Turn left on Rte. 60, two blocks to inn.

RIVERSIDE INN
Pence Springs, West Virginia

I was enjoying a special lunch by reservation on the screened porch of the Riverside Inn, and this was made all the more enjoyable because my luncheon companions were Kelley and Ashby Berkeley, the innkeepers.

Through the open door I could see the low ceilings and rugged, massive fireplace at the far end of the main dining room. The beautiful oak tables were set off by the pewter underplates and pistol-handled knives at each place setting. The walls are made of logs with white plastering in between.

Ashby proudly presented me with the brochure for the inn, with a handsome picture of himself and Kelley serving in the dining room. Kelley is wearing a linsey-woolsey type of gown with a petite white collar and a typical Early American duster cap.

Ashby has a long leather vest over a dashing white shirt with billowy sleeves. His mustache and spade-shaped black beard, I'm sure, adorned the faces of many of the early Jamestown settlers.

It is in this impressive log building that Kelley and Ashby, who grew up in the Greenbrier River Valley, have created an inn with an atmosphere

akin to early 17th-century Jamestown, Virginia. The Riverside Inn has the intimacy of a Colonial roadside tavern where travel-weary guests once refreshed themselves with the tablefare of their hosts.

Today's tablefare features fruit-stuffed duckling for two, Colonial meat pies, mountain rainbow trout, fresh seafood pie in a cheese pastry, baked glazed chicken, lamb chops, and steak—all served with local fresh vegetables. The famous scalded English slaw, a hot cabbage salad with bacon-vinegar dressing, dates to the Jamestown era. The English mulled cider served before each meal is made from fresh cider pressed especially at the nearby Morgan Orchard.

"We're particularly proud of our vegetables," Kelley declared. "Most of these are from local gardens. We have, among other things, orange baked and glazed carrots, bourbon sweet potatoes, braised celery with almonds, green peas with mushrooms, baked apples with cranberry glaze, and stuffed acorn squash."

"We make all our own soups," Ashby said. "I couldn't function without my stockpot. We also do all the breads and pastries. For desserts we have many fresh fruit cobblers, steamed raisin bread pudding in rum raisin sauce, plum pudding, baked egg custard in walnut sauce, and rum and eggnog pies during the holidays.

"We just received word that Riverside has again been chosen as one of the 'top ten' dining establishments in West Virginia. This selection is made by the food critic at the *Charleston Gazette* and is the most sought-after designation by restaurants in this state."

Ashby explained that at the moment there are only token lodgings available and these are always booked in advance. "However, on your next visit we may have a sensational surprise for you and I'll give you a hint—it has to do with our lodging facilities."

That afternoon, as I was returning to Lewisburg, Kelley and Ashby walked out to the car with me. "On a day like this it is easy to see why West Virginia has been named 'Little Switzerland,'" said Kelley. "It is also easy to see why Ashby and I remain here. Maybe it's a little off the beaten track; however, I've yet to talk to anyone who has not said it was worth it and who does not intend to return—sometime!"

RIVERSIDE INN, Rte. 3 Pence Springs, WV 24962; 304-445-7469. A country restaurant on the Greenbrier River on Rte. 3 in the beautiful West Va. mountains, between Hinton and Alderson; 12 mi. from Lake Bluestone. Limited lodgings. Dinner served 5 to 9 p.m. Mon. thru Sat. from May 31 to Labor Day; open Wed. thru Sat., April 15 to May 31 and Labor Day to Oct. 31; open Fri. and Sat., Nov., Dec. Closed Christmas and Jan. to April 15. Lunch served by special reservation only. Skiing, boating, hiking, swimming, spelunking, white water canoeing nearby. O. Ashby and Kelley Berkley, Innkeepers.

Directions: From the east, take Alta exit off I-64, follow Rte. 12S to Alderson then Rte. 3W, 8 mi. to Pence Springs. From the west, from W. Va. Tpke. follow Rte. 3 from Beckley through Hinton to Pence Springs. The inn is located in Pence Springs on Rte. 3 between Hinton and Alderson.

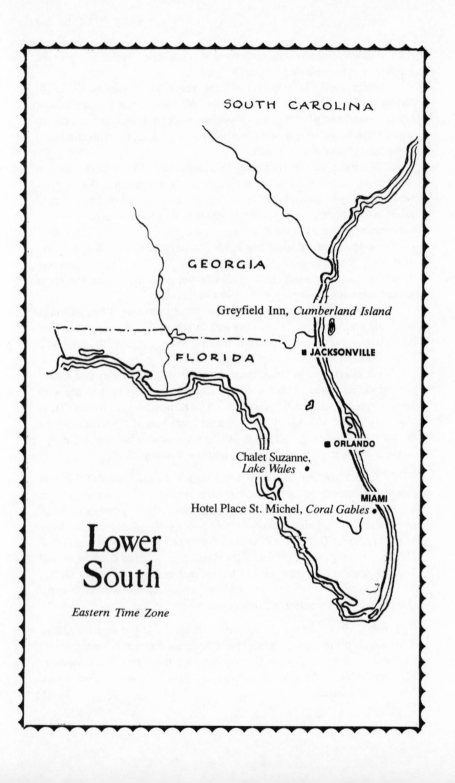

SOUTH CAROLINA

GEORGIA

Greyfield Inn, *Cumberland Island*

FLORIDA

■ **JACKSONVILLE**

■ **ORLANDO**

Chalet Suzanne,
Lake Wales •

MIAMI
Hotel Place St. Michel, *Coral Gables* •

Lower
South

Eastern Time Zone

CUMBERLAND ISLAND

Cumberland Island is the southernmost and largest of a chain of barrier islands that starts at Cape Hatteras and extends to the Florida-Georgia border. It is eighteen miles long and three miles wide at its widest point. There are 26 varieties of wild animals and 323 species of birds identified. The island has one road, Grand Avenue, a dirt and shell affair, which traverses the length of the island through the live oak.

In recent years the National Park Service acquired a great portion of the island and has taken the necessary action to forever maintain it as a nature preserve.

Marshland fringes much of Cumberland's shores protecting them from the current and the tide. Its principal inhabitants are the ubiquitous fiddler crabs and long-legged wading birds. The live oak avenues create an atmosphere akin to a cathedral.

The eighteen-mile beach is the most striking feature of the island and one can walk for hours in delicious solitude except for the sanderlings that scurry out of the clutching fingers of the waves, and the pelicans skimming the water. Shells abound and it's impossible to come back empty-handed.

The dunes, which are carefully protected, provide still another intriguing atmosphere. At the edge of the forest there is a group of lakes, which have their own particular wildlife. Egrets and herons fish these waters as well as ducks who stop off as they travel north and south.

Besides the wildlife there is a rich history of the island that covers pre-Columbian times as well as occupation by the Spaniards, the British, and later on some enterprising men from the new American republic. In the early 1800s there were a few plantations on the island, but after the War Between the States the island was dominated by the presence of the Carnegie family who raised an impressive mansion of brick and stone at Dungeness with formal gardens, swimming pool and stables. Unfortunately, it burned in 1959.

GREYFIELD INN
Cumberland Island, Georgia

This is the story of Grandma Ferguson, who was once married to Thomas Carnegie (brother of Andrew), and the Ferguson family—including her great-grandsons, Andy and Mitty—and of the flora and fauna of one of the last remaining impressive nature preserves on the East Coast. It is only a part of the story of Greyfield Inn, located on Cumberland Island, off the southern coast of Georgia.

I paid my first visit to this gorgeous, haunting part of the world in 1975. I had the pleasure then of spending part of a day with Lucy Ferguson, known to everyone as "Grandma." It was Grandma who first introduced me to Cumberland Island, with its seventeen-mile stretch of beach, fascinating dunes, and secret ponds. She also showed me the ruins of Dungeness, built by her great-grandparents, which unfortunately burned in 1959.

Once again, as on my first visit, I was on the ferry boat, *R.W. Ferguson,* and Captain Mitty Ferguson was updating me on Greyfield Inn. We left Fernandina Beach at 3:00 p.m. and were making the hour-and-a-quarter run up the passage between the island and mainland to the Greyfield dock.

"Of course, everything is much the same as it was when you were here the first time," he said, keeping a guiding hand on the wheel. "The Fergusons, including Grandmother, are still very much in the picture, so that we are a family team dividing the chores. We also have some excellent staff, which makes everything much more of a pleasure."

By this time the ferry was within sight of the Greyfield dock, and I could see once again the gleaming, three-story mansion through the mysterious grove of live oaks. Andy waved to us, and soon, with the other guests, I was bundled into the jeep and driven to the impressive front entrance of the inn with its majestic steps and broad veranda. As soon as I stepped inside, it all returned to me: the paintings, the oriental rugs, the mahogany furniture, the silver on the sideboard, the great fireplaces, and the great collection of books. Andy showed me to my corner room and then joined me in front of the fire for a cup of late afternoon tea as we renewed our acquaintance.

I joined the other guests at dinner in the candlelit dining room and the conversation dealt with the wonders of the unspoiled beach, where the magnificent loggerhead sea turtles lay their eggs, and where guests sometimes can see the young hatching. The shore birds and the marine life are there, as are deer, wild horses, wild turkeys, and the dense live oak forest.

The newest acquisition is a gazebo that stands in the meadow between the primary and secondary dunes—a great spot in which to get out of the sun at midday, to watch the sun rise and set, or just to lie about reading and watching the shore birds.

There were several guests who had been at Greyfield for many days who were saying, "It takes a day just to find out what is here, and at least two days more to explore it."

Several of the guests had seen a recent issue of *Audubon Magazine* with the article by John Mitchell on Cumberland Island and Greyfield Inn.

It was wonderful to be back at Greyfield once again.

Do not plan on visiting the Greyfield Inn if you have only one night, and be certain to check with the inn about the ferry schedules. Incidentally, the 1735 House in Fernandina Beach is an excellent overnight stop before taking the afternoon boat to the island. The Greyfield Inn is the only public overnight accommodation on Cumberland Island.

GREYFIELD INN, Cumberland Island, GA (mailing address: Fernandina Beach, FL 32034); 904-261-6408. An 8-guestroom mansion on an island off the coast of southern Georgia. Accessible from Fernandina Beach, Fla., or on a Natl. Park Service ferry from St. Mary's, Ga. Check with inn on ferry times. Rates include full breakfast and dinner, as well as either box lunch or informal noon meal. Open every day in the year by reservation only. Beachcombing, swimming, fishing, clam digging, photography, birdwatching, bicycles, walking and driving tours, natural history tour. No pets. The Ferguson Family, Innkeepers.

Directions: The R. W. Ferguson *leaves from the public dock at Fernandina Beach, Fla., at either 3 or 5 p.m., depending upon the day of the week (check with inn). Also check with inn on National Park Service ferry schedule from St. Mary's, Ga. Autos are left on the mainland. Island also accessible by small plane or helicopter.*

CHALET SUZANNE
Lake Wales, Florida

After my first visit to Chalet Suzanne a number of years ago, I wondered if it really did happen or was it like the musical *Brigadoon*, in which the fictional Scottish village returns for one day every 100 years. This is a reaction I frequently get from guests who visit this unusual country inn in central Florida. Sometimes they can hardly believe it.

However, there is no doubt that Chalet Suzanne is a real place. The bridges, steeples, cupolas, minarets, peaked roofs, flat roofs, castle towers, domes, treasures, antiques, and pagodas are all there. It's a world of pastels in Bavarian, Swiss, Oriental, French, English, Turkish,

Chinese, and every other style you can think of, and the nice part of it is that the guest rooms are all comfortably furnished in this wonderful Arabian Nights atmosphere.

It was all started in the early 1930s by Bertha Hinshaw, and now her son, Carl, and his wife, Vita, are continuing with their own touches—the newest of which are pedal boats and canoes on the dreamy lake, seen from many of the windows of the dining room.

To the people who live in Florida, Chalet Suzanne is best known for its exceptional food. In fact, it was recently awarded the "Golden Spoon" for the seventeenth consecutive year of being listed among the top twelve restaurants in Florida. *Mobil Guide* has given it four stars and it has the *Travel-Holiday Magazine* award for fine dining.

Dinner is served in the wonderful around-the-world ambience of the dining room, with Persian tile tables, Venetian glass lamps, clocks, statuary, stained glass windows, an old piano, and an eclectic collection of goblets and stemware—no two tables are set alike. By the way, there is a very intriguing little table for two set in the front window, which is reserved for honeymooners, if possible.

Most of the guests visiting Chalet Suzanne for the first time order the well-known chicken Suzanne, beautifully browned and glazed. It is prepared by Carl, who, in addition to being the "chief pilot" of the airfield (oh, I forgot to mention the airfield), is also the "principal stirrer" in the soup factory, and in addition to everything else is the chef at the inn.

Dinner also can include the original baked grapefruit centered with a sautéed chicken liver, the famed Chalet Suzanne romaine soup, hearts of artichoke salad, petite peas in cream and butter, a grilled tomato slice, deliciously hot homemade rolls, a mint ice, and tiny crêpes Suzanne.

The remark "It's almost like a Disney movie" is frequently heard at Chalet Suzanne, and I guess it's more than a coincidence that Disney World and many other famous attractions, including the beautiful Cypress Gardens waterskiing shows, are just a short distance away.

Oh yes, there is a 2,450-foot airstrip at Chalet Suzanne and it comes out of Carl Hinshaw's lifelong love of flying. The flying tradition continues because Carl and Tina's son, Eric, is also a pilot. Some of the best news of all is that Eric's wife, Denise, presented the Hinshaw family with their first and only grandson, Marcus.

CHALET SUZANNE, P.O. Drawer AC, Lake Wales, FL 33859; 813-676-6011. A 30-guestroom phantasmagoric country inn and gourmet restaurant, 4 mi. north of Lake Wales, between Cypress Gardens and the Bok Singing Tower near Disney World. European plan. Dining room open from 8 a.m. to 9:30 p.m. Closed Mon. from June to Nov. Pool on grounds. Golf, tennis nearby. Lots of opportunity for good jogging. Not inexpensive. The Hinshaw Family, Innkeepers.

Directions: From Interstate 4 turn south on U.S. 27 toward Lake Wales. From Sunshine State Pkwy., exit at Yeehaw Junction and head west on Rte. 60 to U.S. 27 (60 mi.). Proceed north on U.S. 27 at Lake Wales. Inn is 4 mi. north of Lake Wales on 17A. ◢

I do not include lodging rates in the descriptions, for the very nature of an inn means that there are lodgings of various sizes, with and without baths, in and out of season, and with plain and fancy decoration. Travelers should call ahead and inquire about the availability and rates of the many different types of rooms.

HOTEL PLACE ST. MICHEL
Coral Gables, Florida

As soon as I walked through the canopied entrance between the potted trees and into the long, narrow lobby of the Hotel Place St. Michel I felt that I had been there before.

Its very stylish three-story facade, with many vines and awnings, is as European as one could possibly imagine, maybe even more Parisian than Paris itself.

As I continued strolling through the hotel, seeing the gleaming hand-tiled floors, soaring arches, and vaulted ceilings, I thought here was a place that should have an "in-house" poet or at least an artist-in-residence. This gave me a clue to my sense of *déjà vu*; and I leafed through the pages of *Country Inns and Back Roads, Continental Europe* to find the Hotel de France in Luxeuil-les-Bains, France. The Hotel Place St. Michel, like its French counterpart, has all the elements of a stage setting.

The original inspiration for this Coral Gables hostelry was the Art Deco world of Paris in the 1920s. Fortunately, Stuart Bornstein and Alan Potamkin, the present owners, decided to return it to its former style and elegance, and this small hotel has undergone a refurbishing that does it proud.

The concierge's desk is on the lobby level, where there is a parquet floor and a European brass and glass chandelier. The adjoining Charcuterie St. Michel offers take-out cuisine, and there is a florist shop and a hair-styling salon.

The Restaurant St. Michel, off the lobby, has banks of greenery, Art Nouveau lighting fixtures, and framed prints reflecting an old-world elegance and a discerning attention to detail.

My notes about some of the bedrooms include Number 302, which has parquet floors, built-in bookcases, and two double beds with very handsomely carved headboards. The decorations are a combination of Art Nouveau and Art Deco with some sensible contemporary furniture. This particular room had dried flowers and some attractive stenciling on the walls. Guests' shoes left outside the door at night are polished and returned early the next morning, along with a morning newspaper. The air conditioning in the guest rooms is supplemented by overhead fans— very Paris!

A continental breakfast of freshly baked croissants with an assortment of marmalades and jams, fruit juice, and hot coffee is included in the room rate, and may be taken in the guest room, if preferred.

The dinner menu includes such intriguing main dishes as breast of chicken sautéed with wild mushrooms, several scrumptious crêpes, as well as filet mignon served in a green mustard sauce. The dessert tray had

a Charlotte Russe, a chocolate mocha torte, and many kinds of little cookies, cakes, and fruits. It was simply terrific.

Luncheon is served with a selection of crêpes, quiches, omelets, salads, and patés.

At one end of the dining room is a white baby grand piano, which at the time of my visit was adorned with a stylish table-sized Christmas tree. There is also a group of framed posters from various French and American art galleries.

Stuart Bornstein pointed out that a strict building and zoning code has kept Coral Gables, an integral part of Miami, visually attractive and appealing. White-pillared plantation-type homes on broad green lawns, Spanish haciendas with barrel tiled roofs, and large coral rock homes dominate the architectural scene. Residential streets are shaded by decades-old gigantic oak and banyan trees.

HOTEL PLACE ST. MICHEL, 162 Alcazar, Coral Gables, FL 33134; 305-444-1666. A 30-guestroom charming, restored, 1926 European-style hotel in the heart of Coral Gables, 7 min. from Miami Int. Airport and 10 min. from downtown Miami. All rooms with private baths and air conditioning. Open year-round. Continental breakfast included in room tariff. Dining room open daily for breakfast, luncheon, and dinner. Sunday brunch. Within 3 blocks of shopping mecca of Miracle Mile, and easy walking distance to theaters, galleries, and boutiques. Children welcome. No pets. Stuart Bornstein and Alan Potamkin, Owners.

Directions: Follow I-95 south into U.S. 1 (Dixie Hwy.). Continue south to Ponce de Leon Blvd. Turn right onto Ponce, continuing to 2135 Ponce. Turn right onto Alcazar.

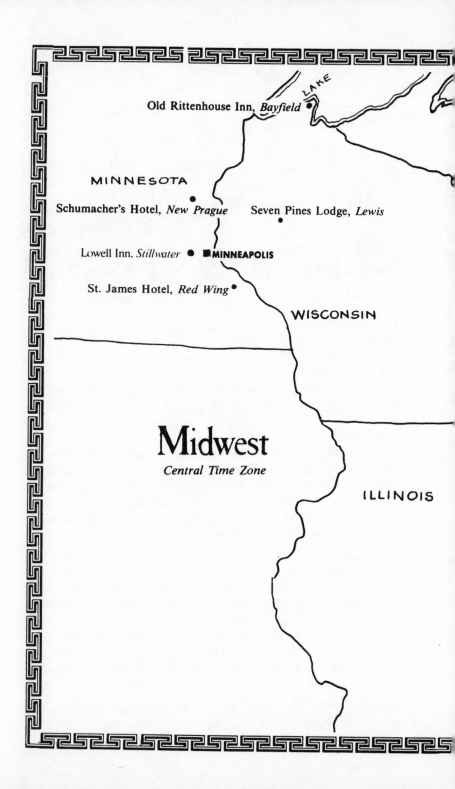

Old Rittenhouse Inn, *Bayfield*

LAKE

MINNESOTA

Schumacher's Hotel, *New Prague*

Seven Pines Lodge, *Lewis*

Lowell Inn, *Stillwater* ■MINNEAPOLIS

WISCONSIN

St. James Hotel, *Red Wing*

Midwest
Central Time Zone

ILLINOIS

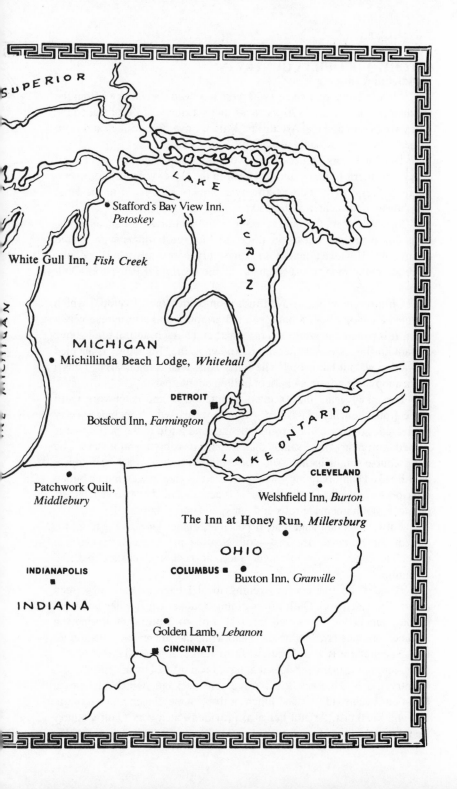

SUPERIOR

LAKE HURON

Stafford's Bay View Inn, *Petoskey*

White Gull Inn, *Fish Creek*

THE MICHIGAN

MICHIGAN

Michillinda Beach Lodge, *Whitehall*

DETROIT

Botsford Inn, *Farmington*

LAKE ONTARIO

CLEVELAND

Patchwork Quilt, *Middlebury*

Welshfield Inn, *Burton*

The Inn at Honey Run, *Millersburg*

OHIO

INDIANAPOLIS

COLUMBUS

Buxton Inn, *Granville*

INDIANA

Golden Lamb, *Lebanon*

CINCINNATI

PATCHWORK QUILT COUNTRY INN
Middlebury, Indiana

Almost every year since 1970 there has been special news from the Patchwork Quilt. I say 1970, because that was the year I first visited the Patchwork Quilt and met Arletta and Milton Lovejoy and Treva and Herb Swarm. First, a word of explanation:

The Patchwork Quilt is a real working farm in the rich agricultural area of northern Indiana, and has been in the Lovejoy family for over a hundred years. Five-course farm-style dinners are served in the large farmhouse in the center of the 260 acres.

In recent years the inn has offered bed-and-breakfast accommodations for overnight guests in three double guest rooms with shared bathrooms. However, thanks to some very cooperative local people, there are many more guest rooms available nearby for Patchwork Quilt guests.

On a recent visit, I stayed in a room called the "Treetop," which features a canopy bed, a hand-painted armoire, and a turquoise velvet chair. It is paneled in white and turquoise and has a beautiful print above a Franklin fireplace. Another room, known as the "Meadow," is paneled in wattled walnut hardwood. The Early American cannonball bed has a minicanopy made from an apricot quilted counterpane.

For many years the excellent reputation of the Patchwork Quilt came from the truly munificent evening meals, which include a zesty homemade soup or chilled fruit appetizer and a trip to the buffet that is loaded with many more salads than I could possibly mention here. The main course might include such offerings as herbed roast beef, open-hearth baked ham, burgundy steak, or Arletta's great prizewinning buttermilk-pecan chicken. The main course is accompanied by two vegetables, potatoes, hot homemade rolls and jams, and coffee or tea.

I always recommend that, if possible, dinner guests save room for one of the fantastic desserts—coffee-toffee pie, three-layer German chocolate cake, lemon meringue pie, old-fashioned custard pie...ad infinitum.

Besides the five-course evening meal I have partially described above, the Patchwork Quilt offers dining options. On Tuesday and Wednesday, luncheons are served from 11 a.m. to 2 p.m. and during the summer on Tuesday, Wednesday, and Thursday there are light dinner menus, called Early Bird Specials, from 4:30 p.m. to 6:00 p.m.

Among the many services that have been offered by this farmhouse-country inn is the Back Road Adventure package, which includes a five-hour back road tour and lunch, a five-course dinner, and overnight bed-and-breakfast. Arletta has also provided Patchwork Quilt Country Retreats at various times during the year. These are midweek, three-day

tours of the Amish community—meeting the Amish people, visiting in their homes and shops, and also enjoying dinners at the Patchwork Quilt.

Over the years the Patchwork Quilt has received much recognition in national magazines. Articles and stories have appeared in many different media. I guess the first real recognition came just about the time of my very first visit, when Arletta's famous pecan chicken recipe (still on the menu) won a national award.

I realize that I've been visiting the Patchwork Quilt Country Inn in Middlebury, Indiana, for almost three-quarters of the total of twenty-one years that there has been a *Country Inns and Back Roads.*

PATCHWORK QUILT COUNTRY INN, 11748 C.R. 2, Middlebury, IN 46540; 219-825-2417. A working farm restaurant and bed-and-breakfast inn about 20 mi. east of Elkhart. Dinner served by reservation only. Lodging rooms available only on Tues., Wed., Thurs., and Fri. evenings. Rates include continental breakfast. Closed Sun., Mon., Thanksgiving, Christmas, and New Year's. Thresher's Lunch served Tues., Wed., and Thurs. 11 a.m. to 2 p.m. during June, July, and Aug. No credit cards. Arletta Lovejoy, Innkeeper.

Directions: From east or west, exit Indiana Toll Rd. at Middlebury (Exit 107) and go north ¼ mi. to Country Rd. 2 and proceed west 1 mi. to inn. From Middlebury, follow Indiana Rte. 13 for 8 mi. north to Country Rd. 2 and west 1 mi.

BOTSFORD INN
Farmington Hills, Michigan

"We're celebrating 150 years of history and hospitality—1986 is going to be a great year at the Botsford Inn!" innkeeper John Anhut exclaimed. John, whom I first met back in the late 1960s, and I were having a very pleasant lunch at the inn while he told me of the many plans for the celebration.

With the assistance of many local people, John has been preparing a year of gala events to celebrate the construction in 1836 of the oldest operating inn in the state.

The inn was originally a stagecoach stop in Clarenceville on the Grand River Plank Road, which followed the Indian Trail to Lake Michigan, and it became a popular meeting place for drovers, farmers, and travelers to and from Detroit.

Henry Ford met his wife, Clara, here, and as a romantic gesture, bought the inn and kept it in operation until after Clara's death in 1951, when he sold it to the Anhut family. Many of the Fords' antiques and treasures are still here—a beautiful little inlaid spinet, a handsome horsehair sofa, music boxes, a Simon Willard clock, an exquisitely inlaid mahogany table, and an attractive late-19th-century oil painting of the Botsford Inn, showing people in the costume of the day.

John tells me a new book about the Botsford Inn, entitled *More Than a Tavern—150 Years of the Botsford Inn*, researched and written by local historian, Jean Fox, was published in January.

The guest rooms in the old, original section have been refurbished, and such considerate amenities as TV sets inside the armoires are worthy of note. I've always been impressed by the dining room, and how the combination of low ceilings and wall decorations, plus the big window with a view of the courtyard, creates a very warm and cozy feeling.

The menu has always featured American dishes, and one of my favorites is sliced steak salad—very thin slices of lightly sautéed beef on a big mound of lettuce, topped off with Parmesan cheese. It makes a wonderful luncheon dish.

But I'm straying from the big news for 1986—the sesquicentennial anniversary festivities, which will be celebrated throughout the entire year! The raising of an 1836 American flag, complete with a full color guard, the American Legion, a community band, and local officials, heralded the beginning of the celebration in January. Among the many festivities still to be held will be a gala costume ball in May; performances by eighty Sweet Adelines regional winners in June; a "First Ladies Historical Pageant"—an evening of music and drama—in September, and many other interesting and exciting events.

John's son, Jim, who is carrying on the Anhut innkeeping tradition, joined us at the table. He, too, was full of news about the year-long celebration. "I hope you'll be here for Founders' Day on July 19," he exclaimed. "There'll be a parade of Model T's, an ice cream social, a barbershop quartet, banjo music, and other fun events all day long!"

Meanwhile, the dessert menu was passed around, and although there were several homemade dishes, including cherry pie, strawberry shortcake, and cheesecake, as usual, I chose the Botsford homemade deep-dish apple pie.

The Botsford tradition of hospitality, begun during the Indian Trail days, is continuing now with the Anhut family. In 1836, it was a day's journey from the banks of the river, where Detroit was a burgeoning city;

today, it is just a short drive from the hustle and bustle of the Motor City. Worthwhile reminders of the past have been preserved and, best of all, the spirit of country innkeeping and community service is very much alive.

BOTSFORD INN, 28000 Grand River Ave., Farmington Hills, MI 40824; 313-474-4800. A 62-guestroom village inn on the city line of Detroit. European plan. Dinner served daily except Monday. Breakfast and lunch Tues. thru Sat. Sun. brunch. Closed Christmas and New Year's Day. Tennis on grounds. Greenfield Village, skiing, and state parks nearby. John Anhut, Innkeeper.

Directions: Located in Farmington Hills on I-96, easily accessible from major highways in Michigan.

MICHILLINDA BEACH LODGE
Whitehall, Michigan

Every evening between 9:30 and 10:00, as if drawn by some interesting and magical magnet, the guests at Michillinda gather in the main living room to enjoy coffee or hot chocolate or lemonade and cookies.

On this particular evening there were several little groups of people, some playing cards, some mapping their activities for the next day, and others just visiting. One such group included a Japanese couple, who were at Michillinda for the first time, and in fact spending their first vacation in the United States. Innkeeper Don Eilers commented on this to me. "Yes, we have people from many foreign countries who find their way to the shores of Lake Michigan and our little lodge."

The scope of a Michillinda vacation with all of the recreational activities, both on the grounds and in the nearby town and countryside, is succinctly woven together in a very colorful brochure where the

photographs show happy, sun-tanned holiday-seekers of all ages sitting in the sun overlooking the lake, walking through the unusually expansive flower gardens, playing tennis, swimming in the pool, playing miniature golf or tetherball, riding the tandem bicycle among the chalets at lakeside, or relaxing in the pine-paneled library and living room. I have seven pages of typewritten notes about my visit.

Don and Sue are ideal people to be involved in a family-oriented resort-inn. They are young and enthusiastic and have growing children of their own. As Don says, "Basically we don't run organized activities, we have all of the recreation any young person could enjoy, and yet we don't have a social director encouraging guests to 'sign-up' for this or that, and putting them into a series of time slots. We have enough grounds here and enough indoor recreation at the Surfside building so that kids can have their own fun and their parents don't have to worry about them."

Sue joined in, "I think we've always had an ideal mix of senior citizens and young children. Many of the older people don't see children as much anymore and they become 'vacation grandparents.'"

Accommodations are in lakeview bedrooms with resort-furniture in both the main house and a series of small cottages and chalets on the grounds.

"One of the most essential things in running a summer resort is to have a staff that can identify with all types of guests. I think we have always been fortunate in having an excellent staff. We put their photographs on the bulletin board so our guests can identify them, and a great many of them help to make our guests' stays most enjoyable."

"With all of this outdoor activity, we serve three full meals a day," said Don, as we walked through the dining room and the kitchen. "We have a choice of three entrées every night and always have an eye towards what kids would like to eat, because kids are part of what this whole place is about."

I did something that I'm sure almost every Michillinda guest does just before departing: I walked out to the edge of the grassy bluff overlooking the beach and took one last look at the blue waters and indefinable horizon of Lake Michigan. I was caught up by the sound of the wind and waves and the warmth of the sunshine. I felt the tug of a small hand at my trousers, and there beside me was a little boy who asked me if I could help him tie his shoes.

MICHILLINDA BEACH LODGE, 5207 Scenic Dr., Box C, Whitehall, MI 49461; 616-893-1895. A 51-guestroom American plan resort-inn 15 mi. north of Muskegon. Located on the shore of Lake Michigan. Blue Lake Fine Arts Camp nearby. Open June 21 to Sept. 13. Lodging only after Sept. 2. Tennis, swimming, mini-golf, shuffleboard on grounds; 6 golf courses, charter fishing nearby. No pets. No credit cards; personal checks accepted. Don and Sue Eilers, Innkeepers.

Directions: Follow U.S. 31 north from Muskegon, exit at White Lake Dr., drive west to South Shore Dr. (4 mi.), left (5 mi.) on South Shore Dr. Follow signs to Scenic Dr., turn left (1 mi.) to lodge.

STAFFORD'S BAY VIEW INN
Petoskey, Michigan

Stafford's, on the edge of the Bay View section of Petoskey, is a summer resort community that grew up around a program of music, drama, art, and religious lectures and services. The community began in the late 1800s when people rode on the Grand Rapids/Indiana railroad or on lake steamers to reach this part of Michigan. The early residents built Victorian homes that are scattered throughout Bay View today.

With that as a background, let me share a letter that will put us all into the picture as far as 1986 is concerned. It is from Janice Smith.

"Dear Norman: It's here! The start of something big, bigger, biggest! The summer of 1986—the beginning of the Bay View Inn's 100th anniversary, and our twenty-fifth wedding anniversary. These two facts, noteworthy in themselves, will be the focal point for a celebration for the entire year.

"Since Duff and I met here (you well remember that story, Norm), we always include the inn in any of our anniversary celebrations. For our twentieth, we completely restored the cottage-Victorian decor of the

lobby and dining rooms. And for our twenty-fifth, we are continuing this restoration project on the third floor, starting with the front tower section. In fact, an elevator shaft has already been started and will be completed in time. Not only will our third-floor guests have a magnificent view of Little Traverse Bay, they will also get to ride up to it in our new elevator. The guest rooms in this restoration will be a little larger than the others and will include a parlor as well as a comfortable sleeping area.

"We will begin this year's festivities the third weekend of June with our twenty-fifth wedding anniversary party. (And Norm, you are expected, so mark your calendar now.) This same weekend is the Historical Festival time in our area, an activity used to promote the start of the summer resort season. The inn is involved in two special events: the 'Taste of the North,' a waterfront tent filled with restaurants serving 'tastes' of their special dishes, and the World's Longest Tug of War between our staff and the staff at the Harbor Inn. The tug is across the bay! A three-mile-long rope that floats is stretched across the bay between the two inns. Both teams pull like the 'dickens' for fifteen minutes, and the team that pulls the most rope out of the water wins.

"Our anniversary party will be the first event to mark the year-long celebration of the inn's centennial year. We are planning all kinds of special historical activities and menus to commemorate it.

"Constant hard work and dedication to people, to service, and to quality have been our watchwords. The inn is no longer a 'quaint, homespun, charming' hotel. We have become a first-class, sophisticated delight—a pleasure to own and to share with the discriminating guest. That nice young couple who took over this business in 1961 has matured and so has their business."

Do I really have to tell any reader where I will be during the third weekend of June in 1986?

STAFFORD'S BAY VIEW INN, Box 3, Petoskey, MI 49770; 616-347-2771. A 23-guestroom resort-inn on Little Traverse Bay in the Bay View section of Petoskey. Bed-and-breakfast plan includes full breakfast. Breakfast, lunch, and dinner served daily to travelers. Open daily May 18 to Nov. 1; Thanksgiving weekend; Christmas week, and long weekends during the winter sports season. Lake swimming and xc skiing on grounds. Historical Festival events, 3rd weekend in June. Bay View cultural programs in July and Aug. Golfing, boating, tennis, fishing, hiking, alpine ski trails, scenic and historic drives and excellent shopping nearby. Stafford and Janice Smith; Judy Honor, Innkeepers.

Directions: From Detroit take Gaylord Exit from I-75 and follow Michigan Rte. 32 to Rte. 131, north to Petoskey. From Chicago, use Rte. 131, north to Petoskey.

LOWELL INN
Stillwater, Minnesota

This time I approached Stillwater from the north, following the course of the St. Croix River on Route 95. I began to understand why Art Palmer of the Lowell Inn was so enthusiastic about this part of the world. The rolling countryside, with its frequent glimpses of the river and the gentle touch of spring in the air, indeed creates a warm feeling for the generous gifts of middle America.

Just outside of Stillwater, the road drops down alongside the river, where there were dozens of watercraft, some of them already in use on the river here in late April.

Now the town of Stillwater came into view, dominated by a tall church spire, and a sign announced that this was indeed the birthplace of Minnesota in 1843. I passed the Washington County Historical Museum, and one block from the main street was the familiar building of the Lowell Inn with its Mount Vernon columns.

I stepped inside the reception area where all was quite serene. The grandfather clock told me that it was ten after one, and in the spacious George Washington Room on the right there were many people still enjoying lunch.

The lobby was bright and cheerful, with an oil painting of innkeeper Art Palmer's father over the mantel and a full-length painting of his beautiful mother on another wall. The Palmers have always been innovators—it runs in the family. It all started when Art's mother and father, who spent a great deal of their youth and young adulthood in show business, met here in Stillwater and were married. The opportunity arose to manage the inn, and so they stayed on and eventually became the owners in 1945. There's no doubt that the inn is a family enterprise, because there are several pictures of the Palmer family at various celebrations, including many weddings. There's a succession of growing children in a growing family.

The Palmer tradition of innovation is reflected in some of the unusual guest rooms at the Lowell Inn, some of which have circular bathtubs for two (if need be), a shower, and a jacuzzi. Each of the rooms is a true model of elegance. One has a circular glass standing shower and a washbowl of pink and white marble with very fancy fixtures. The bed with its decorator sheets and pillowcases looks almost too good to sit on. Each of the bedrooms has a small china cat carefully placed on each bed. "This is one of the most frequently mentioned of our ideas," smiled Arthur.

Barbara Cook, a very nice lady, came up and introduced herself to me. Barbara was here when Arthur's mother, Nelle, was here, and I was hungry for information about this very unusual woman. "Was she in evidence, was she here among the guests?" I asked. "Did she move among the tables and talk to people in the lobby?"

"Oh, yes. She always sat right in the dining room and watched everything. She was a very impressive woman."

"What are some of the things that are still going on here that she probably originated?"

"Well, our service. We've kept our service as it was when she was here, and she watched to make sure that it was always the best. I think it's wonderful that Mr. and Mrs. Palmer and the family have continued in that same tradition. She was a remarkable woman."

Barbara moved on to other duties and I sat down to lunch. I enjoyed the chicken livers that arrived in a small copper chafing dish and were kept warm by a lighted candle underneath, served with some absolutely smashing red cabbage and excellent chutney that went very well with liver.

As I passed through the lobby again, of course I looked up at that painting of Nelle on the wall. I felt as if I were getting to know her very well.

LOWELL INN, 102 N. Second St., Stillwater, MN 55082; 612-439-1100. A 22-guestroom village inn 18 mi. from St. Paul, near all the cultural attractions of the Twin Cities. European plan. Lunch and dinner served daily except Christmas Eve and Christmas Day. Open year-round. Canoeing, tennis, hiking, skiing, and swimming nearby, including 4 ski resorts within 15 mi. No pets. Arthur and Maureen Palmer, Innkeepers.

Directions: Stillwater is on the St. Croix River at the junction of Minn. 95 (north and south) and Minn. 36 (east and west). It is 7 mi. north of I-94 on Hwy. 95.

THE ST. JAMES HOTEL
Red Wing, Minnesota

The original St. James Hotel was built in the mid-1870s and according to the history of the hotel, was a very impressively designed and decorated building with various reception rooms, parlors, and a large ballroom, and was well known for its excellent food and service.

However, even at the top of its form it could not begin to approach today's *restored* St. James Hotel.

The entire project is a tribute to the fact that American ingenuity, capital, and know-how are able to reproduce successfully almost every type of furniture, ornamentation, decoration, and design of a hundred years ago, and still maintain the very best quality.

Almost all the furnishings in the St. James are copies of lamps, bureaus, tables, chairs, beds, and carpets originally manufactured during the Victorian era. All of this furniture is solid, well made, and sturdy, and doesn't have the rickety feeling that sometimes occurs. Even the small details have been considered, including brass soap holders, towel racks, doorknobs, hinges, and the like.

The hotel is a modern accommodation of today, but serves as a reminder of opulent days gone by. In addition to excellent reproductions, the photographs and prints taken in a bygone era are further reminders of the past. Many of the walls are hung with pictures of Red Wing, taken over a hundred years ago, both of the town and of the river steamers that made the town a regular stop.

What excites me most is that this small hotel in the heart of America could have been torn down and gone the way of so many others, but instead, it is making a contribution that bids fair to endure for at least another hundred years.

Turn-down bed service and the morning newspaper at the door are a couple of the niceties that add to the pleasure of a visit to the St. James. Bed linens and towels are of first-rate quality and the quilts for each bed were especially designed and made to harmonize with the furnishings and colors of the room. Many of the rooms look out upon the Mississippi River, where the unending flow of barges provides constant entertainment. An excursion boat is available for guests who would like a closer look at the river.

The Amtrak station is just across the street from St. James and many of the guests arrive in this most convenient fashion.

The lobby of the old original hotel has been restored, but it is not used as the lobby of today's St. James. Instead, it has been set aside for parties, banquets, and special occasions. Photographs of the original 1870s investors, who put up all of $60,000, look down upon today's travelers with a certain undisguised smugness.

For six weeks during the summer of 1985 the much loved "Prairie Home Companion" program on public radio was broadcast from the T.B. Sheldon Memorial Auditorium in Red Wing and was a major event. On the night of August 24, the Red Wing Madrigal Singers did some numbers and I'm sure I heard general manager Gene Foster's voice among them.

The new-old St. James, always a familiar landmark in Red Wing, is making even greater strides in the 1980s.

ST. JAMES HOTEL, 406 Main St., Red Wing, MN 55066; 612-388-2846. A 60-guestroom restored country town hotel on the Mississippi River, 50 mi. from Minneapolis. Open all year. Breakfast, lunch, and dinner served to travelers. This is an in-town hotel with no sports or recreation on the grounds, but swimming, tennis, hiking, golf, bicycling, backroading, and river sightseeing trips are all very convenient. No pets. Gene Foster, General Manager.

Directions: From Minneapolis/St. Paul Airport take Hwy. 5 east, exit on Hwy. 55 to cross Mendota Bridge. Follow Hwy. 55 to Hastings where it joins Hwy. 61. Follow Hwy. 61, 22 mi. south into Red Wing. Accessible by Amtrak.

SCHUMACHER'S NEW PRAGUE HOTEL
New Prague, Minnesota

John Schumacher and I were talking about one of the original recipes he prepares at Schumacher's New Prague Hotel. "We call it quail Helenka," he said. "It is named for my mother."

"First," he said, with a mischievous look in his eye, "you catch two quail. Actually, the thing that's different is the fact that each quail is stuffed with a plum and then wrapped in two strips of bacon and baked for forty minutes at 350°; when they are done I spoon some brown sauce over them. They're particularly good served with red cabbage and hash-browned potatoes topped with melted swiss cheese."

John is a very innovative chef, having graduated first in his class from the Culinary Institute of America. His extensive dinner menu includes rabbit, pike, veal, pork, chicken, and homemade sausage, and all of the orders are cooked by him, except when he takes an occasional day off.

A good example of a new breed of young innkeepers who gain great satisfaction and personal fulfillment in running a country inn, John declares, "It's been a wonderful experience since 1974 when I discovered

New Prague and this hotel. Right from the start there were many things that had to be done, but it's been a highly satisfactory arrangement. Fortunately, I am the chef and I feel that a great deal of our reputation centers around the fact that the food is something I can control.

"The building was built in 1898 and originally was called the Broz Hotel. It was designed by the same man who designed the George Washington Bridge, the Supreme Court building in Washington, and the state capitol in St. Paul. His name was Cass Gilbert."

Abovestairs, each of the inn's twelve bedrooms is named for a different month and has an atmosphere and personality all of its own. One has a large semicircular bed with a white eyelet canopy, an antique couch, and a genuine Bavarian wall bouquet.

"I've been in central Europe several times," John commented, "and I believe the decorations and the cuisine here reflect my identification with Germany and Czechoslovakia. We have imported cotton-covered goosedown comforters and pillows and there are many, many central-European decorative touches. We have hand-painted Bavarian folk scenes and patterns by Pipka, a native Czech, who lives in Minneapolis.

"We don't have any television or telephones in the rooms, but our guests will find fresh arrangements of flowers and live plants, complimentary local newspapers, lots of books and magazines, and we even put candy under the pillows."

One of the things I found most intriguing about Schumacher's is that it has rapidly gained a reputation for being a place that honeymooners and anniversary couples enjoy. They often request a room that corresponds with their wedding month.

My latest communication with John indicates that in the very near future he will be starting a gift and antique shop right next to the inn. This ought to make a visit to the New Prague Hotel even more inviting.

New Prague is just thirty-five miles south of the Minneapolis-St. Paul metropolitan area, and besides the fun of staying at Schumacher's there is a surprising number of things to do nearby, including golf on an 18-hole course, tennis, and cross-country skiing in the winter. The Minnesota River is just nine miles away and is ideal for canoeing. It is a good place for ten-speed biking as well.

SCHUMACHER'S NEW PRAGUE HOTEL, 212 West Main St., New Prague, MN 56071; 612-758-2133. (Metro line: 612-455-7285.) A 12-guestroom Czechoslovakian and German inn located in a small country town approx. 35 mi. south of Minneapolis and St. Paul. European plan. Breakfast, lunch, and dinner served to travelers all year except 3 days at Christmas. Good bicycling and backroading nearby; also xc skiing, tennis, and golf. No entertainment available to amuse children. No pets. No credit cards. Kathleen and John Schumacher, Innkeepers.

Directions: From Minneapolis, take Rte. 494 west to Rte. 169 south to Jordan exit. Turn south on Rte. 21 for 9 mi. to New Prague. Turn left to Main St. at the stop sign, and the hotel is in the second block on the right.

THE BUXTON INN
Granville, Ohio

I always seem to be arriving in Granville at the height of the foliage season. Once again it was a beautiful day in mid-fall and this attractive little town, whose founders came from Granville, Massachusetts, was showing off its autumn finery.

The first thing I noticed at the Buxton Inn was a tasteful arrangement of wicker furniture on the front porch, occupied at the moment by some of the luncheon guests of the inn. The gazebo and wading pool with the fountain were now completed, and there was a new brick smokehouse and patio in evidence, as well.

A coal-black, half-grown kitten rubbed up against my legs purring contentedly. I learned later that its name is "Spirit."

The Buxton was originally built in 1812, and the Orr family, Orville and Audrey and their daughters, Melanie and Amy, have recreated the atmosphere of an inn of that period, even to the point of having waitresses and hosts and hostesses dressed in carefully researched costumes of the time.

My first visit to Granville was in 1974 and ever since that first day I've been noting with great pleasure and pride the progress made by the inn and the innkeepers.

For example, Amy Orr, who was my first guide in Granville, has graduated from high school and has finished her sophomore year at Ohio State, in nearby Columbus. Her sister, Melanie, now home from a year in France, is finishing her senior year at Indiana University. She is very much involved in the cuisine at the inn.

There was some time before lunch, so Audrey took me on a tour of the three bedrooms at the main inn. As we passed through a little passageway on the second floor, I noticed a working loom, and she explained that there is a weaver at the inn on Fridays, Saturdays, and Sundays. All three of the bedrooms are furnished with beautiful carved Victorian beds, marble-top dressers, and other Victorian accessories.

Audrey and Orville are very proud of the inn's reputation for excellent food and service. There are several different dining rooms. One of them has a low ceiling, and the posts and beams are painted with colors that are similar to the salmon-pink exterior hues.

I've always been very intrigued by the printed menus at the Buxton Inn, not only because they contain the very interesting history of the inn, but also because the listing of the menu items is sure to start the digestive juices flowing. For example, there is always fresh fish every day and, in fact, the seafood menu is quite impressive. There is an extensive selection of salads as well. Some of the robust main dishes include shrimp Provençal, tournedos Thomas, veal sweetbreads with marchand de vin sauce, honey-butter almond chicken, and roast duckling with orange-cranberry sauce. Incidentally, a discreet menu note suggests that beef entrées be prepared rare to medium, and that the chef is not responsible for the juiciness and flavor of well-done meats.

We had a very lively lunch and I asked the attractive young waitress to recite all of the luncheon desserts into my tape recorder, and this is what she said:

"Fudge-walnut cake, pistachio cake served warm with ice cream, pecan pie with whipped cream, cheesecake either plain or with a strawberry topping, gingerbread served hot with lemon sauce, a double-dark

chocolate cake with icing and served chilled with mint-chocolate ice cream, triple mousse cake with whipped cream, raspberry or rainbow sherbet, mint-chocolate chip or vanilla ice cream."

The first five rooms in the Warner House Annex are now open, and the response has been so encouraging that the Orrs are continuing on through the next stage; the Annex will have twelve guest rooms. The Glass House is now completed and provides comfort and joy for people and plants year around.

THE BUXTON INN, 313 E. Broadway, Granville, OH 43023; 614-587-0001. A 15-guestroom inn in a college town in central Ohio near Denison University, the Indian Mounds Museum, and the Heisey Glass Museum. European plan. Lunch and dinner served daily. Closed Christmas Day. Golf, tennis, horseback riding, cultural activities nearby. No pets. Orville and Audrey Orr, Innkeepers.

Directions: Take Granville exit from I-70. Travel north 8 mi. on Rte. 37 into Granville.

THE GOLDEN LAMB
Lebanon, Ohio

Sandra Reynolds and I were seated in the lobby of the Golden Lamb, waiting for Jack Reynolds to finish a telephone call, and then we were all going to walk up the street to the Warren County Museum.

Just to be in this lobby is to partake of a generous helping of the American past. Among other things, there was a lamp, the base of which was made out of a candle mold, and a curly maple table. An old coal stove that was used 100 years or more ago is still in use today. Always on hand is a big punch bowl, where guests and friends may enjoy a modicum of refreshment. There are quite a few examples of Shaker crafts in the lobby and elsewhere in the inn, including Shaker boxes, dowels, chests, and Shaker-style furniture in the dining room.

"The Shakers came to this section of Ohio during the 19th century and attracted buyers from all over the country with their fine farm stock, medicinal herbs, furniture, and other household essentials," explained Sandra. "Their community, Union Village, was sold by them over a half-century ago, but we have a lot of local interest in their culture, and the Warren County Museum has a considerable area devoted to Shaker memorabilia."

If Ohio could be called the "mother of presidents," the Golden Lamb might be called the "mother of country inns," because it is a significant force in providing inspiration for many innkeepers to preserve the best of the old, and at the same time to back it up with good innkeeping. Throughout the inn are found artifacts, furniture, and furnishings that have been collected from America's past that in a sense give us a real feeling of appreciation for what our forebears thought was beautiful, useful, and promising.

The building dates back to 1815 and was built on the site of an original log cabin erected by Jonas Seaman, who was granted a license in

1803 to operate "a house of public entertainment." Even before roads were built many guests came on foot or horseback to the inn. Here, in the warmth of the tavern's public rooms, they exchanged news of the world and related their own experiences. Many famous people have stopped here, including ten United States presidents as well as Henry Clay, Mark Twain, and Charles Dickens. Overnight guests may stay in rooms that are named for some of the great and near-great, both national and international, who have enjoyed accommodations here in the past.

Since this lovely old inn is a part of the heartland of America, it stands to reason that the main dishes would be representative of American cooking. There is beef in many forms, rainbow trout, and fried Kentucky ham steak. Roast duckling with wild rice dressing, flounder, Warren County turkey, and pork tenderloin are some of the principal entrées. When possible, vegetables from the nearby verdant Ohio countryside are used.

One of the most rewarding times to visit this inn is during the Christmas holiday season, when it is decorated literally "to the nines." Planning starts in July, with decisions on the theme and the menu. It is also the scene for the Cincinnati Art Club annual show.

THE GOLDEN LAMB INN, 27 S. Broadway, Lebanon, OH 45036; 513-932-5065. A historic 20-guestroom (19 private baths) village inn in the heart of Ohio farming country on U.S. Hwys. 63, 42, and 48. European plan. Breakfast served only on Sundays. Lunch and dinner served daily except Christmas. Golf and tennis nearby. No pets. Jackson Reynolds, Innkeeper.

Directions: From I-71, exit Rte. 48N, 3 mi. north to Lebanon. From I-75, exit Rte. 63E, 7 mi. east to Lebanon.

THE INN AT HONEY RUN
Millersburg, Ohio

This is the heartland of America at its very best. The road follows the contour of the land, and in mid-fall there were many trees with colorful reminders of the passing of the seasons. The sky staged a spectacular cloud-and-sun show through the scrim of a light, misty rain. I was pleased to see so many windmills, because they've disappeared for the most part from the New England farming scene.

Marjorie Stock's letter had warned, "This is Amish country, and there are many horse-drawn buggies on the roads, so please be careful."

Well, the road to Millersburg leads through the rolling Ohio countryside, southwest of Canton, and there were dozens and dozens of neat Amish farms and, indeed, the roads had several of the black horse-drawn buggies.

Following Marjorie's directions, I found my way to the front door of a truly outstanding contemporary country inn. I had first visited it when it was in the final stages of completion; now, most of Marjorie's ideals have been realized.

Designed to harmonize completely with the rolling countryside and set amidst a stand of maple, ash, oak, poplar, black walnut, butternut, and hickory trees, the inn is a bird watcher's delight. It is multilevel, with many rooms that give the impression of actually dwelling in the forest.

The twenty-five guest rooms are a potpourri of styles, including Shaker and Early American. The woods used in the guest rooms reflect the trees of the forest. Everything has been made in Ohio, much of it in Holmes County. Many of the woven and quilted wall-hangings are also done by Ohio craftspeople. Guests are greeted with baskets of fruit upon their arrival.

Meals are made from scratch and include such admirable offerings as freshly squeezed orange juice in the morning, pan-fried trout from Holmes County waters, vegetables carefully steamed to perfection, and a menu that is impressive for both its offerings and its reasonable prices.

Marjorie described a recent innovation during the winter months, called "Tuesday Tastings." "A buffet of about twenty-seven items is on display and guests are asked to rate the various dishes, which could include minestrone or cheddar cheese soup, steaks, ice cream pies, four versions of cheesecake, and many other dishes from our constantly changing menus." Marjorie also plans some outdoor barbecues and steak fries on the new redwood deck in warm weather. I have seen the reviews of several Ohio food writers, all of whom have given the inn very high marks.

Looking back over my visit to the Inn at Honey Run, I could see that Marjorie Stock has taken great pains to preserve within the inn dining rooms, bedrooms, and public rooms the most important feature of the forest environment: a peaceful and secluded tranquility. It is this quality that also makes it an ideal setting for a business conference, and two meeting rooms have been set aside for just such a purpose.

One of Marjorie's really fascinating new projects now in the designing stage is the "hobbit house," to contain eight guest rooms. This will be an earth-sheltered building, and each room will have a full sliding glass door opening out onto a wildflower pasture. In typical fashion, this alert,

attractive woman is breaking new ground. "No one has done this before," she exclaimed, "and I am curious to see what happens. If they turn out as I imagine, they will be fantastic!" I think the Inn at Honey Run is well on its way to making a significant name for itself among American country inns.

Congratulations, Marjorie, on your imagination and ingenuity.

THE INN AT HONEY RUN, 6920 County Road 203, Millersburg, OH 44654; 216-674-0011. A 25-guestroom country inn located in north-central Ohio's beautiful, wooded countryside. Open all year. Lunch and dinner served Mon. thru Sat. Advance reservations only. Sun. breakfast and lunch served to houseguests only. Breakfast is included in the overnight rate. Ample opportunities for recreation and backroading in Ohio's Amish country. No facilities for small children. No pets. Marjorie Stock, Innkeeper.

Directions: From Millersburg, proceed on E. Jackson St. (Rtes. 39 and 62) past courthouse and gas station on right. At next corner turn left onto Rte. 241. At 1 mi. the road goes downhill. At 1¾ mi. it crosses the bridge over Honey Run; turn right immediately around the small hill onto Rte. 203 (not well marked). After about 1 ½ mi. turn right at inn sign. (Watch out for the Amish horse-drawn buggies.)

WELSHFIELD INN RESTAURANT
Burton, Ohio

I've been visiting the Welshfield since the late 60s. Skillet-fried chicken, baked ham, fresh fillet of sole, salmon, and apple pie are some of the specialties. Brian Holmes says, "We never use mixes. Our rolls and bread are made from scratch." This is a real country restaurant with real country cooking.

Brian says that the recipe for indian pudding came from Cape Cod. "We took it as a compliment when one of our guests said it tasted exactly like the pudding at the Red Inn in Provincetown."

The restaurant has a very interesting collection of 19th-century antiques and bric-a-brac. The center of interest is an old nickelodeon. The music has a nostalgic flavor and sounds like a combination of mandolin, flute, violin, and piano.

WELSHFIELD INN RESTAURANT, Rte. 422, Burton, OH 44021; 216-834-4164. A country restaurant on Rte. 422, 28 mi. east of Cleveland. No lodgings. Lunch and dinner served weekdays. Dinner only served on Sun. and holidays. Closed the week of July 4 and 3 wks. after Jan. 1. Closed Mon. except Labor Day. Near Sea World and Holden Arboretum. Brian and Polly Holmes, Innkeepers.

Directions: On U.S. 422 at intersection of Ohio 700, midway between Cleveland and Youngstown, Ohio.

Favorite Back Roads

One of our most striking back roads is the delightful, winding, sixteen-foot-wide blacktop roadway that threads its way along the bluff for 21 miles from Harbor Springs to Cross Village. There is a steady succession of tunnels, shaded bowers and bosky dells, as well as historic touches. This is historic Indian country, graced with lingering softwood greens, tinged with hardwood red and purple and gold.

You start at the main intersection in Harbor Springs, head north up the high hill above the town, past Bluff Gardens, and continue on past the well-manicured links of the Harbor Springs Golf Club. This is followed by a solid mile of tree cover that leaps the road overhead; mostly maple, beech, oak, and cedar, with summer homes tucked away, barely in sight.

Continuing through West Traverse, the road passes an old country school and about five miles from Harbor Springs crosses Five-Mile Creek where there is an old mill. Next to it is a tiny "mom and pop" general store, typical of those to be found in Michigan's lumbering communities. Soon, one comes to a unique barnyard golf course where there are no greens fees. Its sporting, rolling, cobby terrain has plenty of hazards and gorse-type rough.

After three miles of winding, woodsy road, you arrive at a scenic turnout high above the rocky beach of Lake Michigan. On the far shore of Little Traverse Bay, the huge greenish globe of the Big Rock Nuclear Plant looks like a marble perched on the beach.

The road continues past the old Indian mission church and on into Good Hart, which has a combination general store–antique shop–post office. About fifteen miles from Harbor Springs, there's a century-old cemetery, nicely kept in its setting of leafy dignity, and then a two-mile stretch of very old, very high, wind-blown sand dunes.

Now the road has taken you to Cross Village, where you can continue along Emmett County Scenic Route 1—twenty miles to Mackinaw City by way of a magnificent array of sand dunes and open beach—or return the way you came, but nearer the lake by taking a couple of optional turns.

Stafford Smith
Stafford's Bay View Inn
Petoskey, Michigan

OLD RITTENHOUSE INN
Bayfield, Wisconsin

Mary Phillips' letter was right to the point: "Nineteen eighty-five was the most intense growth year of our lives. As you know, we completed five new guest rooms, all with working fireplaces and private baths in the main inn. The construction started in September of 1984 and our inn was filled to capacity on Memorial Day weekend of 1985.

"During the process our builder, Greg Carrier, Jerry, and I purchased the mansion that you saw when you were here in April. By June 28, after many fourteen-hour days with double crews, we opened five guest rooms in Le Chateau Boutin. It is beautiful right now and we are planning to work on it all winter. Response has been fantastic. This has been our busiest season ever.

"Our very first Christmas brochure of our gourmet food items goes into the mail very shortly. The photography is beautiful and was done here locally. We're very excited about it."

Well do I remember my visit last April. On the morning of my arrival I swung my car around to park on the side street next to the Old Rittenhouse Inn, and realized that since my last visit the inn had grown to almost twice its size! This was the first of many surprises. The beautiful, graceful Victorian lines of the original mansion, built in 1890, had been extended with new curves, angles, and a turret. I could see that when all the new shingles were painted it would be impossible to tell where the old left off and the new began. On that visit Mary and Jerry and Greg walked me through the five new bedrooms, and it was wonderful to feel their great enthusiasm and dedication.

However, Mary, Jerry, and Greg were not finished. With a wonderful, mysterious air, and along with some members of the inn staff, we all piled into Jerry's exotic van and drove four blocks away. There was the biggest surprise of all. It was a strikingly handsome Victorian mansion whose first- and second-floor porches and windows enjoy a spectacular view of the lake.

"It's ours," quoth Jerry. "We just bought it and now we're going to call it Le Chateau Boutin and make it a part of the Rittenhouse." Jerry explained that Greg was part of the partnership for this new project, and since he is a builder, everything is going to be done as close to perfection as possible. As many times as he'd seen it, Greg was still wandering around, running his hands over the English oak woodwork, and marveling at the workmanship of the original builders. The rich wood is enhanced by silver door pulls and stained-glass windows.

Well, this is a fitting continuation of Mary and Jerry Phillips' first visit to Bayfield in 1969 and the subsequent establishment of what has become Wisconsin's premiere inn.

The cuisine and the service at the Old Rittenhouse Inn are a wonderful story in themselves. There is an innovative menu of at least six entrées every night, with many enticing side dishes. These have been prepared by Mary, who is the artist in the kitchen; however, Jerry does all the desserts.

Another new addition at the Old Rittenhouse is lunch. Guests may have either soup, a meal-sized salad, and beverage, or an entrée and accompaniments. A lunch entrée might be sautéed lake trout flavored with champagne and almonds or a chicken breast stuffed with walnuts and ricotta, glazed with apple cider and marmalade.

There's really much ado at the Old Rittenhouse and still more to come!

OLD RITTENHOUSE INN, 301 Rittenhouse Ave., Bayfield, WI 54818; 715-779-5765. A 15-guestroom Victorian inn in an area of historic and natural beauty, 70 mi. east of Duluth, Minn., on the shore of Lake Superior. European plan. Breakfast, lunch, and dinner served to travelers. Open May 1 to Nov. 1; weekends through the winter. Advance reservations most desirable. Extensive recreational activity of all kinds available throughout the year, including tours, hiking, and cycling on the nearby Apostle and Madeline Islands. Not comfortable for small children. No pets. Jerry and Mary Phillips, Innkeepers.

Directions: From the Duluth Airport, follow Rte. 53-S through the city of Duluth over the bridge to Superior, Wis. Turn east on Rte. 2 near Ashland (1½ hrs.), turn north on 13-N to Bayfield.

SEVEN PINES LODGE
Lewis, Wisconsin

I parked my car among the tall pine trees and immediately became aware of the sounds of the woods—a combination of water, birds, and wind. The front door of the lodge opened and out scampered a beautiful little golden Labrador retriever, and to the forest sounds were added the delighted and welcoming squeals of what Joan Simpson refers to as "our official greeter."

Joan and David Simpson, along with their son, John-David, and daughter, Tina, are the innkeepers of this rustic hideaway in the Wisconsin forest. It was built in 1903 by Charles Lewis, a grain broker and financier from Minneapolis. Constructed of handhewn logs, the lodge has retained its original appeal and surprising elegance, including an array of interesting antiques that are an integral part of the decor. Ninety percent of the furniture and decorations have been here since Mr. Lewis's time.

Immediately upon my arrival I took a pleasant stroll with Joan, scuffing through the dried leaves to the trout stream, and we passed through a grove of original pine trees, some of which are 115 feet high. Passing over a rustic bridge beside a melodious waterfall, we entered an almost pagodalike, two-story log building with a full screened porch around four sides of the second floor. This is a summer sleeping porch, and I can just imagine the good times enjoyed by families in this woodland setting.

We followed the stream a short distance and came to a sylvan pool with a stone statue of a young Indian boy. As we were drinking in the quiet loveliness of the scene, Joan pointed to a finny denizen and said, "There goes a dinner."

She explained that the brownies, rainbows, and brook trout, all of which are raised on the property, often appear on the menu.

Joan does all the cooking, and David and John-David take care of the tables. Guests frequently sit at the kitchen table while she prepares the Scandinavian bread, desserts, trout dinners, and the hearty meals that are welcomed by guests who usually have spent most of the day outdoors, whether it be summer or winter. There are miles of cross-country ski trails. "When guests make reservations they are given a choice of one of three main dishes, although most returning guests like the trout."

Accommodations at Seven Pines Lodge are in the main building, where there are five year-round bedrooms, and also in log outbuildings, used only during temperate weather. These have a real "woodsy" feeling.

That evening I joined the other guests around the dinner table, and then we all adjourned to the friendly confines of the living room, where there is a big oval table with an overhead lamp that provides convenient lighting by which to enjoy albums of fascinating photographs of the for 1922 provided us all with a good deal of entertainment and laughs. There was a picture of the Portland Beavers of 1922, among whom was the great athlete Jim Thorpe.

Joan and a friend had done a wildflower study that catalogued 181 different wildflowers. The fly fishermen oohed and aahed over the brand-new fly display case with beautiful specimens tied by David Crooks. And so the evening passed quite pleasantly in the big rustic living room, where there is no television. There is only one telephone in the lodge itself. There's nothing to disturb the peace and serenity at Seven Pines Lodge.

SEVEN PINES LODGE, Lewis, WI 54851; 715-653-2323. A 10-guest-room rustic resort-inn (most rooms have shared baths) in the Wisconsin woods about 1½ hrs. from Minneapolis. Open year-round. Closed Thanksgiving and Christmas Day. Trout fishing on grounds. St. Croix Falls, Taylors Falls, National Wild River Scenic Waterway nearby. Tennis, swimming, golf, woodswalking, xc, downhill skiing, backroading nearby. Very attractive for children of all ages since the innkeepers also have children. No pets. No credit cards. Joan and David Simpson, Innkeepers.

Directions: From Minneapolis/St. Paul: follow 135W or 135E north to U.S. 8 at Forest Lake, Minn. East on U.S. 8 through Taylors Falls, Minn./St. Croix Falls, Wisc., to Wisc. 35 north to Lewis. Turn right at gas station to T, right 1 mi. to fork in road and turn left ½ mi. to 7 Pines Lodge entrance.

THE WHITE GULL INN
Fish Creek, Wisconsin

Let me share with you a portion of a letter from Andy Coulson from the White Gull Inn: "The ash trees here are now about crimson and the sugar maples, a bright, reddish orange. When Jan and I first came to Door County in 1972, the fall color was a well-kept secret, enjoyed by a knowing few. Last weekend, people from all over the Midwest streamed onto the Peninsula to witness this spectacular show, recently described on national television as 'the caviar of fall color.' Those who really seek the quiet are now coming later in the fall, when they have the area to themselves. Often, they are the ones who see the herds of deer and other wildlife that is so abundant. Some come in the quiet winter when the state parks open their miles of cross-country ski trails. These are the guests we have time to get to know the best."

The White Gull was built as part of a large resort area more than 75 years ago, when hundreds of tourists would arrive in Fish Creek from Chicago and Milwaukee aboard such steamships as the *Georgia, Carolina,* and *Alabama*. They would be escorted from the dock to the inn, known in those days as Henrietta's Cottage. Nowadays guests drive or fly to Fish Creek because the main street, the beautiful waterfront, and the sparkling atmosphere have remained unchanged.

The main building is a white clapboard, three-story building that doesn't put on airs at all. There is a definite shared informality among the innkeepers, staff, and guests. The rooms, which have been steadily increasing in numbers over recent years, are tidy and neat, and some of them in the main house share baths.

The White Gull is justifiably famous in the Midwest for its traditional Fish Boils, featuring freshly caught lake fish, boiled potatoes, homemade cole slaw, fresh-baked bread, and cherry pie. Russ, the master boiler, prepares a roaring fire and the fish are boiled in two huge iron cauldrons. He also plays the accordion and leads everybody in lots of singing and clapping hands. Incidentally, the recipe for this famous dish can be found in the *Country Inns and Back Roads Cookbook*.

Jan and Andy and the staff have remodeled the Cliff House, a two-story cottage behind the main building. It now has four antique-furnished rooms, all with bathrooms and even TV's that slide out of sight when not being used.

As if this weren't enough, no sooner had the paint dried on the Cliff House than the Coulsons had the opportunity to purchase a rambling turn-of-the-century home, not a block distant from the inn, that can be made into an annex, adding four more bedrooms.

The Coulsons' elder daughter, Meredith, is now seven years old. It seems like just the day before yesterday when Jan and Andy sent me her

birth announcement. She, like Elena Pavloff at Goose Cove Lodge in Sunset, Maine, is now playing the Suzuki violin. The Coulsons' other daughter, Emilie Lindsley, is a little over two years old now and I'm sure we'll have continuing news of her progress in the years to come. Incidentally, the dessert menu at the White Gull features two interesting confections worthy of note: "Raspberries Meredith" and "Strawberries Emilie."

Before this edition went to press, Andy sent me a note saying that there would be something really exciting and new to report on in the 1987 edition. Don't miss it!

THE WHITE GULL INN, Fish Creek, WI 54212; 414-868-3517. A 13-guestroom inn with 4 cottages (private and shared baths) in a most scenic area in Door County, 23 mi. north of Sturgeon Bay. Open year-round. European plan. Breakfast, lunch, and dinner except Thanksgiving and Christmas. Fish Boils: Wed., Fri., Sat., Sun. nights May thru Oct.; Wed. and Sat. nights Nov. thru April. All meals open to travelers; reservations requested. Considerable outdoor and cultural attractions; golf, tennis, swimming, fishing, biking, sailing, xc skiing, and other summer and winter sports nearby. Excellent for children of all ages. No pets. Andy and Jan Coulson, Joan Holliday, and Nancy Vaughn, Innkeepers.

Directions: From Chicago: take I-94 to Milwaukee. Follow Rte. I-43 from Milwaukee to Manitowoc; Rte. 42 from Manitowoc to Fish Creek. Turn left at stop sign at the bottom of the hill, go 2½ blocks to inn. From Grey Bay: take Rte. 57 to Sturgeon Bay; Rte. 42 to Fish Creek.

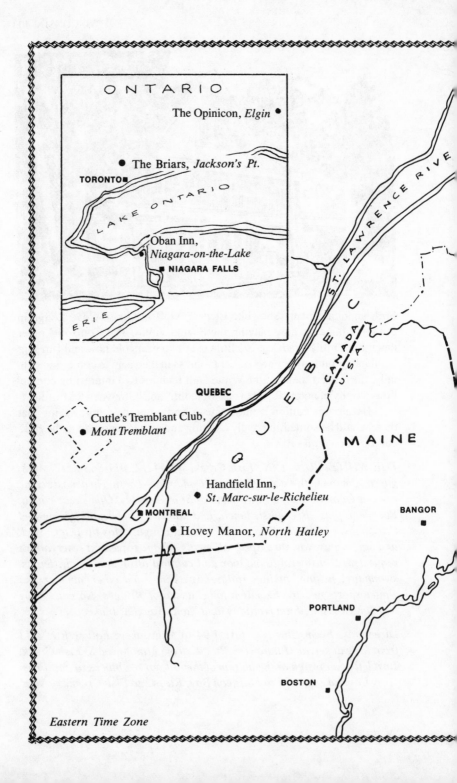

ONTARIO

The Opinicon, *Elgin* ●

● The Briars, *Jackson's Pt.*

TORONTO■

LAKE ONTARIO

Oban Inn,
● *Niagara-on-the-Lake*
■ NIAGARA FALLS

ERIE

ST. LAWRENCE RIVE

QUEBEC

QUEBEC■

Cuttle's Tremblant Club,
● *Mont Tremblant*

CANADA
U.S.A.

MAINE

Handfield Inn,
● *St. Marc-sur-le-Richelieu*

BANGOR
■

■ MONTREAL
● Hovey Manor, *North Hatley*

PORTLAND
■

BOSTON
■

Eastern Time Zone

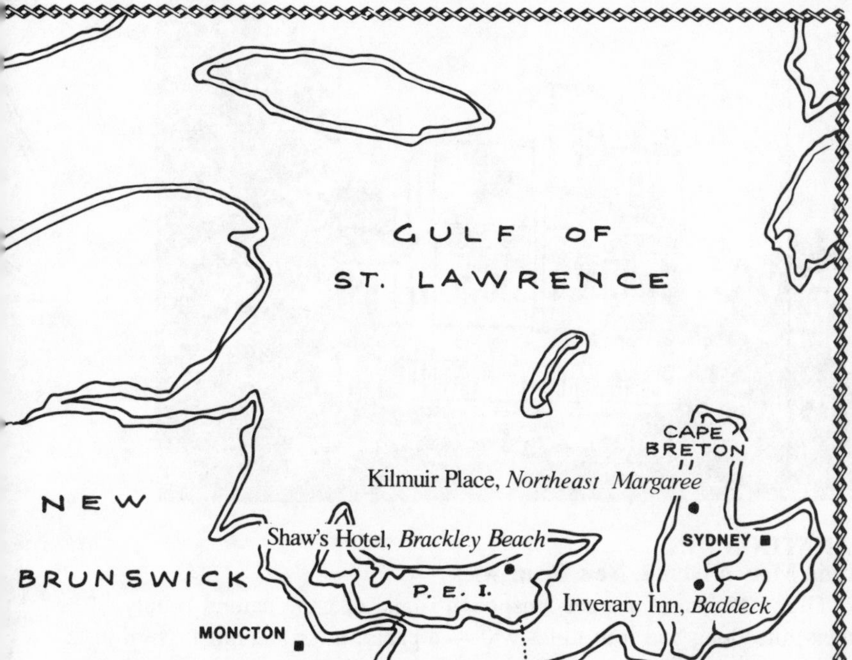

GULF OF
ST. LAWRENCE

NEW

BRUNSWICK

CAPE
BRETON

Kilmuir Place, *Northeast Margaree*

Shaw's Hotel, *Brackley Beach*

SYDNEY

P. E. I.

Inverary Inn, *Baddeck*

MONCTON

Marshlands, *Sackville*

NOVA SCOTIA

CALAIS

HALIFAX

Marathon Hotel, *Grand Manan Island*

ATLANTIC

ANNAPOLIS ROYAL

Milford House, *South Milford*

YARMOUTH

OCEAN

Eastern and Maritime
Canada

Atlantic Time Zone

MARATHON INN
Grand Manan Island, New Brunswick

Grand Manan is a quiet, unspoiled island of great natural beauty fifteen miles long and four miles wide—a paradise for naturalists, bird watchers, photographers, artists, divers, and rock hounds. The best way to experience the island is by walking.

As the ferry from Black's Harbour approached the wharf at North Head on Grand Manan Island, I could readily see that this was a place where men made their living from the sea. There were fishing boats, seining weirs, and weathered docks on tall stilts; a necessity because of the very high tides in the Bay of Fundy. I could see the Marathon Inn at the top of the hill—a gleaming, three-story building with a mansard roof.

On this particular trip Jim Leslie had suggested in a very mysterious way that something unusual and exciting had been going on at the inn on at least two occasions during the year, and said that he would fill me in when we had a chance to chat.

The owner-innkeepers of the inn are Jim and Judy Leslie, and Jim's mother, Fern. The Leslies are all Canadians. Fern is from Saskatchewan, and both Judy and Jim were brought up in Toronto.

The first thing I did on arrival was to take a plunge in the heated swimming pool and arrange for a game of tennis. Jim joined me about an hour before dinner on the front porch overlooking the harbor.

"Our guests often like to take advantage of the chance to go deep sea fishing for herring, pollock, and haddock with the island fishermen. There are also boating trips to Gannet Rock, Machias Seal Island, and Tent Island. Children seem to have a wonderful time here, and that is very gratifying.

"We have some excellent spring programs that are available to our guests at a slight additional charge," Jim said. "There are three four-day birdwatching tours in May and June conducted by Mary Majka. Also in June we have a special photographic workshop conducted by Freeman Patterson and a watercolor seminar by John Austen. We also have a super dark room.

"During the fall months we have a program called 'Ocean Search' that enables our guests to learn more about the great whales off the island and also to go out on the sea in boats. Our naturalist shows slides several evenings during the week with special emphasis on those great mammals during that time."

Finally, I could contain myself no longer. "What is this mystery you're talking about?" Jim smiled broadly and replied, "That's exactly what it is: an old-fashioned 'whodunit' mystery, in which our guests can hunt down clues and suspects. We supply them with a complete kit of clues when they arrive on Fridays. Before the weekend is out we've had a 'crime' with suspects and detectives, and finally we solve the mystery by figuring out who the culprit was.

"We did two of these last year and they were a huge success. We're already booked for some additional weekends this year, as well. You don't have to be a fan of Miss Marple or Sherlock Holmes, but it helps to get into the swing of things. Everybody has a terrific time. Tell your readers that they will have to telephone in advance to make a reservation."

So, I have now solved part of the mystery; however, I made a reservation on the spot for one of the "whodunit" weekends at the Marathon Inn during 1986. Doesn't the idea sound intriguing?

MARATHON INN, North Head at Grand Manan, New Brunswick, Canada EOG 2MO; 506-662-8144. A 38-guestroom resort-inn on Grand Manan Island in the Bay of Fundy, 40 mi. from St. John in New Brunswick. Modified American and European plans. Closed in winter months. Breakfast and dinner served to travelers daily. Heated swimming pool, tennis courts on grounds. Beachcombing, bird watching, swimming, fishing, hiking, diving, bicycles, golf nearby. Whale watching in season. Pets allowed on ground floor annex. Jim, Judy, and Fern Leslie, Innkeepers.

Directions: Grand Manan Island is reached by ferry from Black's Harbour, just off Rte. 1, midway between Calais, Maine, and St. John, New Brunswick. Check inn for schedule.

MARSHLANDS INN
Sackville, New Brunswick

We were an interesting little group. There was a gentleman from Saskatchewan, who was on his way to Cape Breton to do some fishing. A lady and gentleman from Toronto were on their way home from visiting some relatives in Halifax, Nova Scotia. There was also a young honeymooning couple from Detroit, who had stayed in a different *CIBR* inn each of the past four nights. They would be leaving in the morning for the Inverary at Baddeck, Nova Scotia.

We were all sitting together in front of the fireplace in the living room, sipping the delicious hot chocolate offered every evening at the Marshlands. Innkeeper John Blakely said, "This is for guests who simply aren't able to wait until breakfast time."

The Marshlands Inn is literally at the crossroads. It is a perfect, single day's drive from the two inns in Cape Breton, or the Milford House, near Annapolis Royal. It is also a comfortable day's ride on the land route from Calais, Maine, or St. Stephen, New Brunswick, if the traveler is using the land route to Nova Scotia and Prince Edward Island. Many of the guests stay on for an extra night or two to see the famous "tidal bore," visible in the nearby Bay of Fundy, or to play some golf and enjoy some hiking and swimming. There is also curling.

Almost all of the letters I get from our readers who have visited here mention two things: first, the unusually extensive collection of 19th-century antiques throughout the inn and guest rooms, which have obviously been here from the very beginning; and second, the food.

We were talking about the food while enjoying the hot chocolate that evening. The gentleman from Saskatchewan had had the Atlantic salmon and couldn't say enough about it. I had thoroughly enjoyed one of my favorite dishes, curried lamb served with the Marshlands' own chutney. The young honeymooning couple had tried the fresh Miramichi salmon. His was served grilled and hers was poached with an egg sauce. Everyone agreed that the fiddlehead greens were a delicacy.

While we were exchanging travel experiences, I somewhat shamefacedly admitted that before my first visit I thought that Sackville was about fifteen miles south of the polar icecap. The Canadian couple came to my rescue by admitting that they, too, had a total misconception of New Brunswick.

The hour was getting late. Someone remarked that breakfast was served from 7 a.m., so we could get an early start.

We all said good night and promised to meet for breakfast, unwilling to break the chain of friendship we had begun in the handsome inn in not-so-faraway New Brunswick.

There has been a change recently at the Marshlands Inn. My dear friends, Herb and Alice Read, have leased the inn to Mary and John Blakely. Mary worked for four years at Marshlands as a hostess, and she and John both come from Derbyshire in England, where Mary's parents had an English-style country inn. They have two beautiful daughters.

However, Herb and Alice are still very much on the scene in Sackville, and they are extremely pleased with the way the Blakelys are doing things.

Another item of note is the visit by the Queen of England to Marshlands on her Canadian trip in the fall of 1984. John and Mary have some wonderful photographs of Her Majesty's visit, and they were tremendously enthusiastic about what a lovely, real person she is. I'm sure that the occasion was the most auspicious moment in the career of the Marshlands Inn.

MARSHLANDS INN, Box 1440, Sackville, N.B., Canada EOA 3 CO; 506-536-0170. A 10-guestroom (mostly private baths) village inn near Tantramar Marshes and Fundy Tides. European plan. Breakfast, lunch, and dinner served to travelers daily. Closed during the Christmas season. Golf, xc skiing, curling, hiking, and swimming nearby. John and Mary Blakely, Innkeepers.

Directions: Follow Trans-Canada Highway to Sackville, then Rte. 6, 1 mi. to center of town.

INVERARY INN
Baddeck, Cape Breton, Nova Scotia

It was good to be back at Baddeck and the Inverary Inn once again for what I could guess was at least my tenth visit. It was a sunshiny morning, and the sounds of schoolchildren playing on the other side of the high hedge were a most pleasant experience.

As usual, I was up for an early morning walk down to the shore of Lake Bras d'Or, another practice that has become almost a tradition with me. Besides being a wonderful way to greet the Nova Scotia morning, it also provides me with the opportunity to observe what the MacAulay family has accomplished since my last visit.

Indeed, there have been many changes since I first visited Isobel and Danny MacAuley, when they were just contemplating purchasing this property. There has been a particular surge during recent years with the building of a swimming pool that is very handy for warm-weather dips during midsummer.

The years have also seen the development of many other features at the inn. The one that stands out as the most important in Isobel MacAulay's mind is the wee chapel on the grounds of the inn.

"It was the gift of one of our guests," she says. "For everyone it has become a haven of quiet and peaceful serenity. I'm sure to visit there almost every day myself."

With 1985 came the completion of three new lochside tennis courts, with a fine view of the water and the hills beyond. In addition to having a fine place to play, guests can also work on their game with the new tennis pro. This really puts the Inverary in the position that Isobel MacAuley had in mind about five years ago, when she said that she wanted it to become a complete resort where people would stay for more than just one or two nights.

Besides the main dining room, where the menu includes many hearty offerings to satisfy the outdoor appetites developed by guests who have been traveling on the Cabot Trail, there is also, during the season, a waterside seafood restaurant, set among the pine trees on the shore of one of the bays of the lake, where lobsters, fresh fish chowder, and other Nova Scotia seafood are offered. The restaurant has a most attractive view of a boatyard, and some of the fishing boats and sailboats can easily be seen while enjoying one of those delicious Nova Scotia lobsters. A pontoon boat, moored next to the Fish House, takes inn guests out in the evening, and Dan MacAulay is the proud skipper most of the time.

While Isobel and Dan MacAulay are very much on the scene, it is really their son, Scott, and his wife, Terri, who are picking up the Inverary banner and carrying it to even greater heights.

Returning to the main entrance from my morning walk, I stepped

inside the living room. There was a low fire in the familiar stone fireplace and I recalled with pleasure the cup of tea I took there, before retiring the previous night—sitting and talking about travel with many guests of the inn.

The Inverary Inn has several types of accommodations; some are in the main house and others are in adjoining outbuildings and cottages. The newer lodging rooms are principally used to accommodate bus tours.

I would be remiss if I failed to mention the Scottish breakfasts that have been offered ever since my first visit. I think I receive more letters about them than any other of the many features of the inn.

The Inverary, which had such modest beginnings during my first visits, has now become one of the most popular travel objectives in Nova Scotia—a well-deserved reputation.

INVERARY INN, Box 190, Baddeck, Cape Breton, N.S., Canada; 902-295-2674. A 40-guestroom (some shared baths) village inn on the Cabot Trail, 52 mi. from Sydney, N.S. On the shore of Lake Bras d'Or. European plan. Breakfast and dinner served to travelers daily. Open from May 15 to Nov. 1. Bicycles and children's playground on grounds. Boating and small golf course nearby. Isobel MacAulay, Innkeeper.

Directions: Follow Trans-Canada Hwy. to Canso Causeway to Baddeck.

I do not include lodging rates in the descriptions, for the very nature of an inn means that there are lodgings of various sizes, with and without baths, in and out of season, and with plain and fancy decoration. Travelers should call ahead and inquire about the availability and rates of the many different types of rooms.

KILMUIR PLACE
Northeast Margaree, Cape Breton, Nova Scotia

"I've never used a mix in my life, and never will." Isabel Taylor stood with her hands on her hips and tossed her head back, her eyes flashing. "After all, my mother and father started this place over fifty-five years ago and our guests love the old-fashioned ways. I can tell the difference when something is made from a mix and I'm sure that everybody else can, too."

"Indeed, they do, and I'm a guest who's been coming for forty straight years."

This time the speaker was a lady from Philadelphia, who walked into the Kilmuir Place kitchen as if on cue.

"In those days it took some persistence and motivation to come out to the Margaree," she said, settling down into one of the comfortable upholstered chairs in one corner of the kitchen. "Now you can get here from Sydney in about an hour and a half and from Halifax in about three and a half hours. In the old days the roads weren't paved and sometimes it was necessary to get a team to pull us out of the mud."

Built by a merchant, deep in the unspoiled Nova Scotia countryside in 1885, Kilmuir Place was named for a parish house on the Isle of Skye, off the northwest coast of Scotland. The inn can accommodate six people comfortably, and operates on the modified American plan, serving breakfast and dinner to houseguests only. It's necessary to have firm reservations. The home is filled with treasures and other dear things collected over the years. In the dining room, the beautiful mahogany set and the silver are outstanding. It is an old-fashioned country inn offering a unique, almost rustic, and peaceful lifestyle. Homegrown vegetables accent meals of old-fashioned Nova Scotia fare, including, of course, the famous salmon served in the family dining room along with hot coffee and good conversation.

The inn is on the Cabot Trail that winds between the Gulf of St. Lawrence and the Atlantic Ocean, claiming some of the world's most breathtaking scenery.

Kilmuir Place is a delightful home base for salmon and trout fishing, bicycling, hiking or picnicking. Community suppers and dances in the area are plentiful, and summertime's many Canadian holidays provide stimulating cultural activities, including Canada Day, July 1, featuring the traditional Gathering of the Clans and the Fisherman's Regatta. The end of July brings Margaree Days, and in August the Gaelic Mod presents bagpipe music, Gaelic singing, and Scottish cultural programs.

There are guides available for fishing on the world-famous Margaree River for Atlantic salmon and trout, and the beaches are twelve to fifteen miles away on the warm waters of the Gulf Coast on the Northumberland

Strait. Incidentally, there's excellent bird watching, with many bald eagles.

In recent years Isabel Taylor has given over the innkeeping chores to her daughter and son-in-law, Nancy and Guy Parry; however, she still is in residence and eager to talk on any subject in the world to her many returning guests.

Nancy asked the Philadelphia guest whether she would like to have another piece of the famous Kilmuir chocolate cake; however, the lady demurred, saying that she couldn't possibly eat another bite. I'm also

happy to report that the blueberry crop was sensational during the past year, so there were lots of blueberry muffins and marvelous blueberry cake to add to the repertoire, as well as a great blueberry meringue for dessert.

When you come to Kilmuir, be prepared to wish fervently on the day you leave that you could stay several days longer.

KILMUIR PLACE, Northeast Margaree, Cape Breton, N.S., Canada BOE 2HO; 902-248-2877. (U.S.A. reservations: 800-341-6096; Maine: 800-492-0643). A 5-guestroom country inn on Rte. 19, 28 mi. from Baddeck. Some rooms with shared baths. Modified American plan. Breakfast and dinner served to houseguests only. Open from June to mid-Oct. Salmon fishing in the Margaree River, touring the Cabot Trail, and both fresh-water and salt-water swimming nearby. Not suitable for children under 12. Mrs. Ross Taylor, Guy and Nancy Parry, Innkeepers.

Directions: After crossing Canso Causeway to Cape Breton, follow either Rte. 19 (coast road to Inverness) and turn right on Cabot Trail at Margaree Forks, or Rte. 105 and turn left on Cabot Trail at Nyanza.

MILFORD HOUSE
South Milford, Nova Scotia

The time was 7:30 a.m. I awakened to the sound of the lake water lapping against the shore, and looked out of the window of my cabin to see an errant canoeist drifting by in the middle of the lake. I bounded out of bed, in and out of the shower, and dressed rapidly so as not to miss a single moment of my time at this "almost-wilderness" resort-inn in southern Nova Scotia.

My accommodations, like all the others, were in a tidy, rustic cabin where there were two bedrooms and a large combination sitting and dining room with windows overlooking still another view of the lake. There are over two dozen of these cottages situated well apart along the wooded shores of two lakes, within walking distance of the main lodge. Each cottage has its own lakeside dock, two to five bedrooms, a living room with a fireplace, electricity, and a bathroom with a tub or a shower. Some of them are insulated and contain housekeeping facilities ideal for a cross-country skiing holiday or just a secluded winter vacation. There were fresh flowers in my cabin and although the furnishings were plain, everything was absolutely spic and span. All the cottages are provided with maid service, ice, wood, and kindling, delivered daily.

I walked down to the end of the lane and up the woods road toward the main lodge for breakfast, happening to meet another guest bound in the same direction. "Oh I think it's a wonderful place here," she said. "We left the windows open and just loved listening to the loons. My husband and I are going to stay and take a canoe trip."

We continued on up to the main lodge with its comfortable living room, large dining room, library and games room. Milford House guests take their breakfasts and dinners at the main lodge, where there are vegetables from the garden, roasts, fresh fish, native blueberries, raspberries, and ample home-baked breads and pastries. Breakfast consisted of bacon, eggs, pancakes, homemade muffins, and coffee—and, especially, lots of conversation with other guests.

For a number of years, even before my first visit in 1973, the Milford House has been expertly managed by Margaret and Bud Miller. It was their daughter Wendy who gave me my first tour, and about whom I have written continuously over the years. For the benefit of Wendy's many friends, she has joined the Canadian Armed Forces and is at the Officers' Training Center for the Air Force in British Columbia. I do miss seeing that twelve-year-old young lady who showed me around not so very many years ago.

The Millers' other daughter Linda visited in August, too, with her three children, who are becoming well known at the inn. Linda designed and hooked a wall hanging of the Milford Inn with symbolic figures

around the outside of the oval picture. It has truly been a conversation piece. Margaret told me that she was planning to have some Christmas cards made of it.

What has made the Milford House attractive to many repeating guests is the fact that the area is virtually unspoiled; however, it is easily traversable by canoe.

When I left, the remaining guests stood on the porch waving. And when I passed the big tree at the corner, true to the Milford House tradition, I didn't look back. A lovely, old-fashioned custom.

MILFORD HOUSE, South Milford, R.R. 4, Annapolis Royal, N.S., Canada BOS 1AO; 902-532-2617. A rustic resort-inn with 27 cabins on 600 acres of woodlands and lakes, 90 mi. from Yarmouth, N.S., near Kejimkujik National Park. Modified American plan. Breakfast and dinner served daily with picnic lunches available. Open from June 15 to Sept. 15; fall and winter by special reservation. Tennis, fishing, croquet, canoeing, birdwatching, and swimming on grounds. Deep-sea fishing and golf nearby. Warren and Margaret Miller, Innkeepers.

Directions: From Yarmouth follow Rte. 1 to traffic lights in Annapolis Royal. Turn right and continue on Rte. 8, 15 mi. to inn. The Blue Nose Ferry from Bar Harbor to Yarmouth N.S., arrives in time for guests to make dinner at the Milford House.

SHAW'S HOTEL
Brackley Beach, Prince Edward Island

Prince Edward Island is one of the great surprises of North America. For one thing, ocean water temperatures along the wide P.E.I. beaches average sixty-eight to seventy degrees in summer and the sun is excellent for tanning. It has one of Canada's finest national parks, stretching twenty-five miles along the Gulf of St. Lawrence. There are wild seascapes, breathtaking views, and an atmosphere of hospitality, because this has been a resort area for more than a century.

During the summer months there is an excellent theatre at the Confederation Centre of the Arts of Charlottetown, offering a choice of musicals that play to capacity houses almost every night.

Prince Edward Island is very popular in July and August, so reserve well in advance and be sure to obtain ferry information.

I first visited P.E.I. and Shaw's Hotel in 1974 and never thought that I could be this far north and find ocean water so wonderfully warm and enjoyable.

I had taken the ferry from Caribou, Nova Scotia, that morning. There is another ferry from Cape Tormentine, New Brunswick. It is possible to stay at the Marshlands Inn in Sackville and take the ferry over the next morning. I had driven down from the Inverary Inn on Cape Breton in northern Nova Scotia, so the Caribou crossing was more convenient.

I found that Shaw's was part of an original pioneer farm started in 1793; had become a hotel in 1860; and today, still has many of the characteristics of an operating farm.

Some of the accommodations are single and double rooms in the main building, a Victorian house with a brilliant red mansard third story. There are also individual cottages, accommodating from two to eight people. This is most convenient for families who return every summer. The cottages are spaced far enough apart to insure privacy. Five of them have their own fireplaces.

Shaw's Hotel is surrounded by many trees and broad meadows. The view from the dining room might include a sailboat bobbing along on the bay. There is a good mix of both Canadian and American guests, and Robbie Shaw says that there are always a few people from California, Washington, and New York.

One of the most attractive features about Shaw's Hotel is the fact that it is only a short distance through the woods to the beach. All of this summertime outdoor activity, including swimming, sailing on the bay, deep sea tuna fishing, golf, tennis, bicycling, walking, and horseback riding, contribute to very big appetites, so the main dishes include fresh salmon, lobster, mackerel, cod, and halibut. Dinners are fun because

everyone is eager for a hearty meal, and enthusiasm is high after a day of recreation.

Children are particularly happy in this atmosphere. Robbie Shaw said he has had as many as twenty to thirty children at one time at the height of the season. "There is always plenty of elbow room," he said. "We don't have any trouble keeping the parents of the children amused either. Besides the beach, there are riding horses nearby, and it is fun to ride along the beach and on the bridle paths. I have been doing it all my life. My father, who passed away in 1985, always loved the children."

One of our readers summed up her and her family's experience at Shaw's Hotel like this:

"It is not easy to get from Hannibal, Missouri, to Brackley Beach, Prince Edward Island. But my husband and I and our two children, nine and eleven, made an adventure out of it, stopping at inns in your book all along the way. When those golden retrievers bounded out to greet us as we pulled up to the hotel, I knew that we were in the right place."

SHAWS'S HOTEL, Brackley Beach, Prince Edward Island, Canada C0A 2H0; 902-672-2022. A 24-guestroom and 10 guest cottages (some shared baths) country hotel within walking distance of Brackley Beach, 15 mi. from Charlottetown. American plan. Breakfast and dinner served to travelers daily. Open from June 15 to Sept. 15. Tennis, golf, bicycles, riding, sailing, beach and summer theater nearby. Pets allowed in cottages only. Robbie Shaw, Innkeeper

Directions: Prince Edward Island is reached by ferry from either Cape Tormentine, New Brunswick (near Moncton), or Caribou, Nova Scotia. In both cases, after arriving on P.E.I., follow Rte.1 to Charlottetown, then Rte. 15 to Brackley Beach. P.E.I. is also reached by Eastern Provincial Airway, VIA Rail Canada, and Air Canada.

THE BRIARS
Jackson's Point, Ontario

When prospective guests contact the Briars for information, in addition to some very informative literature, they also have the benefit of an unusually large full-color map of the Briars and Lake Simcoe, prepared by innkeeper John Sibbald.

I'll go into details about this map in just a moment, but first let me tell you about the Briars; a lush 200-acre estate on the south shore of Lake Simcoe, about forty-five miles north of Toronto. Guests are accommodated in cottages clustered by the lake or in handsome guest rooms in the Manor and its new wings. The inn is set in expanses of deep green lawns surrounded by sculpted hedges and giant pines. A peaceful river meanders through the golf course, and little streams wander under wooden bridges in the scenic woods and fields. I would term the Briars a distinctive Canadian resort that blends its rich past with modern facilities to offer an attractive holiday for guests with family or friends.

In the more than twenty years that I've been traveling in North America, I've come to the conclusion that while Canadians and Americans have lived side by side for many years and both speak the same language, there are still some subtle differences. For one thing, Canadians are basically more conservative than Americans. In this respect they are more like the English. I found that they prefer some of the more quiet things of life, such as good walking, quiet fireside reading, and a little less flamboyant approach to life in general.

I think this is typical of the atmosphere at the Briars and I bring it up at this time to emphasize to my many American friends who will be visiting the Briars in future years, to recognize and appreciate this Canadian lifestyle. It is found in almost all the other Canadian inns that I write about in *Country Inns and Back Roads*.

And now to the map. In one corner it details a most interesting history since 1819, and traces ownership through more than 170 years to the present Sibbald family.

Actually, the Briars takes in so much territory and so many activities that it really requires this map to give a good overview. It shows the relationship of the Briars to the Red Barn and Peacock House, the gardens, the tennis courts, the wilderness, and of course the 18-hole golf course, the lake, and the village of Jackson's Point.

It shows the location of all of the many lakeside cottages and the golf clubhouse, as well as Saint George's Church, and the route of a great circle tour around Lake Simcoe with many points of interest.

With this map in hand it's easy for the guest to locate the many recreational possibilities at the Briars. In winter the property becomes a snowy paradise for walking and cross-country skiing, skating, toboggan-

ing, and snowshoeing. When the temperature falls there is a beautiful indoor pool, sauna, and whirlpool.

In summer, there are two outdoor pools, all of the lake's recreational advantages, the golf course, lighted tennis courts, lawn sports, and wooded walking trails. There's fishing every day of the year on Lake Simcoe.

Early on, one of the things that intrigued me greatly about the Briars was the fact that the Canadian novelist Mazo de la Roche lived in this area, which undoubtedly supplied her with the atmosphere later portrayed in her famous *Whiteoaks of Jalna* books. She was a guest in one of the cottages at the Briars during the last five summers of her life.

I pored over this map for at least an hour, discovering things that I had never known before about the Briars and Lake Simcoe. Then I turned it over and discovered some wonderful full-color photographs of all of the many four-season activities at this resort-inn.

THE BRIARS, P.O. Box 100, Jackson's Point, Ontario, LOE 1LO Canada; 416-722-3271. A resort-inn on the shore of Lake Simcoe, approx. 45 mi. north of Toronto. Open every day. Breakfast, lunch, and dinner served to non-residents. Recreation includes 18-hole golf course, two outdoor swimming pools, indoor swimming pool, whirlpool, sauna, lakeshore swimming, fishing, two all-weather tennis courts, and many lawn sports. Winter sports include xc skiing, skating, tobogganing, snowmobiling, ice-fishing, and curling. There is an excellent children's program during the summer and Christmas holidays. Excellent for families in all seasons. John and Barbara Sibbald, Innkeepers.

Directions: Jackson's Point is located near Sutton, Ontario. From Hwy. 401, via Hwy. 404/Woodbine. Continue to Sutton and then to Jackson's Point, ½ mi. east on Hatch Rd.

THE OBAN INN
Niagara-on-the-Lake, Ontario

"January, February, and March are wonderful times to be here in Niagara-on-the-Lake."

We were passing through the reception area, and innkeeper Gary Burroughs deftly drew an Oban Inn brochure from the rack and pointed out that there were two photographs of the inn, one in summer, showing the flowers and lawns, and the other in winter, with ample snow and a beautifully decorated Christmas tree.

"The village and shops are still here, but this is before our famous Shaw Festival brings crowds, and summer folks come in, and the feeling here at the inn is slower and more relaxed and such great fun. As you know, we do not salt our roads; instead they are rolled after each snowstorm, so once again there's a lovely sort of country-village feeling

during the wintertime. Also I want to point out that the really exceptional Niagara Historical Society and Museum is open and it provides both Canadians and Americans with an extensive and interesting background of the area. We have a wonderful collection of beautiful old homes, along with English-style shops, that make our village one of the most pleasant places to walk on a brisk winter's day."

Well, it was far from winter during my last visit, and Gary and I were touring the golf course that almost surrounds the inn on two sides. When we got to a point where there is a little lighthouse, he pointed out that we could see the lights of Toronto in the distance, across the corner of the lake, and on the other side, almost close enough to throw a dollar across the river, is Fort Niagara on the American side. "It was originally a French fort and it was right here that there were some skirmishes between the Canadians and the Americans during the War of 1812. That's the mouth of the Niagara River out there," he pointed out.

I can well understand why I get letters from guests who enjoyed their stay, not only in Niagara-on-the-Lake, but also at the Oban itself. There is a wonderful, distinctively Canadian feeling to this inn, and while literally thousands of Americans visit the town and the inn each year, that wonderful Canadian feeling continues undisturbed.

For example, in the inn there is a pub with a magnificent oil painting of George Bernard Shaw, along with photographs of stars of theater and cinema who have appeared at the Shaw Festival during past years. The luncheon fare is typical of what I've enjoyed at pubs in England many times. Real English porridge is served at breakfast.

The dining room overlooking the lake is considerably enhanced by the care and attention given to the flowers by Gary's mother, and here is still another Canadian quality reflected in the inn—the love of flowers.

The dinner menu also reveals the Oban's mix of the old world and the new. For example, among the appetizers is a homemade paté, a tradition in England and on the Continent. The main menu items have the ring of the English countryside: roast prime ribs of beef with Yorkshire pudding and calves' sweetbreads with bacon served on toast. The patrons of the inn include businessmen from the town, as well as a few Canadian-American visitors. In the evening, there are informal, jolly sing-alongs around the piano in the corner, as well as quiet entertainment.

Our swing around the golf course was coming to an end, but we were being treated to a really sensational sunset. Here, in mid-July, nightfall takes its time about coming, and even well after nine o'clock there were sailboats returning from the lake or the river. Gary even found a golf ball. It was obvious that this generous and sensitive man really loves the town and loves the inn, and it was such a pleasure to be with him. "I think it's dinnertime now and I know Sarah will be waiting. Are you ready?"

You bet I was.

THE OBAN INN, 160 Front St., Box 94, Niagara-on-the-Lake, Ontario, Canada L0S 1J0; 416-468-2165. A 23-guestroom village inn on a quiet street in one of Canada's historic villages, approx. 12 mi. from Niagara Falls, N.Y., on the shores of Lake Ontario. All plans available. Breakfast, lunch, dinner served daily to travelers. Open every day of the year. Near Ft. George and Ft. Niagara, and the Shaw Festival. Golf, xc skiing, sailing, fishing, tennis nearby. Owner-controlled pets welcome. Gary Burroughs, Innkeeper.

Directions: Exit Hwy. 55 at St. Catharines from the Queen Elizabeth Hwy. Follow signs to Niagara-on-the-Lake.

THE OPINICON
Chaffey's Locks, Elgin, Ontario

Ever since I was a boy I've been hearing about those wonderful, almost inaccessible, fishing and hunting resorts in Canada that are always situated on sylvan lakes and surrounded by primeval forests. Friends of my father would disappear a couple of times each year and return with tales of fish that practically leapt into the boat and game in Paul Bunyan dimensions. There were stories about highly voluble guides and idyllic days spent in the forest and on the water, followed by trenchermen's meals, very often including the day's catch.

In the summer of 1980 I found such a Canadian retreat with all of the virtues listed above, plus many more that make it a wonderful place for a rusticated vacation.

The Opinicon resort-inn is situated on a lovely wooded hill overlooking Opinicon Lake, and surrounded by seventeen acres of well-groomed lawns, giant oaks, a large flower garden, and quiet spots in the woods or on the lake from which to observe nature. Accommodations are in the main building, an old-fashioned, two-storied, yellow clapboard residence with completely modernized rooms, many opening onto a porch or balcony. In the woods, set back from the lakeshore, are a series of cottages accommodating from two to eight persons each.

The cheerful dining room offers three sumptuous meals a day under the American plan, and I understand they've had the same chef for twenty years. Guests' freshly caught fish can be cooked and served at any meal, and the dining room is conducted like many old resort inns that have now disappeared. I sat at the same table and had the same waitress for all my meals. She and the other waitresses were friendly young ladies from the area.

Innkeeper Al Cross, whose Bay State accent I recognized immediately, is from Newton, Massachusetts. His wife Janice's family has been running this resort-inn for many generations. Al is a somewhat rumpled type of man who is always on the go, greeting guests, taking care of their needs, and keeping the staff members on their toes.

With over 200 lakes in the area, the Opinicon is known for its great fishing. It appeared to me that about fifty percent of the guests in residence during my visit were interested in this sport, for which boats and experienced local guides can be arranged. The inn provides basket lunches, if desired.

On the other hand, many people enjoy the great variety of recreational activities available, including boating, lake and pool swimming, tennis, croquet, shuffleboard, horseshoes, ping-pong, volleyball, and for the occasional inclement days, a good lending library. There's also an honest-to-gosh country store.

One of the most interesting things to do is to take the short walk to Chaffey's Locks, which are a part of the Rideau Canal System. This system was opened in 1832 to connect Kingston with Ottawa, thus avoiding the rapids of the St. Lawrence. It is still a navigable waterway, and the locks, models of stone engineering construction, are operated by hand by two gatekeepers.

The Opinicon is a great place to take the entire family for a real Canadian woods holiday. Rates have been structured in such a way that it is within the financial means of the average North American family, especially when you think of hungry kids eating three meals a day.

THE OPINICON, Chaffey's Locks, RR 1, Elgin, Ontario, Canada KOG 1CO; 613-359-5233. An 18-guestroom resort-inn on Opinicon Lake, part of the Rideau Canal System of eastern Ontario; accommodations also available in rustic cottages. Full American and modified American plan. Open early April to late November. Fishing, boating, tennis, heated swimming pool, shuffleboard, bicycles on grounds, golf course nearby. Excellent for children of all ages. No credit cards. Personal checks accepted. Albert and Janice Cross, Innkeepers.

Directions: From south: Interstate 81 to 1000 Island Bridge to Ontario Rte. 401 west. Turn off Exit No. 645 at Rte. 32 (right), go north to Rte. 15, turning right (north). Follow to 2 miles beyond Elgin (bypassed). Turn left on Chaffey's Locks Rd. From east: Rte. 401 west to Exit No. 696 (Brockville), turn north (right) on Rte. 42, follow Rte. 42 to Crosby, turn south (left) on Rte. 15 for 2 miles and turn right on Chaffey's Locks Rd.

CUTTLE'S TREMBLANT CLUB
Mont Tremblant, Quebec

It was early morning and I was once again at Cuttle's. I bounded out of bed (as is my usual wont) to look at the thrilling panorama of lake and mountain. However, my attention was arrested by a great flock of grosbeaks feeding on the lawn and advancing toward my window. First one would dart ahead, and then another, and then a third and a fourth would jump over the first as if they were chessmen. I had a peculiar feeling that they were a delegation of some kind. They stopped just below my window and then all of a sudden flew away as a group.

Jim and Betty Cuttle, who are as active a pair of innkeepers as I have ever met, have taken advantage of the wonderful combination of lake and mountains here in the Laurentians, north of Montreal, to create a multi-season country inn.

It is their love of outdoor activity that has been a central factor in the inn's growing success. They themselves were ski instructors when they first came here, and even today the inn ski school, which includes videotape recordings as part of their teaching method, is an important part of the winter activity.

During earlier trips I enjoyed the skiing at Mont Tremblant, riding the ski lift with Jim and Betty; learned some fine points of sailing from Jim; and had several good sets of mixed doubles. Later, on the afternoon of this visit, the Cuttles shared their latest enthusiasm with me.

"We started windsurfing about six years ago," Jim said. "We were in Mexico in the early spring on a holiday, liked the idea, and said let's take four or five days to learn the sport."

"Windsurfing is a combination of skiing, surfing, and sailing," explained Betty. "Now we've been holding a windsurfing regatta in front of the club for the last four years and last summer there were over 200 boards. It's unbelievable to see 200 sails of different colors."

We left the little piano lounge area where a very talented gentleman was playing the electric keyboard and singing, and continued on to the dining room. We sat at a table beside the window that offers a truly spectacular view of Lac Tremblant and the famous skiing mountain on the other side. As dusk fell, little pinpoints of light began to appear on the lakeshore and in homes on the opposite side.

"Have I told you about our Tour de Gourmet?" asked Jim. "We have combined with three other Laurentian inns, and during the summer season guests on the modified American plan can pick one or more of the other inns on a given night and enjoy dinner at one of the other three."

The dinner menu at Cuttle's has an emphasis on French cuisine, including onion soup, a cold seafood plate with fish from the Gaspé Peninsula, roast leg of veal, braised calves' sweetbreads, and boned

chicken Bayonnaise. The menus are bilingual so everyone can practice his or her French or English, as the case may be.

Cuttle's is a good place to bring active, outdoor-minded young people of all ages. There is a game room for them to enjoy in the evening.

Although the word "club" is used in the name of this somewhat sophisticated resort-inn, it is, nonetheless, open to the public. Guests come in all seasons and stay from one night to three weeks. There are lots of Americans because the Canadian exchange rate is very favorable.

CUTTLE'S TREMBLANT CLUB, Mont Tremblant, Quebec, Canada JOT IZO; 819-425-2731. A 62-guestroom resort-inn on Lac Tremblant facing Mont Tremblant, the highest peak in the Laurentians. Modified American plan omits lunch. Breakfast, lunch, and dinner served daily to travelers. Open year-round. Tennis, swimming, sailing, windsurfing, boating, fishing, and xc skiing on grounds. Golf, riding, trap shooting, alpine skiing nearby. No pets. Jim and Betty Cuttle, Innkeepers.

Directions: From Montreal, 85 mi. northwest via Laurentian Autoroute 15 to St. Jovite. Turn right on Rte. 327 north 7 mi. to Lac Tremblant. Cuttle's is on the west shore facing the mountain.

HANDFIELD INN (Auberge Handfield)
St. Marc-sur-le-Richelieu, Quebec

I will certainly never forget my first visit in late March to the Handfield Inn and the "sugaring-off party" held by innkeeper Conrad Handfield at his own maple sugar grove a few miles from the inn. The spell of winter was on the land with much snow and many cross-country skiers.

The "sugar shack" was a low-ceilinged rough building where great iron cauldrons of maple syrup were boiling down over a roaring fire. About eighty French-Canadian innkeepers and their wives were enjoying a great feast of pancakes, maple-cured ham, and eggs, all served with maple syrup. A fiddler and an accordion player accompanied while *all* were singing at the top of their lungs.

Innkeeper Handfield explained that these sugaring parties start at the beginning of March and run to the end of April and are very popular with the inn guests. "They are part of the fun of visiting Auberge Handfield at this time of year," he said.

On my second visit, the Richelieu River (part of the waterway that carries boats down to the St. Lawrence and to the tip of Florida) was blue and sparkling in the summer sun. The marina in front of the inn had several visiting boats, and there were people sitting around the swimming pool enjoying animated conversations in both French and English. The fields were bursting with ripening grain, and I could see a number of farm animals, including sheep, goats, ducks, and geese.

I was greeted upon my arrival by Madame Huguette Handfield, who enthusiastically told me about all the things there were to do, both on the inn grounds and in the immediate area. She also explained that theatrical performances were given on the converted ferry boat, *l'Escale*, moored on the river a few hundred yards from the inn.

With her help in translating the menu, I found that among the main courses that evening were a homemade paté (quite traditional among the European restaurants), salmon from the Gaspé, duck, chicken in wine, filet mignon, and steak au poivre.

Accommodations were in rustic rooms decorated and furnished in the old Quebec style, but with touches of modern comfort, including tile bathrooms and controlled heating. My room had rough wooden walls and casement windows overlooking broad fields. Madame Handfield explained to me later that most of the inn is decorated either with antiques or furniture made by local craftsmen.

I have two recent letters; one from Mary Virginia and Jim Mellow of St. Louis, who tell me that they visited Auberge Handfield recently and found the entire experience most memorable. They particularly mentioned the superb brown-sugar pie for dessert. The other letter is from

Conrad and Huguette Handfield, who tell me that they have completely renovated the exterior of the inn and made a new veranda, which is possibly open year around with a greenhouse and a new patio. Everything is now Wedgwood blue and white. I will certainly be visiting there during the upcoming year.

The Handfield Inn is a great many things: it is a venerable mansion that has seen a century and a half of history; an enjoyable French restaurant; a four-season resort; and perhaps best of all, it is an opportunity to visit a French-Canadian village that has remained relatively free from the invasion of developers. Its ancient stone houses remain untouched and its farms still raise good stock and poultry.

HANDFIELD INN (Auberge Handfield), St. Marc-sur-le-Richelieu, Quebec, JOL 2EO, Canada; 514-584-2226. A 45-guestroom (some shared baths) French-Canadian country inn about 25 mi. from Montreal. Different lodging plans available. Please consult with inn in advance. Open every day all year. Breakfast, lunch, and dinner served daily to travelers. Ladies are expected to wear a skirt or dress and gentlemen a coat at dinner. All summer and winter active sports easily available. Many handcrafts, antique, and historical tours in the area. No pets. M. and Mme. Conrad Handfield, Innkeepers.

Directions: From Champlain, Victoria, or the Jacques Cartier bridges, take Hwy. 3 to Sorel, turn right at Hwy. 20. From the east end of Montreal, go through the Hyppolite LaFontaine Tunnel. Rte. 20 passes through St. Julie, St. Bruno, and Beloeil. Leave Hwy. 20 at Exit 112, turning left on Rte. 223 north. Handfield is 7 mi. distant.

HOVEY MANOR
North Hatley, Quebec

The entire six pages of an article on Hovey Manor which appeared in the June issue of *Sel & Poivre*, Quebec's leading food magazine, were in French, and even if my French is a bit sketchy I could see that there were many, many compliments for some of the wonderful dishes prepared by the new chef from Belgium, Marc de Canck.

A letter from Steve and Kathy Stafford at Hovey Manor indicated that they were both very pleased that the magazine was in agreement with them regarding Marc's talent. "Marc loves Hovey Manor and I believe he will be here for many years to come. By the way, we'll be receiving new dinnerware from Europe shortly with our own logo."

Hovey Manor is a traditional inn with all the resort facilities for a complete vacation experience. In the summer there is sailing, canoes, paddle boats, water skiing, fishing, and tennis on the grounds. There is also a free tennis clinic with André Marois. It appears that M. Marois is a golf professional as well.

Steve's letter continues, "Windsurfing has proved to be very popular with the guests, and arrangements for lessons are available for everyone from kids to grandmothers. It's a fine, exhilarating exercise and offers a good escape without taking too much time. By the way, there are ten golf courses within a half-hour's ride, and there is summer stock at the Piggery Theatre and concerts at the Mount Orford Arts Center nearby."

There seems to be something special going on at all times during the summer—beach barbecues, a lake cruise to Ripplecove Inn at Ayer's Cliff where you can have lunch if you like, chamber music concerts, poetry readings with wine and cheese, and various other events.

Festival Lac Massawippi runs from mid-July to mid-August, and the Abenaki Room at Hovey Manor will be the site of one of Festival Lac Massawippi's art exhibits, featuring the works of Eastern Township artists.

Some other news is that nine new bedrooms and an expansion of the dining room will be completed by spring of 1986. As Steve describes them, the bedrooms will be quite deluxe, many with fireplaces, private balconies, four-poster beds, and whirlpool baths, which are particularly attractive to cross-country and alpine skiers. Steve hastens to add that Hovey's atmosphere will not change.

The new guest rooms are going to be furnished with a combination of antiques, antique reproductions, and works of local cabinetmakers, as well as artwork by Eastern Township artists.

I mentioned skiing, and actually, Hovey has 125 kilometers of groomed cross-country ski trails right from their door, and also a ski package offering inn-to-inn skiing, where the inn transfers the cars and

the baggage. Downhill skiers enjoy the interchangeable ticket, valid at four big mountains in the area, all with extensive snowmaking equipment. Guests can also play indoor tennis, squash, and racquet ball at an excellent club nearby.

Steve concludes his letter with, "The two-language menu is quite European, and chef Marc de Canck is putting emphasis on contemporary cuisine featuring beautiful presentation and lighter sauces. Desserts are sinfully good—or bad—depending on your viewpoint."

Steve called me just before we went to press to say that they have been awarded a "four-forks" rating by the Ministry of Tourism for their contemporary cuisine. This is the highest restaurant rating in Quebec.

HOVEY MANOR, North Hatley, Quebec, Canada JOB 2CO; 819-842-2421. A 38-guestroom resort inn (8 with woodburning fireplaces) on Lake Massawippi, ½ hr. from U.S./Canada border. Modified American and European plans. Breakfast, lunch, dinner served every day. Open all year. Lighted tennis court, two beaches, sailing, canoeing, paddleboats, water skiing, windsurfing, fishing, xc skiing on grounds. Downhill skiing, horseback riding, year-round tennis, racquet sports, and golf (10 courses); also many scenic and cultural attractions nearby. Sorry, no pets. Stephen and Kathryn Stafford, Innkeepers.

Directions: Take Vermont I-91 to Vermont/Quebec border and follow Rte. 55 to No. Hatley Exit 29). Follow Rte. 108E for 5 mi. to T junction at Lake Massawippi in North Hatley. Turn right for ¾ mi. to Hovey Manor sign and private drive on left.

Favorite Back Roads

There are many fine drives to be taken from Hovey Manor in North Hatley, Quebec, and Lake Massawippi and its valley are the focus for one of the most scenic and, fortunately, one of the most convenient. A series of paved and dirt roads are available to take you right around the lake, offering a mosaic of rural farms, picturesque villages, and spectacular countryside. The total distance is only 25 miles and a morning drive is recommended to take advantage of the sun's striking the mountain ridge along the lake's west side. In autumn, this is particularly impressive.

Driving around the lake in a counterclockwise direction, the recommended stops, in order, are as follows:

1) Boutique Les Arrivants (North Hatley)—a good choice of Scottish woolens and the work of local artisans.

2) Brandt Farm (Route 143)—fresh organic asparagus (in season).

3) Du Moulin and Montrency Antiques (Ayers Cliff)—an eclectic assortment of Canadian and Victorian antiques at reasonable prices.

4) Ripplecove Inn (Ayers Cliff)—lunch on the lakeside patio.

5) Covered Bridge Park (Ayers Cliff)—a good spot for a picnic lunch.

6) Catholic Church (Katevale)—an excellent example of a rural Quebec church—very large in proportion to the tiny village.

Steve and Kathy Stafford
Hovey Manor
North Hatley, Quebec

This drive starts in the village of Bear River in Annapolis Royal, Nova Scotia. Turn left at the service station and follow the road about one kilometer to the head of the river. Continue straight toward the hydro tower, and at the sign of the Bear River Indian Reservation take the lower right-hand road following along the river. At first the riverbed is very rocky with massive outcroppings containing examples of fossils. These are remnants of the action of the glaciers. We shall follow the west branch of the river until the river widens and, farther along, there is a lovely quiet pool in the upper river where one can stop, take pictures, watch for water movement of fish, muskrat, or beaver, or listen for bird songs.

At approximately five kilometers from the beginning, we come to an intersection in the road and at the center is a neat farmstead; at this point take the left-hand road and continue through the forest leaving the river for about four more kilometers to the fire tower. There is a sign here that says, "Visitors Welcome—Climb at Your Own Risk." I am sure the view *from this sixty-foot tower is spectacular, inasmuch as from the ground you can already see a large lake in the distance.*

Leaving the fire tower, on the road, we soon catch sight of this lake in the distance and it is indeed a beautiful lake. Along the six-kilometer road to the lake we can see where old farmsteads had once been beside the open fields, and old apple trees once grew there. We finally come right to the shore of the lake—there is nothing remaining here of the once-prosperous community, and in the field above the lake, the Boy Scouts come every spring to plant trees and camp out. It is interesting to read of the history of this once-thriving community that has completely disappeared.

In the early 1900s this was the site of a unique industrial venture. By the side of the lake, a large sawmill was built, powered by one of the first steam units in western Nova Scotia. A clothespin factory was part of the complex. Because of the distance from Bear River village, a number of workers were housed in permanent lodges containing dormitories. There were also quarters for families and a small school and community social hall.

In the spring, logs were yarded in the lake and sent on their tumultuous journey down the river. Logrolling was a favorite sport on the lake and continued to be a feature of all carnivals in Bear River for a number of years. In the winter, it would be a sight to see the convoy of logging teams working out of here and bringing provisions the sixteen long kilometers we have just traveled so easily on this good gravel road.

Apart from the historical significance of this lake, it is a great place for a picnic or a swim and, from the Milford House, a slight change of scenery and a good way to spend a few hours or a whole day.

Warren and Margaret Miller
Milford House
Annapolis Royal, Nova Scotia, Canada

WHAT IS INNKEEPING REALLY LIKE?

Each year I receive many dozens of letters from readers who are considering a second career in country innkeeping. There is a common refrain in each of these letters that has a most familiar ring: "We have visited many of the country inns listed in your book, and we both agree that we would like to get away from the hurly-burly of the city and take up residence in the country where the pace is much slower and more agreeable to us."

These letter-writers usually reveal that on the average they are somewhere between forty and forty-five years old with approximately two and a half children, eight to thirteen years old. They have a certain amount of equity in the mortgage on their surburban home, and with that, plus a family loan, they are able to muster an adequate amount of negotiable cash and securities toward the new venture.

Inquiries are almost always made as to books and also other sources such as government pamphlets that might be available on operating inns. May we suggest that you ask your local bookshop for a copy of *How To Open A Country Inn* by Karen Etsell and Elaine Brennan, formerly of the Bramble Inn on Cape Cod. It is published by the Berkshire Traveller Press, and will provide you with a good insight into some of the practical problems and solutions of innkeeping.

Written in a lively style with quite a few humorous touches, this book may well answer some of the principal questions that you have about innkeeping today.

Some of the typical questions are: Is there a specific way to find out when an inn is for sale? Where are the best real estate agents to assist in finding inn property? How much money is needed for a down payment? How much should be kept in escrow against emergencies? How many operating dollars are necessary? What are some of the absolute essentials necessary to go into the country-inn business?

My response to these letters is to try to paint the most realistic picture possible for the prospective innkeepers. One of the frequent problems is undercapitalization. Country innkeeping is a very demanding and at times difficult business. Prospective innkeepers very quickly need or must acquire some very practical knowledge in bookkeeping, carpentry, plumbing, and engineering. They also need unusual patience and tact in dealing with the public. Furthermore, all of these qualities must be exercised twenty-four hours a day.

If a full-scale food operation is involved, it would be most preferable for one of the principals to have had some practical experience in all phases of restaurant operation. New innkeepers discover all too soon that someone had better be prepared to cook the menu, because the position of chef or cook is one of the most unstable in the entire business. I bow to no one in my admiration of cooks and chefs at country inns; however, very frequently circumstances arise that cause them to leave the night before Easter or Thanksgiving, and someone has to step in and do the job.

I have talked with many, many people over the past twenty-one years about the prospects and problems of going into the country-inn business. Many conversations proceed along the following lines: "My wife and I know that we are very capable in dealing with people," says the eager husband. "I have been running an office for the past twenty years and my wife and I have been great partygivers. She is a wonderful cook!"

My first bit of advice is never to allow the woman in the partnership to go behind the range unless she really has been a professional cook. It's one thing to prepare a dinner party for twenty-four people once every four months, and still another to turn out fifty or sixty dinners six nights a week, and at the same time deal with all of the provisioners, suppliers, and the other tradespeople who are essential to this business. It's been my observation that this is one of the best ways to break up a marriage or a partnership.

During more recent years a new type of accommodation has emerged—the bed and breakfast. After careful scrutiny and much travel, I have included a number of these inns in this book; however, these are very superior places that have been chosen for their special ambience, decor, and unusual location, as well as the extremely high quality of the accommodations and affability of their innkeepers. All too frequently the new bed and breakfast innkeeper has failed to do his homework in terms of exactly how many nights a year the seven or eight bedrooms must be filled in order for a break-even point to be reached.

A bed and breakfast inn is not usually the answer to becoming a financially independent innkeeper. Most generally, one of the innkeepers must be employed at an outside job, and this ordinarily means the woman in the partnership stays home and changes all the linens and cleans all the rooms when the chambermaid fails to appear.

The additional amenities offered by full-service inns, such as swimming pools, tennis courts, full meals, refreshment services, and so forth, provide for longer stays and returning guests, both of which are essential for success in the inn business.

I have touched only lightly upon the real problems that are connected with the inn business. Where a couple is involved, I can truthfully say that being together twenty-four hours a day, trying not to tread on each other's toes, and learning to departmentalize all of the demands will shatter a relationship that is unstable, and will create serious cracks in one thought to be perfect.

If you can make it through the first five years and show a steady growth (much less profit), and if you have survived several business and personal crises along the way, then perhaps innkeeping is for you.

You will not get rich overnight, or probably ever, but if you would be happy with the country life (it gets pretty quiet on rainy Tuesdays in March and during "mud season") and you are really "service-minded"— willing to extend yourself on behalf of cantankerous, demanding guests who look for TVs and room service, then you have a good start.

The remainder of these comments consists mostly of excerpts from letters to me from *CIBR* innkeepers. I have tried to keep a balance between the pros and cons of innkeeping, and hope that these will provide an insight into what innkeeping is really like.

Anyone involved in any aspect of 'serving the public' knows that it takes up a good part of every day, and not just the hours you happen to be open, and so suddenly it's autumn. My mother brought me up by saying, 'if a thing's worth doing, it's worth doing well,' and so we all work hard and are rewarded by the pleasure of seeing a fine old stagecoach building being well cared for, and being appreciated by our customers.

Most of our longtime employees are still with us, which means a lot. They know our service so well and can greet customers by name and know where they prefer to dine . . . —New York

Christmas was truly lovely, our guests arriving laden with gifts as well as with luggage. The traditional Christmas feast which featured roast goose and English Trifle was followed by an evening before the fire, sharing wine, conversation, and games. Unfortunately, the one ingredient missing for a perfect Christmas was snow. And that brings us to a 'down'—no Christmas sleigh-ride and many cancellations after the holidays. True, some people came anyway, just to get away—to read, to relax, to enjoy good food, and even to skate on the pond. But those bent on skiing were doomed to disappointment.

Spring was similar—quiet and guest-less. The inn-take for March and April did pay the mortgage but little else. This condition has led us to decide to close from March 1 to April 15. As we told you during our brief visit this summer, our truck was totalled this March while we were away. While this was quite a shock as well as a down, we turned it into an up by sinking the insurance money into a much needed well. And sink we did, all 560 feet of it. Expensive, yes, but it brought to an end a two-year water problem.

With the summer approaching we contracted to have our pond set up for the limited use of which we wrote last year. Our contractor never arrived until too late in August and at this time we decided to postpone this project indefinitely . . . —Maine

This hasn't been one of our better years. Business has been fine but we have suffered through a series of calamities that seem beyond belief. Two major problems affecting the inn: The first week in June lightning struck a big maple, toppling the tree onto our newly renovated guest cottage. The cottage was flattened and had to be completely rebuilt. As you might suspect, having just finished the cottage, we had not yet contacted the insurance agent to cover the building. The second disaster happened two weeks ago, when our beautiful old barn burned to the ground.

The cottage has been rebuilt and we are now deeply involved in plans to rebuild our barn. Hopefully this time we will be able to include twelve new guest rooms in the new barn.

Don't get me wrong, we have had some sunny days as well this year. In January, we completely renovated our kitchen at the inn; it turned out beautifully. Now we have a kitchen that we are proud to bring our guests into . . . —New York

We had a wonderful Fourth of July celebration with our guests this year. Not one guest stayed behind. As in past years, we packed a delicious (if I do say so myself!) picnic and took everyone to the park, where the symphony orchestra was performing. When we left the inn none knew anyone else, but when we came back, several couples were in each others' rooms, and when our evening desk person left to go home at midnight that evening, there were still a few guests sitting on the porch drinking their iced tea, and talking. What a good feeling that gives an innkeeper—to see strangers leave your inn friends . . . —Colorado

We have had a very successful year with our occupancy up about five percentage points over the previous year. I think that for the entire year it will probably run an average of 85%. Of course, now during the summertime we run 97-98%, which means I can't complain too loudly . . . —California

The last guest has departed, and rugs and curtains stored and sign taken down. It has been a season to remember. We ran about 42% ahead of last season but one has to do that well to stay even . . . —Maine

Here we are in Bermuda—'basket cases' as we always are on arrival! The inn is closed till the 13th (and we go back the next day). Hopefully a lot has begun to happen there—new carpeting downstairs and up, painting in the lobby and stairways, an enlarged and rebuilt storeroom, and some much-needed steam cleaning on the kitchen. None of it is very glamorous.

This November vacation in Bermuda has become a real need for us. It's a time for the four of us to have time together once again. As much as we dearly love the inn, when we're home it is the 'family member' whose needs must usually come first. I know other innkeepers feel differently, but we'll always have to be a working part of our inn . . . —New Hampshire

Thank you for forwarding the letters of complaint. One hates to have someone complain about something one has put so much time, energy, and love into, but I guess you can't please everybody!! I remember these people, they were two couples traveling together. I'd like to tell you their interesting story: (1) They wrote for our brochure and room chart in June. Our floor plan is printed out and every room is explained as to what floor and what facilities are included. (2) They wrote back for reservations on August 13 for September 17 and 18, requesting rooms #6 and #8 (our most popular rooms!). We wrote back and told them that those two particular rooms had been previously booked and we had given them the next best available accommodations. We booked them into other rooms, sent along another room chart, and asked that if these accommodations were unacceptable that they contact us immediately. We did not hear from them so we assumed all was well. We do all our correspondence on three-part forms. (3) They arrived requesting that their rooms be changed to 6 and 8, which of course was out of the question as those rooms had been booked for some time. Our desk girl pulled out all of our very well-kept correspondence and explained the situation again. (4) They complained all the way upstairs and after about a half hour came downstairs, made a few phone calls, and off they went!! . . . —New Hampshire

The sixteen acres behind our buildings on our property are now partly utilized in two ways: 3,000 white pines have been planted, and a local farmer has planted many acres of corn, tomatoes, beans, cucumbers, squash, and peppers. We feel good about this as we don't want to extend building and do like to see the land utilized. Hope to plant Christmas trees also this fall . . . —Maine

This has been our most exciting year ever. Maybe it's because we're so established as this coming year will be our sixth year of business! There are problems, but they are minor compared to the satisfaction we get from serving the public as country innkeepers . . . —Massachusetts

We've been fortunate in having young families come. Some of these folks came with parents and grandparents years before (the inn is 29 years old). One cute young lady said, 'It's great—just like I remembered—only thing different is new wallpaper and fabrics—it looks the same, just fresh and clean!' (She came with her grandmother long ago.)

We know how lucky we are to have an inn among the oldest mountains in the world—and in today's world to be within one day's driving of 50% of the U.S. population. But we also realize it takes lots of energy and a desire to serve people (as you told us one time years ago, Norm!) in order for a place like ours to succeed. Country inns are 'in' now, but people will never return if we as innkeepers don't get across the feeling of caring. This is needed in today's world.

We are told our help is a real 'first-string team.' We know we could never carry out our plan here without a good office staff, excellent cooks, courteous and efficient dining room help, fastidious room ladies, and our 'man Friday'! It's been said, 'When the boss is away and things run smoothly, it's the sign of a superior team and super leader.' John must be that, because while we were away recently for a wedding, no one seemed to know we were gone until greetings were not exchanged!

With no phones, no TVs, no golf (only within one hour), no decision as to hours of meals (breakfast 8:30 and dinner 6 p.m.) or where to sit (John tries to seat people who are congenial at the same table—and they mostly return to that place each meal), no decision about menu as the food is on the lazy-Susan tables. These are the factors to give one rest and change from busy schedules and decision-making routines . . . —North Carolina

Remember the table we sat at in the front yard? During the night someone robbed us of the whole set, plus three wrought iron arm-chairs. We felt sick. Now we must bury chains in concrete under the ground and bolt everything down. How awful, and so different from the casualness we want. We'll cover it up well with vines and flowers . . . —California

With a new lease on life after a good strong season, we are now in the process of doing or have done many exciting and glamorous things as:

1. reshingled the last third of the inn roofs—project now complete, entire inn has been reshingled.

2. installed a new hot water heater—this will make life a lot less adventuresome for the shower lovers—no more alternate blasts of hot and cold water.

3. installed a new kitchen exhaust fan and relocated same—no longer will the folks in room #9 know exactly what the chef's whim is going to be, as the exhaust is no longer located outside their window.

4. various and sundry other small upgrading projects, such as wall to wall carpeting in two bedrooms; new carpet and drapes in the sitting room, plus a paddle fan to recirculate the heat from the wood stove; brand new shower heads on all the showers . . . —New Hampshire

We had an excellent season. We had some anxiety at the beginning of the season about what would happen to us with the gas shortage— especially since we are out at the tip of nowhere where we can't even get deliveries because it's 'too far off Route 1.'

Although we 'opened' on May 1, we had no guests until mid-May when a couple from Unionville, Connecticut, arrived, having had no previous inn experiences. They loved it and returned in October for our last weekend (bringing along friends) and ended our season with us. I use them as an example of the way it went this summer—many guests coming two times during the season and others sending children, parents, friends, etc.

Best of all we made more new friends who enjoyed our 'real country inn.' Those returning say they're pleased to find things the way they remembered them and ask us to please not to make to many changes— and we've about decided that's the thing to do—just keep it simple and offer good beds and food and hospitality and enjoy what we're doing and the people who continue to take the time and make the effort to enjoy what we offer . . . —Maine

We have no training schools here; therefore, we have to train green help every year. When they get good they get permanent jobs and we have to go back to the training. It is from cooks right on down the line. Guests are mostly cooperative for they realize most of my staff are school kids in their first job in the hospitality field . . . —Prince Edward Island

Our starting philosophy (tho I'm not sure we ever articulated it as such) seem to be working. Life is a seven-day-a-week houseparty; we have an absolute ball (we like the job!) and 98% of our guests feel free to join in. Not all our guests are as articulate, but this excerpt from a recent note kind of sums it up: 'Looking back on our stay with you . . . I realize that you made us feel so much like houseguests of personal friends that I will not feel right until I get off a thank-you note!

One thing we have learned that neither of us foresaw when we elected to become innkeepers—I suppose it is most important for small inns like ours: You are never *Off Duty! You are 'on' from 7 a.m. to about midnight and even from 12 midnight to 7 a.m., you are 'on call.' We have adjusted as best we can, hiring a housekeeper this summer to help with the physical plant to give us about eight hours 'off' one day a week.*

But, lest that sound too downbeat, taken all-in-all, my only regret is that we didn't become innkeepers about ten years before we did. How else, I ask you, could we find ourselves lacking only the USSR, PRC, and the Indian sub-continent in terms of people we have met in just eighteen months! . . . —Massachusetts

The greatest joy of innkeeping is meeting the wonderful guests who come our way. The greatest compliment we have received is when folks tell us that their visit is 'like being a personal guest in your home' . . . —South Carolina

Once, on a particularly harried day, a guest asked if I still enjoyed innkeeping now that I was 'working' at it. I paused, broke out in a big grin, and told him I loved it and couldn't dream of doing anything else. All the aggravation and problems don't add up to an ounce compared to the many pounds of pleasure and friends we have made. There are times we are busy eighteen hours a day and we also have had moments, but the major difference is we control our destiny and we are careful that we don't let our business consume us . . . —Virginia

NOTE

A deposit is required for a confirmed reservation. Guests are requested to please note arrival and departure dates carefully. The deposit will be forfeited if the guest arrives after date specified or departs before final date of reservation. Refund will be made only if cancelled from 7 to 14 days (depending on the policy of the individual inn) in advance of arrival date and a service charge will be deducted from the deposit.

It must be understood that a deposit insures that your accommodations will be available as confirmed, and also assures the inn that the accommodations are sold as confirmed. Therefore, when situations arise necessitating your cancellation less than the allowed number of days in advance, your deposit will not be refunded.

INDEX